MW00512621

WALES AND THE FRENCH REVOLUTION

General Editors: Mary-Ann Constantine and Dafydd Johnston

'Richard Price, D.D. F.R.S.', engraving by Thomas Holloway, 1793,
after a painting by Benjamin West.

Liberty's Apostle
Richard Price, his Life and Times

PAUL FRAME

UNIVERSITY OF WALES PRESS
2015

© Paul Frame, 2015

All rights reserved. No part of this book may be reproduced in any material form (including photocopying or storing it in any medium by electronic means and whether or not transiently or incidentally to some other use of this publication) without the written permission of the copyright owner except in accordance with the provisions of the Copyright, Designs and Patents Act 1988. Applications for the copyright owner's written permission to reproduce any part of this publication should be addressed to The University of Wales Press, 10 Columbus Walk, Brigantine Place, Cardiff CF10 4UP.

www.uwp.co.uk

British Library Cataloguing-in-Publication Data
A catalogue record for this book is available from the British Library.

ISBN   978-1-78316-216-1
e-ISBN 978-1-78316-217-8

The right of Paul Frame to be identified as author of this work has been asserted by him in accordance with sections 77, 78 and 79 of the Copyright, Designs and Patents Act 1988.

Typeset in Wales by Eira Fenn Gaunt, Cardiff
Printed by CPI Antony Rowe, Chippenham, Wiltshire

For my brother Jonathan
and to the memory of our parents
Gwen and Geoff Frame

WALES AND THE FRENCH REVOLUTION

The French Revolution of 1789 was perhaps the defining event of the Romantic period in Europe. It unsettled not only the ordering of society but language and thought itself: its effects were profoundly cultural, and they were long-lasting. The last twenty years have radically altered our understanding of the impact of the Revolution and its aftermath on British culture. In literature, as critical attention has shifted from a handful of major poets to the non-canonical edges, we can now see how the works of women writers, self-educated authors, radical pamphleteers, prophets and loyalist propagandists both shaped and were shaped by the language and ideas of the period. Yet surprising gaps remain, and even recent studies of the 'British' reaction to the Revolution remain poorly informed about responses from the regions. In literary and historical discussions of the so-called 'four nations' of Britain, Wales has been virtually invisible; many researchers working in this period are unaware of the kinds of sources available for comparative study.

The Wales and the French Revolution Series is the product of a four-year project funded by the AHRC and the University of Wales at the Centre for Advanced Welsh and Celtic Studies. It makes available a wide range of Welsh material from the decades spanning the Revolution and the subsequent wars with France. Each volume, edited by an expert in the field, presents a collection of texts (including, where relevant, translations) from a particular genre with a critical essay situating the material in its historical and literary context. A great deal of material is published here for the first time, and all kinds of genres are explored. From ballads and pamphlets to personal letters and prize-winning poems, essays, journals, sermons, songs and satires, the range of texts covered by this series is a stimulating reflection of the political and cultural complexity of the time. We hope these volumes will encourage scholars and students of Welsh history and literature to rediscover this fascinating period, and will offer ample comparative scope for those working further afield.

Mary-Ann Constantine and Dafydd Johnston
General Editors

Theologian, philosopher, mathematician;
Friend to Freedom as to Virtue;
Brother of Man;
Lover of Truth as of God;
His eminent talents were matched by his integrity,
Simplicity, and goodness of heart;
His moral dignity by his profound humility.

Few have been more useful in their generation,
Or more valued by the wise and good;
None more pure and disinterested.
Honoured be his name!
Imitated his example!

> Inscription on Richard Price's memorial in
> Newington Green chapel, London.

Give me Dr. Price's political principles and I will move all kings out of their thrones, and all subjection out of the world.

> John William Fletcher, *American Patriotism Further
> Confronted with Reason, Scripture and the Constitution:
> Being Observations on the Dangerous Politicks Taught
> by the Rev. Mr. Evans and the Rev. Dr. Price. With a
> Scriptural Plea for the Revolted Colonies* (Shrewsbury,
> 1776).

Contents

Figures and Plates

Preface

In his preface to *The Honest Mind: The Thought and Work of Richard Price*, the late D. O. Thomas warned that the most intrepid biographer faced a daunting prospect and 'herculean task' in trying to do justice to all the details of Price's achievements. The question of whether I have done them justice or not I am happy to leave to the judgement of the reader, but the herculean nature of the task has been made far less daunting thanks to the diligent scholarship and wide-ranging nature of David Thomas's own publications on Price.[1] To these, and in particular the three volumes of Price's collected correspondence which Thomas edited with Bernard Peach, I owe the greatest debt. Shortly before he died David told me that one reviewer of these volumes had criticized them for the number and detail of the footnotes they contain. I am simply thankful for them.

Mention must also be made of David's wife, Beryl Thomas, who in deciphering Price's private shorthand journal has provided this and any future biographer with a rare insight into Price's deeper personality and character; something generally hidden in his correspondence and published works. My profound thanks also go to Martin Fitzpatrick for his interest in the project, for his reading of the text a number of times over many years, and for useful comments shared during enjoyable meetings in Aberystwyth and at his home in mid-Wales, where the welcome more than lived up to the traditions of Welsh hospitality.

To Mary-Ann Constantine of the University of Wales Centre for Advanced Welsh and Celtic Studies in Aberystwyth I also owe an enormous debt of gratitude. Though I am essentially an amateur historian, she showed no hesitation in collaborating with me on this project. Mary-Ann has edited the text with great skill and with a candour of which Price would be proud and for which I am grateful. The book reads far better for her 'amazonian

---

[1] See James Dybikowski, 'A Bibliography of D. O. Thomas', *E&D*, 19 (2000), 214–23. Thomas's papers on Price are currently held at the Dr Williams Library in London.

efforts' on my behalf. My thanks also go to Dafydd Johnston and the editorial skills of Gwen Gruffudd at the Aberystwyth Centre for all their help and for allowing me to publish my work as part of their excellent 'Wales and the French Revolution' series.

As a sometimes punctuation-averse post-war child I am eternally grateful for the grammatical skills and valuable insights of a slightly earlier generation in the shape of my uncle, Lyndon Frame, and the always direct and truthful encouragement and candour of my late aunt, Pamela Frame.

To the staff of the gloriously positioned National Library of Wales at Aberystwyth (in particular Emyr Evans) and to the British Library in London with its courtyard haven in bustling King's Cross, my thanks. Also to those who have supplied various pieces of valuable and illuminating information in the Price story. They include: Nicola Bennetts, John Morgan, David Perry, Peter Davies, Lyndall Gordon, Sharon Bertsch McGrayne, Rory McLaggan, Tony Rail, Paul Joyner (National Library of Wales), Roy E. Goodman (American Philosophical Society) and Susan Klein (Beinecke Library, Yale University).

My thanks to Sarah Lewis, Siân Chapman and Dafydd Jones at the University of Wales Press for their guidance, encouragement and patience, and to the Press-appointed external reader for many useful comments. Thanks also to all who have taken the time to read and comment on the text at various stages in its near-twelve-year gestation, and to those who have simply encouraged me by their continuing friendship or by asking 'Is it done yet?' They include: Martyn Hooper and Dave and Lynne Ward of the Richard Price Society for reading parts of the text, Gerald Jarvis for photographs, and all other members of the Society for their support. Also: John Harrington, Ron Woollam, Marcelle Fadel, Firoze Din, Rob Hulsbos, David Smith, Steve Poole, Sabat Prasetyo, Angela Crompton, all at Core Laboratories, Bob Wynn Jones, Ken Brassil, Derek Harrison, John Athersuch, Antoine Wonders and Ginger Smith. Finally, if she should find her way to this book, my love to Sally. If I have inadvertently missed anyone out I apologize as I do for any other mistakes which are, of course, entirely my responsibility.

February 2015   Paul Frame

Acknowledgements

Gerald Jarvis: Fig. 2
Robert Wynn Jones: Figs. 4, 5b, 23
The London Borough of Hackney Archives: Fig. 5a
The National Library of Wales: Figs. 6, 17, 22; Plate 1a
The Royal Society: Fig. 7
The National Portrait Gallery: Fig. 14; Plates 1b, 2a, 2b, 3a, 3b
Nicola Bennetts: Fig. 19
David and Lynne Ward: Fig. 24
The Library of Congress: Plates 4a, 4b

Abbreviations

Bibliography	D. O. Thomas, John Stephens and P. A. L. Jones, *A Bibliography of the Works of Richard Price* (Aldershot, 1993)
CC	Carl B. Cone, *Torchbearer of Freedom: The Influence of Richard Price on Eighteenth Century Thought* (Lexington, 1952)
CRP	W. Bernard Peach and D. O. Thomas (eds.), *The Correspondence of Richard Price* (3 vols., Durham, NC, 1983–94)
E&D	*Enlightenment and Dissent*
HM	D. O. Thomas, *The Honest Mind: The Thought and Work of Richard Price* (Oxford, 1977)
'Journal'	Beryl Thomas and D. O. Thomas, 'Richard Price's Journal for the Period 25 March 1787 to 6 February 1791. Deciphered by Beryl Thomas with an Introduction by D. O. Thomas', *National Library of Wales Journal*, XXI, no. 4 (1980), 366–413
Memoirs	William Morgan, *Memoirs of the Life of the Rev. Richard Price* (London, 1815)
NLW	National Library of Wales
Ogborn	Maurice Edward Ogborn, *Equitable Assurances: The Story of Life Assurance in the Experience of the Equitable Life Assurance Society, 1762–1962* (London, 1962)

ORP   Richard Price, *Observations on Reversionary Payments; on Schemes for Providing Annuities for Widows, and for Persons in Old Age; on the Method of Calculating the Values of Assurances on Lives; and on the National Debt* (4th edn., 2 vols., London, 1783)

PW   D. O. Thomas (ed.), *Richard Price: Political Writings* (Cambridge, 1991)

Raphael   D. D. Raphael (ed.), *A Review of the Principal Questions in Morals by Richard Price* (Oxford, 1974)

Sermons   Richard Price, *Sermons on the Security and Happiness of a Virtuous Course, on the Goodness of God and the Resurrection of Lazarus. To Which are Added Sermons on the Christian Doctrine as Received by the Different Denominations of Christians* (Philadelphia, 1788)

Travels   Mary-Ann Constantine and Paul Frame (eds.), *Travels in Revolutionary France & A Journey Across America by George Cadogan Morgan & Richard Price Morgan* (Cardiff, 2012)

Introduction: Rediscovering Richard Price

History has neglected the man who possessed, according to Condorcet, 'one of the formative minds of the century'. The verdict of history is unjust; Benjamin Franklin would be shocked by it.[1]

At the height of the War of Independence with Britain, the Congress of the fledgling United States offered to bring him to America so that he could become a citizen and their first financial adviser. To the French revolutionaries of 1789 he was 'the implacable enemy of tyrants', a 'benefactor of humanity' and the 'Apostle of Liberty'. Many in Britain, however, were less enthusiastic about this London-based Dissenting minister from south Wales. As the troubles in France spread across Europe they saw him not as Liberty's apostle but as a dangerous and seditious radical, intent on fomenting a similar revolution in Britain. He was, in his time, a key political thinker with an international reach and reputation. But history has not been kind to Dr Richard Price.

My own first meeting with Richard Price came in the early 1980s when I worked for a short time in a tower block in the City of London. Disliking the corporate atmosphere in the office canteen I sometimes took sandwiches to the nearby oasis of Bunhill Fields cemetery. There I sat and ate among the more constructively dissenting shades of William Blake, John Bunyan, Daniel Defoe and Richard Price. As a Welshman myself, the name 'Richard Price' on the cemetery notice board and, though somewhat faded, on a nearby weathered tomb, attracted my attention: but on discovering he was only being remembered in Bunhill at that time for his major contribution to the development of life assurance, my interest quickly waned. It was not a subject close to my heart. His name did not crop up again until 2000 when I read Dr John Davies's seminal *Hanes Cymru / History of Wales*, in which he describes Price as a supporter of the American Revolution of 1776 and of the opening events of the French Revolution in 1789. As I researched further I found his story gripping, and could not understand why, despite

years of education in Wales, I and many of my fellow citizens had so little
knowledge of a man Dr Davies describes as the greatest thinker Wales has
thus far produced.

Though Price's major contribution to the development of life assurance
and annuities would always be remembered, neglect of his contribution to
moral philosophy and civil liberties began shortly after his death in 1791.
As the bloodier events of the French Revolution gathered pace and attempts
at political reform in Britain were stifled, Price's welcoming of the fateful
events in France in July 1789 seemed not only mistaken but highly dangerous
and even seditious. He came to be seen in the guise created for him by
Edmund Burke in his *Reflections on the Revolution in France* and gleefully
elaborated by the caricaturists of the day: a dangerous radical and metaphysical
speculator opposed to traditional hierarchies and a culture of deference.
Moreover, Price would soon be overtaken in the setting of a radical agenda
by Thomas Paine, and his Arian theology eclipsed by the more aggressive
Unitarianism of Joseph Priestley. When Sir Leslie Stephen published his
history of English eighteenth-century thought in the latter part of the nineteenth century he largely dismissed both Price's theological thinking – 'too
far removed from the general current of speculation to have much influence'
– and his philosophical ideas.[2]

In spite of Stephen's criticism Price's work did continue to elicit periodic
revivals of interest within academia. In 1942 W. H. F. Barnes published a
reappraisal and response in *Richard Price: A Neglected Eighteenth Century
Moralist* and in 1966 Antonio Cua published *Reason and Virtue: A Study in
the Ethics of Richard Price*. By 1974 D. D. Raphael, in his edition of Price's
Review of the Principal Questions in Morals, found Stephen's earlier view 'lacking
in understanding and sympathy'. Other works devoted to Price's thinking
subsequently appeared. They include Bernard Peach's 1979 work on *Richard
Price and the Ethical Foundations of the American Revolution* and P. A. L. Jones's
1989 commemorative Welsh and English bilingual edition of *Cariad at ein
Gwlad / A Discourse on the Love of our Country*, in which Price had welcomed
the early events of the French Revolution. In 1991 all Price's political
writings, edited by D. O. Thomas, were republished in the 'Cambridge
Texts in the History of Political Thought' series, and in 1993 Thomas,
Stephens and Jones published *A Bibliography of the Works of Richard Price*
which contains details of all Price's work, including their British and overseas
editions and other literature on Price published up to 1993.

Yet, as my own experience of discovering Price makes clear, he remains
relatively little known beyond academia; and this is particularly the case,
perhaps, in his own home country of Wales. This despite a number of
publications ranging from the short 1836 memoir by D.W. (Lledrod) in

Seren Gomer to W. J. Rees's *Richard Price (1723–1791)* in 1992, which detailed Price's life, moral philosophy and theology for the general reader. A wealth of new work on writers and thinkers of late eighteenth-century Wales has brought the period into new focus; it is a good time, then, to bring the contribution of Richard Price to more general attention because, as any modern reader of his work will quickly discover, he remains profoundly relevant.

Richard Price was born in the south Wales village of Llangeinor, near Bridgend, in 1723; he died in Hackney, London, in 1791. His life thus spans not only most of the eighteenth century but much of the period we call the Enlightenment: a time when rational thought and scientific knowledge seemed to offer liberation from old oppressions, ideas and habits and helped create an agenda for social progress and political change. In over thirty works published in his lifetime, many in multiple editions at home and abroad, Price made a significant contribution to this agenda. It is by any standards an impressive legacy, reflected not only in the importance of his major works on moral philosophy and life assurance, and his championing of old age pensions, religious toleration, parliamentary and electoral reform and the civil liberties that lie at the heart of our society today, but also in the sheer quality of his writing. This is a voice that speaks across the centuries. When we read Price, sentences of great lucidity, power and relevance seem to leap from the page. His fear of national bankruptcy resulting from the scale of Britain's debt and the possible consequences of the policies implemented to deal with it resonate powerfully in the early twenty-first century. Our concern over increasing disparities of wealth, religious intolerance, constraints on freedom of speech and the press and the moral justification of military interventions, drone strikes and torture can all be viewed in the light of Price's work on politics and moral philosophy. So too can lobbying in the House of Commons, a practice surely as pernicious as the influence of 'placemen' in the Parliament of Price's own time.

The aim of this book is not so much to provide an exhaustive account of every aspect of Price's work as to situate it in the context of the chronology of his life and times: to gain some sense of the man, as it were, through his ideas. My work draws a great deal on Price's own writings, and quotes from him liberally, but it is also indebted to a number of important scholarly contributions.

Price's nephew, George Cadogan Morgan, had intended to write the first biography of his uncle, but pulled back from doing so in the wake of the French Revolution, and the resulting clampdown on the reformist agenda in Britain by William Pitt's government.[3] George Morgan died in 1798 and so the first full biography, by Price's other nephew, William Morgan, was not actually published until 1815, at the close of the wars with revolutionary and Napoleonic France. No further volume appeared until Roland Thomas's work of 1924, which was the first to make extensive use of archival material available in this country. Then, with the publication of Carl Cone's lively and very readable *Torchbearer of Freedom: The Influence of Richard Price on Eighteenth Century Thought* in 1952, the extensive American sources were fully utilized for the first time. Henri Laboucheix's French-language biographic study and analysis of Price's philosophical and political thinking was published in 1970, with an English translation by Sylvia and David Raphael appearing in 1982. By far the most complete exploration of Price's life and contribution published so far however is that published by D. O. Thomas in 1977 as *The Honest Mind: The Thought and Work of Richard Price*. As its title suggests, this work, like most of the others mentioned above, adopts a thematic narrative structure with biographical detail interwoven into discussion of Price's work. The present contribution differs by taking, for the first time, a purely chronological approach aimed at placing Price's life and work firmly within the context of his times. It is also the first to make full use of Price's collected, and very extensive, correspondence, which was published and edited in three volumes between 1983 and 1994, with D. O. Thomas and Bernard Peach as editors. These letters, together with Beryl Thomas's transcription of the shorthand journal Price kept late in his life, have allowed, I hope, a fuller picture of Price's personality to emerge, as well as an even fuller appreciation of the extent of his contribution to Enlightenment thought. I am also indebted to the many scholarly articles published in recent years, particularly through the auspices of *The Price-Priestley Newsletter* and its descendant journal *Enlightenment and Dissent*.

For more detailed explorations of particular strands of Price's thought, the reader is referred to the notes for each chapter and the extensive bibliography. My hope is that the book will help to bring this important and neglected thinker to much wider attention, and inspire new readers to read his words for themselves. I have always believed that if we know little of our past we cannot hope to understand the present, and if we do not understand the present we have little hope of planning sensibly for our future. The shape of that future is very much where my interest lies.

Price once wrote of his belief and hope that sometime in the future, 'A scheme of government may be imagined that shall, by annihilating property and reducing mankind to their natural equality, remove most of the causes of contention and wickedness' in the world.[4] It is hardly surprising therefore that his work should have been referenced (favourably and unfavourably) by Karl Marx in *Das Kapital*, and that the historian J. G. A. Pocock declared him to be Britain's 'first and original Left-Wing Intellectual'.[5] Seen in this light he is the largely forgotten progenitor of that honourable line of Welsh social and political reformers stretching from the eighteenth century, and the cooperative and trade union movements of Robert Owen and Chartism of John Frost in the nineteenth, to the achievements of Lloyd George (old age pensions, disestablishment of the Church in Wales), Aneurin Bevan (National Health Service) and Jim Griffiths (National Insurance) in the twentieth. But Price also sensed in the Britain of his time, as I do in mine, a political stasis in the face of much-needed reform; a sense of old ideologies having failed and there being little to replace them. We continue with the same rhetoric and repeat the same actions in the face of a creeping certainty that what is really needed is radical reform, coupled with a renewed willingness to ask fundamental questions about the society in which we live and the one we want to see develop. In short, we need to rethink old certainties and ideas and to 'redefine the limits of the possible'.[6] This is an urgent need in a world of growing inequality and intolerance, where we have globalized markets but not the politics to deal with them, and in which environmental concerns will – and I say this as a historian at heart, a geologist by training and profession, and an environmentalist by conviction – force change upon us.

In spite of his relative obscurity, at least beyond academia, many of the ideas Price expressed in his published works on political reform and civil liberties became the norm in the years following his death in 1791, but as we have seen he also opposed some eighteenth-century trends that were destined to become dominant in nineteenth- and twentieth-century Britain and with whose legacy we still live today – imperialism and utilitarianism amongst them. His last public address, delivered on 4 November 1789 and published as *A Discourse on the Love of our Country*, brought together a lifetime's thought on everything from education to the concept of the nation under the heading of 'universal benevolence', which he regarded as 'an unspeakably nobler principle than any partial affections'.[7]

Price believed that any people had a right to self-determination as a nation, if they so chose, but this did not in any sense mean an exclusive and narrow focus on nationality. Instead, he believed in the individual and the nation as playing their part in a wider international context. His discussion of this issue alone is profoundly inspiring to read in the twenty-first century: as the late Geoff Powell has written, Price's belief in universal benevolence is underwritten by 'an economic order in which the individual participants are not self-centred competitors but benevolent cooperators. His liberty is not freedom of choice to do anything for self-gratification because it is governed by a determination to have the same expectation for others that we have for ourselves, and, since we are to be citizens of the world, the "others" are, literally everyone.'[8] It is a simple and profoundly moving idea, and, utopian as it may seem, it can be seen at work in our own time in, for example, recent concern for the working conditions of overseas workers who produce the goods we buy.

Price argues that as citizens we all have a responsibility, even a duty, to be actively involved in, and to ask questions of, the society to which we belong. As this book will show, he had questions for his own society in abundance. He questions the nature of the relationship between religious belief, the State and science. He asks how we know right from wrong, and where our ideas of right and wrong originate. He asks how power should be exercised in society – and how it should be controlled. That constantly questioning attitude can be, in part, attributed to Price's own south-Walian upbringing in a particular kind of intellectual environment, that of religious Dissent. And it is with Dissent that his story really begins.

1

A Background of Dissent

And because the passion and uncharitableness of the times have produced several opinions in religion, by which men are engaged in parties and animosities against each other (which, when they shall hereafter unite in a freedom of conversation, will be composed or better understood), we do declare a liberty to tender consciences, and that no man shall be disquieted or called in question for differences of opinion in matter of religion, which do not disturb the peace of the kingdom.[1]

When in May 1660 King Charles II entered London, the city where eleven years before his father had been publicly executed as a tyrant and an enemy of the Protestant Church, hopes were high that he would be able to keep his promise, made at Breda the previous month, to 'declare a liberty to tender consciences' and that no one would, any longer, be 'called in question for differences of opinion in matter of religion'.[2] Instead, however, the Cavalier Parliament of 1661 set about passing a series of acts aimed at restoring the supremacy of the Anglican Church, enacting revenge upon the Puritan dissenters and continuing the persecution of Catholics and Quakers.

Under the terms of the Corporation Act of 1661 anyone who did not receive communion according to the rites of the Church of England was excluded from holding municipal office. In 1662 the Act of Uniformity, perhaps the most divisive of the canon of legislation and the one having the most immediate impact on the forebears of Richard Price, decreed that all ministers of religion and teachers were obliged to give 'unfeigned assent, and consent to all, and everything contained, and prescribed' in the Book of Common Prayer. The 1664 Conventicle Act made religious meetings outside the Church of England with five or more non-family persons present punishable by imprisonment. Finally, the Five Mile Act of 1665 barred any clergyman from approaching within five miles of a city or corporate town unless he swore, under oath, not to attempt an 'alteration of government either in Church or State'. He was also forbidden from teaching in any school.[3] The impact of this legislation, known as the Clarendon Code, and the Act of Uniformity in particular, was felt throughout Wales and England with as many as 2,000 clergy losing their livings in England (one fifth of the total). In Wales, although the effects were less trenchant thanks to a more lenient interpretation and imposition of the legislation, thirty-one ministers were ejected.[4]

Among those who suffered under the expulsions in Wales was one Samuel Jones who had been posted to his living of Llangynwyd, a small hamlet in the Llynfi Valley in Glamorganshire, in 1657. Unable to conform to the demands of the Act of Uniformity, he was removed from his position and only by the good fortune of his marriage to Mary Powell, the daughter of a man of means, was he able to move a few miles away to a dowry property of Mary's at Brynllywarch. Here he established a Dissenting meeting place at which he preached and an academy at which he taught. Born in Chirk, Denbighshire, and educated at Merton and Jesus College Oxford, Jones was a philosopher, linguist and Orientalist and came well qualified to his role as teacher.[5]

Among those of Jones's Llangynwyd congregation who moved with him to Brynllywarch were Rees and Katherine Price, the paternal grandparents of Richard. The couple seem to have been of the 'middling sort' and they lived quite prosperously at Tynton, a substantial late seventeenth-century farmhouse still standing on the banks of the Garw River at Llangeinor, a village just north of Bridgend and in the next valley to Brynllywarch.[6] It was at Tynton that Katherine gave birth to five children. The eldest, Rice Price, was Richard's father, born in 1673. He was followed in 1676 by Samuel, who would later play a part in Richard's early life in London, and then three daughters: Catherine *c.*1675, Jennet in 1683 and Barbara (date unknown).[7]

Rice first married Mary Gibbon, a lady said to be of a parsimonious nature despite significant personal wealth. Before her early death she gave birth to four children: John, Samuel, Mary and Ann. Rice's second marriage was to Catherine Richards, the reputedly beautiful daughter of David Richards, a doctor from Old Castle, near Bridgend, and a lady much loved by the three of her six children who lived to adulthood: Richard, Sarah and Elizabeth.

Richard Price, the eldest of Catherine's surviving children (David, an older brother by one year, having died when Richard was six), was born at Tynton on 23 February 1723. Little is known of his formative years but his education certainly started at home; first under a governess, then with a Mr Peters who lived locally. Whether Price spoke Welsh at this time is unknown. Certainly he is likely to have first had the Bible in that language, and his library in later life contained a number of Welsh language bibles.[8] We also know that his sister Sarah spoke the language fluently; as did at least

Figure 1. Tynton, the Price family home and Price's birthplace at Llangeinor, south Wales. Possibly dating from the late seventeenth century, the listed house is currently in private ownership and under extensive renovation.

one of her sons (William Morgan) who was so fluent he could transpose a Welsh song into English on the spur of the moment.[9] In such a linguistic environment it seems likely that Price was bilingual. Indeed, this may have proved a necessity for, by the age of eight, he had been taken out of a school in nearby Bridgend 'on account of the moroseness and ill temper of his master'[10] and sent away to a succession of schools, each progressively further from home but within the western heartland of the language. First came the school of the Revd Mr Simmons at Neath, where he remained for four years. Then he attended Pentwyn, near Llan-non in Carmarthenshire, a school run by the second Samuel Jones to enter Richard's life and a man renowned for possessing candid and liberal religious views. Although no details of Price's time at Pentwyn survive some idea of his life there can be gleaned from the occasional diary and notebooks kept by another student, Thomas Morgan, who entered the school in September 1741 while it was still under the tutelage of Samuel Jones.[11]

A typical day began with prayers at eight o'clock followed by a theology lesson during which biblical extracts for translation by the students were read in Hebrew, Greek and Latin – a course of study borne out by the significant number of classical textbooks Morgan purchased while at Pentwyn (his acquisition of an Italian Grammar at 2d. and a copy of *Robinson Crusoe* at 1s. must have represented a welcome departure into modernity and light relief). The afternoon teaching session began at three and was given over to both theoretical science and to practical experimentation.

Science plays a pivotal role in the life of Richard Price and his interest in it was encouraged during his time at Pentwyn. He did not forget the debt he owed to this early encouragement. Many years later, in 1773, a gentleman informed the *Cambrian Magazine* of the acquisition by another Dissenter institution, the Carmarthen Academy, of 'the most curious Philosophical, Optical, and Mathematical Instruments and Machines'. Not only were these scientific apparatus 'the most curious things of art' with an elegance that could 'scarcely be conceived', they were also 'made under the direction of the judicious, and learned Dr. Price'.[12] It is not clear whether Price actually donated these instruments to the Carmarthen Academy or whether he simply oversaw their manufacture and purchase. A combination of both is certainly possible since in 1789 he would undertake a similar commission for Yale University in America.[13]

Having completed a week of theological and scientific study at Pentwyn, Sunday was spent practising the preacher's art at Dissenter places of worship. Unfortunately for Richard the liberal religious views of his tutor Samuel Jones, upon which he probably drew for his sermonizing, proved too liberal for his father Rice Price. Barely a year after enrolling his son at Pentwyn, Rice removed Richard and sent him instead to the school at Chancefield near Talgarth in Breconshire established by Vavasour Griffiths,[14] a man whose religious convictions were more in line with Rice's own (Richard Price's nephew, William Morgan, would later describe them as 'narrow, selfish and gloomy').[15] Rice Price certainly held High Calvinist views and there is little doubt that he wished to instil in his son their central doctrine of predestination and the concept of an elect: that God had chosen some for salvation.

Rice Price had been born in 1673, the year in which a final piece of Clarendon Code legislation passed through Parliament and a Declaration of Indulgence declared by Charles II in 1672, which had attempted to suspend the Code's worst elements, was revoked. As a fourteen-year-old in 1687 Rice may well have hoped to see the Code's restrictions changed as a result of further 'Indulgences' declared by James II in 1687 and 1688. But he would also have sensed the unease that grew in the country as the king's tolerance came to be seen as support for Catholicism rather than a move toward religious freedom and Dissenter rights. This unease ultimately led to James's exile and the accession to the throne of Protestant William III in 1689, whose reign would begin with the passing of a Toleration Act allowing limited freedom for Dissenting worship (other than for Catholics).

Figure 2. Memorial to Richard Price's paternal grandparents, Rees and
Katherine Price, in Bettws church, south Wales. The tone of the
inscription to Rees gives some idea of the family's religious zeal.

Yet, despite this limited toleration, the Clarendon Code legislation still
denied Rice a university place, the chance to teach openly and the opportunity
to better himself through gaining a position in civic society. Furthermore,
he lived through these events in a Welsh and British society that, although
changing, remained strongly conservative in its beliefs and practices. It was
a stratified society in which one's position in the hierarchical structure was
generally considered to be divinely ordained. It is no surprise therefore that
he, and others like him, should embrace a Calvinistic belief system which
gave him a place in a different hierarchy, one preordained by God, and
which assured him of a better life to come. He would have been anxious
to pass on the perceived benefit of these High Calvinist beliefs to his son
Richard, who seemed destined to face the same social, educational and
religious discrimination as he grew older. Yet, although Richard followed
his father in becoming a convinced and lifelong dissenter from established
religion, he would, with the benefit of his more liberal education and his
intellect, subject his father's views to rational analysis and clearly find those
views wanting. In a sermon many years later he publicly dissected the High

Calvinist view of Christianity before reaching the conclusion that it was 'a system inconsistent with reason, injurious to the character of the ever-blessed deity, and, in the highest degree, comfortless and discouraging'.[16]

Such contrasting views between father and son on a subject as central to eighteenth-century family life as religion appear to have created some tension at Tynton, as evidenced by an incident Richard later recounted to his nephew William Morgan. Returning home to Tynton one day, Rice Price came upon Richard sitting besides the fire reading a volume of the works of Samuel Clarke, another man of liberal theological views. Rice grabbed the book and threw it into the fire while uttering 'bitter invectives' against his son 'for his want of faith and orthodoxy'.[17] Even at a young age, Richard was clearly well advanced along the road of religious exploration and freethinking that would soon take him away from his father's Calvinism to Arianism, with its controversial denial of the Trinity and unorthodox views of Christ's divinity.

Although we can only guess how Catherine, Richard's mother, may have reacted to such moments of tension, we might speculate that she sided with her son and so set herself, however reluctantly, against the will of her husband. It is a suggestion that would go some way to explaining the comparatively harsh treatment she received under the terms of her husband's last will and testament.

Rice Price died on 28 June 1739 and his will makes clear his wish to be buried next to his first wife. To Catherine he left only a feather bed and its bedclothes, together with all the other goods she had brought to Tynton at the time of their marriage. Tynton itself he left to Samuel, his son by his first marriage and the executor of his will. The only obligation on Samuel was to provide Catherine with meat, drink, washing and lodging at Tynton for one year from the day of Rice's death, provided 'she be contented to dwell with [Samuel] so long'; she was not. Within a short time of her husband's death Catherine left Tynton with her daughters Sarah and Elizabeth and went to live closer to her own family at Old Castle in Bridgend; although not so close as to invalidate her husband's bequest to her daughters, who were each left £200 to be received on their coming of age, on condition that they would not live at Old Castle because Rice desired them to have above all things 'a pious education in a religious family'. This seems as much a sideswipe at Catherine's family as it is an instruction to his daughters. Richard received a cash sum of £50 in order to complete his education and to establish himself 'in a way of business trade or profession which his inclination shall lead him too [sic].' He also received two houses at Bridgend, which he thoughtfully put aside for use by his mother and his sisters. The remaining and more substantial part of Rice's estate went to the children of his first marriage.[18]

Following his father's death and the settling of his mother at Bridgend Richard Price returned to Chancefield to continue his education. His stay was soon cut short by news that his mother was ill. During 'the great frost' of the winter of 1739/40 he walked home to visit her and a short time later, on 4 June 1740, found himself at her bedside with his sisters when she died aged forty-seven, two weeks before the first anniversary of her husband's death. In barely a year Richard's whole world had been torn apart. We might expect such tragedies to have given him cause to question his most deeply held religious beliefs. If they did, they did not undermine them, for he would later recount how much he admired the tranquillity with which his mother had viewed her approaching death and, with it, the prospect of a better world. From this time on the thought of a better world after death becomes a lifelong preoccupation for Richard and one of the principal reasons for his continuing, though never unquestioned, belief in Christianity. He did not return to Chancefield. Instead, eschewing the business life his father had suggested for him, he set out for London.

2

A London Life

Y ddinas ddihenydd, bedlam fawr yr holl ddaear, cysgod o uffern ei hun.
(The city of destruction, the world's great bedlam, a reflection of hell itself.)[1]

London – this vast emporium of happiness and misery, splendour and wretched-
ness, the mart of all the world, the residence of the voluptuous and the frugal,
the idle and the busy, the merchant and the man of learning.[2]

Richard Price entered London at the age of seventeen sitting atop a conveyance he described as little more than a broad-wheeled wagon. Although he
would return nearly every year to visit his family in south Wales, London
now became home for the rest of his life: a city in which he eventually
became so well known that the costermongers of Covent Garden would
clear a path for him as he rode by on his half-blind horse and from which,
in a wonderfully Hogarthian moment, he was once thrown into a basketful
of their beans.[3]

Like many a Welsh émigré to the metropolis, Price was not without his
London-Welsh contacts. Before leaving south Wales he sought the advice
of his uncle Samuel, who had settled in London in 1703. It was Samuel who
now procured spartan lodgings for his nephew above a barber's shop in
Pudding Lane while at the same time enrolling him in the Tenter Alley
Academy in Moorfields, near the modern Barbican. This first taste of city
life was brief for, within a few months, Price developed a case of jaundice.
This was quite possibly hepatitis contracted either from the drinking water,
the unsanitary conditions in which he lived at Pudding Lane – 'a close and
confined abode, which was rendered more noxious by the want of those
ordinary conveniences which are necessary to health and cleanliness'– or
through swimming in the less-than-clean pools and rivers of the city.[4]
Whatever the cause, he went home to Wales to recuperate before returning
to London and the Tenter Alley Academy in the winter of 1741, anxious
to continue his education with the aim of entering the Dissenting ministry.

Founded in 1701 by William Coward, a wealthy Dissenter, the Tenter Academy originally subscribed to the strict Calvinist views of its first tutor, Isaac Chauncy. By the time Price arrived in 1740, however, it had changed considerably, being then under the tutelage of John Eames, an erudite man of 'candid and liberal disposition and a friend of free-enquiry'.[5] This was the man whose abilities his ex-pupil recalled many years later 'with the greatest respect and esteem'.[6]

The education provided by the Dissenting academies concentrated on theology and the training of students for the ministry, yet, as at Pentwyn in Wales, the curriculum could be broad in scope and progressive in terms of subject matter. At the best academies students were taught to a university standard so high that members of the Established Church were known to attend them in preference to Oxford or Cambridge – where, if the verdicts of men such as Swift, Defoe, Gray and Gibbon are to be believed, hard drinking rather than hard thinking had become the order of the day. The cheaper fees generally charged by Dissenter academies may also have been a consideration.[7]

The friendship of Price's tutor John Eames with the now deceased Isaac Newton, coupled with Eames's membership of the Royal Society and reputation as a natural philosopher, meant that Tenter Alley had become a leading centre for the teaching of natural philosophy. Eames appears to have been an inspired teacher in a multiplicity of subjects including 'divinity, the classics, mathematics, anatomy and natural and moral philosophy'. His course in applied mathematics, a subject Price came to love, included lectures in 'mechanics, statistics, hydrostatics and optics', some of them given in Latin.[8] Eames's assistant, James Densham, gave courses in 'logic, geography, algebra, trigonometry, physics and conic sections'.[9]

With such a quantity of knowledge to absorb it is unlikely a studious and religious young man like Richard, who applied himself 'with ardour and delight' to his studies, found much time for frivolity, entertainment or other forms of dissipation.[10] Consequently, it is easy when reading his works and reviewing his life to allow his ardent seriousness to divorce him from the raucous city in which he found himself, a city which must have been an influence on the moral, political and religious ideas that were soon to pre-occupy him.

The geography and buildings of eighteenth-century London presented as complex a mix of the past shadowing the present as they do today. After the Great Fire of 1666, which began in a baker's shop in Pudding Lane where Price first lodged, the city that rose from the ashes, although of modern stone and brick, still largely followed the old medieval street pattern. Even London Bridge, the only fixed crossing of the Thames until 1750 and barely a stone's throw from Price's lodgings, stood upon nineteen piers laid down in 1176. It was these same nineteen piers that allowed the shallower, pre-Embankment Thames to freeze in harsh winters like that of 1739/40, and Richard, who loved cold and frosty weather, soon became familiar with the frost fairs held on the river at such times.[11]

For a young man used to the quietude of Tynton and the rarefied atmosphere of study at country academies it must have been extraordinary to step out onto a London street, jammed with every type of conveyance, from common carts to the carriages and sedan chairs of the well-to-do, and thronging with a veritable army of street traders, peddlers and Abraham men (common beggars). He would have been assailed by the stinks of the city, both animal and human. Even Casanova, who visited in 1763, complained at seeing people 'attending to their needs and showing their behinds to the passers-by' without turning up an alley or to the wall.[12]

Extremes of wealth and poverty, riot and ribaldry were just as visibly displayed. In 1766 the construction of Spencer House in St James's Place cost £35,000; the annual wage of a common housemaid stood at six to eight pounds a year.[13] Fagin-led gangs of child pickpockets and muggings by footpads were rife, although the unfortunate footpad who assailed Price on one of his country walks probably regretted his demand for Richard's (silver?) shoe buckles. Seemingly unconcerned, Price simply turned and lectured the man on the folly of his ways.[14] The follies and tragedies of many others formed a visible part of the city and were often a source of its entertainment. Carts carrying felons to jail, the pillory, a public flogging or hanging (the last accompanied by a coffin for their body and a minister for their soul) were a regular feature of the streets; traitors' heads still appeared on spikes above Temple Bar in Fleet Street. Riot was endemic to the city and could erupt anywhere, and at any time: from the general tumult of a disgruntled mob to the trashing of brothels by equally disgruntled sailors or a theatre audience livid at price rises for seats at Covent Garden. Price lived through many such events, but none was more dangerous than the anti-Catholic Gordon Riots of 1780 that left large parts of the city devastated. As the rioters destroyed Newgate prison and attempted to storm the Bank of England he must have been concerned for the fate of a house he owned in nearby Leadenhall Street.

The city was renowned for ribaldry and sexual dissipation. A 1749 engraving of Ludgate Hill, near the London Coffee House (a place that would later play an important part in Richard's life), shows prostitutes advertising themselves by raising the edge of their skirts.[15] Printed guides were available to the often more extreme delights of the numerous bordellos around Covent Garden; places where, as the contemporary adage put it, many a gentleman discovered that one night with Venus (or a molly-house Apollo) could lead to a lifetime with Mercury.[16]

Various writers have rightly drawn attention to Price's puritan concentration on 'industry, sobriety, thrift and prudence' and above all his devotion to, and promotion of, the concept of a virtuous life. It is something of a surprise therefore to find relatively little use in his writing of the word 'sin', nor any sign of his preaching hellfire and damnation. In the early years of his life he had a very strong conception of heaven and hell and a conviction that the virtuous and right-thinking would receive their reward in heaven, but he did not believe in a hell of eternal damnation and punishment, preferring instead the idea that the wrongdoer would simply cease to exist after death. 'Eternal misery there cannot be under the Divine government, and I wonder how many men of reflexion and humanity can admit a thought of it into their minds', he wrote. 'But I am not so well satisfy'd that *extermination* may not be inflicted as a punishment for vice; and there is nothing that alarms me more, or that has a greater tendency to deter me from vice, than the consideration that it is at least *possible* this may happen.'[17] Price never believed in the perfect human being entirely free of sin and wholly virtuous. As he wrote: 'God remembers we are dust: perfection is above human capacity, and cannot be the condition of our acceptance. All that is necessary is, not *innocence*, but *integrity* of character; not *sinless*, but *true* virtue . . .'[18]

Considering the lives led by some of his circle of friends it is perhaps just as well he held such views. In his diary of 1762, Boswell, whom Price knew quite well, recounts 'taking' ladies in various courts of the city and once on the 'noble edifice' of Westminster Bridge while 'in armour complete', i.e. wearing a sheep-gut condom tied on with a ribbon.[19] Price was also a friend and mentor of Mary Wollstonecraft, a woman much maligned by later, more prudish, generations for leading an unconventional life. Even Benjamin Franklin, probably Price's closest friend, sired a son, William, in circumstances of some mystery (nowhere in Franklin's autobiography or papers does he mention the name of the boy's mother). Something of a ladies' man, Franklin even wrote notes for the younger generation on the advantages of having an older woman as a mistress.

Though Price did distinguish between public and private, he could become censorious when the private lives of some individuals, such as Charles James Fox and John Wilkes, spilled into the public domain and made the distinction hard to maintain. During the regency crisis, when the unbalanced state of mind of George III meant power might pass to his son the Prince of Wales, Price wrote: 'Is it not astonishing that the person [the Prince of Wales] who is the object of contention [in Parliament] should not, at a time when it is particularly incumbent upon him to maintain a dignity of conduct, have sense enough to avoid such an indecency as appearing drunk in public? This together with the loose and dissipated characters of his adherents, particularly, *Sheridan*, cannot but excite strong prejudices in the minds of the virtuous part of the public.'[20]

Sheridan, of course, as a politician and playwright was just one starry name in a London positively glittering with talent. On the stage, Garrick appeared to great success as Richard III in 1741 and would soon become manager of Drury Lane. Handel was already making music in the city and the young Mozart would make his appearance in 1764. In art, Canalletto, whose views of the city present such a contrast to its Hogarthian image, was at work by 1746. Thomas Gainsborough arrived, like Price, in 1740 and Joshua Reynolds became the first president of the Royal Academy in 1768, just as another of the Academy's founder members, the Welsh painter Richard Wilson, set about reinventing the painting of landscapes.

As a Dissenter, and thus in many respects a second-class citizen, Price would have been aware during his early days in the city of the all-pervasive power of the State and its established religion. After all, the dome of St Paul's loomed over his early lodgings in Pudding Lane and the spires and towers of Wren's churches pierced the skyline all around. Nor did he have to look far to see how easily and swiftly the rational, post-Newtonian thinking he championed could be overtaken by irrational religious bigotry. At the end of Pudding Lane was the monument to the Great Fire of 1666. Built by Wren and Hooke and completed in 1677 it stands 202 ft high (its precise distance from the starting place of the fire) and it once acted as a zenith telescope for members of the Royal Society to make astronomical obser-vations.[21] Yet, at the same time, on the northern panel of the four that surround its pediment and which illustrate various episodes from the fire were the words, in Latin: 'But Popish frenzy, which wrought such horrors, is not yet quenched.' Added to the original inscription in 1681 at the height of the Popish Plot, they referred to the commonly held belief that Catholic sympathizers had been instrumental in setting London ablaze. The offending words were removed during the reign of James II only to be re-carved more deeply than before in the reign of William III. No stranger to Latin, Price may well have pondered on the words as he passed by. They were finally removed in 1831.[22]

In 1744, having completed four years of education at Tenter Alley, Richard set about looking for a position in which to begin his ministry. He found one as assistant to Samuel Chandler at a meeting house in Old Jewry and once there soon achieved some popularity as a preacher. He may even have produced something of the emotional *hwyl* preachers at home in Wales employed in their sermons, for Chandler requested him 'to be less energetic in his manner, and to deliver his discourse with more diffidence and modesty'. Price obliged but then seems to have run 'into the opposite extreme of cold and lifeless delivery' to which his congregation were far less receptive. Price himself noted that: 'having preached in the afternoon on the *future judgement* with all the force and energy in his power, he had the mortification to find that neither his delivery nor the importance of the subject could keep a great part of his hearers from sleeping!'[23] Later, though, the poet Samuel Rogers records that Price 'in the pulpit . . . was great indeed, – making his hearers forget the *preacher* and think only of the *subject*'.[24]

In addition to the work at Old Jewry, Samuel Price also helped establish his nephew's career by recommending him for a position as chaplain and companion to the family of the prominent and wealthy Dissenter George Streatfield of Stoke Newington. Price took the opportunity and spent the next thirteen years with the family, only leaving when George Streatfield died in 1757, barely a year after Samuel Price's death in 1756. Richard now found himself in the fortunate position of being financially secure, having received a legacy of money from Streatfield and a house in Leadenhall Street in the City of London from his uncle Samuel.

By 1758 Price was earning a salary of £50 a year, rising to £52 10s. 0d. in 1760.[25] During this period cheese generally cost between 4d. and 6d. a pound, a pound of candles 2s. 10d., and a pair of strong shoes 7s. A man's suit cost £8, while 10s. 6d. bought a ticket to hear the *Messiah* at the Foundling Hospital, with Handel at the organ. £32 purchased a young Negro.[26] Price appears to have been a willing investor in what he judged to be sound propositions, as his neighbour Mary Rogers records in a letter to her husband Thomas. 'Dr. and Mrs. Price spent the evening with us last night, and Dr. P was speaking on what very advantageous terms they were granting annuities on the Douglas and Heron Bank – provided the security was good – upon which he and Mary Mitchell agreed to go to London this morning to hear Mr. Welch's opinion of it, and if they should hear a satisfactory account of it to risk about £200 pounds apiece.'[27]

A relatively prosperous man, at least by his middle years, Price regularly gave a fifth of his income to charity, saying to Joseph Priestley that even if he had children he would still have given a tenth.[28] Later, he made practical gifts of scientific instruments and books to a number of institutions, both at home and in America. Yet, despite this relative prosperity, the spectre of bankruptcy seems to have been ever-present in his life. His private journal and his letters record on a number of occasions the bankruptcy of close friends and acquaintances, some of them members of his congregation. One reason for his concern is likely to have been his personal knowledge of the distress bankruptcy caused to one family in particular, that of his wife-to-be

Figure 3. 'Stoke Newington Church, 1750', unattributed engraving in
Walter Thornbury, *Old and New London* (London, n.d.). Price married
Sarah Blundell here on 16 June 1757.

Sarah Blundell. Sarah came from Belgrave in Leicestershire and the bursting
of the South Sea Bubble in 1720 had ruined her father, a previously wealthy
speculator. Having moved to London after his demise, she lived with her
mother in a private lodging before moving to Hackney on her mother's
death. There, she lived on what remained of the family's wealth and, in
1757, married Richard Price.

There has been a church at Stoke Newington for at least 1,000 years and
the Tudor red-brick St Mary's Old Church, although touched by later
restorations and dominated by its Victorian successor across the road, survives
to this day. Standing in its tiny churchyard amid the tilted tombs and rustling
trees it is not hard to imagine Richard and Sarah appearing in its doorway
on 16 June 1757. Yet, even at so happy an event, Richard's status as a
Dissenter would have been a consideration. Prior to the Hardwicke Act of
1753 Dissenters had been allowed to marry in their own meeting houses.
The act however made it compulsory for every marriage (other than Jewish
or Quaker) to be conducted within the churches of the Church of England.
Still, it is unlikely to have marred their day, especially since Sarah was an

Figure 4. Price's home in Newington Green. Built c.1658, Price's house has been identified as today's number 54, which is the property with the squared-off top to the left (as viewed) of the central arch. It was here Price received many eminent eighteenth-century figures including Joseph Priestley, Benjamin Franklin, John Adams and Mary Wollstonecraft. At number 52 (far right) lived Price's friends Thomas and Mary Rogers and their son Samuel.

Anglican, and it is clear that Richard had found in her the love of his life and his greatest friend.[29]

Their first year together was spent in a noisy house in a narrow street in Hackney but they soon moved to the quieter surroundings of Newington Green where they were to spend the best part of twenty-nine years together. Even today, despite traffic and built-up surroundings, the area still evokes something of the atmosphere of eighteenth-century village life on the northern outskirts of London. Enclosed by 1742, the green remains a public space and Price's house still stands on its western side. It is one of a row of four recently restored seventeenth-century brick-fronted houses with a narrow arch at the centre of the row through which it is likely Richard led his horse to be stabled.[30]

To the north of the green, close by their front door, stands the meeting house where in 1758, following the death of George Streatfield, Richard took up an appointment as morning and afternoon preacher.[31] Sarah, however, would not have accompanied her husband to his services. She remained a devout Anglican throughout her life and no doubt left him each Sunday to

Figure 5a. 'Newington Green Chapel in 1860' unattributed photograph, taken before the remodelling that took place that year, and so still as Price would have known it.

Figure 5b. Newington Green chapel as it is today, the oldest Nonconformist place of worship still in use in London.

continue her stroll along Church Walk to the nearby Stoke Newington church where she had been married – an example, from within the bosom of his own family, of the precept of religious toleration Price would preach throughout his life and a marked contrast to the attitude of his father.

Sarah's life with Richard is poorly documented. She appears most often in her husband's letters when wishing to be remembered to his correspondent or when thanking the likes of William Hazlitt, senior, for his gift of brawn or lord Shelburne for his more exotic pineapples or the loan of a book on travel to China from the library of Bowood, Shelburne's country home. Such interests at least reveal Sarah as a literate lady and probably fully engaged in her husband's social and working life. This is borne out by the warm and affectionate compliments paid to her in many letters received by Price. From 1762 onward, however, her life would be plagued by illness, which must have precluded much in the way of travel: even, sometimes, their yearly visits to south Wales, Brighton or Eastbourne for the sea swimming that Richard loved. Sadly, too, we know next to nothing of Sarah's attitude to people of Price's acquaintance. We can only wonder what she made of Benjamin Franklin, Joseph Priestley, Mary Wollstonecraft or the ladies of the 'Blue Stockings', the informal literary club a number of whose members Price knew well. Nor do we know anything of her attitude to her husband's work, other than her desire at the height of the American War of Independence to protect him from the threatening and abusive letters to which he was subjected.[32]

A prevailing but always private sadness in their life together may have been their childless state; if so, it is a situation given added poignancy by Richard's well-documented affection for the children of Thomas and Mary Rogers, his immediate neighbours at Newington. Their son, Samuel Rogers, has left us a number of touching portraits of Price during his time on the Green. He records that Price not only loved being with children but possessed 'that boyishness and love of frolic which have often characterised men of genius'. Rogers presents a vivid picture of this pious clergyman and intellectual giant leaping the New River at Stoke Newington before attempting the same feat over a honeysuckle bush in the Rogerses' back garden, only to become so entangled that 'away went the doctor and the bush together.' It is also clear from Samuel's account that despite his natural or perhaps cultivated reserve, Price had a competitive side, which he displayed during the visit of a Mr Hulton to Newington Green. Described as being a 'much taller and more robust' man than the good doctor, Price nevertheless challenged him to a hopping race along the length of Cowslip Meadow between the meeting house on the Green and nearby Stoke Newington; Price won.[33] Nor did he mind taking time to explain his scientific experiments to his young neighbours, or to show them the telescope and other 'philosophical instruments' he possessed. So fond was Samuel of his neighbour that when asked by his father what he wished to be when he grew up, this future banker and poet replied 'a preacher', for he believed 'there was nothing on earth so *grand*'.[34]

In his early years at Newington Green Price's social life revolved around the meeting house and its congregation. Built in 1708 after the passing of the 1689 Toleration Act, by which Dissenters were allowed to engage in public worship for the first time, it was extended to its present form in 1860 and served an area with a long Dissenter tradition. Daniel Defoe attended an academy in Newington and the prison reformer John Howard, who probably knew Price at the Tenter Academy, lived nearby and became a close friend. Thomas Rogers, Price's neighbour, became treasurer of the meeting house in 1767 and once travelled with him to visit the Price family in south Wales. Another member of the congregation was James Burgh, a man of radical politics and philosophic interests similar to Price. He ran an academy at Stoke Newington and his pupils were regular attendees at Price's sermons. It was with Burgh, Thomas Rogers and Ralph Thoresby, the rector of Stoke Newington church, that Price formed a club that met once a week at a member's home. This comfortable if circumscribed world was now about to change. During his thirteen years with the Streatfield family in Stoke Newington, Price had found time to write a substantial work of moral philosophy. In 1758, while still living with his new wife in the noisy house in Hackney, this work – A *Review of the Principal Questions and Difficulties in Morals* – had been published.[35] Through it he became more widely known and with subsequent publications on many subjects written at Newington Green, he soon established a public reputation as a man of intellect and radical views. In consequence, his social milieu quickly extended well beyond the good folk of Newington Green.

3

The Virtues of Virtue

VIRTUE is the foundation of honour and esteem, and the source of all beauty, order, and happiness in nature.

Beauty and *wit* will die, *learning* will vanish away, and all the *arts of life* be soon forgot; but *virtue* will remain for ever.[1]

Between 1758 and 1767, as he left Hackney, married Sarah and settled into life in Newington Green, Richard Price published a number of important books, papers and sermons. They include his magnum opus, *A Review of the Principal Questions and Difficulties in Morals*, in 1758 as well as *Four Dissertations* in 1767, a sermon on *The Nature and Dignity of the Human Soul* in 1766 and *An Essay on the Doctrine of Chances* which, though written by his friend Thomas Bayes, was revised, edited and published by Price in 1764. He also published his own supplement to the Bayes essay in 1765.

In all these works Newtonian physics, astronomy and mathematics play a significant part, the latter particularly so in the *Essay on the Doctrine of Chances*, which, though recognized today as crucial for its contribution to the theory of probability (see chapter 4) was also attractive to Bayes and Price for the 'scientific' support it appeared to give to arguments for the existence of God. But 'science', in the way we know it today, was only just emerging in Price's time. What he really outlined in these works is closer to the older concept of a 'natural philosophy' derived not only from the study of creation through mathematics, physics and astronomy, but also philosophy and theology. In order fully to understand what motivated Price as a political and social thinker, we need to have some sense of the religious foundations of his morality.

By studying the world around him Price saw in it a 'regularity and order' that he took as evidence for its art and design. This implied, in turn, the presence of an intelligent creator since 'an unintelligent agent cannot produce order and regularity, and therefore wherever *these* appear, they *demonstrate*

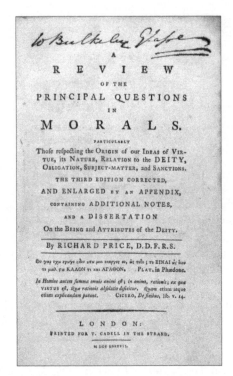

Figure 6. Title page of *A Review of the Principal Questions and Difficulties in Morals*
(1758; 3rd edn., London, 1787). This work established Price as one of the most
important British rationalist philosophers of the eighteenth century.

design and wisdom in the cause'.[2] This creator provided not only regular
and constant attention to creation, but also gave initial life and motion to
the otherwise inert matter from which it first came. Price illustrated this
conclusion in *Four Dissertations* by reference to Newton's Laws of Motion.
Since matter is inert, a force is needed to impart initial movement to it. But
what is the source of that force? If we say it comes from the first piece of
matter being struck by a second, then what gave movement to that second
piece? If we say a third, then what gave movement to that? We are left with
three options to explain the initial movement of matter. First, that there was
'an endless progression of motions communicated from matter to matter,
without any *first mover*'. Second, that 'the first impelling matter moved itself',
or, thirdly, there had to be a non-mechanical, non-material source of the
first movement in the form of a creator.[3]

Price realized that this cause and effect problem as it relates to the first movement of matter is just as applicable to the existence of a creator. Atheistical
writers, he observed, will ask the question, who then created the creator.[4]

In *Four Dissertations* Price tried to resolve this problem while at the same time admitting 'the difficulty . . . in giving a just explanation of the subject' because our language and our conceptions of God 'are *always* extremely defective and inadequate, and *often* very erroneous'.[5]

Price's solution, which acknowledges his debt to the work of the English philosopher Samuel Clarke (1675–1729),[6] is that a creator, and our conception of that creator, is necessary in the same way as we find 'abstract duration and space . . . necessary to the conception of all existence'. It was impossible, he continued, for us to think of space without a conception of distance, or of life without a conception of time and so, in the same manner, we cannot conceive of creation without actually thinking of a creator. As a result the non-existence of the creator is rendered impossible. Yet, he realized that this is not a truly satisfactory answer. Even though we may instinctively think of a creator when we ponder creation, it still remains open to us to deny that such an entity exists. To counter this he argues further that the non-existence of the creator is an impossibility not 'grounded upon or deduced from any facts or arguments, but an impossibility appearing *immediately*, and carrying its own evidence with it; an impossibility in the *nature of the thing itself*'.[7] Thus, he continued, 'the NECESSITY (or SELF-EXISTENCE) of the Deity is an attribute of the same kind with the SELF-EVIDENCE of those primary truths on which all science depends'.[8] Essentially, Price is saying that our perception of the creator's existence is as intuitive or self-evident as our appreciation of space and time and our acceptance of 2 + 2 = 4.

Price turned next to a consideration of the creator's true nature. Here he acknowledged his debt to Isaac Newton's idea that 'The Deity . . . by existing *always and everywhere* CONSTITUTES infinite space and duration.'[9] To Price this was a most important sentiment, and one reflected in his own assertion that the Deity 'is always present with all beings, not merely by his notice and influence, but by his essence'. Therefore God

> is intelligent, not by the *apprehension* of truth, but by *being* truth; and wise, not by knowing all that is knowable, but by being that intellectual light which enlightens all other beings, and which makes them wise and knowing. He is therefore, WISDOM, rather than *wise*; and REASON rather than *reasonable*. In like manner; he is ETERNITY, rather than *eternal*; IMMENSITY, rather than *immense*, and POWER rather than *powerful*. In a word; he is not *benevolent* only, but *benevolence*; not absolutely *perfect* only, but absolute *perfection* itself; the root, the original . . . the substratum of all that is great and wise and good and excellent.[10]

In his discussion of creation Price never doubts the existence of a creator as a first cause, nor does he question the six-thousand-year biblical time frame for creation's existence established by James Ussher (1625–56), archbishop of Armagh, who famously 'dated' the creation to October 4004 BC. Instead, he suggests that within that time frame 'the preservation of all things appears to be indeed very little different from a continual creation':

> The vanishing of old stars, and the appearance of new ones, is probably owing to the destruction of old worlds, and the creation of new worlds. It is reasonable to believe that events of this kind are continually happening in the immense universe; and it is certain, that they must be brought under the direction of some superior power. There is, therefore, the constant exertion of such power in the universe. Why must it be thought that, in the lapse of six thousand years, there have been no occasions on which it has been exerted on our globe?[11]

Clearly Price is no apologist for the Creationists of our own time, but neither is he advocating a form of Darwinian evolution. The process whereby continuous evolution takes place is still the result of the workings of providence and the kindly care and constant action of the creator.

It was probably little more than a year or two before publishing these ideas in *Four Dissertations* in 1767 that Price had made the acquaintance of Joseph Priestley, who was destined to become a close and lifelong friend despite their differing religious and philosophical views.[12] In religion, both men had rejected the Calvinism of their youth but they went on to adopt differing Protestant beliefs. Price followed the Arian doctrine, which denied the Holy Trinity and the concept of original sin and believed Christ to be not wholly of the same substance as God but still partially divine; such divinity being a prerequisite for humanity's redemption and our ultimate resurrection. Priestley, by contrast, followed the Socinian and, later, the Unitarian doctrine. This too denied the Trinity and original sin but saw Christ as wholly human and someone appointed by God to be our teacher and an example of moral perfection to which we could aspire.

The two men's differences did not end there. In 1777 Priestley published *Disquisitions Relating to Matter and Spirit*[13] and *The Doctrine of Philosophical Necessity*,[14] in which he advanced views at odds with some of those adopted by Price in the three early works considered here. These differences later resulted in a lengthy correspondence between the two men, published in 1778 as *A Free Discussion of Materialism and Philosophical Necessity in a Correspondence between Dr. Price and Dr. Priestley*.[15] The work not only illustrates their basic argument, but also shows how civilized debate between two people with differing views could be carried on without resort to the abuse common in the literary and social world of the time. Though both men would suffer from such abuse in their publishing lives, they wanted to debate 'without the mixing of any thing personal, or foreign to the subject' and with the aim, as Priestley put it, of achieving '*truth* not *victory*'.[16]

The issues they debated concerned the nature of matter and its relation to the spirit or soul and to our possession of free will. Even Price perfectly understood that such issues might appear 'dry and metaphysical',[17] but they are, nevertheless, important in his life for two principal reasons. First, they open out onto wider concepts of liberty, principally the civil and religious liberty that so concerns Price later on. Second, they help us to understand his compulsion in the years ahead to contribute to the well-being of the society in which he lived and to questions of moral, religious and civil liberty.

As regards the nature of matter and its relation to the soul, Price adopted a 'dualist' position. He believed that arguments from both reason and scripture demonstrated that 'there is in man, something . . . distinct from his body' and that this 'spirit or soul' is not only immortal but that it represents the 'higher parts of our nature'. On death the body decayed but the soul continued and would be resurrected.

Priestley by contrast adopts what is called the monist or materialist position. Though he does not deny the existence or importance of the spirit/soul there is no separation of it from the body. Instead, the soul is 'part of the system of the body and is created as that system is created. When the system dissolves so does the soul, "till it shall please the Almighty being who called it into existence to restore it to life again"'.[18] Our higher functions, such as sensation and thought, Priestley suggested, might 'necessarily result from the organization of the brain, when the powers of mere life are given to the system'; though he did not know precisely how this happened.[19]

The appeal of Priestley's monist/materialist position to nineteenth- and twentieth-century thinking in which science competes so powerfully with ideas of indefinable spirituality is obvious, and is surely one reason why Price and his ideas became relatively overshadowed. Another relates to both men's differing conception of how we acquire knowledge of the world. Both understood the value and importance of gaining knowledge, but their views on how we actually obtain it differed and led them into another debate, one still ongoing today, between empiricism and rationalism.

Empiricists such as John Locke, Joseph Priestley, and David Hume (whom Price knew and with whom he corresponded)[20] believed our knowledge of the world derived principally from our experience and sensation of it as filtered through our sensory faculties. This is another theory in tune with modern thinking as it forms the basis of the scientific method of experimentation. In the moral sphere, however, such ideas meant the question of whether we deem an action to be truly 'right' or 'wrong' depended upon how it affected us. Its corollary is the utilitarian concept that, because we naturally desire to be happy, an action is morally right or good if it results in our happiness, and morally wrong or evil if it results in the contrary. Price believed this argument to be 'destitute of all proof', one which, when pursued to its natural consequences, would surely end 'in the destruction of all truth and the subversion of our intellectual faculties'.[21] In the *Review of Morals*, he set about exposing flaws in the empiricist doctrine.

Sensation, he argued, could never provide a complete knowledge of the world since it saw only 'the *outside* of things', perceiving in a work of art, for example, no more than what the artist presents to the eye. Only our intellect allows us to see in a painting the 'order and proportion; variety and regularity' and the 'infinity of particulars' that enable us to discover general truths about the picture. Similarly, while feeling pain 'is the effect of sense', it is our understanding that is employed when our mind reflects on the pain and we try to 'discover its nature and causes'.[22] To Price any suggestion that morality derived solely from sense perceptions, and that arbitration between good and evil depended on how these perceptions affected us, reduced morality to little more than blind instinct in the cause of hedonistic self-satisfaction. Our natural desire for pleasure and happiness is not, therefore, always the arbiter when we make moral choices. We sometimes choose a moral course knowing it will bring unhappiness and even, in some cases, physical or mental pain. Clearly, therefore, considerations other than those of sensation or a pursuit of happiness must be at work when we make moral choices.

Price appealed instead to the primacy of reason and the use of intellect over sensation, arguing that morality is a necessary truth existing independently from external sensation and experience. It is perceived through reason, the use of our intellectual faculties, and through the particular faculty within us that intuits distinctions of right and wrong. It is this intuitive faculty which comprises the building blocks of reason for 'Every process of reasoning is composed of intuitions, and all the several steps in [reasoning] are so many distinct intuitions.'[23] Significantly, however, despite his appeal to the dominance of reason, Price does concede that occasions may still arise where we see 'moral beauty' in a particular action, and that this might engender in us a sensation of happiness. Thus, when we judge the actions of moral agents, namely ourselves, both our understanding and our heart may actually be involved.[24]

Despite their different approaches to understanding how we gain knowledge of the world, both Price and Priestley believed in the importance of knowledge itself. It formed part of their shared belief in the continual progress of humanity. Price agreed with many of Priestley's ideas on the subject, but for him, knowledge was not all. As a dualist, Price believed that the soul, with its higher functions and separation from the physical body, is most 'properly ourselves' and its cultivation and care consisted not only in furnishing it with knowledge but also with virtue since both these qualities constitute our 'perfection and glory':

> Virtue must be added to *knowledge*, or we shall remain poor and miserable. These ought never to be separated. There is always a greatness in knowledge; but, when separated from virtue, it is the greatness of a demon. There is likewise always an amiableness in virtue; but, when separated from knowledge, it is the amiableness of a well-meaning bigot, or a good-natured enthusiast. It is the union of these two qualities that gives the soul its complete excellence.

Despite this symbiotic relationship virtue remains superior:

> One virtuous disposition of soul is preferable to the greatest natural accomplishments and abilities, and of more value than all the treasures of the world. – If you are wise then, study virtue, and contemn every thing that can come in competition with it. Remember, that nothing else deserves one anxious thought or wish. Remember, that this alone is honour, glory, wealth, and happiness. Secure this, and you secure every thing. Lose this, and all is lost.[25]

Not surprisingly, therefore, Price devoted a large part of his *Review of Morals* to discussing our obligation to virtue and morality, its nature and its manifestation within us. He outlines the 'subject-matter of virtue' to which, he believed, we are all obligated and which we intuitively perceive. Foremost is 'Duty to God': 'our first and sovereign principle of conduct'.[26] Next is duty to ourselves since, 'If it is my duty to promote the good of *another*, and to abstain from hurting him; the same, most certainly, must be my duty with regard to *myself*.'[27] Then follow Beneficence: the study of the good of others;[28] Gratitude: because our receipt of benefits lays us under an obligation to the persons who have conferred them,[29] and, finally, Veracity[30] and Justice in all our dealings with others.[31]

In this creed of virtue Price prefigures by twenty years one of the most famous philosophical ideas: the *Categorical Imperative* described by Immanuel Kant in his *Critique of Pure Reason* in 1781. Both men believed there was a disposition to virtue within all of us, together with an imperative to act morally and virtuously that all rational and thinking people intuitively perceive. But Price understood that this did not mean we would always act rationally and virtuously. 'God has given no human a security against error' and temptations of many different kinds might lead us to stray from the rational and virtuous path. Furthermore, when faced with making moral judgements our intuitions, often so 'clear and unquestionable' as to produce 'demonstration and certainty', are sometimes 'faint and obscure' and produce only 'opinion and probability', wherein lies the possibility of error.[32] Human knowledge is never complete and often contradictory, so it is inevitable that the law of morality will sometimes be broken and the obligations of virtue ignored. That is why we constantly need to educate ourselves, to study morality and to take our time in reaching moral judgements.[33] Price then comes to a conclusion of prime importance in our understanding the life he subsequently came to lead. 'Practical virtue', of the sort just outlined, 'supposes LIBERTY' in the sense of our having 'the power of *acting* and *determining*: And it is self-evident, that where such a power is wanting, there can be no moral capacities'.[34]

Moral choice, therefore, lies at the heart of Price's philosophical work: but achieving practical virtue through such choice implies our possession of free will. Here he faces a seemingly insurmountable objection for, like Joseph Priestley, in a belief carried over from their Calvinist upbringing, Price believed in an all-seeing, all-powerful, omniscient and omnipotent creator working through providence to guide creation according to a divine plan. This would seem to preclude any possibility that we possess free will.

Priestley addressed the problem by accepting the omniscience and omnipotence of the creator. Consequently, as Robert Schofield has put it, for Priestley, 'Man's actions are determined', but 'the determination is not merely mechanical. Man has a power of reason that, through experience, represents a change in circumstances and influences the motivation of his will.'[35] With regard therefore to the question of moral virtue, man was 'both an instrument and an object in a system of unerring direction, and though the chain of events was subject to the established laws of nature, his determinations were part of that chain. The success or failure of a farmer's crops was in the determination of God, but no farmer is thereby excused from sowing his fields.'[36]

By contrast, Price overcomes the same problem by asserting our liberty from any form of determinism external to ourselves. 'Virtue', he argues, 'supposes determination, and determination supposes a determiner' but 'a determiner that determines not himself, is a palpable contradiction. Determination requires an efficient cause. If this cause is the being himself, I plead for no more.'[37]

In *Four Dissertations* Price went further by considering the presence of wrongdoing within the world. In Price's moral system its existence is a necessary precondition for the existence of morality and crucial to confirming our possession of free will. Without wrongdoing we could all aspire to perfection but that would place us on a par with God, which was impossible – 'God has given no human being a security against error; nor was it possible he should, without making us omniscient.'

The introduction of wrongdoing into Price's moral system also raises another interesting problem for if, as he argues in *Four Dissertations,* God's nature is such that he is 'the intellectual light which enlightens all other beings, and which makes them wise and knowing', how is it possible we can ever be unwise or act wrongly? Any unwise act or choice on our part would surely imply fallibility in the deity, something Price believed impossible. His answer is that by making the right moral choice we unite ourselves with God, who is not to be found in a particular moral virtue but in the pathway to that virtue. Price conceived of God as 'present with us, in all we think, as well as in all we do [. . .] His sense penetrates ours'.[38] So, whenever we are unwise or unreasonable because of bad choices we have freely made in the face of temptation, we sin not only against ourselves but also against God:

> . . . whenever any passion becomes predominant within us, or causes us to contradict our sentiments of rectitude, we lose our liberty, and fall into a state of slavery. When any one of our instinctive desires assumes the direction of our conduct in opposition to our reason, then reason is overpowered and enslaved. On the other hand, when our reason maintains its rights, and possesses its proper seat of sovereignty within us; when it controls our desires and directs our actions so as never to yield to the forces of passion, then are we masters of ourselves, and free in the truest possible sense. A person governed by his appetites is most properly a slave.

Moral choice, therefore, besides being at the heart of Price's philosophical work, and his life, is always seen as an act of volition, an act of our will. Predestination plays no part in this philosophy, despite his Calvinist up-bringing. Instead, we are autonomous individuals possessed of the moral freedom to make our own moral judgements, and to do so mindful of our obligations to morality and virtue.

There are, of course, other problems with these ideas. For example, if we intuitively understand right from wrong, as Price argues, then surely our morality lies wholly within us. So why do God and religion have to enter into questions of morality at all? Such problems led D. O. Thomas to suggest that 'it is doubtful whether at all points [Price] succeeds in reconciling his theology with his moral philosophy and even whether the latter is consistent with a Christian ethic'.[39]

There are dangers too in our being slaves to knowledge, for it may bring us to believe that a course of action is right because it makes rational sense even though, by all other measures, it is morally wrong:

> You well know that actions may have all the form of virtue without any of its realities. Works of charity may be nothing but ostentation and religious zeal; nothing but an attachment to opinions taken up blindly and capriciously. Honesty may be the effect of worldly policy; and achievements the mot [*sic*] brilliant, the effect of a passion for fame. Repentance may proceed more from a sorrow for losses sustained, or disgrace incurred, than from a hatred of vice as such, and shame for having done wrong.[40]

When allied to knowledge and virtue, rationalism too can impart a form of tyranny; when, for example, rather than simply ensuring the freedom of an individual or state by removing the obstacles in their path to it we then proceed to tell them how they should use the freedom gained. Price was aware of such problems. He believed they presented themselves unavoidably 'to all thinking persons, and . . . in all ages have puzzled human wisdom. Perhaps', he continued, 'we have not faculties for understanding the full answer to them, and for my own part I am very willing in this instance to acquiesce in my own ignorance.' He was happy to ascribe what puzzled him to his 'imperfect knowledge, partial views, and disadvantageous situation'.[41] But, he goes on, 'we need not rest the solution of this difficulty entirely on our ignorance'. Perfection in our ideas, just as in man himself, is impossible because 'There is not . . . any circumstance of our existence, or any one of our bodily or our mental powers, which has not in it something to perplex us; and one of the greatest mysteries to man is man.'[42] In light of such difficulties in making moral judgements, Price appeals not only for us to take our time in reaching them, but also to the power of our conscience (for 'whatever conquers this, puts us into a state of oppression') and to two virtues he possessed to an unusual degree for a Dissenter of his time – doubt and toleration.

To enter the world of Richard Price through the medium of his writing is to enter a world where doubt is supreme – not cynical doubt, but rather the constructive doubt of the rationalist. It is a world where every idea or belief, no matter how deeply held, is open to question and must stand on its merits before the test of reasoned argument and debate. Price knew, of course, that such a world was not a comfortable place in which to live. As he wrote, 'There are, probably, few speculative and enquiring men who do not sometimes find themselves in a state of dejection, which takes from them much of the satisfaction arising from their faith in very important and interesting truths. Happy, indeed, is the person who enjoys a flow of spirits so even and constant never to have experienced this. Of myself I must say, that I have been far from being so happy. Doubts and difficulties have often perplexed me, and thrown a cloud over truths which, in the general course of my life, are my support and consolation.'[43] This even extended to his religious beliefs, which certainly evolved during his lifetime. As a young man he had dissented from the orthodoxies of the Established Church and the Calvinistic predestination espoused by his father, and, by the time of writing his *Review of Morals*, he had found a spiritual home in Arianism, which rejected the Trinity and had an unorthodox attitude to the true extent of Christ's divinity. Toward the very end of his life he would even tend toward Unitarianism, with its still greater emphasis on Christ's humanity.

Questioning and doubt also extended to his belief in Christianity itself. As he later told the earl of Shelburne, 'Your Lordship has mistaken me if you think that my belief of Christianity is an *assurance* of its truth. I feel difficulties and wonder at the confidence of the men who think that on this point no honest man can doubt. This affords no argument in their favour, for it generally happens that there is the most confidence where there is the least reason for it . . . My conviction on most points is only a preponderance on one side.'[44]

Such pervasive doubt is often criticized today as leading to a debilitating relativism, the idea that what is right and wrong for one individual or society may not hold true for another with different cultural or social values. Thus the prospect of a set of core universal values, so essential to Price's later work on civil liberties, is rendered impossible. That Price understood this problem is made clear in his *Review of Morals*:

> . . . though all men, in all cases, judged rightly what is virtue and right behaviour, there would still prevail a very considerable variety in their moral practices in different ages and countries. The reason is obvious: In different ages and circumstances of the world, the same practices often have not the same connexions, tendencies, and effects. The state of human affairs is perpetually changing, and, in the same period of time, it is very different in different nations. Amidst this variety, it is impossible that the subject-matter of virtue should continue precisely the same. New obligations must arise, and the properties of conduct must vary, as new connexions take place, and new customs, laws, and political constitutions are introduced.[45]

This did not mean there were 'no principles of truth in themselves certain and invariable, and forcing universal assent'.[46] He was clear that 'the grand lines and primary principles of morality are so deeply wrought into our hearts, and one with our minds, that they will be for ever legible'.[47] Yet, it is in his willingness to also recognize that 'new obligations' must arise and 'new customs, laws, and political constitutions' be introduced that we see the germination of his unwavering support for the revolutionary situations soon to develop in America and France. But as the latter event in particular would show, there are always instances when we desire to turn doubts into certainties. To avoid this, and any descent into rigid dogma and fanaticism, one further virtue, toleration, is essential.

Price's tolerance stemmed from the simplicity of his religious beliefs, which centred on the existence of a creator and the Christian hope of resurrection rather than outward customs and modes of worship. Indeed, doctrinal and religious differences actually seem to have been of very little consequence to him. 'Give me but this single truth, that ETERNAL LIFE is the gift of God through Jesus Christ . . ., and I shall be perfectly easy with respect to the contrary opinions which are entertained about the dignity of Christ, about his nature, person, and offices, and the manner in which he saves.' He had an intense dislike too of proselytism and all forms of religious fanaticism. 'The rage for proselytism is one of the curses of the world. I wish to make no proselytes except to candour, and charity, and honest enquiry . . . In truth; ecclesiastical history in general . . . is little more than a history of the worst passions of the human heart worked up by ecclesiastical zeal into a diabolical virulence and madness.'[48]

This degree of tolerance surely explains why he found it so easy to remain friendly with those of differing views amongst the Dissenting community, and, more significantly, Anglicans, though usually of a liberal or latitudinarian outlook. They were, however, a minority, for leading members of the Church of England (to which his wife belonged) would later vociferously attack his views on religious freedom and civil liberties and use their episcopal power in the House of Lords to oppose some of the social and political reforms close to his heart. Though a true eighteenth-century Protestant in his dislike of Catholic beliefs and practices and in his hope that one day they, and the world, would come to see the superior nature of Protestantism, Price still saw certainty of belief as inherently dangerous:

[W]hen men come to annex notions of sacredness to particular formularies of faith, and to think it their duty to do all they can to bring men over to the belief of them: when they come to look upon persons who do not receive them with horror, and to consider them as enemies to the Deity, then the most horrid evils begin, – the flames of persecution are kindled, – numberless innocent victims are sacrificed, – and religion becomes a cruel and pernicious superstition.[49]

As we shall see, this generally undogmatic and tolerant nature would lead Price not only to question his own religious beliefs and, through science, the nature of the creation around him, but also the society in which he lived. It brought him to believe that things were not as they should be and that this, in accordance with the demands of virtue for contribution and improvement, was a situation that needed to be addressed. Price's belief in the possession of free will is essential in understanding his need to contribute to society in the years ahead, and his championing of liberty in particular. As Carl Cone has written, 'human freedom was always at the heart of Price's thoughts and acts' and so 'just as there should be moral autonomy, there should be political and religious autonomy. Without understanding the emphasis Price placed upon freedom of action and will, one misses the integration of his moral, religious and political thought.'[50]

In the nineteenth century Priestley's empiricism and utilitarianism, and even acceptance of divine providence, would come to overshadow Price's thinking. It would be false, though, to claim a complete antithesis between the thinking of the two friends. There was much they shared in common and the philosophies they both adopted gave rise to degrees of improvement and moral activity. Yet, there is in Priestley's thinking a tendency to accept that 'whatever is, is right'[51] and it is certainly true that he was less actively involved in the politics of reform than Price. In true puritan fashion Price believed that 'You may go idle into misery. But you must work and strive if you would be happy.'[52] Determined to avoid the former, he became addicted to the latter. As a consequence, he would make substantive practical contributions in the years ahead to the happiness of the society around him and to the cause of civil liberty and freedom. Somewhat surprisingly, his tentative start on this road came in a sermon ostensibly celebrating war.

* * *

War, both national and international, had been a backdrop to Richard Price's London life from the time of his arrival in 1740. In 1745, as he completed his education and settled into life with the Streatfield family at Stoke Newington, Charles Edward Stuart, the exiled Young Pretender to the British Crown and better known to history as Bonnie Prince Charlie, landed in Scotland with barely a dozen supporters at the start of what became known as 'the 45', the last Jacobite rebellion in Britain. Within a few weeks the prince's support had risen to over 1,500 men and on 21 September they marched south taking a route via Carlisle down the western side of Britain. By the first week of December they had reached Derby, with their numbers swollen to over 5,000; at this point no substantial military presence stood between the Jacobite army and London. We do not know how Price reacted to these events, or to the Government's hasty mustering of troops at Finchley, barely four miles from Stoke Newington, but one aspect of the uprising does seem to have had a lasting and tangible effect on him: on 6 December 1745, as news of the Jacobite advance spread through London, there was a run on the Bank of England. Dubbed 'Black Friday', it may well have coloured Price's later calls for Government to maintain public confidence in the fiscal system by supporting the Bank whenever military conflict seemed likely. On this occasion, the Bank survived. The Jacobites turned around and headed back to Scotland, where they defeated another army sent against them at Falkirk in January 1746, before succumbing at Culloden in April that same year. By July the heads of several participants in the rebellion appeared on spikes above Temple Bar.

Between 1741 and 1748 the War of Austrian Succession, of which the 1745 Jacobite rising indirectly formed a part, pitted Austria (supported by Britain) against Prussia (supported by France and Spain). Though this war ended with the signing of the Treaty of Aix La Chapelle in 1748, two years later, as Price worked on his *Review of Morals* and continued to minister to the Streatfield family, Robert Clive reopened hostilities against the French in India. This provided just one of the pretexts for yet another sustained conflict.

The Seven Years War (known in North America as the French and Indian War) officially began in 1756 and saw Britain ally herself this time with Prussia against a coalition of France, Austria, Russia and later Spain. Despite early British setbacks in India and the Mediterranean the tide of this war began to turn in Britain's favour in 1759 and such was the scale of British victories that year that the Government appointed 29 November as a day of General Thanksgiving. To help celebrate it, Price, fresh from publishing his *Review of Morals*, recently married and by now the morning and afternoon preacher at Newington Green chapel, entered his pulpit and preached on a theme taken from verse 20 of Psalm 147: 'He hath not dealt so with any nation: And as for his judgments, they have not known them. Praise ye the Lord.'

The sermon is in two parts. The first is designed to show, in the light of Britain's victories, how the nation was distinguished in its happiness; the second suggests what effect such a distinction should have with regard to further improving that happiness. Price begins by reflecting on the background of war against which Britons lead their daily lives. 'We *hear* indeed of the dreadful calamities and desolations of war, but we only *hear* of them. We neither *feel* nor *see* them. And so little is the difference between the state of most of us now, and what it was before the commencement of war, that, was it not for the accounts we read and the reports conveyed to us, we should scarcely know that we are engaged in war.'[53]

He goes on to applaud the 'plenty and opulence' Britain enjoys. It is, he says, a place where even the poor are satisfied with bread and, 'Notwithstanding all the drains of war, we feel no very sensible scarcity of any kind. Our wealth increases continually; and it may be questioned whether any nation ever raised, with so much ease, such large expences as have been laid out by this nation in the present war.'[54] In keeping with the celebratory purpose of the day, he praises the events and victories of the *annus mirabilis* 1759. 'Our counsels have been wise, our measures vigorous and our enterprizes successful. Our Navy and our Army have gained the highest honour by their unanimity and bravery. Our enemies have been taught to fear and to feel our superiority. They have fled before us everywhere.'[55] Even though such glories had cost 'some of the best blood that was ever shed', he went on, 'let us remember how gloriously [the soldiers] have fallen, and that they are more the objects of envy than lamentation. Their example, we may expect, will kindle courage in others, and their spirit be transfused into thousands who will emulate their virtues and aspire to their glory.'[56] But it is not only Britain's military strength Price celebrates. He also extols the liberty Britons are blessed with since, in this country, 'No life can be taken away, or any punishment inflicted on any one, without a fair and equitable trial.' Britons were blessed too by their possession of religious liberty, 'the crown of all our national advantages',[57] and they lived in a place where 'free and publick discussion is allowed on all points' and 'All sects enjoy the benefit of toleration'.[58]

Such eulogizing of Britain's military prowess and its civil and religious freedom appears so at odds with his later views that for Price to arrive at them from the position he adopts here would seem to require a conversion as dramatic as that of Paul on the road to Damascus. The second half of his sermon shows, however, that he is aware of problems with the picture he has just painted. 'Is it not too sadly notorious, and has it not been often lamented by the wisest and best men amongst us, that, in our constitution, both civil and ecclesiastical there are many particulars, which greatly want amendment, and some of which are inconsistent with that liberty, which is the chief subject of our boast and triumph, and really a scandal to a great and wise people?'[59] Here, one feels, is the more recognizable voice of the future champion of civil and religious liberties, and it is perhaps a sign of the already politically charged nature of his times that he treads very cautiously at this point: 'I will not enlarge here, lest I should offend any worthy men, and deviate into what would be inconsistent with the design of this day.'[60] Yet, then, in what becomes a typical Price trait, he ignores his own call for caution and goes on to deliver not the celebratory peroration his previous eulogizing might lead us to expect, but one that directly challenges his listeners to confront civil and religious injustice:

> [I]t is, I think, our duty, as private men, to do what we can towards removing those offences which dishonour our country, by declaring our sentiments about them, on all proper occasions, with modesty and humility; by never complying in any instance contrary to our sentiments; and giving as far as possible, a publick testimony in favour of universal liberty and the simplicity of the Gospel. As long as wise men will not do this, or indulge timidity and indolence, it is certain, that corruptions must continue, and that no alterations or improvements can ever be expected.[61]

In conclusion, he notes, many in Britain have 'nobly distinguished themselves' in attempting to amend for the better human affairs and he hopes their names may 'be had in everlasting remembrance and honour'.[62]

Having raised his concerns and published his sermon as a pamphlet entitled *Britain's Happiness and the Proper Improvement of It*,[63] he at this point seems to have been content to leave political concerns aside in order to make less controversial but no less valuable improvements to such happiness.

4

The Equitable Life[1]

Permit me to thank you, not only on my own Account for the book itself you have so kindly sent me, but in [*sic*] Behalf of the Publick for Writing it. It being in my Opinion (considering the profound Study, and steady Application of Mind that the work required, the sound Judgment with which it is executed, and its great and important Utility to the Nation) the foremost Production of Human Understanding that this Century has afforded us.[2]

Price's earliest attempt at a contribution to 'Britain's happiness' came in 1771 with the publication of his second major work, *Observations on Reversionary Payments; on schemes for providing annuities for widows, and for persons in old age; on the method of calculating the values of assurances on lives and on the national debt.* It is to this that his great friend Benjamin Franklin is referring in the quotation above, but the work's genesis lay in an even earlier Price publication; one that, like *Observations on Reversionary Payments*, to which we shall return, is of considerable significance not only to Price's own time but also our own.

In 1761, the year of George III's coronation, Price's friend Thomas Bayes died. A Dissenting minister in Tunbridge Wells and a mathematician of note, Bayes had, like Price, attended the Tenter Alley Academy in Moorfields, although being older by twenty years had not known Price there as a pupil. They most likely met through their mutual acquaintance with John Eames, who tutored both men during their respective student days.

Having been asked to look through his deceased friend's papers by the Bayes family Price came upon a mathematical essay he recognized as important in the field of probability theory; he proceeded to edit the paper with a view to publication. This proved a lengthy process, principally because his sense of duty required 'he should be very sparing of the time he allotted to any other studies than those immediately connected with his profession as a dissenting minister'.[3] At the same time in 1762 both he and his wife Sarah fell ill – the latter's sickness rendering Price 'indifferent to almost every other event'.[4] In November he turned down the offer of a position as tutor in his

Alma Mater at Tenter Alley; he also declined a chance to edit the works of
Isaac Newton and, in 1763, to become a preacher in Bristol.[5] Two other
offers he did accept. In 1762 he became evening preacher at Poor Jewry
Lane (he would relinquish this post by 1770).[6] He also joined the board of
the trust founded by fellow expatriate Welshman Daniel Williams, who, on
his death in 1716, had left funds for the education of Dissenting ministers,
the founding of schools in north Wales and the establishment of the library
in London which bears his name to this day. As a consequence Price did
not finish editing Bayes's essay until late in 1763, when he sent it in the
form of a long and mathematically detailed letter to his friend John Canton,
a member of the Royal Society. The paper was read there on 23 December
and subsequently published in the Society's *Philosophical Transactions* under
the title 'An Essay Toward Solving a Problem in the Doctrine of Chances'.

Price remained diffident as to his part in editing the essay and it is difficult
to know precisely how much work of his it contains. He certainly replaced
Bayes's introduction with one of his own and chose the more satisfactory
of the two solutions to the problem of probability Bayes discussed.[7] For the
rest we must be satisfied with Price's comment that 'I have in some places
writ short notes, and to the whole I have added an application of the rules
in the essay to some particular cases, in order to convey a clearer idea of the
nature of the problem, and to show how far the solution of it has been
carried.'[8] Price went on to publish his own paper on the subject in 1765 – a
'Supplement to the Essay in the Doctrine of Chances'– in which he attempted
to improve on some of the solutions in the Bayes essay. On 5 December
that same year, in recognition of 'his great skill in mathematics and philosophy', he was elected a Fellow of the Royal Society.[9]

Bayes's essay essentially suggests that the probability of future events
happening could be predicted by calculating the frequency of their earlier
occurrence. The essay has since been called 'one of the most famous in the
history of science'[10] and a theorem it contains is now widely known as Bayes
Theorem, Bayes Rule or Bayes Law; though very recently it has been
suggested that 'By modern standards, we should refer to the Bayes-Price
Rule. Price discovered Bayes's work, recognised its importance, corrected
it, contributed to the article, and found a use for it.'[11] Today, the Bayes-Price
rule is used by a wide variety of practitioners, including lawyers and statis-
ticians, medical and environmental researchers, astrophysicists, those interested
in molecular evolution and even by Google and Microsoft for filtering
spam mail. In eighteenth-century Britain, however, the principal value of
the essay, a value Price would be the one to fully reveal, was to those involved
in actuarial studies and the associated and burgeoning business of life
insurance.

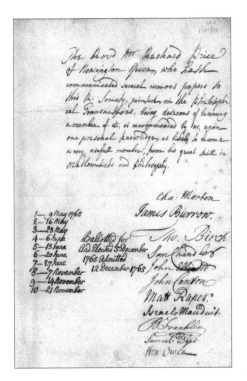

Figure 7. Richard Price's certificate of election to the Royal Society,
December 1765. Among those who signed his certificate and
proposed his membership as a man with 'great skill in
mathematics and philosophy' are his friends
Benjamin Franklin and John Canton.

Short-term insurance of a traveller's life for a single journey or the provision
of an annuity for an individual's old age had long been available. Yet, although
some aspects of the mathematics involved in assessing life expectancy (essential
for determining the premiums to be paid) were understood by Price's time,
assessments were not accurate enough to guarantee the success of large-scale
and more long-term life-annuities schemes. The danger, of course, was that
not enough funds might be collected to support the number of participating
annuitants. With the advent of Bayesian probability it finally became possible
to determine life expectancy with something like the required accuracy.
Unsurprisingly, therefore, Price now found himself consulted on the subject
of annuities and life assurance with increasing frequency.

Among the first to seek his advice was a group of lawyers who proposed
to establish a society to provide annuities or pensions to the widows of those
connected with the law; they desired to know Price's opinion as to the

$$p(\Theta|y) \; = \; \frac{p(\Theta)p(y|\Theta)}{\int p(\eta)p(y|\eta)d\eta}$$

Figure 8. The Bayes-Price theorem on probabilities and the
foundation of many aspects of our modern life.

viability of their scheme. He was not impressed, and so persuaded were the
lawyers by his arguments that the 'whole design was laid aside'.[12] Another
consultation, this time by the Society for Equitable Assurances, now known
as the Equitable Life Assurance Society, led to a much longer association.

The first record of Price's involvement with the Equitable dates from
1768, when the Society clearly found satisfactory his reply to their initial
annuities enquiry, for the Society's actuary, John Edwards, submitted its
entire printed accounts to Price for his examination and comment. The
Society, Price concluded, 'may be of great service if proper care is taken'.[13]
Encouraged by this response, Edwards submitted many more queries over
the coming months.

In addition to answering the Society's questions, Price also began formu-
lating tables aimed at simplifying survivorship and annuities calculations.
These he forwarded to the Equitable together with notes on the best method
of their construction and calculation. As a consequence, tables of survivorships
and annuities soon became an essential element of his work for the Society.
However, Price was soon overwhelmed by the enormous number of calculations required to derive the tables, and felt, more importantly, that the
work took him away from his other responsibilities, in particular his ministry.
Though he searched for ways to shorten the method of calculating the tables,
he found none that was 'consistent with sufficient exactness'.[14] By mid-1769
he suggested that he withdraw from his consultative position with the
Equitable. Yet, on 9 June he answered a further query from the Society and
as late as August 1770 the directors were still asking for his assistance in 'the
calculation of tables of survivorships, endowments and deferred annuities
on children's lives and similar contracts on adult lives'.[15] Thereafter, the flow
of consultations continued much as before.

Why did Price find it so difficult to withdraw from a position that had
clearly become burdensome to him? After all, he received no formal payment
for his work with the Equitable. Instead, the Society paid its debt to him
via gifts of a mostly practical kind, which can be traced in his correspondence.
In 1768 Price wrote to thank Actuary Edwards 'for two volumes on the Greek
Testament';[16] in 1770, the Society presented him with a set of 'mathematical

instruments' worth £51 4s.[17] These may well have been the telescope, electrical machine and microscope that Price so enjoyed showing to Samuel Rogers, his seven-year-old neighbour at Newington Green.

Perhaps the more likely reason for Price's failure to withdraw from the Equitable is a combination of persuasion by the Society's officers for him to continue his service, coupled with his own belief in the necessity for a virtuous man to involve himself in wider society and its improvement. As Price himself grew older, this latter consideration would often override his parallel desire to withdraw from general society and cut down on his commitments. Consequently, his advisory association with the Equitable ultimately lasted nearly fifteen years, and gave rise to an even longer familial involvement with the Society in the shape of his nephew, and first biographer, William Morgan.

William Morgan, the son of Price's sister Sarah and her husband William Morgan, senior, had left Wales in 1767 to come and live with his uncle Richard and aunt Sarah at Newington Green. Nineteen at the time, he was inclined to follow in his father's footsteps and train to be a doctor. Price, for his part, had agreed to help fund the young man's studies. William's steps on the medical ladder, however, were not a great success and although he returned home to Bridgend on the death of his father in 1772 with the intention of taking over his practice, he soon returned to London.

Following his nephew's return, and knowing of his desire to find employment, Price asked him one day whether he had any knowledge of mathematics. 'No, uncle,' William is said to have answered, 'but I can learn.' At the Equitable the new post of Assistant Actuary had just been created with a salary of £100 per annum and, after an intensive year studying mathematics with Price, William was appointed to the post in 1774. He did well and in 1775 became actuary at the age of twenty-three. It was a post he would hold until 1830. During his fifty-five year tenure as actuary the Society rose, as Morgan himself put it in his retirement speech, 'from a puny Institution, consisting of a few Members and possessing a Capital of a few thousands, to a magnificent Establishment consisting of many thousand Members and many millions of Capital, diffusing its benefits to the families of its deceased Members, and holding forth the prospect of equal benefits to those of its living Members'.[18]

Price, in the meantime, was aware of the fact that a great many societies similar to the Equitable were being founded at the time, often 'on plans alike improper and insufficient'. So he set out to provide the public with information on annuities and assurance subjects in the hope that this would lead to the 'establishment of stable societies and ultimately more certain benefits to their members'. This work was of course additional to that

Figure 9. 'William Morgan', engraving by William Say, 1803,
after a painting by George Hounsom.

with the Equitable, and involved more time and trouble than he originally
expected. 'I was led to undertake this work imagining that it might soon be
finished, and that all I could say might be brought into a very narrow compass.
But in this I have been much mistaken. A design, which I at first thought
would give little trouble, has carried me far into a very wide field of enquiry;
and engaged me in many calculations that have taken up much time and
labour.'[19]

The first public fruit of Price's labour came in the form of a detailed letter on the population of London sent to his close friend, the visiting American and Royal Society Fellow, Benjamin Franklin. The choice of Franklin as recipient was apt, for he had written on population studies as early as 1751 and had long been interested in the development of reliable insurance for which, of course, accurate population statistics were essential. Price's letter was read to the Royal Society on 27 April and 4 May 1769 and published in the *Philosophical Transactions* under the title 'Observations on the Expectations of Lives'.

In this work Price attempted to analyse the contemporary state of London 'with respect to healthfulness and number of inhabitants'. In the coming years, as this kind of demographic work progressed alongside that on annuities, Price became adept at collecting and collating historical and contemporary population data from across Europe and the British Isles.[20] But the database he used for this first work on population comprised the London Bills of Mortality. These were a weekly total of the births, marriages, deaths and causes of deaths within the city walls and a number of parishes beyond them. They had been kept since the sixteenth century and were notoriously un-reliable. For example, they did not record the births of Jews, Quakers or Catholics, and even though Parliament passed acts in 1695 and 1700 to ensure local Anglican priests noted Dissenter births these records too were often incomplete. Added to this was the problem of knowing how many people were leaving and entering the city in any one year. Price did, though, have other data to hand including the window-tax records that he had been studying since at least 1765.[21]

Using this less than perfect database, Price concluded in his essay that earlier estimates of London's population, such as the near a million of Corbyn Morris in 1751, were too high; his own total for the year 1769 was just 650,000. In this conclusion he may well have been correct.[22] However, having reached his conclusion, he then applied his population formula back to the year 1736, concluding that London's population had fallen between 1736 and 1769 by 84,260. This conclusion of an overall fall between 1736 and 1769 was erroneous, a result of the inadequacies of the database from which he worked and, to a degree, his misinterpretation of the data he possessed. He later compounded this mistake in a further population study, in which he suggests the population of England and Wales was also falling despite persuasive evidence to the contrary presented by his contemporaries.

In true Dissenter fashion, Price attributed the decline he believed he saw in London's population to 'the tenderness, the luxury, and the corruptions introduced by the vices and false refinements of civil society'. This, he believed, was an urban phenomenon, breeding 'that rottenness of constitution which is the effect of indolence, intemperance and debauchery'.[23] Like many others, Price favoured country living with its simpler lifestyle, making an interesting early complaint against London's already growing atmospheric pollution. 'The great evils which produce the unhealthfulness of towns are the closeness and foulness of the air, and the irregular modes of living.'[24] This 'foulness', he concluded, injured life's delicacy 'by every breath of air' and even though there had been some recent improvement in the general quality of London's air 'the truth may be' that it had 'not much extended itself to the lower ranks of people in *London*, who form the body of the inhabitants'.[25] Benjamin Franklin agreed. Writing home to his wife Deborah in Philadelphia he too complained that 'The whole Town is one great smoky House, and every Street a Chimney, the Air full of floating Sea Coal Soot, and you never get a sweet Breath of what is pure, without riding some Miles for it into the Country.'[26]

Although Price's suggestion of a fall in London's population between 1736 and 1769 was mistaken, he was fully aware of the inadequacies of his statistical database and, from this time on, he became a passionate and lifelong champion of the need for accurate population statistics, principally via a regular national census. Above all, he desired that the data gathered 'should contain not only a list of the distempers of which all die, like that of the London Bills; but they should specify particularly the numbers dying of these distempers, in the several divisions of life'[27] – a comment which has recently seen him suggested as a founder of epidemiology.[28] Such data, he concluded, would 'shew the different degrees of healthfulness of different situations, mark the progress of population from year to year, keep always in view the number of people in the kingdom' and, importantly in the light of his current and future work on the subject, allow the determination of 'the precise law according to which human life wastes in its different stages; and thus supply the necessary *data* for computing accurately the values of all *life-annuities* and *reversions*'.[29] As always, his theorizing had an eye to practicality and now, with his first work on demographics behind him and with his mind still very much concerned with life insurance, he published another short paper, called 'Observations on the Proper Method of Calculating the Values of Reversions'. This was read to the Royal Society on 10 May 1770 and published in the *Philosophical Transactions* shortly afterwards.

That same year Price also relinquished his post as evening preacher at Poor Jewry in the City of London in favour of becoming the morning preacher at Gravel Pit in Hackney, which was closer to Newington Green where he remained the afternoon preacher. Yet, despite wishing to concentrate on this ministry, and to reduce his commitments to the Equitable,

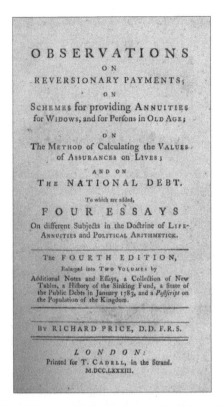

Figure 10. Title page of *Observations on Reversionary Payments*
(1771; 4th edn., London, 1783).

Price now began working on a book on annuities that took up 'all [his] time
and attention' in the winter of 1770/1. This book, though rather daunting
to the lay reader, can be justifiably called his second major contribution.

*Observations on Reversionary Payments; on Schemes for providing Annuities for
Widows, and for persons in Old Age; on the method of calculating the values of
assurances on lives: and on the National Debt* is a substantial volume published
in 1771 and written with the aim of fulfilling his desire to see the 'establishment of stable [annuities] societies and ultimately more certain benefits
to their members'. The first chapter essentially mirrors his work with the
Equitable in that it comprises a series of 'questions relating to schemes
for granting reversionary annuities, and the values of assurances on lives'.
Each question is answered in detail with mathematical examples, notes and
comments. Price's purpose in asking these questions is made clear in chapter
two which contains 'an application of the questions . . . to the schemes of
the societies' then being established in Britain, with the aim of assessing their

viability. Later editions of the work would also include an examination of annuities societies from across Continental Europe.

Among the British societies Price studied were the London Annuity Society, the Laudable Society for the Benefit of Widows and 'the Association among the London Clergy, and the Ministers in Scotland for providing annuities for their widows'. He also included an account of the Society for Equitable Assurances and the annuities scheme established among the commanders of the East India Company. Following his review, the Society for Equitable Assurances prospered into the early years of the twenty-first century and even though the East India Commanders Society eventually closed, it was thanks to Price's review of it that each member received the full value of his share at the Society's termination. Despite a few reservations, Price had good hopes too for the provision made by the ministers in Scotland for their wives.

In contrast to these schemes, Price knew that many other British annuities societies had been formed 'just as fancy has dictated, without any knowledge of the principles on which the values of reversionary annuities ought to be calculated'. He did not impugn the motives of the societies' 'contrivers' but he did think 'they ought . . . to have informed themselves better'.[30] This was something his work set out to help them achieve. 'How barbarous', he declared, no doubt remembering his wife's exposure to near penury following her father's losses in the South Sea Bubble of 1720, 'is it thus to draw money from the public by promises of advantages that *cannot* be obtained? Have we not already suffered too much by *bubbles*?'[31]

But Price reserved his main criticisms in *Observations on Reversionary Payments* for the other London-based societies, as he made clear in a letter to another Dissenting minister and mathematician, George Walker, on 3 August 1771. 'I wish I may prove the means of either breaking them or engaging them to reform. They have in their present state a very pernicious tendency.'[32]

By October, six months after publication of his tome, Price felt hopeful that his criticisms were being heeded. 'I am happy to find, that the time and attention I have bestowed on this work are not likely to be quite in vain', he wrote. 'The London societies were laying the foundation of a great deal of mischief; and they are now in general alarmed, and some of them are reforming.'[33] The London Annuity Society was certainly among the latter. Having revised its scale of payments in light of Price's criticism by 1790, when Price and William Morgan came to examine its accounts, the Society was so well founded they felt able to recommend an increase in the annuities paid out.

By contrast the Laudable Society for the Benefit of Widows, which paid no heed to Price's criticisms, was forced to reduce annuities by 35% while increasing premiums by 20%, a situation that so concerned Price he petitioned

Parliament on their account in March 1774. 'It appears', he declared, 'that in nine years (supposing no new Members admitted) the Society, if it persists in its old Plan, will begin to break into its Capital; and that in 21 years the whole Capital will be spent, 200 Widows left in distress, and the Expectations of 187 Members be disappointed, after going on for 21 years in making their payments.'[34] Although Parliament instituted limited reforms as a result of his intervention, these warnings went unheeded. By 1790 the annuities payable to existing annuitants of the Laudable had been reduced by half and those to all future annuitants by one fifth.

Having dealt comprehensively with annuities in the first two chapters of *Observations on Reversionary Payments*, Price turned in the third chapter to another topic that would become a lifelong preoccupation – the public credit and the national debt.[35] He understood that this might appear 'foreign to [his] chief purpose'[36] in a book principally concerned with annuities and reversionary payments but he firmly believed the subject to be of primary importance: 'what I most wish is that the Observations I have made on the national debt may be attended to'.[37]

His concern over the national debt stemmed not only from its ever increasing size (it had risen from £52 million in 1726 to £140 million by 1772), but the harm the constant servicing of it did to the social and constitutional fabric of Britain, and the threat it posed of national bankruptcy. His offered solution in *Observations* was to call for a return to the use of a sinking fund. This was a method by which the Government would establish a surplus of revenue over expenditure and use this surplus to purchase Government stocks. The income from these could then be used, along with the following year's surplus, to purchase more stocks. Compound interest would be earned and in forty years, he estimated, an annual surplus of one million could discharge a debt of £100 million; provided ministers did not raid the fund to remedy any unforeseen emergencies. Price later expanded his thoughts on the problem into a full-blown pamphlet, which was published in February 1772 as *An Appeal to the Public on the Subject of the National Debt*. A second edition followed in March by which time, despite his other commitments, an appendix containing calculations and tables showing the progress to be achieved by various kinds of sinking funds had been added.

The chapters on annuities, the annuities societies and the national debt form the bulk of the text in *Observations on Reversionary Payments*. All that remained, following their completion, was to add a final section of four essays 'on different subjects in the doctrine of life annuities and political arithmetic', and an appendix comprising 'four new tables, shewing the probabilities of life in London, Norwich and Northampton; and the values of joint lives'. Yet, despite the substantial nature of this work, Price was dismissive of his efforts. Writing to the Bluestocking Elizabeth Montagu on Friday, 22 March 1771, he expressed the belief that the public would 'be a good deal concerned in parts of it; but I do not expect that it will be much attended to'.[38] His reaction stems from a natural humility, on which many of his friends would comment, but also from considering the public's reaction to the *Review of Morals* which, although an important contribution to the subject of moral philosophy, had not truly set the eighteenth-century intellectual and literary world alight. Not for the last time, however, Price was proved wrong in an appraisal of his own work. Demand for *Observations on Reversionary Payments* was immediate, and by the autumn of 1771 he could write to his friend, the Dissenting minister and scientist Joseph Priestley, 'My work on annuities has gone off very fast and I am now very busy preparing a 2nd edition of it. I shall make many additions but they shall be published separately for the purchasers of the first edition. Equity, I think, requires this.'[39] A third edition followed in 1773 and the fourth, in 1783, had to be split into two volumes to incorporate the large amount of additional data and tables he had calculated and collected by that time. He would be working on a fifth edition at the time of his death in 1791 and this, along with a sixth edition in 1802 and a seventh in 1812, would be edited and published by his nephew, William Morgan.

Looking at Price's *Observations on Reversionary Payments* today, as well as his work for the Equitable and the annuities tables and population studies he produced, it is impossible not to admire the concentration of mind and self-discipline in the face of the thousands of calculations such a body of work required. This was work done with little or no financial reward to be expected and without the prospect of being able to withdraw. There was, inevitably, a cost. As William Morgan records, while engrossed in the mathematical calculations involved in preparing one of his papers for publication Price's hair, 'which was naturally black, became changed in different parts of his head into spots of perfect white'.[40] It is also easy in the face of such a volume of work to perceive Price as a theoretical wizard divorced from practical experience of the issues he was analysing and writing upon. In reality he was nothing of the kind. For at the same time as producing this body of work he was also involved in two very practical attempts to establish annuities societies; one on a small scale, akin to the schemes he had outlined and critiqued in his book, and a second, far larger one, that, if successful, would give Britain something approaching a national scheme of social insurance for the first time.

In April 1771, shortly before publication of *Observations on Reversionary Payments*, a group called The General Body of Protestant Dissenting Ministers in London and Westminster[41] decided to look into the possibility of founding an annuities society 'for the relief and support of aged Protestant Dissenting Ministers'. Having been appointed to the committee established to help achieve this, Price drew up a plan for the scheme and produced the actuarial tables necessary to ensure its reliability. These tables also formed the basis of his involvement in a second annuities scheme, which was proposed by Francis Maseres.

A lawyer, historian and mathematician recently returned from Canada, where he had been attorney general from 1766 to 1769, Maseres presented a rather old-fashioned face to the world. He was often to be seen wandering around the Inns of Court off the Strand in London in a 'three-cornered hat, tye wig and ruffles'. Yet, despite this fusty appearance, Maseres outlined in 1771 a radical scheme to provide, through annuities granted by parish authorities, monetary relief to Britain's 'industrious poor'. Prior to publishing his idea for the scheme, Maseres, or his editor, sent a draft of the work to Price for his opinion. Price welcomed the proposal but demurred over the fact that Maseres had based his annuities calculations for the whole country on the London life-expectancy tables of Thomas Simpson. From his previous demographic work, Price knew that life expectancy was greater in the countryside than in London and that it was therefore wrong to make the London tables the basis for a countrywide annuity charge. He also felt that Maseres proposed to start paying out annuities at too young an age. Price believed they should be paid at a later time: '55 or 60, because I would not give men any temptation to relax their industry while capable of it'.[42] He also suggested the scheme might be improved 'if annuities increased with the age of the annuitants'. These criticisms and suggestions, however, came too late to be incorporated into the article, which was published by Maseres under the pen name 'Eumenes', in the *Public Advertiser* on 22 July 1771.[43]

Through the autumn and winter of 1771 Price continued his involvement with both the Annuities Committee and with Francis Maseres, whose scheme he discussed in the second edition of *Observations on Reversionary Payments*, which appeared in January 1772. Price also included tables showing how his own suggestions might work in practice. He then remodelled these tables and included them in the proposals being developed by the Annuity Committee for the General Body of Protestant Dissenting Ministers. In November the Committee thanked him for his efforts and his three tables were copied into their minute book. Then, in December, they 'desired Dr. Price and Dr. Kippis to prepare a copy of what is intended to be printed relating to the annuity scheme', 2,000 copies of the proposals were printed and circulated throughout England and Wales.[44]

In the meantime, Francis Maseres had gone to press again, this time publishing details of his nationwide scheme in a pamphlet entitled *A Proposal*

for Establishing Life Annuities in Parishes for the Benefit of the Industrious Poor.
In it he accepted Price's recommendation not to use the London-based
life-expectancy tables of Thomas Simpson.

Despite these positive early developments, Price now faced the first of a
number of disappointments relating to proposed social reforms with which
he would be associated. In December 1772 he and the other members of
the Annuity Committee had to report to the Body of Protestant Dissenting
Ministers that despite all their efforts, Dissenting ministers generally had
shown insufficient interest in the proposed annuities scheme. Consequently,
the proposals could not be adopted.

By contrast the Maseres scheme looked more hopeful, at least at first. A
parliamentary committee established to look into the proposals, with a view
to drafting a bill to Parliament, requested Price to calculate the actuarial
tables necessary for operating the scheme. These would be appended to the
bill to be put before Parliament. Price obliged and a bill incorporating the
Maseres scheme and Price's tables was proposed to the House of Commons
on 11 December 1772. Sponsored by William Dowdeswell and Sir George
Savile, the bill was also supported by Edmund Burke, a man who would
later play a significant part in Price's life and posthumous reputation. Although
the Commons approved the bill on a vote of 62 to 34 on 5 March 1773 it
met its fate in the House of Lords where it was objected to on the grounds
that the bill's provisions would produce a greater burden on the poor rate.
In fact, since Maseres had designed the scheme to aid those who could live
on the first three days of their week's earnings, allowing them to save the
rest by purchasing the annuities proposed, it would in all likelihood have
reduced the poor rate burden through a decreased demand upon it.[45]

Despite these political disappointments Price did not lose heart and his
interest in, and work on, annuities and life insurance would be lifelong.
Even by this stage he had greatly furthered the progress of the study and its
potential for benefiting his fellow citizens. Not only was he a principal
founder of a system of life assurance who 'developed actuarial theory far
beyond his precursors Edmond Halley, Thomas Simpson, and James Dodson'
but he was 'the only one of these pioneers to advise on the "practical steering
of a life office"'.[46] This refers to another aspect of Price's annuities work
for the Equitable – the numerous papers he wrote for the Society that
often resulted in important changes to its business practice. As far back as
1771, for example, he had been instrumental in the Society changing its
rules on the insurance of women's lives. Price had enquired why the Society
considered women's lives more hazardous than men's for the purposes of
insurance. Price convinced the Society's president that based on his knowledge
of survivorships women's lives were no more hazardous than those of men.

From then on the Society insured women's lives on the same terms as men.

It was in a paper submitted to the Equitable in 1774, however, that Price made what is regarded as his major contribution to the business side of life insurance and annuities. As the historian of the Equitable M. E. Ogborn wrote in his bicentennial history of the Society in 1962, Price was the first 'to show how the business of a life office should be arranged and valued'. He did so in 'Observations on the Proper Method of Keeping the Accounts and Determining, from Year to Year, the State of the Society for Equitable Assurances on Lives and Survivorships'. Among its many recommendations was a call for the periodic valuation of the Equitable Society because 'No trouble should be avoided that is proper to throw light on the affairs of the Society and to give a more clear and satisfactory view of its state.' It would be Price's nephew, William Morgan, who undertook the first such valuation in 1776, using one of the methods Price had outlined in his paper.

Of all the praise that came Price's way for his annuities work in his own lifetime, none is likely to have meant more to him than that of his friend Benjamin Franklin, who, on receiving a gift of the second edition of *Observations on Reversionary Payments*, sat down on 11 February 1772 in his London lodgings and wrote the glowing tribute with which this chapter opened. But if Franklin risks hyperbole in order to successfully convey the importance he attached to Price's work, it is Andrew Kippis's much later graveside eulogy for Price that captures its true spirit:

> The blessings of those who might otherwise have perished came upon him; and he has given cause to many a widow's heart, that knew him not, to sing for joy.[47]

5

Science and Society

Be a philosopher but amidst all your philosophy be still a man.[1]

Prior to writing *Observations on Reversionary Payments* in the winter of 1770, Price not only composed another work on annuities – *Observations on the Proper Method of Calculating the Values of Reversions*[2] – he also wrote a paper on astronomy, a subject that along with mathematical probability had helped open up his mind to belief in a creator and to the wonders and mysteries of creation. At home in Newington Green he kept a large number of scientific instruments and these included the telescope he had received as a gift from the Equitable Society. It was this that now allowed him to make a contribution to one of the great astronomical events of his time.

Twice each century the alignment of the earth, the sun and the planet Venus permits observation of the transit of Venus across the sun's face. In 1677 an early member of the Royal Society, Edmond Halley, had observed a similar phenomenon regarding the planet Mercury during his visit to the Atlantic island of Saint Helena. Knowing he would not live to see the next transit of Venus, Halley urged the Society to observe that event carefully and to measure the planet's transit time from various locations on the earth's surface. This would help determine more accurately the earth's distance from both the sun and Venus, while widely spaced observations would help overcome the problems of parallax when making such measurements. By the eighteenth century, Venus transits were due to occur on 6 June 1761 and 3 June 1769, and Halley's appeal was not forgotten. Under the watchful eye of the Revd Nevil Maskelyne, a Royal Society-sponsored expedition returned to Saint Helena in 1761 to observe the planet's transit. Price, a fellow member of the Society, knew Maskelyne and corresponded with him after Maskelyne became the fifth Astronomer Royal in February 1765.[3]

For a variety of reasons, not least bad weather, the observations made of the 1761 transit were not a great success and a memorandum from the Royal Society to George III proposed a further expedition in order to measure the

second transit in 1769. In submitting their proposal the Society members
were at pains to stress the importance of the event for Britain. It would,
they noted, 'contribute greatly to the improvement of Astronomy, on which
Navigation so much depends'; an important consideration for a naval power
when several other European powers were also 'making . . . proper dis-
positions for the Observations' of the transit. Consequently, an expedition
at a cost of 'about £4000, exclusive of the expense of the ship' was required
but the Royal Society was 'in no condition to defray this expense'.[4]

The king agreed to the Society's appeal and after some initial problems
appointing a captain, command of the expedition fell to James Cook, who
sailed from Plymouth in the barque *Endeavour* on 26 August 1768. At Tahiti
on 3 June 1769 in a temperature approaching 119 degrees Fahrenheit, Cook
observed and measured the second Venus transit.

On 6 September that same year John Winthrop, the Harvard professor
of mathematics and natural philosophy who had led an Anglo-American
expedition to Newfoundland in order to measure the first Venus transit,
wrote to Benjamin Franklin in London. In his letter Winthrop claimed that
the planet's apparent transit time across the face of the sun was retarded by
an equation for the aberration of light. This conclusion ran counter to
prevailing opinion, which saw the same equation as accelerating the transit
time. Before forwarding Winthrop's letter to the Royal Society Franklin
showed it to Price, an act which pleased Winthrop as he later made clear:
'I look on myself as under singular obligation for your friendship in com-
municating my paper on the aberration to the Rev. Mr. Price, before you
ventured it in public. It gives me pleasure to find myself supported by so
judicious a person.'[5]

Though Price agreed with Winthrop's conclusion regarding the retard-
ation of the transit time, he also put forward his own idea that it was further
retarded by an aberration of the sun, an observation he believed 'not to
have been attended to by the astronomers'. This letter, an early draft of
which Franklin forwarded to Winthrop, was read to the Royal Society on
20 December and published in the Society's *Philosophical Transactions*.[6]
Winthrop's letter to Franklin appeared in the same volume and was fully
acknowledged by Price.

Both Benjamin Franklin and John Winthrop became good friends of
Richard Price and, as we saw earlier in chapter 3, it was shortly before
1767/8 that he had also developed his lifelong friendship with the scientist
and Dissenting minister Joseph Priestley. The date of their first meeting
remains uncertain, though it is clear that by the time Priestley visited London
in 1765/6, to meet with John Canton and Benjamin Franklin with the aim
of eliciting their help in writing his history of electricity, his friendship with

Price was well established. We know, for example, that Price took Priestley to a meeting of the Royal Society on 9 January 1766[7] and that he was a sponsor of Priestley's election to the Society in June. Furthermore, Price's involvement with Priestley's *History and Present State of Electricity*, published in 1767, was considerable. In his introduction Priestley thanks Price, among others, for 'the attention they have given to the work, and for the many important services they have rendered me with respect to it'.[8] The public, he also notes

is indebted [to those who had helped him] for whatever they may think of value in the *original experiments* which I have related of my own. It was from conversing with them that I was first lead to entertain the thought of attempting anything new in this way, and it was their example, and favourable attention to my experiments, that animated me in the pursuit of them. In short, without them, neither my experiments, nor this work would have had any existence.[9]

Apart from the general conversations that must have taken place between Price and Priestley concerning this particular work, Price's principal contribution was to draw up of a list of analogies between magnetism and electricity 'in an abridgement of [the work of] Aepinus'.[10] Price's other contribution consisted of comments on the 'large circular spots' Priestley had noted as appearing on metal plates 'after discharging a battery of about 40 sq. ft. with a smooth brass knob'. Priestley records Price as having suggested that they might be akin to so-called 'fairy rings, which consist of grass of deeper green in pasture fields, and which have by some been imagined to be occasioned by lightning'. Fairy rings however, as Price noted, lacked the central spot Priestley also saw from his experiments. In fact, Priestley's rings are 'a variety of "Newton's rings" which are produced when thin films of metal are oxidized by spark discharge on a metallic plate'.[11]

Price also helped correct proofs of Priestley's works and in October 1771, for example, Priestley wrote informing him that he was sending '200 more pages of my work'; in this case *The History and Present State of Discoveries relating to Vision, Light and Colours* which would be published in 1772.

Price was candid to a degree bordering on abruptness in his comments on the various works. But this does not seem to have bothered Priestley, who urged him 'to continue your remarks with the same, or greater freedom'.[12] And Price (known to have a great affection for his old horse) seems not to have been unduly perturbed by Priestley's descriptions of his electrical experiments on animals. Price's love of animals is sometimes used by later writers to illustrate his love of liberty, as when he turned upright a beetle struggling on its back, or when he released a whole flock of larks trapped in a net on Newington Green (this was an act about which he felt so guilty he later returned to the spot and left some coins for the bird trapper). We can only imagine his thoughts on reading of Priestley's electrocution of a 'pretty kitten' and the large dog that exhibited convulsions, rattling in the throat, profuse saliva, 'flux of rheum' from the eyes and blindness. The poor creature was finally dispatched prior to autopsy when Priestley shot him 'through the hinder part of his head'.[13]

Details of Priestley's electrical experiments fill his early letters to Price, but later on the great concern is with his attempts to isolate various gases. Clearly impressed with the work he was producing in this field, Price, in response to one gas experiment, suggested Priestley 'communicate it to the Royal Society. I am sure it will deserve a prize medal and I hope you will obtain it.'[14] This proved prescient, for Priestley won the Copley Medal, the highest honour of the Royal Society, in 1773. On other occasions Priestley's work acted as a spur to Price's own, as on 16 December 1773 when Priestley's paper 'On the Noxious Quality of the Effluvia of Putrid Marshes' was read at the Royal Society. This spurred Price to submit one of his own, entitled 'Farther Proofs of the Insalubrity of Marshy Situations', read to the Society on 13 January the following year. Scientific and editorial assistance, however, was not the only kind of help Price gave to Priestley during their long friendship. He also became intimately involved in Priestley's more personal affairs.

In 1768 the botanist Joseph Banks had sailed with James Cook to Tahiti as part of the Royal Society's expedition for measuring the second transit of Venus. It was a successful and epic journey that included the famous landing at Botany Bay. The travellers returned to Britain on 13 July 1771 and even before the year's end Cook was busy preparing a further expedition to the South Seas. This time the aim was to settle the question of whether a southern continent existed and, if it did, to claim it in the name of the king. Banks was to accompany this new expedition and he proposed to Priestley that he too should take part, 'in the character of an astronomer, with a handsome provision' being made to himself and his family.[15] On 5 December Priestley, whose 'favourite employment' was, like Price, that of a Dissenting minister, found himself in two minds on the offer and he wrote from Leeds wishing to know Price's 'real thoughts' on the subject, as well 'as that of some others of my friends'. Shortly afterwards Price spoke to Banks at the Royal Society and then informed Priestley that the proposal made to him 'was the product of some mistake'. Adding, quickly, that he had also consulted with two of their closest mutual friends – Benjamin Franklin and John Canton – and that Franklin thought the journey too 'long and dangerous' while Canton joined with Price in thinking Priestley 'would scarcely find the company [he was] to go with entirely agreeable'.[16] Though it now seems likely that Banks had made a mistake inviting Priestley onto the trip without proper authorization, Priestley asserts in his later *Memoirs* that the 'mistake' arose because 'some clergymen in the Board of Longitude, who had the direction of the business' had objected to his religious principles, an instance of religious discrimination that would not have been lost on Price as a fellow Dissenter. Whatever the truth of the matter, this was not the only case of possible religious discrimination involving Priestley to which Price became privy.

Despite a salary of one hundred guineas a year and the provision of a house, Priestley was not content with his position as a minister in Leeds. In a letter to Price in July 1772, he notes that if he ever moved, 'it must be to America, where it will be more easy for me to dispose of my children to their advantage'.[17] Franklin, who visited the family in Leeds that year, had been distressed at the conditions in which he found his friend and had written to John Winthrop in New England in the hope of finding Priestley a suitable post at an American university. Unfortunately, as both Franklin and Winthrop realized, Priestley's theological views were insufficiently orthodox for him to be able to gain such a place. By the first week of August, Price, 'much concerned for Dr Priestley', found himself in a position to offer help thanks to his new friendship with William Petty, the earl of Shelburne, a friendship arising from Price's earlier publication of *Four Dissertations*.

Born in 1737 and entering the Lords on the death of his father in 1761 Shelburne had, by the time of his meeting Price in 1771, served in the ministry of the elder Pitt as president of the Board of Trade and as Southern Secretary. At this time the latter post included responsibility for the American Colonies. Shelburne would go on to become Home Secretary in 1782, give his support to the Americans in their revolutionary struggles and, as Prime Minister from 1782–3, begin Britain's recognition of their independence.

In January 1771 Shelburne had been left in a melancholy state of mind following the death of his first wife. His sadness had been relieved by his reading of Price's *Four Dissertations*, following a recommendation made at a literary soirée he attended at the home of Elizabeth Montagu. Particularly comforted by Price's third dissertation on the 'future happiness' or, as Price had termed it, *On the REASONS for Expecting that Virtuous Men Shall Meet after Death in a State of Happiness*, Shelburne asked Mrs Montagu to introduce him to its author. She obliged by passing the request on to fellow Bluestocking and wealthy widow Mrs Hester Chapone, who ran a literary gathering at which Price was a regular attendee. Mrs Chapone informed Price of Shelburne's desire to ride out and meet him at Newington Green. Price, disinclined to put Shelburne to this trouble, offered instead to call at Lansdowne House, the earl's London home in Berkeley Square.[18] Despite his worries at being 'a plain man; and an utter stranger to the formalities of the world',[19] the meeting proved a great success and the start of a lifelong friendship. Shelburne became as frequent a visitor to Newington Green as Price was to Lansdowne House and Bowood, the earl's country estate in Wiltshire.[20]

In May 1771 Shelburne set out on a half-year tour of France and Italy leaving to Price's attention two of his most pressing problems – the need to find a tutor for his children, and a librarian for his books. In a letter to Shelburne on the subject of a suitable tutor, Price gives us a glimpse of his early attitude to education:

> The principal part of education is certainly not teaching the languages or the sciences, but directing the passions and forming the mind and temper; and this is a work that requires greater abilities and more wisdom than the generality of even Scholars and Philosophers possess.[21]

Price asked Priestley if he knew of a suitable candidate as tutor, to which Priestley replied that he himself would be suited for the job since the education of children was a subject to which he had 'given very particular attention' and with which he had 'a good deal of experience'. But, he added, 'every thing of this nature I consider superseded by the tutor his lordship will appoint for them'.[22] Shelburne, meanwhile, having learnt during his travels in Europe of the respect in which Priestley was held there wanted to secure his services as librarian. On Price's recommendation the vacant tutorship eventually went to Thomas Jarvis, a man well educated in the classics and mathematics, but the appointment of Joseph Priestley as Shelburne's librarian proved a more protracted affair.

Problems arose over Priestley's concern about his independence of action should he come into Shelburne's employ, and that his scientific researches might take up too much time and detract from the work he was paid to do by the earl. Many of Priestley's friends urged caution while Price, writing to Shelburne, tried to remain as impartial as he could. 'I have myself been very cautious with respect to advising him . . . I have studied, with the faithfulness of a friend, to allow every objection its just weight, and to leave him to be determined by his own views and feelings and judgment.' The main problem, he continued, arose from Priestley's 'apprehension that in the new sphere of life to which he is invited he will not be sufficiently master of his own conduct, and that he will be brought into such a state of obligation as will deprive him of that Philosophical ease and liberty and independence which are preferable to all other advantages'. Personally, though, Price looked forward to Priestley taking up the position. 'Should he at last resolve to accept, I shall receive a considerable addition to my happiness from his nearness to me, and I believe your Lordship would be in possession of a valuable treasure.'[23] Nevertheless, Price could sympathize with Priestley's concern over the question of his independence of thought and action. Some years after this event Price faced a similar dilemma when asked to become private secretary to Shelburne during the latter's tenure as Prime Minister. Price refused, probably on similar grounds. He enjoyed his independence and the freedom it gave him to candidly speak his mind, just as he did in this instance on the subject of Priestley's wages. Shelburne had offered £200 per annum for life and a willingness to do more as Price and Priestley saw fit; the eventual salary decided upon was the £250 per annum suggested by Price. As a result, Priestley began work at Bowood in March 1773. He would remain there until 1780 and, although he was not entirely happy, it would be where he performed many of his most famous experiments, including the identification of oxygen in 1774.

By the time of Priestley's appointment to Bowood, Price was about to turn fifty, a time of life when many draw back from the radicalism and idealism of their youth. This was not the case with Richard Price, whose life reflects the reverse scenario, in direct contradiction of his own wish, as he grew older, to withdraw from public life and its pressures and commitments. Driving him on was his belief in moral virtue and its demanding creed of rationally considered contribution and improvement undertaken in an atmosphere of mutual respect and toleration, coupled with our possession of free will. Freedom to act, moral virtue and toleration were the east, west and south of Price's life compass and they, in turn, held out the prospect of hope – his true north. Hope implied the possibility of improvement, for though the '*natural improvableness* of the human race has never taken its complete effect' this did not mean improvement was unattainable:[24]

> One of the most remarkable and distinguishing properties of human nature is, its capacity of improvement . . . by the invention of arts and sciences, and the establishment of the best schemes of civil policy.[25]

Up to this point in his life Price had devoted his public energies principally to the arts of philosophy and theology and to the sciences of mathematical probability and astronomy. But the circumstances of his life as a Dissenter, and the condition of the society of which he was a part, now led him to consider whether Britain truly did have one of 'the best schemes of civil policy'.

6

Freedoms Denied

The best way, certainly, of attaching men to true principles is to enable them to examine impartially all principles. Every truth that is necessary to be believed and really sacred, must be attended with the clearest evidence. Free enquiry can be hostile to nothing but absurdity and bigotry. It is only falsehood and delusion which fly from discussion and choose to skulk in the dark.[1]

There is nothing that requires more to be watched than power.[2]

Seventeen years separate the approaching American Revolution of 1776 from Price's 1759 sermon on *Britain's Happiness and the Proper Improvement of It* in which he had briefly touched upon issues of civil liberty and religious freedom. They were seventeen years during which three public events brought these issues to ever greater prominence.

The first occurred in 1763, a few months before the reading of Price's essay on Bayesian probability to the Royal Society. In April that year John Wilkes, a journalist and Member of Parliament, published anonymously in issue 45 of his paper the *North Briton* an article critical of the king's speech made at the close of the parliamentary session that year.[3] Such speeches normally occurred at the start of a session and were followed by a parliamentary debate that gave the opposition an opportunity to criticize its contents. A closing speech allowed for no such debate and since the purpose of this one was to praise the terms of the Treaty of Paris, which had recently ended the Seven Years War, Wilkes suggested in his article that it was little more than a propaganda coup on the part of a government who had both negotiated the treaty and written the speech for the king. He also intimated, in a sentence laden with irony, that the king had been unwittingly 'brought to give the sanction of his sacred name to the most odious measures, and to the most unjustifiable, public declarations, from a throne ever renowned for truth, honour, and unsullied virtue'.[4] Rather than rousing Government ministers to anger, it was the king who was most furious over the article, demanding that one of his Secretaries of State take legal advice with a view to the Government prosecuting the article's author. Keen to please a monarch increasingly involved in political affairs, the Government dutifully obliged. *North Briton*, issue 45, was declared a treasonable and seditious libel and its author was to be found and prosecuted.

Wilkes was ultimately arrested under a general warrant, which was essentially a licence for arbitrary arrest since no person or persons were actually named in such warrants, and no evidence as to the possible guilt of any party need be presented in order to obtain them. Within three days of the warrant being issued forty people had been arrested 'on suspicion', among them the *North Briton*'s publisher George Kearsley and his printer Richard Balfe. From Kearsley it was discovered, or at least confirmed, that Wilkes had authored the offending article and he was then arrested following a two-hour stand-off at his home, during which he repeatedly protested his immunity from arrest as an MP and denounced the use of a general warrant to achieve it as 'a ridiculous warrant against the whole English Nation'.[5] He was committed to the Tower and denied visitors, including his legal adviser.

After one adjournment a court freed Wilkes on grounds of an MP's right to parliamentary privilege, a privilege that could only be suspended when a Member committed treason, a felony or a disturbance of the peace. Not satisfied with this verdict the Government remained determined to prosecute the alleged libel. To do so now, however, required a parliamentary ruling overturning Wilkes's claim to parliamentary privilege. The campaign to achieve this came to a head on 15 November 1763 when Wilkes attempted to raise a point of order in the House of Commons concerning the breach of privilege he had recently suffered. The point of order was denied in favour of the House first hearing a message from the king, which sought to remind the House that parliamentary privilege had been used by Wilkes to obstruct justice. The likely course of the ensuing debate was thus made abundantly clear to Wilkes from the outset. Later that day a defamation campaign against him began in the House of Lords when extracts from his *Essay on Woman* were read out. Intended as a parody of Alexander Pope's *Essay on Man*, the *Essay on Woman* was sexually explicit – 'Since Life can little more supply / Than just a few good fucks, and then we die' – and filled with scurrilous innuendo against well-known personages, including the recent Prime Minister lord Bute: 'in the scale of various Pricks, 'tis plain, Godlike erect, Bute stands the foremost Man'.[6] Though many recognized the hypocrisy of extracts from the *Essay* being read out in Parliament by lord Sandwich – a onetime friend of Wilkes and, like him, a member of the Hell-Fire Club, notorious for its heady mix of orgiastic sex, drinking and black magic – the damage was done and the House was asked to declare the *Essay on Woman* 'a most scurrilous, impious and obscene libel'.[7]

As if this were not enough, in the earlier Commons debate Wilkes had also been accused of being a 'cowardly rascal' by his fellow MP Samuel Martin, a man who had himself been the butt of Wilkes's journalism in the *North Briton*. A duel followed in Hyde Park and though Martin, widely believed to be a Government agent provocateur who had practised with his pistols beforehand, missed with his first shot his second hit Wilkes in the stomach or groin. As Wilkes later recuperated from his wound at home, Parliament revoked his privilege as an MP on the grounds that it did not extend to the writing or publishing of seditious, blasphemous and obscene libels that might invoke a breach of the peace by those who read them. Sensing a new warrant for his arrest would now be issued Wilkes left for France where his daughter was living. In November 1763 Parliament declared the *North Briton* article to be a seditious libel and Wilkes, tried in his absence and found guilty, was expelled from Parliament on 19 January 1764 and made an outlaw.

Outlaw Wilkes nevertheless returned to Britain early in 1768; no attempt was made to arrest him on his arrival. Emboldened by this apparent lack of interest he stood for Parliament in the general election of March that year. Though he polled last out of the seven candidates for the City of London seats he swiftly announced his candidacy for one of the two upcoming seats of Middlesex county. To this seat he was elected five days later with a substantial majority, and to Government and royal consternation.

The year 1768 was a time of economic recession in Britain and social unrest was commonplace. In London there were strikes by sailors, coal heavers and the silk-weavers of Spitalfields and these disputes inevitably became interwoven with popular support for Wilkes and his defence of individual liberty. Indeed, the London mob had already taken to the streets in his support when they prevented the public hangman from carrying out the court-ordered burning of copies of the libellous *North Briton*, issue 45. But now, with the Middlesex result announced, they gathered to celebrate their hero's re-election to Parliament by knocking off hats that did not display the number '45' in their brim and by insisting that people lit cele-bratory candles in their windows to avoid having them smashed.

Wilkes's determination to take his seat in Parliament now became some-thing of a political football. At the same time as the Cabinet hatched a plan to again expel him from the House of Commons, Wilkes made well-advertised attempts to surrender himself to justice so that he might legally challenge the libel cases against him and his continuing status as an outlaw. To this end, and having cannily informed the Attorney General of his intention beforehand, he surrendered himself to the Court of King's Bench on 20 April 1768 only to be released on a legal technicality and consideration of the fact that he had voluntarily offered himself up. Next day, embarrassed that it had allowed an outlaw to freely roam the country, the Government finally issued a warrant for his arrest.

On his second appearance before the court Wilkes was refused bail and committed to the King's Bench prison in Southwark to await trial. From there he continued his defiance by issuing on 5 May an address to his Middle-sex constituents stating his belief that he was being imprisoned because of his 'support of the liberties of this country against the arbitrary rule of ministers'; an address certain to have been noticed by Price who, as a resident of Newington Green, was one of those constituents. Popular support for Wilkes in the ensuing two weeks culminated on 10 May 1768 when a vociferous crowd of some 15,000 people stood in St George's Fields, just outside the prison walls, chanting 'Wilkes and Liberty! No Liberty, No King! Damn the Government! Damn the Justices!' As a result of incidents between the demonstrators, the troops and the officials present, a Justice of the Peace read the Riot Act, only to find himself felled by a piece of brick. He ordered the troops to open fire and seven of the crowd were shot and killed in what became known as the Massacre of St George's Fields. Disturbances then erupted across the city and on 11 May a royal proclamation had to be issued for the suppressing of all 'Riots, Tumults and Unlawful Assemblies'.

On 18 June, with a semblance of calm restored, Wilkes received a fine and a twenty-two-month prison sentence, which proved less than onerous as he received numerous visitors to his rooms and accepted a host of gifts including wine, ale and, significantly, '*forty-five* hogsheads of tobacco from Maryland'.[8] Parliament, meanwhile, after a series of past-midnight sittings to discuss the constitutional and legal ramifications of their action, voted to expel him from the House.

Undaunted, Wilkes stood again as a parliamentary candidate for his now vacant Middlesex seat in February 1769, only to have his second victory there overturned by Parliament. The same thing happened in two further elections held in March and April. Finally, after the April election, Parliament took a decision. After another lengthy debate on the constitutional and legal position, it appointed Colonel Henry Lawes Luttrell to the seat; he had been runner-up to Wilkes in the election and could be promoted as 'a young man of great courage and sense' who had fought in the recently ended Seven Years War. But the constitutional precedent set by this action, and by the whole Wilkes affair, was far from glorious, and its ramifications were definitely on Richard Price's mind at the time.

Figure 11. 'Watkin Lewes Esqr Presenting the Addresses from the Counties of Pembroke, Carmarthen, and Cardigan, to the Lord Mayor, Alderman Wilkes, and Alderman Oliver in the Tower', unattributed engraving. In this political cartoon of 1771 Watkin Lewes (far right, as viewed), who originally came from Pembrokeshire and went on to become lord mayor of London, is seen presenting petitions of support to Brass Crosby (2nd from left, lord mayor of London in 1771), John Wilkes (3rd from left and identifiable by his marked squint) and Richard Oliver (far left, a founder member of the Bill of Rights Society, a Price correspondent and fellow member of the Club of Honest Whigs), who were imprisoned in the Tower of London during the campaign to allow press reporting of parliamentary debates.

Both men were members of the Royal Society, but, aside from our knowledge that Price corresponded with Wilkes's daughter in France from at least 1784,[9] we only have a single 1785 letter from Price to Wilkes to confirm their acquaintance.[10] Though Price said 'he could trample [Wilkes] underfoot' (an allusion to his distaste for the personal character of Wilkes) he also believed Wilkes's private conduct 'was irrelevant to the constitutional issue'.[11] In its narrowest sense that 'constitutional issue' was the spectacle of Parliament ignoring the wishes of the voters, whom Price considered sovereign. As he would write later, in 1777, 'there was a time when the kingdom could not have been brought to acquiesce in what was done in the case of the Middlesex election. This is a precedent which, by giving the House of Commons the power of excluding its members at discretion and of introducing others in their room on a minority of votes, has a tendency to make it a self-created House and to destroy entirely the right of representation. And a few more such precedents would completely overthrow the constitution.'[12]

But the Wilkes affair had further constitutional significance. It directly contradicted Price's assertion in his 1758 sermon that in Britain 'No life [could be] taken away, or any punishment inflicted on anyone, without a fair and equitable trial.' Though Wilkes had received a trial, his arrest had been made under a warrant that bore no name or charge, and Government actions since his initial acquittal could certainly be seen as a form of persecution. Parliamentary privilege too, an essential right if MPs were to speak freely on any issue, had been called into question by the affair, as had State censorship and freedom of publication and speech in general. As a passionate opponent of censorship and a vocal champion of freedom of publication and speech the right of Wilkes to publish what he chose would not have been in question for Price. As he wrote in *Four Dissertations*, which was published at the height of the Wilkes affair, 'who shall have the power of determining whether a book against an established opinion is writ *decently*, in order to give a right of punishing? There are no hands in which such a power can be lodged, without the utmost danger to what, as reasonable beings, we ought most to value.'[13] Civil powers, he contended, were not competent to rule on such matters. Indeed, 'the civil magistrate ought not to interpose in the defence of truth, till it has appeared that he is a competent judge of truth. This, certainly, he is not. On the contrary; universal experience has, hitherto, proved him one of its worst enemies.'[14]

That such a method as general warrants and the laws of libel could be used to silence critics was, to Price, not only an affront to freedom of expression and individual liberty but also evidence of a growing trend towards arbitrary government. And it was a further instance of that arbitrariness revealed by the Wilkes affair – the growing influence of the king over both the legislative and executive branches of government – that became the second issue to concentrate his mind on civil liberties in the years following his 1758 sermon.

Royal influence in the Wilkes affair had begun when George III became the chief instigator of the libel prosecution. He had then sacked Wilkes from his position as colonel of the Buckinghamshire militia *before* the trial of the alleged *North Briton* libel took place; this proved not only the king's general attitude to the case but his apparent disregard of the maxim 'innocent till proven guilty'. Furthermore, the king's order for Wilkes's dismissal had been carried out by Lord Temple, the Lord Lieutenant of the county. As a friend, Temple had written to Wilkes offering a degree of regret over the action he was required to take. This angered the king so much that he had Temple dismissed. Three more serious examples of undue royal influence followed.

The first came in the wake of the parliamentary vote on the first expulsion of Wilkes from the House of Commons; a vote in favour of expulsion by 258 to 133. One who voted against expulsion was the MP General Conway, a Groom of the Bedchamber. Informed of Conway's vote by Prime Minister Grenville, the king immediately wrote back proposing Conway's dismissal along with 'any others who have . . . gone steadily against us'.[15] The king then delayed Conway's actual dismissal until the first furore over the Wilkes affair had died down. It was also made quite clear that others would suffer Conway's fate if they did not suitably 'amend their conduct'.[16]

Then, in April 1768, the king wrote to Lord North declaring that the expulsion of Wilkes 'appears to be very essential and must be effected'.[17] Since North at the time headed a parliamentary commission looking into the whole issue of the second expulsion of Wilkes from Parliament, this instance of royal influence bordered on gross interference in parliamentary affairs. Finally, following his government's success in expelling Wilkes in 1768, and in appointing Colonel Luttrell to the Middlesex seat over the heads of its voters, the king found himself inundated with petitions from across the country opposing the action. In the main he ignored them, a presage of his attitude to petitions from the American colonies whose anger over taxation formed a potentially volatile background to these so far domestic British affairs.

Aside from such *public* instances of royal influence at work there would have been many more kept private, a matter for the king, his court and his ministers. Yet, there were methods by which the wider public, including Price, gleaned information as to affairs at court. Gossips in the many clubs to which Price belonged would no doubt have broached such issues, as would close friends such as Benjamin Franklin, who was busily engaged with various Government ministers over American tax problems. Price's friendship with the earl of Shelburne, though it only began in 1771, would have given him a retrospective view. As a minister in the Chatham administration of 1766–8 Shelburne was in government when the main events of the Wilkes affair took place. He also knew at first hand the powerful influence the king could exert. Near the end of Chatham's premiership, daily 'instigations to remove Lord Shelburne' from his post had come from the king.[18] Lastly, Price would have gleaned much information from the full reporting of parliamentary debates that became legal for the first time in 1771. This was in no small part due to the further efforts of John Wilkes, in the face of intense parliamentary opposition.

Although Price's surviving correspondence and other writings from this time are silent on the issue of the king's growing influence, those from a slightly later date clearly reflect his views. For example, in a letter to his friend William Adams in 1778, with Britain by then at war with revolutionary America, Price writes: 'I have seldom been more shocked than by the doctrine which is now avowed . . . that the King has power, without the consent of Parliament, to raise troops and to accept benevolences for paying them. The open avowal of such a doctrine shews indeed that we are got very far towards the loss of all that is valuable to a free people.'[19] Nor was the importance of the issue lost on other prominent figures. As Horace Walpole wrote, in the wake of the dismissal of Conway 'when the context . . . appeared to be, that military men in Parliament were to forfeit their profession and the merit of their services, unless implicitly devoted to the Court; could these reflections, when coupled with the arbitrary measures which the nation has observed to be the system of the Court, fail to occasion the bleakest presages?' Writing under the pseudonym Junius in the *Public Advertiser* of December 1769, another author had the temerity to suggest exactly what Walpole's 'bleakest presages' might entail, for any king who 'plumes himself upon the security of his title to the crown, should remember that, as it was acquired by one revolution, it may be lost by another'.[20] The king, for his part, also saw danger in the Wilkes affair, declaring it to be an issue 'whereon almost my Crown depends'.[21]

There is considerable discussion among historians over the true extent of George III's influence on his government, but since Parliament at this time was not made up of parties as we know them today, patronage, both royal and aristocratic, was essential to political life in order to create ministries with any chance of long-term survival. Such ministries were, in reality, coalitions relying on patronage from above and from those MPs who had sought and gained royal favour. The most obvious way for the king to exert such patronage was through his right to ennoble, and so bring into the

House of Lords, supporters who shared his opinions and who could ensure defeat of legislation he disliked. However George III did not really abuse this privilege. He preferred instead to ennoble only when an aristocratic line had become extinct. The more important power, and one he certainly exercised, was his right under the royal prerogative to appoint his own prime minister, subject to that person having a majority in Parliament, as well as most of his other ministers, judges, bishops and army officers. This had significant consequences since the appointed ministers were themselves possessed of considerable powers of patronage. As men appointed by the king they could undoubtedly choose to use this power in order to influence the make up of Parliament.

Over the next few years the problems of royal influence and arbitrary government became inextricably linked in Price's thinking with the need for a comprehensive root and branch reform of Parliament. This was something for which he would later campaign vigorously; for the moment though, we must turn to the third issue of importance in Price's political thinking following his overly confident assertion of Britain's 'happiness' in 1758. This concerns the ever-vexed issue of religious freedom; and here too the king's influence would play its part.

The Toleration Act of 1689 guaranteed Dissenters freedom of worship in their own licensed meeting houses. But the Corporation Act of 1661, a remnant of the Clarendon Code legislation still on the statute book, required all prospective members of town corporations to take the sacrament in accordance with Church of England rites. The Test Act of 1673 extended this condition to any holder of civil or military office and this act too remained on the statute book. Together they acted as a deterrent to Dissenter involvement in civic affairs. Furthermore, Dissenters were obliged to pay tithes to the Established Church for the upkeep of a clergy to whose religious beliefs they did not themselves subscribe.

It was also a requirement under the Toleration Act that Dissenting ministers, tutors and schoolteachers subscribe to the doctrinal articles at the heart of the established Anglican faith. These articles however were contentious not only to the protestant Dissenters but also to some liberal clergymen, and on 17 July 1771, at a meeting in the Feathers Tavern in London these clergymen drew up a petition to Parliament asking for relief from the need to subscribe to the articles. During the parliamentary debate on the petition on 6 February 1772, the Prime Minister, now Lord North, voiced his opinion that were the Protestant Dissenters to put forward a similar request it would, in all likelihood, receive a favourable hearing. As a result the General Body of Dissenting Ministers met in March that year to elect a committee to make such an appeal. Price, along with his friend Andrew Kippis, was elected a member.

The Committee worked fast in preparing the bill and soon began canvassing support for it from a number of prominent people. Among them was lord Shelburne who, as well as being a good friend to Price by this time, had 'professed a warm regard to Dissenters as friends of liberty' and promised, 'if he ever came into power, to exert himself in supporting their rights, and placing them on the same footing with other Protestant subjects.' Shelburne now agreed to canvass support for the Dissenters bill in Parliament and he began by approaching the earl of Chatham (the elder Pitt), in whose government of 1766 to 1768 he had recently served. Writing on 18 March Shelburne outlined the wish of Price and other members of the Dissenter Committee to call upon Chatham and enlist his support for their cause. Chatham replied on 3 April 1772 welcoming both the bill and the proposed visit. That same day leave was granted for the Dissenters bill to be brought before the Commons.

The Committee's visit to Chatham did not take place until Wednesday, 13 May, by which time the bill had passed through its third reading in the Commons by a vote of 70 for to 9 against. It had then been carried to the Lords for its first reading. The successful passage of the bill thus far gave 'great encouragement to the dissenters' but Price harboured no illusions as to its chance of ultimate success in the Lords. Having met Chatham on 13 May with his fellow Committee members, he sat down that same evening and wrote to the earl of the Committee's expectation that the bill would be 'strongly opposed' in the Lords. For this reason they were 'united and earnest' in their request that Chatham, his health permitting, might favour them with his support. Then, in typically forthright fashion, Price concludes his letter with his own thoughts on why the bill was so important. 'In my opinion,' he wrote, 'a Toleration, limited by law to those who believe the doctrinal articles of the Church of England, deserves not the name.' Nor was he coy when it came to pointing his finger at those most likely to oppose the bill in the Lords. 'We have reason to think that in this application we should have met with no difficulties, had not the Bishops resolved to oppose us.'[22] He was right. Despite Chatham's appearance in the Lords' debate and his delivery of an eloquent and famous speech in which he declared his support 'because I am for toleration, that sacred right of nature and bulwark of truth and most interesting of all objects to fallible man', the bill was defeated by 102 votes to 27, and by a combination of the bishops supported by the ministry.[23] What Price would not have known, but certainly suspected, is that the king had made his opposition to the Dissenters bill known to his government. Indeed, he had written as much to his Prime Minister:

> I think you ought not to press those gentlemen who are brought on that interest into Parliament to oppose this measure, as that would be driving them out of

those seats in a new Parliament, but I think you ought to oppose it personally through every stage, which will gain you the applause of the Established Church and every real friend of the Constitution, if you should be beat it will be in doing your duty and the House of Lords will prevent any evil; indeed it is the duty of Ministers as much as possible to prevent any alterations in so essential a part of the Constitution as everything that relates to religion, and there is no shadow for this petition as the Crown regularly grants a Noli prosequi[24] if any Justice of the Peace encourages prosecutions.[25]

Price expressed his disappointment at the bill's failure in a further letter to Chatham on 22 May. 'We are indeed concerned to find, that no force of argument could secure success for us; and that we must still continue to owe to the mercy of our governors a security to which we have, as we apprehend, a natural right.'[26] Disappointed Price may have been, but he was not yet deterred. Five months later he suggested to Shelburne that the Committee might apply again 'this Winter' even though 'nothing is yet determined.' By March 1773 Price could inform Chatham that the Committee was now 'determined to apply this Session [of Parliament] partly because the public attention to the subject is now fresh, but principally because we thought it would appear respectful to government to apply now rather than the next session and just at the eve of a general election'. Nevertheless, Price sensed the prospects of the bill passing were still 'dark and doubtful'.[27] He was proved right on 2 April when it was again defeated in the Lords by 86 votes to 28.

This time Price was sorely disappointed, not only because the failure gave the lie to his 1758 sermon assertion that religious liberty was the 'crown of all our advantages' but also because in both bills the Dissenters had made concessions they hoped would answer the bishops' objections. In the first bill, which had attempted to completely repeal the necessity for Dissenter subscription to the Thirty-Nine Articles, the Committee suggested that Dissenters might be asked instead to 'sign a subscription, declaring the Scriptures of the Old and New Testament to be the mind and will of God, and a rule of faith and practice'. The second bill had been less adventurous. Subscription to the Articles would remain on the statute book but this time the Committee suggested that anyone who opposed such subscription might state instead: 'I declare, as in the presence of Almighty God, that I am a Christian and a Protestant, and that as such I receive the Revelation of the will of God contained in the Scriptures of the Old and New Testament as the rule of my faith and practice.' Price, in fact, opposed both these concessions since they seemed to him to undermine the principle dear to his heart of the universality of religious freedom. For Price there could never be legislation for what a person thinks or believes:

It is no less a *contradiction to common sense*, than it is *impiety*, for any men to pretend to a power to oblige their fellow men to worship God in any manner different from that which is most agreeable to their consciences; that is, in any way but that in which alone it is acceptable and right in *them* to do it.[28]

Thus, 'the civil magistrate goes out of his province, when he interposes religious differences. His office is only to secure the liberties and properties of those under his jurisdiction; to protect all good subjects; to preserve the peace amongst contending sects, and to hinder them from encroaching on one another'. Only when our thoughts and beliefs lead us into action might they enter the realm of law and the remit of the civil authorities.

Religious toleration, Price believed, should extend to all sects since:

The maxims of sound policy, as well as the principles of Christianity, require civil governors to protect all good subjects; and to extend toleration to every mode of faith and worship, that is not inconsistent with the safety of the State.[29] It ought not, in our opinion, to be confined within even the limits of the Christian religion; and were a body of Mahometans to apply, as the body of Protestant Dissenters now do, for the permission to exercise their religion without being subject to penal laws, we do not see, that such permission could be reasonably denied them. It is well known that Turks tolerate Christians in the Greek Empire; and, therefore, it would be certainly right in Christians to tolerate Turks.[30]

In consequence, religion should be divorced from the concerns of civil government whose true purpose was as 'an institution of human providence for guarding our persons, our property, and our good name against invasion; and for securing to the members of a community that liberty to which all have an equal right, as far as they do not, by any overt act, use it to injure the liberty of others'.[31] Possessing such a concept of religious toleration and civil liberty, it is hardly surprising that Price disagreed so strongly with the concessions to subscription many of his Dissenter colleagues were willing to make.

As a result of his unhappiness with the original terms of the two bills and their subsequent failure Price now largely withdrew from this particular fight realizing its futility in the current political climate. As he had written to Chatham during the passage of the second bill: 'Should we fail now, I shall for my own part consider this point as decided against us 'till the times alter, and the administration of public affairs falls into hands more favourable to civil and religious liberty.'[32] True to his word, and though his name would still appear in support of later attempts at relief, his energies were never again so fully engaged in the subject. Instead, he turned to a wide-ranging consideration and analysis of civil liberty, including religious freedom, and of the political structures that essentially allowed the maintenance of religious intolerance, the acceptance of arbitrary government and the deprivation of individual freedom and civil liberties he had witnessed in recent years. But before his thinking on these issues could come to fruition in what would be his next major work – *Observations on the Nature of Civil Liberty*, published in 1776 – he needed a crucible in which to discuss his ideas rationally and candidly with people who both opposed and supported them. He also needed a specific cause to which they could be applied.

The cause would prove to be America, whose problems over the mundane issue of taxation form a background to the wider civil liberties concerns occupying Price's thoughts at this time. These, of course, were destined to become the concern of the Americans too, as their cause evolved from a fiscal dispute into a fight for liberty and freedom. But, for the moment, Price began honing his ideas in the atmosphere of a radical club and in his close friendship with a truly remarkable American, Benjamin Franklin.

7

Price, Franklin and the Club of Honest Whigs

I always think with pleasure and gratitude of your friendship. The world owes
to you many important discoveries; and your name must live as long as there is
any knowledge of philosophy among mankind.[1]

Richard Price's friendship with the American polymath and bon viveur
Benjamin Franklin was one of the closest and most enduring of his life. It
was a friendship that survived not only the trials of the coming war with
America, which found both men of like mind on the justice of the American
cause yet on opposing sides in the conflict, but also the long years of separation
that followed and the vicissitudes of old age.

The precise date and circumstance of their first meeting is unknown but
a letter written by Franklin from Philadelphia in March of 1764 asking John
Canton in London to present his 'respectful compliments . . . to Mr. Price,
Mr. Burgh, Mr. Rose, Mr. Cooper and the rest of that happy company with
whom I pass'd so many agreeable Evenings' suggests it took place between
July 1757 and August 1762, during Franklin's second visit to London.[2] Carl
Cone, Price's American biographer, has suggested that this first meeting
may have been at the Royal Society; both men were after all deeply interested
in scientific matters. Franklin became a member of the Society in 1756 (in
absentia, he was in America at the time), and although Price was not admitted
until 1765, when Franklin acted as one of his sponsors, he could have been
present earlier as a member's guest.

What is clear is that by August 1767 Franklin certainly felt confident
enough in their friendship to enlist Price's support in obtaining an honorary
degree of Doctor of Divinity for a certain Mr Elliot, a minister of the New
North church in Boston, Massachusetts. Having already applied for degrees
on behalf of three other American personages (Ezra Stiles, Samuel Cooper
and Eleazer Wheelock), Franklin was concerned that trying for a fourth
from the same university (Edinburgh) might make him appear 'troublesome'.
Consequently, he proposed to apply instead to the University of Glasgow.

Figure 12. 'The Royal Society's House in Crane Court', unattributed engraving in
Walter Thornbury, *Old and New London* (London, n.d.). Price attended meetings
of the Royal Society here until its move to Somerset House in 1780.

Since Price had mentioned being on friendly terms with its principal, William
Leechman, Franklin asked Price to add a recommendation of Elliot to
Franklin's own. Alas, their joint efforts failed and Elliot eventually got his
degree from Edinburgh in 1767 after 'Deacon John Barrett of the New
North (church) obtained the degree . . . by the simpler process of paying
cash'.[3] On 7 August 1769 Price too received an honorary degree – of Doctor
of Divinity from Marischal College, Aberdeen.[4] Proud of this recognition
he would doubtless have been mortified to discover (for according to his
early biographer William Morgan he did not know) that his own honour
had come through the solicitation of his friends and the payment of an
appropriate fee.[5]

Whatever the manner of their first meeting both Price and Franklin had many interests in common, including the 'manly and useful exercise' of swimming. Franklin had not only experimented with swim flippers on his hands and feet but once swam a three-mile length of the river Thames. Price, although reported to have once nearly drowned at Brighton, remained a regular sea-bather there, at Eastbourne, and at Southerndown in south Wales throughout his adult life. In London it was his custom 'everyday at 2pm to run off for a swim at the Peerless Pool', otherwise known as the 'Perilous Pond' on account of the number of youths who drowned there.[6]

Another draw for Franklin may have been Price's Welsh origins. Well acquainted with the Welsh settlements of Pennsylvania, whose echoes are today seen on the indicator boards of Philadelphia's buses,[7] Franklin had been closely involved with two émigré Welsh families. His first business partner had been Hugh Meredith, 'a Welsh Pennsilvanian, thirty years of age, bred to country work; honest, sensible, [with] a great deal of solid observation, was something of a reader, but given to drink'.[8] Together they published some of the earliest Welsh-language texts in America.[9] Franklin also came to know and have various dealings with the 'ingenious engineer' Lewis Evans. Originally from north Wales, Evans mapped a substantial part of Pennsylvania and the Ohio Valley between 1749 and 1755. He also gave some of the earliest public lectures on electricity in America, a subject of special interest to Franklin (and to Price's relatives). Evans had business dealings with Franklin, whose wife became godmother to Evans's daughter.[10]

Welsh history also seems to have been of interest to Franklin for, like John Adams in his 'Novanglus Papers' of 1774, he used the situation exist-ing between Wales, the English Crown and the London parliament in the years from the conquest of Wales in 1286 to the Act of Union or 'annexation' by England in 1536–43, to highlight the eighteenth-century American position. Between 1286 and 1536, it was argued, Wales largely maintained her own laws and, though subject to the English Crown, remained un-represented in the London parliament and untaxed by it. Only when parlia-mentary representation was granted in 1543 did such taxation begin. As in Wales, so in America, for 'although the colonies are bound to the crown of England . . . it does not follow that the colonies are a parcel of the realm or kingdom, and bound by its laws'.[11]

Freemasonry may also have provided a link between Price and Franklin. Franklin had been made Provincial Grand Master of Pennsylvania in 1749 and there is compelling, though circumstantial, evidence from Masonic records for south Wales that Price too was a member of the Society. The name 'Richard Price' occurs in documents relating to the establishment of a Masonic Lodge in Bridgend, south Wales, in the early 1760s (the forerunner of today's Glamorgan Lodge Number 36 that meets at Cardiff's Masonic Temple). In the 1760s a warrant from a lapsed Lodge that had met at The Star and Garter in the Strand in London was reissued to a Lodge meeting in Bridgend. A return from this Lodge made in 1765 bears the names Richard Price, Michael and William Flew and Benjamin Coffin. Furthermore, a replacement warrant was issued in 1777 to David Jones, Jenkin Williams and Richard Price, who now held the position of Worshipful Master. The Lodge seems to have met at the Sign of the Bear, a reference to the Bear Inn whose remains today are believed to form part of the Wyndham Arms Hotel in Bridgend. The Price family had a long association with Bridgend. Richard's mother was born in the town and his sister, Sarah Morgan (née Price), still lived there at this time. The family had also helped to establish Dissenter meeting places in the town; and Tynton, their original family home, was not far away. The most compelling evidence that the Richard Price referred to is our Richard Price comes from his familial connections with several of the other names mentioned in relation to the Bridgend Lodge. Jenkin Williams, for example, married Price's niece, Catherine. William Flew married Richard's sister Elizabeth, and Benjamin Coffin married his stepsister Mary.[12]

With its hierarchical structure and secretive rituals the Masons seems an unlikely society for a man like Price to join. Yet, as Jasper Ridley recounts in his study of Freemasonry, the Society in the eighteenth century attracted supporters of two principal types: 'the philosophical intellectuals and the gentlemen who thought that a Masonic Lodge was a useful and agreeable social gathering'.[13] Benjamin Franklin, Ridley concludes, belonged to the first group and he would certainly have appreciated the toleration shown by the Masons to various religious sects, including those expressing the kind of Deistic beliefs Franklin himself propounded. Price, if he was a member, would also have been attracted to the Society for reasons of philosophical enquiry and religious toleration, but the fact that his name appears in relation to a Lodge in Bridgend, a town he generally visited at most once a year, suggests his membership may have been more of a social than truly active kind. The possibility exists, however, that he first became a Mason in London, perhaps even at The Star and Garter Lodge whose lapsed warrant was issued to that at Bridgend. If so, it might even have been through the Masons that Price first met Franklin.

Whatever the manner of their first meeting or the initial reasons for their taking a liking to each other, three subjects sustained their friendship in the years ahead: science, moral philosophy and politics.

Franklin possessed one of the great enquiring minds of the age, Leonardo-like in the variety of its fascinations and its ability to transform them into ideas for practical experimentation.[14] By contrast, Price's particular genius tended toward the theoretical but always with an eye to the practical value of his theorizing. Despite this difference in approach, both men understood the nature of the other's work and their correspondence with scientific contemporaries, such as Joseph Priestley and John Canton, testifies to the development of a true scientific community at this time. As Priestley would confide to Price: 'Writing upon a philosophical subject to any of you; I would have it considered as writing to you all.'[15]

Although Royal Society meetings largely satisfied Price and Franklin's desire for scientific discussion, the moratorium there on discussing the more contentious moral and political issues that also animated them created the need to find a less formal setting in which to debate these subjects. Home obviously provided one such place, and Franklin frequently visited the Price's house on Newington Green just as Price did Craven Street, where Franklin lodged with Margaret Stephenson and her pretty daughter Polly who became Franklin's lifelong friend.[16] At the same time, though, both men were great 'clubbers'.[17]

Clubs in eighteenth-century London catered for every level of society and covered every topic, from the erudite to the completely bizarre. Thus the antithesis of the brilliance of Samuel Johnson's Literary Club could be found in the Beefsteak Club, that devoted itself to drinking and wit, the Spit-farthing Club that catered to misers and skinflints and the Farting Club of Cripplegate whose members, by their 'Noisy *Crepitations* attempt to outfart one another'.[18]

During the course of his life Price belonged to a variety of clubs and societies ranging from his Stoke Newington 'supping club' and the Friday literary soirées at which he discussed the literature of the day with the likes of wealthy widow Hester Chapone and her fellow Bluestocking Elizabeth Montagu, to the Society for Promoting the Knowledge of the Scriptures with its mix of Dissenters and Anglicans that 'transcended [the] sectarian limitations' Price so disliked.[19] In later years contentious political debates were held at the Society for Promoting Constitutional Information, of which Price was a founder member, and the Society for Commemorating the Revolution in Great Britain, more commonly known as the Revolution Society, which met to celebrate the Glorious Revolution of 1688 and the accession of Protestant King William III.

In America Franklin had established his own club – the Junto – in Philadelphia as early as 1727 and when in London he routinely visited a number of others; among them the Club of Thirteen (or the Wednesdays Club), which he founded with another Welsh friend, David Williams (1738–1816).[20] Williams would later publish the radical *Letters on Political Liberty* (1782), become a French citizen during the Revolution and found what is now the Royal Literary Fund. He was also well known to Price.[21]

The favourite London club of both Price and Franklin however was that dubbed by Franklin the 'Club of Honest Whigs'. It met every other Thursday 'during the season' at the St Paul's Coffee House in St Paul's Churchyard and later, after March 1772, at the London Coffee House, 24–6 Ludgate Hill. Few accounts of the interior of either place survive but a London Directory of 1798 described the London Coffee House as 'perhaps the most elegant and extensive that come under the name of coffee-house in the three kingdoms'. It was also said to be a place where Masonic meetings were occasionally held.[22]

As with the Masons, membership of the Club of Honest Whigs appears to have been entirely male. It included, besides Franklin, Price's other close friends Joseph Priestley, John Canton and Andrew Kippis. The remainder were principally ministers of religion (Dissenters mostly but with the occasional Anglican) and political activists such as Alderman Richard Oliver who founded the Bill of Rights Society and William Rose who co-edited the liberal *Monthly Review* with Ralph Griffiths. One fortuitous membership was that of the diarist James Boswell for, although he rarely attended, his diary provides our only description of a meeting in progress. 'I went to a club to which I belong', he wrote on 21 September 1769. 'It meets every other Thursday at St. Paul's Coffee-House. It consists of clergymen, physicians,[23] and several other professions. There are of it: Dr. Franklin, Rose of Chiswick, Burgh of Newington Green, Mr. Price who writes on morals, Dr. Jeffries, a keen Supporter of the Bill of Rights, and a good many more. We have wine and punch upon the table. Some of us smoke a pipe, conversation goes on pretty formally, sometimes sensibly and sometimes furiously. At nine there is a sideboard with Welsh rabbits and apple-puffs, porter and beer. Our reckoning is about 18d a head.'[24]

It is not difficult to imagine the rest. The large noisy room fuggy with tobacco and candle smoke. Franklin seated by a blazing fire, listening as Price discoursed, with all the animation for which he was renowned, on subjects such as Dissenter rights or the expulsion of Wilkes from Parliament. Their companions, meanwhile, turn from the sideboard with their pots of porter in hand and look on with some amusement as, according to his habit in the heat of debate, Price 'turned his wig round on his head, twisted one leg around the other and folded his cocked hat into a thousand different shapes'.[25]

Sadly, any sense of the actual relationships and friendships that existed between the members of the club, the 'jesting' and 'camaraderie' as well as the candour and openness of their debates, is lost to time. Some inkling of them, however, can be gleaned from a letter one member, James Densham, sent in 1769 to John Canton from Oporto in Portugal, where Densham resided as agent for a London merchant. 'You are a knot of wicked Rogues,' he wrote, 'you Cantons, Prices, Burghs, and some more of you for letting a Body be so long in Exile (tho' not like Wilkes, illustrious) without writing a word.' To accompany his letter Densham sent a box of Guimarine plums. 'A baubling present . . . to quicken and awaken' his friends: he asked Canton to divide the fruit out amongst the members, in particular 'Mr. Cooper for writing me a kind letter (among the first) – Mr. Price for he will write – Mr. Burgh for the long grave Phyz he puts on when catechising me – for which, like his other Boys got away in vacation, I don't care a pin[26] – Dr. Jeffrey's for his favourite Lady, I think he's a courting – and Dr. Franklyn, if in town, for the good Sense he genteelly treats us with at the Club.'[27] Nothing is known of the precise format of an Honest Whig meeting but we might surmise that it ran along similar lines to that of Franklin's Junto and with equivalent aims in mind: 'A club of mutual improvement' at which its members met to discuss issues of 'Morals, Politics, or Natural Philosophy' with debates conducted 'in the sincere spirit of inquiry after truth'.[28]

Many other London clubs were proscriptive regarding topics to be discussed at their meetings. Like the Royal Society, Johnson's Literary Club banned political discussion. Johnson also had a tendency to dominate proceedings and stifle debate in a way that seems unlikely to have been tolerated by the candid members of the Honest Whigs.[29] Price and Franklin certainly seem to have found the more convivial and easy-going atmosphere of the Honest Whigs to their taste. It also satisfied their shared preference for candid discussion among small gatherings of friends and acquaintances rather than overt public dispute.

Along with science, discussion of which often continued at the Honest Whigs straight after a meeting of the Royal Society, another frequently debated topic was likely to have been moral philosophy and the efficacy of virtue. This was a subject of common interest to Price and Franklin; one which originated for both of them in their early experiences of religion, and which underpinned many of their attitudes to life, the society around them and their contribution to that society.

Both men were raised in homes with a strict, paternally imposed religious observance; the Presbyterianism of Franklin's father shared with the High Calvinism of Price's an emphasis on predestination and the assured salvation of an Elect. The early years of Price and Franklin are marked by a journey away from this uncompromising stance toward a more rational and tolerant religious belief. Nevertheless, there remained profound differences between them in the course that journey took and in their ultimate religious positions.

For Price, thanks to his exposure to the liberal religious teachings of men like Samuel Jones and John Eames and his study of the equally liberal writings of Samuel Clarke, there was no great schism in his life with regard to religion and his lifelong, if continually questioned, belief in Christianity. Franklin by contrast had, by the age of fifteen, already begun to seriously question the Christianity he heard preached and taught in Boston and later in Philadelphia. Unlike Price, he did not come under the influence of liberal teachers but instead discovered a number of books written by Christian theologians against the then popular religious philosophy of Deism.

Deist ideas became fashionable in the eighteenth century and Franklin candidly admits in his autobiography that the Christian writers' arguments against the Deist position 'wrought' on him an effect 'quite contrary to what was intended by them; for the arguments of the Deists, which were quoted to be refuted, appeared to me much stronger than the refutations; in short, I soon became a thorough Deist'.[30] Deism had gathered strength in the eighteenth century in light of the discoveries made previously by Copernicus and Galileo – discoveries which effectively removed the earth and its inhabitants from their centrality in God's creation. At the same time, Newton, Hooke and Boyle had begun to discover and explain, with mathematical precision and proof, the physical laws by which nature worked; laws which, even if they originally derived from a creator, appeared in some interpretations not to need the creator's intervention for their continued operation. Furthermore, there had been a widespread realization in a society formed in the shadow of the Reformation that what had once seemed unquestionable religious dogma was actually nothing of the sort. Instead, it was open to reinterpretation and could be used and abused by popes, kings, princes, bishops and clergy for their own ends. Deists believed that a revealed religion derived from biblical texts, doctrine, dogma and priestly assertion could not shed light on the existence and true nature of the creator. Rather, this could only be achieved through a natural religion based on reason, experience and the study of creation.

As the Deist Thomas Paine, soon to be a Founding Father of the United States and a friend to Price and Franklin, put it: 'God [was] the power of first cause, nature . . . the law, and matter . . . the subject acted upon'. And, in building upon this basic creed in *The Age of Reason*, a book he published in 1794 and 1795, Paine provides us with a succinct outline of basic eighteenth-century Deistic belief. 'I believe in one God, and no more', he wrote, 'and I hope for happiness beyond this life. I believe in the equality of man, and I believe that religious duties consist in doing justice, loving mercy, and endeavouring to make our fellow creatures happy.'[31]

At first sight there seems little here that does not conform to Price's own belief in 'rational religion'. Reason and the study of science were certainly integral to his daily life; his understanding of natural laws, such as those revealed by his mathematical studies (particularly relating to probability) was profound. As a Dissenter he had already rejected the Holy Trinity and its idea of 'three in one' (God the Father, Christ the Son and the Holy Spirit) and so divorced himself from the theology of the Established Church. Even Price's conception of God's existence as akin to a self-evident scientific truth, which he had expressed in *Four Dissertations*, is reflected in the Deist idea, again succinctly expressed by Paine, that 'THE WORD OF GOD IS THE CREATION WE BEHOLD: And it is in *this word*, which no human invention can counterfeit or alter, that God speaketh universally to man . . . It is only in the CREATION that all our ideas and conceptions of a *word of God* can unite . . . and this *word of God* reveals to man all that is necessary for man to know of God.'[32] Yet, despite these apparent similarities of belief and conception, Deism was a step too far for Price.

The principal consequence of the changes science had brought to human conceptions of the universe, aside from the removal of humankind from its centre, was a growing sense of creation as a form of machine; this was a concept to which Newton contributed when he likened the workings of the universe to those of a clock. As a result there arose among some Deists the complementary idea of 'God the clockmaker', who, having built and set running the exquisite timepiece called creation was content to leave it run by its own devices. This mechanistic vision of creation provided a powerful image in a mid-eighteenth-century Britain in the embryonic stages of an industrial revolution.[33]

It also fitted Deist emphasis on studying the visible and measurable creation, rather than communion with a spiritual and invisible creator through a formalized religion. But the detached, impersonal nature of the creator these Deist ideas evoked was not that of Price's vision. Just as any machine or clock needed supervision to ensure its smooth and continued running so, he believed, God constantly intervened in his creation to both nurture it and ensure it operated in accordance with the divine plan.

There were other consequences of Deistic beliefs to which Price could not subscribe. If God was not involved in the daily trials and tribulations of humankind – that most fractious part of creation – why bother with conventional religious worship? Why pray, for example, if God was not listening or, even if our prayers were heard, was unlikely to intercede on our behalf? To Price, prayer was crucial; its importance evidenced in *Four Dissertations*, where the second dissertation is entirely devoted to discussing its nature, reasonableness, efficacy and 'importance . . . as an instrumental duty'. Finally, Deist emphasis on the scientific study of the visible creation inevitably led to a degree of ambiguity regarding the question of life after death. As Paine put it in *The Age of Reason*, 'I consider myself in the hands of my Creator, and that he will dispose of me after this life consistently with His justice and goodness. I leave all these matters to Him, as my Creator and friend, and I hold it to be presumption in man to make an article of faith as to what the Creator will do with us hereafter.'[34] On this question Price could not be so non-committal. Although as devoted as any Deist to the pursuit of science and rational religion, he could not wholly give up a revealed religion whose espousal of a life after death gave him succour and consolation. It is hardly surprising therefore that his third essay in *Four Dissertations* was entitled 'The Reasons for Expecting that Virtuous Men Shall Meet after Death in a State of Happiness'.

For Franklin, by contrast, Deist belief meant subscribing, as J. Dybikowski has put it, 'to the existence of a powerful, good, wise and providential God who created the world and towards whom our main service was to do good to our fellows, but he accepted little else'.[35] And, unlike Price, there is little or no concern for the soul or the afterlife. Indeed, in London Franklin's other friend David Williams would write a Deist liturgy that appealed to Franklin, just as it did to Voltaire. Williams went on to found the first Deist place of worship in Europe, at Margaret Street in Cavendish Square in London.

At the age of twenty, however, Franklin had taken his personal Deist beliefs to heights the philosophy could not sustain. He had composed a pamphlet in which he argued that 'from the attributes of God, his infinite wisdom, goodness and power . . . nothing could possibly be wrong in the world, and that vice and virtue were empty distinctions, no such things existing'.[36] He quickly learnt the folly of this position when two friends to whom he had loaned money refused to repay it on the grounds that there was no need since in a world without vice or virtue whatever they did was right. From this experience Franklin developed his lifelong conviction as to the necessity and importance of morality in life and he intended his expression of that belief to take a practical rather than a purely theoretical turn. In 1731 he conceived the idea of writing a book of morals to be entitled the *Art of Virtue*, which, in contrast to Price's later intellectual and theoretical analysis in the *Review of Morals,* was to comprise practical ways of achieving virtue. Yet, despite the work occupying his thoughts for over fifty years, Franklin, unlike Price, never completed his book.[37]

Price's principal virtue, 'our duty to God' is missing from Franklin's list of the most important virtues, but that apart, it would be relatively easy to fit the remainder of his list into the 'heads of virtue' Price outlined in his *Review of Morals* – our duty to ourselves, our duty to others, our gratitude, our veracity and our justice in dealings with others. This, then, was a shared attitude to practical morality centred on illustrating what we need to do in order to live happy and virtuous lives, rather than having virtue imposed upon us through castigations of our moral laxity and denunciations of the evils of sin. This demand for 'ethical and right behaviour' from us as individuals and members of society is the essence of the word 'virtue' in both men's minds and a vital adjunct to their ideas of civil liberty and freedom.

Discussion of morality and virtue was undoubtedly the bread and butter of many an Honest Whigs meeting, but any talk of them in a club so full of ministers of religion must also have led to some debates becoming more theological or religious in nature. It is unlikely that Franklin would have been party to these since he had decided many years before not to engage in any controversy on matters of religion and faith. If he did discuss such matters it was probably in private and with particular individuals and close friends, like Richard Price. In a letter written late in his life Price (not knowing that Franklin had died the previous month) gently rebuked his friend for his lack of belief in Christianity: 'I cannot . . . help wishing that the qualities and talents which produced [your] eminence had been aided by a faith in Christianity and the animating hopes of a resurrection to an endless life with which it inspires. Had this been the case such talents and qualities would I fancy have [been] raised to still greater eminence. But indeed is it not wonderful that the nonsense that has been mistaken for Christianity and the liberality generally encountered with the profession of it should render many wise and upright men *averse* to them.'[38]

Despite their differences with regard to Christianity, Franklin found Price's approach to religion to his taste. One of his main complaints about the religion taught him in Boston and Philadelphia was that so many of the sermons he heard were geared to inculcate the listener with 'the peculiar doctrines of our sect' rather than the moral principles he saw as the purpose of religion. The aim, he felt, was to make 'Presbyterians rather than good citizens'. Such preachers 'made faith the ultimate goal of man and mere morality worthless except as a possible sign of faith'.[39] For Franklin, 'Morality or virtue is the End, faith only a means to obtain that End; and if the End be obtained, it is no matter by what means.'[40] In this he must have found common cause with Price, though Price may well have quibbled over Franklin's utilitarian attitude to 'means'.

The appeal of Price's approach was that although he took a biblical passage as a starting point, his sermons were often philosophical debates. Rarely, if ever, does he succumb to the use of simple homilies or cosy parables. Nor does he often resort to the kind of exhortations to keep 'holy the Sabbath', to be diligent in reading the Holy Scriptures and to pay 'due respect to God's ministers' that Franklin so disliked in his preacher at Philadelphia.[41] That

Price's style appealed to Franklin is evident from the fact that although he never became a regular churchgoer he did find time to attend Price's meeting house at Newington Green on a number of occasions, often bringing with him important visitors from America.

While religion may have been off the agenda when Franklin was present at the Honest Whigs, the final topic of the three that helped deepen his friendship with Price never failed to excite debate; that topic was politics. Even in his short description of an Honest Whigs meeting Boswell had noted that amongst the members present 'Much was said . . . against the Parliament' and, since 'it seemed to be agreed that all Members of Parliament become corrupted, it was better to chose men already bad, and so save good men'.[42]

Politically there was much for the Honest Whigs to discuss, not only concerning the ramifications of specific instances of political abuse, such as the case of John Wilkes or the progress of Dissenter rights, but also the more general state of British politics and its parliamentary government. Discontent was growing over many issues. These included the problem of placemen and political appointees wielding unrepresentative authority in Parliament; the abuse of the voting system through aristocratic or landowner control of parliamentary representation; a system of patronage that amounted to the buying of votes particularly in such anachronisms as the rotten and pocket boroughs; the development of factional politics in a parliament that often seemed more enamoured of individual personalities than ideas and, finally, the growing influence of the king in both Parliament and Government.

The Club of Honest Whigs undoubtedly provided a forum in which Price could hone his ideas on these issues. What he needed now was a cause that would crystallize them into a coherent whole. He found it in the American crisis. In this respect his friendship with Benjamin Franklin proved crucial, for Franklin was in London as a political agent of several American colonies seeking to protest against what ultimately became the issue at the heart of the American situation – taxation without representation.

In February of 1757 Franklin had accepted nomination as the London agent of the Pennsylvania Assembly with a remit to negotiate with Richard and Thomas Penn, descendants of the colony's founder, William Penn, who consistently refused to see their substantial landholdings in the colony taxed by its assembly. On 1 August 1757, six days after his arrival in London, Franklin had met with the Penns but they still refused to be taxed. He conferred with them again in November of 1758, with no success. The issue reached its climax in 1760 when the Board of Trade in London rejected seven of nineteen acts passed by the Pennsylvania Assembly, among them an act to allow taxation of the Penn estates. Though Franklin's appeal to the Privy Council succeeded in overturning the Board's ruling on the Penn taxation issue, the dispute presaged the more serious trade and taxation disputes that were destined to become hallmarks of British policy and American anger in the coming decade. After travels to the Austrian Netherlands and the Dutch Republic, Franklin left Britain in November 1762 for Philadelphia and home. By the time he returned two years later to his Club of Honest Whigs and the company of Richard Price, relations between Britain and her American colonies were taking a marked turn for the worse.

8

On a Perilous Edge

> While . . . in this world, I think it my duty to employ my voice in applauding the opposers of oppression, and to give my vote and interest, as far as they will go, on the side of justice, liberty and virtue.[1]

As Richard Price developed his ideas on civil liberties in the company of the Honest Whigs, life for many in the American colonies was characterized by a simmering discontent punctuated by periods of occasionally violent crisis. Still steadfastly *British* Americans, the colonists' quibbles centred at first not on the questions of liberty and freedom that became their later refrain, but on the more mundane ones of trade, finance and taxation.

Taxation in particular loomed large in colonial affairs because of changes Britain had felt forced to make as a consequence of the Treaty of Paris, which ended the Seven Years War in 1763. With new colonial possessions in North America resulting from the treaty terms, it was estimated that a British army of 7,500 men at an annual cost of £385,000 would now be needed to protect them.[2] This charge, the Government under Grenville decided, should be borne by the colonists, with the money raised through some form of taxation. As a result a whole raft of legislation was proposed including the Currency Act of 1764, which attempted to end the colonists' use of paper money, and the Quartering Act of 1765, which allowed for quartering in empty buildings but with the colonists expected to provide the troops with essentials such as fuel, bedding, candles and cooking pots free of charge.[3] In practice both acts only served to exacerbate the colonists' sense of grievance; they now began to see the prospect of the London government becoming ever more involved in what they had historically considered their own affairs.

Since neither the Currency nor Quartering Acts directly raised revenue, however, the problem of funding the colonial armies in America remained. To solve the problem a Stamp Act, imposing a stamp duty on the colonies' newspapers and a swathe of their legal documentation, was proposed.

Benjamin Franklin's return to London in December 1764, for his third and
final visit to the city, was a direct consequence of this proposal. Since the
end of his second visit in August 1762 he had been heavily involved in
colonial politics in Philadelphia but by February 1765 he was acting as the
London agent for Pennsylvania with a remit to protest against the proposed
stamp duty. His efforts, along with those of the other colonial agents, came
to nothing, for when the Stamp Bill came before Parliament in March 1765
it passed in the Commons with a majority of 156.

When news of the act's passing reached America in April 1765 demon-
strations against it were widespread and sometimes violent. By November
colonial opposition had made the act almost unenforceable and, in January
1766, Chatham, the elder Pitt, spoke out in Parliament in favour of its repeal.
Despite his intervention, support for the act remained strong in Parliament:
if it were to be repealed, by the incoming Rockingham administration
that replaced that of Grenville in July 1765, the opposition would require
an appeasing sweetener. This came in the form of the Declaratory Act,
emphatically declaring Parliament's right to legislate for the colonies 'in all
cases whatsoever'.[4] As a result parliamentary opposition largely evaporated
and on the day that the Declaratory Act passed into law the Stamp Act was
repealed. In America a degree of normality returned and a colonial boycott
of goods imported from Britain ended shortly afterwards.

In July 1766 the British government changed again when the king dismissed
Rockingham and persuaded the elder Pitt to form an administration. This
also brought into Government the earl of Shelburne who became Southern
Secretary, a post that bore responsibility for the American colonies at this
time but not in financial matters, which remained the prerogative of the
new Chancellor of the Exchequer, Charles Townshend. Rather surprisingly
in view of colonial reaction to the Stamp Act, Townshend now returned
to a policy of reasserting Parliament's supremacy in colonial matters via yet
another doomed flirtation with colonial taxation.

The Townshend Duties, as the new taxes quickly became known, were
to be imposed on such imported goods as tea, paint, paper, glass and china.
Although initially devised to fund the army in America, their purpose later
changed to one of helping to offset the cost of government in the colonies,
by paying the salaries of colonial governors, judges and other officials. This
the colonists saw as an attempt by the Westminster government to undermine
the traditional responsibilities of their own state assemblies, making them
ever more reliant on Britain and setting another new and dangerous precedent.

Townshend did not live to see the consequences of his duties for he died
on 4 September. Lord North, who succeeded him as Chancellor, at first
enjoyed a period of relative quiet in the colonies, where opposition to the

new duties developed only slowly. No colonial congresses were called and there was no immediate demand for a boycott of trade with Britain. When it finally materialized the opposition grew out of localized debates, meetings and via the colonial press. Particularly important in this respect were the letters from a 'Farmer in Pennsylvania' that appeared at the end of 1767.[5] Written by John Dickinson, a Philadelphia lawyer, the letters contended that the imposition of the Stamp Act, and now the Townshend Duties, 'FOR THE PURPOSE OF RAISING A REVENUE' was 'an innovation, and a most dangerous innovation'.[6] Dickinson went on to question not only the legality of the Townshend Duties but also the right of Parliament to impose *any* tax on the colonies. This represented a direct challenge to Parliament's supremacy in colonial matters as enshrined in the Declaratory Act of the year before.

It did not take long for Dickinson's challenge to be taken up by others in America. In February 1768 the Massachusetts Assembly in Boston put on record its agreement with Dickinson's position. They conceded the right of Parliament to legislate on trade but they also believed in the cause of no taxation without representation. London responded with a threat to dissolve the Assembly and, on 8 June 1768, dispatched troops and a naval force to Boston. On the 10 June violence erupted in the city when the ship *Liberty*, belonging to local businessman and politician John Hancock, was seized for *allegedly* smuggling dutiable goods.[7] When news of these troubles reached London a further two regiments of troops embarked for America and the British government expected armed conflict when they arrived at Boston. This worry proved unfounded but it then gave rise to the misguided notion in Britain, and in Parliament in particular, that when faced with the ultimate test the Americans would simply cut and run.

Petitions and addresses sent mainly to the king, and so pointedly avoiding a hostile parliament, flooded in from the colonies to little or no effect. The colonists, led by Boston, then attempted a trade embargo with a ban on all imports from Britain. Although only partly successful, it served, together with reports of further disturbances in America, to increase public and parliamentary pressure in Britain for further retaliatory measures against the colonies.

In October 1768 Prime Minister Chatham resigned through ill health, taking Shelburne with him. The premiership now passed to Grafton, Chatham's deputy. Needing to save face over the taxation issue, Grafton's administration decided on a stick and carrot approach. First, the ringleaders of the recent troubles were to be rounded up and prosecuted, not locally but in Britain under an ancient treason statute dating back to the time of Henry VIII. Second, suggestions were put forward that the Massachusetts colonial charter might be changed in order to reduce the power of its colonial assembly. The 'carrot' came in a leaked suggestion from Grafton's government that there would be some form of repeal of the duties, though not until 1770 at the earliest.

Although not yet the nadir in British/American relations it was at this particular low point that Richard Price published his first reflection on the situation. A 'reflection occasioned', he said, 'by the discontents which were then prevalent in the colonies'. It came in his essay *Observations on the Expectations of Lives* that was read to the Royal Society in April 1769 and separately published that same year. In it, in addition to his controversial suggestion of a decrease in London's population between 1736 and 1769 (see chapter 4), he concluded that since the American population was doubling every 25 years there would, '70 years hence, in New England alone, be four millions; and in all North *America* above twice the number of inhabitants in Great-Britain'. To this he added the statement: 'Formerly an increasing number of FRIENDS, but now likely to be converted, by an unjust and fatal policy, into an increasing number of ENEMIES.'[8] This last suggestion caused considerable offence in Britain and when Benjamin Franklin communicated the paper to the Royal Society the words 'unjust and fatal policy' were omitted and the whole sentence removed from subsequent published editions. The reaction is not surprising since with impeccable timing and prescience the comment came just as the colonial position turned from concern with tax and trade to the far more contentious ones of civil liberties, political representation and the right of the British parliament to legislate for the colonies. The change had much to do with the appearance of pamphlets such as Dickinson's *Letters*, a copy of which Price had received from America shortly after its publication.

The Americans were also watching British constitutional developments with interest, as Maryland's present of '45' hogsheads of prime Virginian tobacco to John Wilkes during his imprisonment at this time bears witness. 1769 marked the climax of the Wilkes affair; a matter Price considered of constitutional significance and in whose light he undoubtedly viewed the American situation.

Price's prescience on colonial affairs was a direct result of his being one of the best informed, if not *the* best informed British observer of the American situation. This position he owed to his membership of the Honest Whigs, where he could hear the latest intelligence from the likes of Benjamin Franklin and meet occasional American visitors to the club, such as the Attorney General of Rhode Island, Henry Marchant, who visited between 1771 and 1772, Isaac Smith of Harvard University and the lawyers Josiah Quincy, junior and Francis Dana who visited with the aim of pleading the

American cause and gaining support for it in Britain. Price also benefited from his extensive and highly informative correspondence with many Americans at the forefront of their colonies' social, religious and political life. Henry Marchant, for example, knowing Price to be a 'distinguished Friend' to 'the Publick Good . . . and particularly Religious Liberty' felt that these causes would be best served by 'frequent Communications of Facts and Sentiments from each Side the Water from Honest and Ingenious Men'.[9]

The British government rarely replicated Price's prescience in colonial affairs. Yet, by the end of 1769, those in power did realize that the continuing unrest in the colonies meant concessions on the Townshend Duties would have to be made sooner rather than later. In the closing months of 1769, Prime Minister Grafton finally came out in favour of repealing all the duties; he was defeated on this in a cabinet vote, which determined that the duty on tea should be kept. In January 1770, largely as a result of fallout from the Wilkes affair, Lord North replaced Grafton as Prime Minister and on 5 March 1770, following a House of Commons debate, it was agreed that the Townshend Duties would be repealed, 'exclusive of the tea'. The situation in the colonies then quietened for a time and Lord North basked in what proved to be a premature aura of success in colonial policy.

In May 1773 the folly of the decision to retain the tax on tea became apparent when the East India Company found itself in financial difficulties. These arose as a consequence of a decline in tea sales, which accounted for 90% of its revenue, coupled with a vastly increased expenditure resulting from policing the substantial colonial possessions it had gained in India as a result of the Seven Years War. As a rescue package, Lord North's government offered the company a loan and, via the Tea Act, the right to ship tea directly to the American colonies, where the Townshend Duty would have to be paid by the colonists. They, however, saw this as another attempt at indirect taxation. Anger grew and resulted in the Boston Tea Party of December 1773.

Price, meanwhile, had occupied himself in preparing a third edition of his *Observations on Reversionary Payments* for publication. But it is clear from a letter he wrote on 2 November 1773 to Henry Marchant that his ideas on civil liberties, as they related to both Britain and America, were now crystallizing into a coherent argument:

> You are in a country that is increasing and improving fast, and likely in time to be the seat of the greatest and happiest empire that ever existed. I am in a country that is, I am afraid, declining. Corruption and venality have undermined the foundations of *civil* liberty among us; and as to *religious* liberty, allmost all that we enjoy of it is an indulgence or connivance contrary to law. May our *American*

brethren guard against the evils that threaten us with ruin. I admire the exertions
of the spirit of liberty among them: and I detest the unjust and miserable policy
which our governors have for some time been per[suing] with respect to them.
My heart is indeed with [them], and I am continually attending to the accounts
of what passes among them. *America* is the country to which most of the friends
of liberty in this nation are now looking; and it may be in some future period
the country to which they will all be flying. For our own sakes, therefore, we
have reason to wish they may keep themselves free.[10]

From the end of 1773 Price's earlier prediction that British policy in
America would turn friends into enemies came about. Britons were outraged
at news of the Boston Tea Party when it reached London on 19 January 1774.
Franklin, still in London and a Bostonian by birth, noted that 'we never had
since we were a people, so few friends in Britain. The violent destruction
of the tea seems to have united all parties here against our province.' The
result was British legislation between March and May 1774 designed to
punish Boston and the State of Massachusetts. 'The Coercive and Intolerable
Acts', as the colonists knew this legislation, began at the end of March with
the Boston Port Bill, which closed the port to all trade as of 1 June. At the
same time General Gage, commander of the British forces in America who
was home on leave, sailed with four regiments of soldiers and instructions,
as temporary governor of Massachusetts, to remove the seat of government
from Boston to Salem. He arrived in the colony on 13 May.

Price's American correspondents rushed to inform him of what was going
on. On 30 May, two days before the closure of Boston harbour came into
effect, Charles Chauncy wrote from the city describing the act as 'so palpably
cruel, barbarous, and inhumane, that even those who are called the friends
of Government complain bitterly of it'. Chauncy though was equally convinced that the result of the 'British edict' would make the colonists 'more
strongly spirited than ever to unite in concerting measures to render void its
designed operation'.[11] In sending his letter Chauncy missed his intended post
and the letter arrived at Price's Newington Green home enclosed with another
written on 18 July, almost a month later and after the Port of Boston had been
shut for a month and a half. By then Chauncy's earlier conclusions had been
borne out. Since the closure of the port, he wrote, 'bountiful donations
from one part of the country and another are daily flowing in upon us.
Waggons, loaded with grain, and sheep, hundreds in a drove, are sent to us
from one and another of the towns, not only in this, but the neighbouring
Colonies.'[12] This last fact was important for if the colonists chose to act
together then the British government's legislation would prove largely
ineffective. With the passing of two further bills relating to Massachusetts,[13]

the Harvard professor John Winthrop, writing to Price in September 1774, worried that in America, 'Things are running fast into confusion', and that the British actions were 'designed to irritate the people into something which might be called rebellion. At all events, the people will never submit to the new system. Their minds are universally agitated, to a degree not to be conceived by any person at a distance; and they are determined to abide all extremities, even the horrors of civil war, rather than crouch to so wretched a state of vassalage.'[14]

Winthrop felt he could do little more in a letter than give Price 'a slight sketch of the present situation' in America, 'omitting many matters of great moment', but Price soon heard of these matters at first hand. In the winter of 1774 the young Harvard-educated lawyer Josiah Quincy, junior arrived in London to plead the American cause, having already made a mark at home with his pamphlet *Observations on the Boston Port Bill*, a copy of which Charles Chauncy had sent to Price. On 24 November Quincy attended the Royal Society and from there went directly to a meeting of the Honest Whigs. Price befriended the young man and in December introduced him to the earl of Shelburne at Lansdowne House. Shelburne, Quincy noted in his London Diary, appeared 'a very warm friend to the Americans' and after two hours conversation on 'American affairs' concluded that 'he clearly approves of their conduct and spirit, and said if they continued united, they must have all they ask'.[15]

The British government now implemented another piece of controversial legislation even though its purpose was not directly related to the punishment or control of Boston or Massachusetts. The Quebec Act came before Parliament in May 1774 and effectively moved the border of the British colony of Quebec southward, down to the Ohio River and into what had previously been considered Indian land. In so doing it fixed the western boundary of the more northerly of the original American colonies and denied them the possibility of westward expansion. Furthermore, this larger Quebec would contain more French than British settlers and the act not only allowed Catholic worship to be tolerated there but also, in effect, allowed the establishment of the Roman Catholic Church in Canada. It also waived the Test Act that Price had so long campaigned against in Britain, allowing Catholics to hold public office; something still denied both Catholics and Protestant Dissenters in Britain. Limited financial support was also to be offered to the Catholic Church and elements of French law integrated with English law. This caused significant consternation among Price's correspondents and one of them, Ezra Stiles, gave vent to his feelings in a letter to Price on 10 April 1775. In doing so he also touched upon a secondary problem, one of importance to Price – the power of Church of England bishops to affect legislation in the British parliament. The bishops of the Church of England, Stiles wrote:

> dishonoured themselves . . . in voting for the Quebec Bill for establishing the Romish Idolatry over two Thirds of the Territories of the British [empire], and thereby exciting a Jubilee in Hell and throughout [the] Pontificate . . . This obliging token of friendship from the Bench of Bishops will not be very soon forgotten by the Puritans in America.[16]

It is clear that Stiles's virulent concern was linked not only to the spread of Catholicism but also the possibility that a Protestant episcopacy, of the kind already existing in Britain, might be established in America, a proposal many Anglican colonists certainly favoured. Apart from any concern he had at the passing of the Quebec Act, it is on the subject of American episcopacy that Price now made his second foray into colonial politics, albeit privately.

As early as March 1770 Price had received a letter on the issue of an American episcopacy from Charles Chauncy. 'The Church of England Clergy in the Colonies, those Colonies I mean that lie northward of Maryland, are so high in their principles, and are so set upon that grandeur and power that are attendant on an established Episcopate, that we may depend on their being further troublesome', Chauncy complained. 'We shall watch their motions here, and hope our friends at home will do the same there.'[17] As Price became involved in Dissenter attempts to obtain relief from subscription to the Thirty-Nine Articles in 1772/3 he had done just that, only to see the bishops in the House of Lords vote down any chance of greater toleration for Dissenters. 'They have hitherto shewn themselves enemies to truth and liberty', he informed Ezra Stiles, 'and there is no reason to expect that their natures will be changed in *America*.'[18]

Having watched the coercive legislation strangling Boston and Massachusetts, the remaining colonies now decided to join together in opposition. The result was the First Continental Congress, which sat in session in Philadelphia between 5 September and 26 October 1774, and a trade boycott outlined in a document called the Continental Association. The boycott banned all imports from Britain and of British goods derived from elsewhere. It later included a ban on exports from America to British colonies in the West Indies.

By the end of December Price anxiously waited for a ship from Boston with 'the News from thence . . . likely to grow more and more interesting'.[19] In January 1775 he received another long and detailed calendar of events from Charles Chauncy. In it Chauncy notes the eleven regiments of British troops stationed at Boston under General Gage, the harbour 'encompassed with ships of war' and all the necessaries of life having to be transported twenty-eight miles from Salem. 'Can it in reason be tho't, that Americans, who were freeborn, will submit to such a cruel tyranny? They will sooner lose their heart's blood', Chauncy wrote. Though Americans had not 'the least disposition to contend with the parent-states' and 'shall not betake our selves to the sword, unless necessarily obliged to it in self-defence', it was 'the determination of all north America to exert themselves to the utmost, be the consequence what it may. They chuse death rather [than] to live in slavery; as they must do, if they submit to that despotic government which has been contrived for them.'[20]

In Britain various efforts at conciliation were underway and Price wrote a letter to the earl of Chatham in which he 'could scarcely express the emotions' he had felt on hearing Chatham's proposals in Parliament for the removal of General Gage's troops from Boston. Typically Price then expressed his own view of the current situation in Britain and America:

> The nation is on a perilous edge. Our present governors have brought us upon it; and they are now concerting measures which must hurry us over it . . . The present measures of Government appear to me to be not only unjust, but wild in the highest degree. I am satisfied that they will not succeed. My correspondence with America and my intimacy with some of the first Americans leave me but little room to doubt about this.
>
> The Americans are wise enough to know the value of liberty; and it will, I believe, be found that they have virtue and fortitude enough to defend it against all invaders.[21]

Writing to Charles Chauncy on 25 February 1775 Price had even more to say:

> It is from *themselves* that, our Brethren in America must look for deliverance. They have, in my opinion, infinitely the advantage in this dispute. If they continue firm and unanimous it must have a happy issue, nothing being more certain than that the consequences of the present coercive measures must in a year or two be so felt in this kingdom as to rout the present despotic ministry, and to bring in new men who will establish the rights and liberties of the colonies on a plan of equity, dignity and permanence.[22] In such circumstances, if the *Americans* relax, or suffer themselves to be intimidated or divided, they will indeed deserve to be slaves. For my own part, were I in America I would go barefoot; I would cover myself with skins, and endure any inconveniences sooner than give up the vast stake now depending; and I should be encouraged in this knowing that my difficulties would be temporary, and that I was engaged in a last struggle for liberty, which perseverance would certainly crown with success. I speak with

earnestness, because thoroughly convinced that the authority claimed by this country over the Colonies is (as far as taxation and internal Legislation are concerned) a despotism which would leave none of the rights of freemen; and because also I consider *America* as a future *Asylum* for the friends of liberty here, which it would be a dreadful calamity to lose.[23]

Price went on to outline for Chauncy recent events in Britain and, just as his concern over religious freedom and the bishops' power at home is reflected in his anxiety over the possibility of episcopacy in America, so his concern with threats to freedom and civil liberty at home is paralleled by the threat he sees to them in America from British government actions; in relation to the Quebec Act for example, and through the growing influence of the monarch. 'Indeed the influence of the crown has already in effect subverted liberty here; and should this influence be able to establish itself in America, and gain an accession of strength from thence, our fate would be sealed, and all security for the sacred blessing of liberty would be destroy'd in every part of the British dominions. These are sentiments that dwell much upon my heart, and I am often repeating them.'[24]

Price's worries over Parliament's competence to legislate effectively grew increasingly clear: 'Were there not so many melancholy instances of the pliableness of the House of Commons', he continued in his letter to Chauncy, 'it would be wonderful that the same House that had one day declared *war* against the Colonies, should almost the next day, on a sudden fright in the Cabinet, agree to a Proposal supposed conciliatory. You may learn from hence our condition; and what that Power is which claims a right to make laws for America that shall bind it in all cases whatever.' As a result, he warns America to beware of Britons bearing gifts:

The design of the ministry by this step is to produce differences among the Colonies; or, as Lord North said in the House of Commons, to break at least *one* link in the chain; in consequence of which he thinks the whole may fall to pieces. New-York, in particular, the ministry have in view; and they imagine that they have reason to depend on succeeding there. But frantic must that Colony be that will suffer itself to be so ensnared. Indeed our ministers have all along acted from the persuasion that you are all fools and cowards. I have said that the design of Lord North's motion is to disunite. I must add, that it is intended also (to draw *Odium* on the Colonies in this Country, should they reject it; and, farther) to create delays and gain time: For as with you all depends on *losing no time*; so with us all depends on gaining time (to corrupt and divide).[25]

Although Price had yet to embark on writing down his thoughts on civil liberties as they related to America his general position was already well known and appreciated there, as John Winthrop indicates in a letter from Cambridge, Massachusetts on 10 April 1775: 'All America is greatly indebted to you for the sympathetic concern you express for their distress.' The people of Boston, Winthrop went on, 'pass'd tolerably well thro the winter, by the help of the generous donations of this and other Colonies. I am well informed that not less than 7000 persons depend on these donations for their daily bread.'[26] Ominously, he then adds that while the people in Boston had thought the 'works . . . General [Gage] threw up last fall at the only entrance into the town, were designed merely for his own *defence*', he now appeared to be 'making preparations . . . which indicate *offensive* war'.[27] If Price needed further convincing that war was in the offing it came on 20 March 1775 when Benjamin Franklin finally left London for Portsmouth, there to embark for home.

Price noted the departure of a man he described as the 'ablest friend America had' in a letter of 1775:

Dr Franklin is returned to Philadelphia, and will, I suppose attend the Congress. I have lost by his departure a Friend that I greatly loved and valued. He talked of coming back in the beginning of next winter; but I do not much expect to see him again.[28]

Although their friendship would continue to be maintained through letters, Price's prediction proved to be correct.

As Franklin returned home, events in America moved quickly toward a crisis point and news of its approach came to Price in a letter from New England on 6 June 1775. 'The blow has been struck – the sword is drawn – and I suppose the scabbard thrown away' wrote John Winthrop.[29] Two months earlier, on 19 April, at Lexington, that blow had been the firing of the opening shots of what now became the American revolutionary war. John Winthrop's letter offered a vivid commentary of events from the colonial perspective.

To this day, the question of who fired the first shot at Lexington remains a matter of debate. Winthrop, though, was in no doubt: 'a body [of British soldiers], said to be about 8 or 900 men, were secretly conveyed across the bay from Boston to Cambridge, and marched as silently as possible thro' byways till they got into the high road to Concord; with what design, could not admit of a doubt.' Watched all the way by the colonists the British marched to Lexington where 'a body of less than 100 of our people' were assembled. 'The Regulars without any provocation fired upon them, killed 8 upon the spot, wounded several others, and then persued their march to Concord, where they destroyed what stores they could meet with, and fired on another party of Provincials, and killed some of them; but the Provincials returning the fire killed some of the Regulars.' It was, Winthrop concluded, a 'memorable day, a day that will never be forgotten in America'.[30]

In fact, the colonists were already feeling the consequences of the action, as Winthrop's own situation showed: 'I have quitted my house, and reside in the country, at a considerable distance. The College [Harvard] is all dispersed; there being a large army of Provincials posted in the town, and my house is filled with Soldiers.' Before he sent his letter Winthrop added a postscript: 'All direct communications between you and us is now cut off; so that I am obliged to send my letters by the way of Philadelphia thro' the hands of our good friend Dr F[ranklin].'[31] The situation then deteriorated quickly until, as Benjamin Franklin's son William, a loyalist who was governor of New Jersey put it, 'All legal authority and government seems to be drawing to an end here and that of congresses, conventions and committees establishing in their places.'

On 10 May 1775 the Second Continental Congress met in Philadelphia, ostensibly to promote reconciliation and to send a further petition to King George. But on 14 June the Congress also created an army, under the command of General Washington. Even before the new commander could get to his men one of the first battles of the war had taken place: 'War now rages here on all its fury – bloody battles fought – one maritime town already laid in ashes – and others threatened with the same fate.'[32] The battle to which Winthrop referred was Bunker Hill on 17 June, a fight that resulted in significant losses on the British side and gave the lie to claims, such as those of lord Sandwich in Parliament earlier in the year, that the British merely faced 'a body of Fanatics in New-England, who will bluster and swell when danger is at a distance, but when it comes near, will, like all other mobs, throw down their arms and run away'. As Price wrote some months later, 'The truth is, we expected to find them a cowardly rabble who would lie quietly at our feet; and they have disappointed us'; just as he had long predicted.

On 18 July Charles Chauncy wrote a long and very detailed account of events at Bunker Hill to Price and, in a subsequent letter only four days later (on 22 July), informed him that 'Our continental Congress have published a declaration, setting forth "the reasons why they have taken up arms".' He also said they had sent 'a Petition to the King, and an Address to the People of England'.[33] Both were ignored by the British administration and no reply came from the king to what became known as the Olive Branch Petition. Adopted by Congress on 5 July it arrived London on 21 August – where the king refused to accept it.

Preparations for war were now well under way in America as Chauncy outlined to Price. 'It is intended our army shall be increased to thirty thousand; besides which, our minute-men are so numerous, that, upon alarm, fifty thousand of them might come to the help of the army, should necessity call for it, in two or three days. We have a sufficiency of powder . . . and before next year we shall have a full supply within ourselves. We can make what Cannon, shot, shells, bombs, etc. we want.'[34] Chauncy was convinced that even though 'The ministry may imagine we can't live without Commerce with England; . . . they are greatly mistaken. We have all the necessaries, and many of the comforts and conveniences of life within ourselves; and shall perhaps be better able to go thro' the war than they are.'[35] This no doubt was in Price's mind when he later wrote that America's self-sufficiency was one reason he believed Britain could not win an all-out war with America.

In August 1775 Price travelled home to south Wales for his annual sea-bathing at Southerndown. By his return to London later that month the king had declared all the American colonies to be in a state of rebellion (23 August) and by October the earl of Shelburne looked 'upon the colonies as lost'.[36]

Since 1763, and the start of the Wilkes affair, Price had watched the steady erosion in Britain of freedoms and liberties he considered the basic rights of all. He had witnessed justified demands for representation by the Americans undermined or denied by the British parliament, the duplicitous behaviour of Parliament in offering concessions to the Americans while simultaneously passing coercive acts, and the heaping of abuse upon such loyal friends to America and Britain as Benjamin Franklin. By the winter of 1775/6 the time had come for Price to begin writing down his thoughts on civil liberties – their universality and their application to the cause of America and its independence. This was a cause whose justice and success he never doubted, as long as the Americans kept their resolve:

The Colonies . . . should be upon their guard against insidious offers; and consider this as their time for securing forever their liberties. Perseverance and activity, whatever present sufferings may attend them, cannot but make all end well. The stake is vast and worth any temporary suffering.[37]

9

Revolution in America

Government is an institution for the benefit of the people governed, which they have the power to model as they please; and to say that they can have too much of this power, is to say that there ought to be a power in the state superior to that which gives it being, and from which all jurisdiction in it is derived.[1]

A work in twenty folio volumes will never make a revolution; it's the little books . . . which are to be feared.[2]

Richard Price's defence of the American colonists, a substantial pamphlet entitled *Observations on the Nature of Civil Liberty,* appeared in London on Saturday, 10 February 1776 in an edition of 1,000 copies priced at 2 s. each. Price initially thought 500 copies would suffice but his printer, Thomas Cadell of the Strand, advised that since the work bore Price's name as the author a thousand copies would be a practicable proposition. The edition sold out within three days.

Positive and negative reaction came swiftly. Joseph Priestley, who had received a copy from Price just before publication, sat up reading it till 1 a.m. and by 13 February had forwarded to Benjamin Franklin in America what he called this 'most excellent pamphlet'.[3] Theophilus Lindsey, however, while considering the work 'a noble one indeed', noted that Thomas Cadell had been warned not to print and sell another edition or 'he would be prosecuted by the Directors of the Bank [of England]'.[4]

Official consternation over the pamphlet in Britain centred less on Price's ideas of civil liberty and the role of government and the governed than on his discussion of the potentially disastrous consequences for the British economy if the Government continued with its current American policy. As Horace Walpole wrote, the work 'made a great sensation . . . But the part that hurt Administration was the alarm it gave to the proprietors of the funds by laying open the danger to which they were exposed by ruinous measures of the Court. I think this was the first publication on that

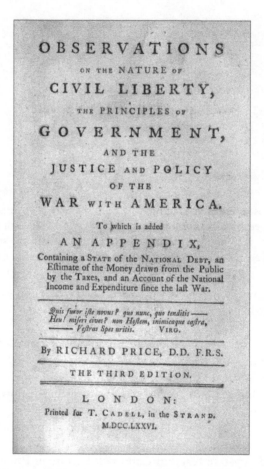

Figure 13. Title page of *Observations on the Nature of Civil Liberty* (1776; 3rd edn.,
London, 1776). Published in February 1776, over 60,000 copies were sold
in a year. In it Price expressed his clear support for the American cause.
The work was also published throughout the American colonies and
translated and published in France, Holland and Germany.

side that made any impression. All the hireling writers were employed to
answer.'[5]

Price's economic worries centred on the vastly increased use of paper
money at a time of coin scarcity, and a worryingly large national debt, which
was certain to increase substantially if war broke out between Britain and
America (it would, in fact, nearly double as a result of the war). To Price,
coin represented a means of exchange that had real value. It could thus 'bear
any alarm, and stand any shock'. By contrast, paper money, which had
become so necessary in the face of a coin shortage that even lottery tickets

had become negotiable, owed 'its currency to opinion', had 'only a local and imaginary value' and could 'stand no shock. It is destroyed by the approach of danger or even the suspicion of danger.'[6] These dangers could be anything from the destruction of a few account books at the Bank of England, to the landing of French troops on British soil or an insurrection threatening a revolution in government.

The American problem presented specific dangers of its own. First, it would upset trade with the American colonies and, second, there would be a deficiency in the revenue due to the loss of customs duties. Any of these dangers might precipitate a crisis in confidence leading the public to demand substantive coin to replace their illusory paper credit, a demand the banks would be unable to meet. Taxes would go unpaid and the Government revenue would eventually fail.

The intimidation of Price's printer Thomas Cadell was, however, to no avail. Price, it appears, had been quietly advised 'without fear, to print as many copies as the public demanded' of his pamphlet, and demand it they certainly did.[7] On 20 February, just ten days after publication of the first edition, a second was announced, with a third following a week later. By 18 March Cadell had begun advertising the fifth, which he quickly followed up with a number of cheaper editions printed in a smaller type so as to reduce the page number from 128 to less than 80. Selling, with Price's agreement, at sixpence each, these editions lost Price his royalties but brought the pamphlet before a much wider public. By the year's end, a work he had been convinced 'might sink in the first edition'[8] had sold, following William Morgan's estimate, 'near 60,000 copies' in Britain alone. Two editions had also appeared in Dublin, another in Edinburgh and translations were soon available in Dutch and French. A number of American editions would also appear in 1776 (see below) and, a year later, two German translations.[9]

The scale of this success is best gauged in relation to the sales figures Cadell gave to Price for some of the other works he had recently published. Even allowing for the exaggerations of a printer wishing to reassure an anxious author, the figures are telling. A pamphlet by a Mr Glover published in 1775 sold around 400 copies while another, *The Rights of Great Britain asserted against the Claims of America* by James Macpherson, sold only 500 'though then in the 6th edition thanks to the Government having been put to the expense of giving it away by thousands'.[10] One of the 'hireling writers' employed by the Government to refute Price's arguments, Macpherson challenged his thesis as 'unnatural and wild, incompatible with practice, and the offspring of the distempered imagination of a man who is biased by party, and who writes to deceive'.[11] There is a certain irony in this comment coming from the man at the heart of the notorious controversy over the

Poems of Ossian, a collection of 'ancient' Gaelic poetry in which all was not quite as it seemed.[12]

Over thirty pamphlets were written against Price's *Observations*, most of them by 'hirelings', but a few came from those truly worried by what Price had to say. Among this latter group was John Wesley who believed that although Price 'wrote with an upright intention', and was a man possessed of 'uncommon abilities', his ideas were dangerous and needed to be countered. 'I began', Wesley wrote in his journal on 14 April 1776, 'an answer to that dangerous Tract, Dr Price's 'Observations upon Liberty'; which, if practised, could overturn all government, and bring universal anarchy.'[13]

Although occasionally dismayed that his work brought forth such 'a torrent of opposition and abuse from the ministerial writers',[14] Price loved a quiet life too much to enter into a protracted controversy. He did not, he said, 'feel the least animosity against any person for differing from me or writing against me. If he does it with temper and decency I think myself obliged to him; and if he does not he is himself the greatest sufferer.' Indeed, Price found himself 'rather gratified' by the 'commotion and alarm' which his work raised among 'the friends of the present measures and the writers for government. I never thought that any thing I could write would produce any such effects. [. . .] My success, therefore, has surprised me.'[15]

Given the public's 'uncommon eagerness' to read his work 'and the rapidity with which it . . . circulated thro' the Kingdom', his conclusion that 'the sense of the nation is more in favour of America than the ministry are willing to believe' is hardly surprising.[16] It was reinforced by the behaviour of some of those around him: Thomas Rogers, Price's neighbour at Newington Green, explained to his children the causes of the American rebellion and how Britain was in the wrong. When news of the battle of Lexington reached London Rogers went so far as to put on mourning dress and when asked if he had lost a friend replied that he had lost several – in New England.[17] A number of military figures resigned their commissions rather than face the prospect of serving in a conflict they regarded as tantamount to a civil war. In the Ordnance Office, which supplied the British Army in America, Granville Sharp resigned, saying that it was not right to ship stores and armaments to put down self-government in the colonies.[18] In London the Recorder of the City also donned mourning dress just as his employers, the City of London Common Council, became the first to honour Price for his publication. On 14 March they voted to thank him 'for having laid down in his late publication . . . those pure principles upon which alone the supreme legislative authority of Great Britain over her Colonies can be justly or beneficially maintained'. They followed their thanks with the

Freedom of the City presented in 'a Gold Box of the value of Fifty Pounds'.[19] Such recognition certainly helped 'make amends' for the 'abuse' of the 'ministerial writers'. Others too, it seems, appreciated Price's efforts. According to Samuel Rogers, as Price listened to a debate at the House of Lords the duke of Cumberland told him he had read his essay on civil liberties 'till he was blind'. 'It is remarkable', replied lord Ashburton, near-by, 'that your Royal Highness should have been blinded by a book that has opened the eyes of all mankind'.[20]

The central political argument of the *Observations* is Price's defence of the American colonists based on his belief in the right of every community to govern itself. From the outset, he stresses the importance of liberty in underpinning this argument. 'There is not a word in the whole compass of language which expresses so much of what is important and excellent. It is, in every view of it, a blessing truly sacred and invaluable . . . It is the foundation of all honour, and the chief privilege and glory of our natures.'[21]

Liberty, Price argued, is comprised of four 'heads' – physical liberty, moral liberty, religious liberty and civil liberty – united by the 'one general idea that runs through them all; . . . the idea of self-direction, or self-government'.[22] Any inability to be self-directed or self-governing had serious and important consequences:

> Without physical liberty, man would be a machine acted upon by mechanical springs, having no principle of motion in himself, or command over events; and therefore incapable of all merit and demerit. Without moral liberty, he is a wicked and detestable thing, being subject to the tyranny of base lusts, and the sport of every vile appetite. And without religious and civil liberty, he is a poor and abject animal, without rights, without property and without a conscience, bending his neck to the yoke, and crouching to the will of every silly creature who has the insolence to pretend to authority over him.[23]

Price then expounded his argument on civil liberty as he believed it related to 'the Principles of Government', the 'Authority of One Country over Another' and, finally, to the situation in the American colonies.

For Price the power of government derived exclusively from the people. 'All civil government, as far as it can be denominated free, is the creature of the people. It originates with them. It is conducted under their direction, and has in view nothing but their happiness . . . In every free state every man is his own Legislator. All taxes are free-gifts for public services. All laws are particular provisions or regulations established by common consent for gaining protection and safety. And all magistrates are trustees or deputies for carrying these regulations into execution.'[24]

In a perfect state 'every independent agent' would be capable of using their individual power to decide upon 'public measures', but in larger states he sees clearly the necessity to appoint 'substitutes or representatives' to whom the public at large may 'entrust the powers of legislation, subject to such restrictions as they think necessary'. Whatever these delegates then do 'within the limits of their trust, may be considered as done by the united voice and counsel of the community'.[25] Price is clear too that for legitimacy such representative government must be based on as wide a franchise as possible. He does not call for a universal franchise, restricting it to those [males] capable of 'independent judgment', a rather nebulous term that could be taken to simply mean all those capable of *rational* judgement but which actually implied, in an eighteenth-century context, a franchise restriction based on property ownership.

Throughout his life Price championed the need for electoral and parliamentary reform, becoming a powerful advocate of the need for more equal representation, the introduction of shorter parliamentary terms and the abolition of political anachronisms such as placemen and rotten boroughs. But on the specific question of the franchise he vacillates between the restricted and universal options. For example, as D. O. Thomas has pointed out, Price endorsed the call in John Cartwright's 1776 pamphlet *Take Your Choice* for a universal male franchise, but in 1783, when advising Ireland on the issue, Price 'wished, that the friends of reformation [in England] had confined their views at present to the extension of the right of voting to Copyholders, and Leaseholders'.[26] The words 'at present' are significant in this context for one explanation of his ambivalence regarding a universal franchise is that he saw it as an ideal, an ultimate aim which needed to be tempered according to the circumstances of the time. It was a conclusion echoed in his moral philosophy where he had argued that 'A moral plan of government must be carried into execution gradually and slowly through successive steps and periods.'[27] At first sight this conclusion is difficult to reconcile with Price's passionate support of the American Revolution, which was the very antithesis of incremental change. Price's approach to change, however, was pragmatic. He believed gradual change to be for the best but also realized that occasions do arise when issues go beyond the dictates of pragmatism. At such times revolutionary change might be necessary, but always as a last resort.

Price next turned in the *Observations* to a consideration of what happens once a representative government is established, arguing passionately that the people remain sovereign at all times because parliaments 'possess no power beyond the limits of the trust for the execution of which they were formed. If they contradict this trust, they betray their constituents and dissolve themselves. All delegated power must be subordinated and limited. If omnipotence can, with any sense, be ascribed to a legislature, it must be lodged where all legislative authority originates; that is, in the people. For their sakes government is instituted and theirs is the only real omnipotence.'[28]

The election of a representative government by a free people also had a larger purpose. He hoped that the widespread establishment of such governments 'would exclude the desolations of war, and produce universal peace and order'.[29] Though this appears utopian in the context of modern realities and twentieth-century history it was, nevertheless, an idea that led Price, while living under the shadow of war in America and Europe, to make an early call for what was, in effect, a united states of Europe:

> Let every state, with respect to all its internal concerns, be continued independent of all the rest, and let a general confederacy be formed by the appointment of a senate consisting of representatives from all the different states. Let this senate possess the power of managing all the common concerns of the united states, and of judging and deciding between them, as a common arbiter or umpire, in all disputes; having at the same time, under its direction the common force of the states to support its decisions. In these circumstances each separate state would be secure against interference of sovereign power in its private concerns, and, therefore, would possess liberty, and at the same time it would be secure against all oppression and insult from every neighbouring state. Thus might the scattered force and abilities of a whole continent be gathered into one point, all litigations settled as they rose, universal peace preserved, and nation prevented *from any more lifting up a sword against nation.*[30]

In the light of this ideal, and with the threat of war in America looming, the final section of part one of Price's *Observations* concerns itself with the right of one country to exercise authority over another. Conquest, he concludes, being 'founded on violence, is never rightful',[31] nor did it impart to the conqueror a right to legislate for the conquered.

Like the French philosopher Montesquieu, who held that civic inactivity is always followed by slavery, Price realized 'there is nothing that requires more to be watched than power'.[32] Government 'is, in the very nature of it, a trust, and all its powers a delegation for gaining particular ends. This trust may be misapplied and abused. It may be employed to defeat the very ends for which it was instituted, and to subvert the very rights it ought to protect.'[33] Such a situation he now believed existed in the relationship between the British administration and the American colonies.

In part two of the *Observations* Price set out to show the injustice of a war with America. After a lengthy review of the background to the conflict he sees the war as a contest for power, one that contained within it the seeds of Britain's financial ruin. It was a dishonourable war, one that contravened Britain's own constitutional principles. 'But alas! it often happens in the political world as it does in religion, that the people who cry out most vehemently for liberty to themselves are the most unwilling to grant it to others.'[34]

Any enquiry as to 'whether the war with the colonies [was] a just war' should be determined by assessing the justice of Britain's claim to the right of jurisdiction over the colonies. This claim was made explicit in the words of the Declaratory Act of March 1766: 'That this kingdom has power, and of right ought to have the power to make laws and statutes to bind the colonies, and people of America, in all cases whatever.' Price is outraged: 'Dreadful power indeed! I defy anyone to express slavery in stronger language.'[35] He then quickly moves from outrage to a comprehensive analysis of the inadequacy of the reasons behind Britain's claim to power over America: the need to preserve the British empire, the inherent superiority of the British state, the fact that Britain had protected the colonies and ran deeply in debt on their account and that the land on which the American colonists had settled was rightfully Britain's.

Pleas to preserve the integrity of empires had, in all ages, Price argued, 'been used to justify tyranny' and produced nothing but 'discord and mischief'. Surely it was better to preserve unity through 'a common relation to one supreme executive head, an exchange of kind offices, types of interest and affection, and compacts'.[36] As to the superiority of the British state – in what did it reside? Was it its wealth? No, this never conferred real dignity. 'On the contrary its effect is always to debase, intoxicate, and corrupt.' Nor was it simply a question of British superiority in numbers or virtue since it was clear that the colonies would 'soon be equal to us in number' and were 'probably equally knowing and more virtuous. There are names among them that will not stoop to any names among the philosophers and politicians of this island.' And, he added, was it not also true that 'all we have done for them has not been more on our own account than on theirs?'[37]

The idea that Britain's hegemony over her colonies was akin to that of a parent over a child was one that had 'fascinated and misled' Britain but it denied the natural law that children grew up and left home. If we in Britain truly believed in this idea 'we should have been gradually relaxing our authority as [the colonists] grew up. But, like mad parents, we have done the contrary . . . No wonder they have turned upon us, and obliged us to remember that they are not children.'[38]

Finally, Price discussed the idea that the land on which the colonists had settled belonged to Britain. In doing so, he gives an interesting insight into his attitude to the rights of the often forgotten Native Americans and how closely this attitude connected his moral philosophy with his ideas on civil liberties. He begins by asking how the land in America first came to be 'ours' and he immediately dismisses as fallacious the argument of ownership by discovery: 'If sailing along a coast can give a right to a country, then might the people of Japan become, as soon as they please, the proprietors of Britain? Nothing can be more chimerical than property founded on such a reason. If the land on which the colonies first settled had any proprietors, they were the natives.' The colonists' right to the land came from the fact that the greatest part of it had been bought from the natives by settlers who 'have since cleared and cultivated it; and, without help from us, converted a wilderness into fruitful and pleasant fields. It is, therefore, now on a double account their property, and no power on earth can have any right to disturb them in the possession of it, or to take from them, without their consent, any part of its produce.'[39]

Price established his concept of property in the *Review of Morals*: 'The origin of the idea of *property* is the same with that of right and wrong in general. It denotes such a relation of a particular object to a particular person, as infers or implies, that it is fit he should have the disposal of it rather than others, and wrong to deprive him of it. This is what every one means by calling a thing his *right*, or saying that it is *his own*.'[40] For John Locke, whose ideas are important to Price, settlement gave entitlement to land while nomadism did not. The whole issue of Native American versus settler rights at this time is of course a fraught one that raises many questions, not least the true nature and extent of the settlers' 'purchases' of Indian land and the differing concepts and attitudes toward property ownership that might have existed between the two groups in the early days of European settlement. But while Price's account of the settlement of America is idealistic it at least *considers* Native Americans' right to the land, and does so in accordance with his ideas of moral and civil liberty. It is a rare example of such concern in the eighteenth century.

In the final section of the *Observations*, which is titled *On the Probability of Succeeding in the War with America*, Price makes it clear, just as his American correspondents had to him, that for Britain 'to think of conquering that whole continent with 30,000 or 40,000 men to be transported across the Atlantic and fed from hence and incapable of being recruited after any defeat' was a 'folly so great that language does not afford a name for it'.[41] The scale of the country and its resources of food and raw materials meant that no matter how effective Britain's military and naval efforts, America would always prove the greater in resources, manpower and resolve. Americans at the forefront of these events had told him, in no uncertain terms, that the strength of their resolution in the face of British aggression would render their victory certain. To emphasize this point to his British readers, Price then deliberately contrasts the American pursuit of freedom with the desperate need for reform of a system at home that he considered 'inflated and ir-religious, enervated by luxury, encumbered with debts, and hanging by a thread'. Could anyone, he asks, 'look without pain to the issue?'[42]

What impact and influence did the *Observations* have in the colonies themselves? With the voyage to America taking up to eight weeks, London editions of the *Observations* would have reached America around the middle of April 1776. This was too late for the work to have made an impact on the push to independence comparable to that already created by Tom Paine's pamphlet, *Common Sense*.

Thomas Paine, a one-time corset-maker and customs official from Thet-ford in Norfolk, had arrived in America in November 1774. *Common Sense*, like Price's *Observations*, is one of Voltaire's 'little books', written in a style John Adams (later Vice President to Washington and ultimately second President of the United States) admired for its 'strength and brevity' and with a content he rightly felt would become the 'common faith'. An instant bestseller from the moment of its publication on 10 January 1776, a month before Price's *Observations*, Paine's *Common Sense* sold many thousands of copies and achieved its purpose of rallying to the cause of independence the numerous colonists who still doubted the efficacy of a final break with Britain.

Reconciliation with Britain had long been the hope of many in the colonies, even those who later became prominent revolutionary figures. In March 1775, while still in London, Benjamin Franklin had assured the earl of Chatham that 'he had never heard in any conversation from any person drunk or sober the least expression of a wish for separation or hint that such a thing would be advantageous to America'.[43] As late as August 1775, and despite the bloody events at Lexington, Concord and Bunker Hill, Thomas Jefferson could still declare himself to be 'looking with fondness towards a reconciliation with Great Britain'.[44] Price had similar hopes, even suggesting in the *Observations* that a form of federal empire might provide a lasting political solution, an empire in which all member states would be represented in a federal imperial parliament with each state maintaining the right to legislate for itself in matters not relating to the empire as a whole. He also reprinted in the conclusions to his *Observations* the text of a speech the earl of Shelburne gave to Parliament on 10 November 1775, which called for Britain to retain the right of external legislation over American affairs but to leave 'internal legislation and all revenue taxation to the colonies'. By February 1776 Shelburne's solution was a forlorn hope. Paine's master stroke in *Common Sense* was to cut through similar equivocation in the colonies by attacking what was, for many colonial reconcilers, the last link binding them to the mother country – their loyalty to the monarchy. Until the publication of *Common Sense* the argument with Britain had been seen in America as essentially one with Parliament and the king's ministers. Many still believed the monarch to be personally and constitutionally above politics; a belief that explains why so many of the addresses and petitions from America at this time were directed to the king rather than to, or through, Parliament. Ironically, however, at precisely the same time many people in Britain, including Price, were becoming concerned at George III's growing influence in parliamentary matters.

In *Common Sense* Paine set out to change the generally favourable view many colonists had of the monarchy and of a king he called a 'hardened sullen-tempered Pharaoh' and 'the Royal Brute of Great Britain'. He did so by launching a blistering attack on the hereditary principle that underlay the monarch's authority, both in relation to the British constitution and to contemporary American affairs. His offering of 'nothing more than simple facts, plain arguments, and common sense' on the subject galvanized the colonies and, from January 1776, independence finally became the issue of the hour.

In February 1776, just as Price's *Observations* first appeared in London, the Second Continental Congress, meeting at Philadelphia, put aside a resolution that denied independence was the American aim. By March Washington had placed cannon on the hills overlooking Boston, forcing the British, under General Howe, to retire to Nova Scotia. In April, in defiance of the London government, Congress ordered the reopening of American ports to trade and, on 10 May, requested all states to form their own governments, an act tantamount to a declaration of independence in itself. On 7 June, Congressman Lee of Virginia moved that 'these colonies are, and of right ought to be free and independent states'; the motion was seconded by John Adams. Despite all this there were still doubters, those who, in Jefferson's words, were 'not yet ripe for bidding adieu to the British Connection'.[45] Nevertheless, on 1 July nine colonies voted for precisely that and the following day, in a final and decisive vote, all but one voted for independence (New York abstained). Two days later, on 4 July 1776, Jefferson's draft of the Declaration of Independence was adopted.

Since all of these events would have happened with or without publication of Price's *Observations* its direct impact on them was probably limited. Nevertheless, it was certainly read by prominent members of Congress and it has been suggested that the influence of the pamphlet can be seen in the famous Declaration itself.

Carl Cone's comment that 'the larger sentiment of [Price's] *Observations* resembles that of the Declaration of Independence' is true and unsurprising.

Figure 14. 'Declaration of Independence, July 4th 1776', engraving by
Asher Brown Durand after a painting by John Trumbull. Among
those pictured are a number of Price correspondents and friends,
including Thomas Jefferson, John Adams, Benjamin Franklin
and Benjamin Rush.

Both Price and Jefferson 'drew upon many of the same sources', especially
the works of John Locke, and their ideas were certainly part of the common
currency of radical eighteenth-century thought.[46] Their achievement was
not so much the generation of wholly new ideas but to elucidate existing
ones in texts that are simply yet intelligently written, concise yet eloquent,
and hugely inspiring. To argue, however, that Jefferson consulted Price's
Observations as he sat drafting the Declaration of Independence in the house
of Mr Graff, a Philadelphia bricklayer, in the warm June of 1776 would be
presumptuous. Jefferson stated openly that he did not consult any book or
pamphlet while undertaking the draft since he wished 'to place before
mankind the common sense of the subject, in terms so plain and firm as to
command their assent, and to justify ourselves in the independent stand we
are compelled to make'.[47] It is however possible, even likely, that Jefferson
saw a copy of the *Observations* beforehand.[48]

Price's *Observations* was certainly widely available in America, with editions
printed in Philadelphia, Boston, Charleston and New York. It was also
reprinted in the *Continental Journal* and as a serialization in the *Connecticut
Courant and Hartford Weekly Intelligencer* between 29 July and 16 September

1776. On current evidence, the earliest of these printings seems to be the edition from Philadelphia, which was advertised in the *Pennsylvania Packet* in the first week of July and in *The Pennsylvania Gazette* on 10 July.[49] In addition, John Adams in responding to a 5 July request from Samuel Chase, another delegate to the Congress, for a copy of Price's *Observations* noted in his reply of 9 July that 'I shall enclose to you Dr. Price. He is an independent, I think.'[50] All these dates clearly indicate that the publication was widely available in America by the beginning of July 1776 and that it was well known and talked about among members of the Congress. An early July, or even late June, publication date in America however was probably too late for Jefferson to have definitely seen an American copy of the pamphlet before beginning his draft of the independence declaration in mid-June.

Another scenario is that Jefferson might have seen a British edition of the *Observations* before beginning his work. As already noted these would have begun reaching America as early as mid-April including, presumably, the copy Joseph Priestley sent to Benjamin Franklin on 13 February, a few days after its London publication. In early June, while attending the Second Continental Congress in Philadelphia, Benjamin Franklin found himself appointed a member of the 'committee of five' charged with drafting the independence declaration; its other members being John Adams of Massachusetts, Roger Sherman of Connecticut, Robert Livingston of New York and Thomas Jefferson of Virginia (to whom the committee quickly delegated the work of writing the document). In this context it seems reasonable to suggest that Franklin may have shown or even given Jefferson his own copy of the *Observations* since it was clearly a work directly related to the business in hand. The French writer Henri Laboucheix has taken the question of Price's influence a step further by suggesting that through his friendship with Franklin, a specific element of Price's thought may have had a direct bearing on the declaration document. Numerous alterations were made to Jefferson's four-page draft before Congress finally approved it and Franklin was supposedly responsible for changing the opening words of the second paragraph from 'We hold these truths to be sacred and undeniable' to the now famous phrase 'We hold these truths to be self-evident' (others suggest Jefferson made the change). Laboucheix argues that 'the word self-evident', with its metaphysical connotations, 'is no more familiar to Franklin and his way of thinking than to Jefferson . . . both had little taste for abstract thought'. To Price, however, the word is a 'key' one, being used in the *Review of Morals*, for example, 'more than twenty times' to express his central idea that morality is inherent to our natures. We intuitively understand right and wrong because they are 'self-evident' to us. Thus, Laboucheix concludes, it could be that 'one of the terms of Price's intellectual intuitionism was used to express more clearly the philosophical justification for the independence of the United States'.[51]

Whatever the truth of Laboucheix's assertion, it does remind us that Price's political philosophy stemmed directly from the moral philosophy he had outlined in the *Review of Morals* eighteen years before. Both philosophies expressed his belief in 'self-direction, or self-government', i.e. the free will of the individual as the essence of all moral and political liberty. By linking his political and moral philosophy in this way, Price's *Observations* certainly helped give to the political nature of the American Revolution an ethical and moral foundation. This was an invaluable contribution to a fledgling nation seeking to develop a new system of government and to justify it before the court of world opinion.

Price's *Observations* continued to be influential in the months following the Declaration of Independence. It touched those committed, yet more conservative, rebels who found the form of government advocated in Tom Paine's *Common Sense* too radical for their tastes, men like John Adams who, though he recognized Paine's genius, still considered him 'a disastrous meteor' and someone better 'at pulling down than building'.[52]

In *Common Sense* Paine had argued that government, which 'even in its best state' he considered a 'necessary evil', is only properly attained through direct democracy and a parliament in which 'every man, by natural right will have a seat'. Like Price, he understood the necessity for representatives to be elected as a state grew in size and population but in Paine's model these representatives must 'never form to themselves an interest separate from the electors'. He wanted representatives who would always act 'in the same manner as the whole body would act were they present'.[53] This was anathema to Price as well as to conservative rebels like Adams for implicit in such a system is a unicameral legislature; one from which the checks and balances in a bicameral system, so vital to protect minorities from the tyranny of the majority, are absent. Adams saw Paine's ideas as so 'without . . . restraint or even an attempt at any equilibrium or counter poise' that they must 'produce confusion and every evil work'. They were, in short, far too 'democratical'; a word that, in contrast to its modern image, conjured up in many an eighteenth-century mind visions of unruly mobs and a perpetual instability in society and public affairs. As a man who wrote that liberty 'can no more exist without virtue and independence than the body can live and move without a soul', Adams, and others like him, surely found in Price's calmer, more philosophical approach to civil liberties the balance they desired.[54] At home in Britain, however, many saw Price's *Observations* as anything but a route to a civil society of equilibrium and counterpoise.

10

Reaction at Home and Abroad

By these publications *I have drawn upon myself a vast deal of abuse*; but the comfort I derive from the consciousness of having in this instance satisfied my judgment and endeavoured to act the part of a good citizen, makes me abundant amends.[1]

Price learnt of the American Declaration of Independence in August 1776, just before setting out for 'Brighthelmstone' (Brighton) on his annual bout of sea-bathing and 'dissipation'. 'You have undoubtedly seen the news published in the Gazette on Saturday night', he wrote to William Adams on 14 August. 'The Congress has declared war and independency, and there is now an end of all hope and reconciliation.'[2] Price also announced in this letter that he was 'thinking of publishing a supplement' to his *Observations*. The publication was originally intended for May or June, but he now resolved to postpone it until October or November. It would eventually appear as the *Additional Observations on the Nature and Value of Civil Liberty, and the War with America* in February 1777.

A follow-up pamphlet became necessary for three reasons. First, he disagreed with the content of a budget speech Lord North had presented to Parliament on 24 April 1776. A substantial part of the *Additional Observations* is given over to arguing that the Government had overestimated the surplus available to redeem the national debt and the amount of gold coin in the kingdom. He also critiqued the administration's method of raising loans and produced an analysis of the current state of the national debt. He even included a timely discussion of the debts and resources of France; a potential ally of America. Second, just as his ideas on civil liberties were giving heart to conservative rebels in America, Price found himself accused at home of being a rabid democrat and republican in the mould of Tom Paine. Third, he realized quite soon after publication of the *Observations* that in Britain his political ideas were manifestly misunderstood, and he wanted to clarify and elaborate those ideas.

Some criticism of the *Observations* was simply crass. Walpole, for example, noted that the Government hack John Shebbeare, a man sentenced in 1758 to the pillory and a jail term for libel, abused 'Dr. Price daily in the papers'. In one pamphlet Shebbeare argued that Price intended to emulate the Cromwellian regicides. 'George the Third,' he stated, 'like Charles the First . . . was to be murdered, to give the people liberty'.[3] This was arrant nonsense. Even though a considerable degree of ambiguity on the subject of monarchy can be detected in Price's later writing he had never, thus far, attacked the concept of monarchy or called for its abolition. He was no Paineite republican. On the contrary, he supported and advocated, in Britain at least, the tradition of a balanced constitution of king, Lords and Commons. What Price did oppose was the idea that 'there are certain men who possess in themselves, independently of the will of the people, a right of governing them, which they derive from the Deity'. Rule by divine right, whether vested in a king or a despot, he considered 'a doctrine which avowedly subverts civil liberty and which represents mankind as a body of vassals . . . to be obliged to look up to a creature no better than ourselves as the master of our fortunes, and to receive his will as our law – what can be more humiliating?'[4]

The more pertinent and perceptive criticism levelled against his ideas came from critics such as Adam Ferguson who saw in Price's conception of liberty nothing more than 'a right or power in every one to act as he likes without any restraint'. Even 'thieves and pickpockets', Ferguson argued, would 'have a right to make laws for themselves' in the kind of free state Price envisaged.[5]

In the *Additional Observations* Price accepts that liberty cannot be better defined than by calling it 'a right or power in every one to act as he likes', but he goes on to say that he will only fully adopt this meaning if 'it is understood with a few limitations'. These limitations derived from his belief in man as a moral being: 'That every man's will, if perfectly free from restraint, would carry him invariably to rectitude and virtue and that no one who acts wickedly acts as he likes, but is conscious of a tyranny within him overpowering his judgment and carrying him into a conduct for which he condemns and hates himself.'[6] His critics believed this view to be unrealistic and argued that the degree of virtue and moral rectitude required for the kind of representative government Price envisaged could not be found in times whose 'universal degeneracy and selfishness . . . were so fatal to representative institutions'. But Price never advocates a liberty that is simply a hedonistic individualism devoid of restraint or 'self-direction, or self-government'. Liberty, including civil liberty, is always paralleled and tempered by his moral philosophy and its concept of virtue. So, just as the virtuous person has a duty to make informed moral choices based on the use of intellect and reason, so the citizen has a duty to do the same with regard to their political and civil liberties.

By revisiting and expanding his ideas in the *Additional Observations*, Price had hoped to answer his critics once and for all. In this he was to be disappointed. The criticism continued, and that from two people in particular gave him cause for further concern. On 21 February 1777, in a sermon preached to the Society for the Propagation of the Gospels in Foreign Parts, William Markham, the archbishop of York, objected to what he called Price's 'loose opinions' and declared that the true essence of liberty was not the sovereignty of the people but the supremacy of the law. In April, in a *Letter to the Sheriffs of Bristol,* the formidable politician Edmund Burke argued that Price's ideas on liberty were 'a speculation which destroys all authority'.[7]

Price replied to both men via the general introduction he wrote for the *Two Tracts*, a compilation volume containing newly edited versions of his *Observations* and *Additional Observations*, which appeared in London on 24 January 1778. In the *Observations* he had argued that 'Liberty . . . is too imperfectly defined when it is said to be a government by laws, and not by men. If the laws are made by one man, or a junto of men in a state, and not by common consent, a government by them does not differ from slavery.'[8] In his introduction to the *Two Tracts* this argument provides the basis for his counterblast to Markham. The archbishop, Price argued, says that liberty comes from 'the supremacy of law . . . whatever the law is, or whoever makes it. In despotic countries government by law is the same with government by the will of one man . . . but, according to this definition, it is liberty.' Price then countered the religious questions Markham had also raised in his sermon, including a suggestion that if the Dissenters continued their politicking they should be subject to similar restraints as Catholics:

> In England formerly the law consigned to the flames all who denied certain established points of faith. Even now, it subjects to fines, imprisonment and banishment all teachers of religion who have not subscribed the doctrinal articles of the Church of England; and the good Archbishop, not thinking the law in this case sufficiently rigorous, has proposed putting the Protestant Dissenters under the same restraints with the Papists. And should this be done, if done by law, it will be the establishment of liberty.
>
> The truth is that a government by law, is or is not liberty, just as the laws are just or unjust; and as the body of the people do or do not participate in the power of making them. The learned prelate seems to have thought otherwise, and therefore has given a definition of liberty which might as well have been given of slavery.[9]

Certain that the revolution in America would be quickly crushed, Markham had also argued for the establishment of an episcopacy in America, another topic guaranteed to raise Price to debate. He answered Markham by noting that the Americans themselves had argued in many states against such an imposition and that the Church of England surely could not insist on its right to impose bishops on the Church of another country.[10]

Edmund Burke's opposition Price found puzzling since he thought it 'scarcely possible his ideas and mine on this subject should be very different'.[11] Burke had been a long-standing champion of the American cause and in terms very similar to Price's own, or so Price thought. Price's view was probably influenced by Burke's 1770 pamphlet *Thoughts on the Cause of the Present Discontents*, in which he spoke of the 'governing part of the state' as being 'the trustees of power'. But as Carl Cone has pointed out, Burke's idea 'of trusteeship was more nearly akin to the idea of *noblesse oblige* than to the democratic philosophy of the sovereignty of the people' advocated by the likes of Price.[12]

Burke was a traditionalist and, despite his general support of the Americans in their opposition to direct taxation from Britain, this stance was reflected in his more general view of the colonies. He desired a return to the status quo and in arguing for it denounced the sort of rights propounded by Price. 'Again, and again, revert to your own principles', Burke urged Parliament:

> *Seek Peace, and ensue it* – leave America, if she has taxable matter in her, to tax herself. I am not here going into the distinctions of rights, nor attempting to mark their boundaries. I do not enter into these metaphysical distinctions; I hate the very sound of them. Leave the Americans as they anciently stood, and these distinctions, born of our unhappy contest, will die along with it. They, and we, and their and our ancestors, have been happy under that system. Let the memory of all actions, in contradiction to that good old mode, on both sides, be extinguished for ever.[13]

Burke also saw the British parliament as being 'at the head of her extensive empire in two capacities: one as the local legislature of this island, providing for all things at home, immediately, and by no other instrument than the executive power. The other, and I think her nobler capacity is what I call her *imperial character*, in which, as from the throne of heaven, she superintends all the several inferior legislatures, and guides, and controls them all without annihilating any.' Inevitably, though, should one of these 'inferior legislatures' run out of line, in the way some American colonial assemblies had, West-minster, as the superior legislature, must reserve the right to enforce its will. Thus, in the present dispute the Americans should, as Burke put it, 'Tax yourselves for the common supply, or parliament will do it for you.'[14]

EDMUND BURKE, ESQ.ᵣ

Figure 15. 'Edmund Burke, Esq.r' by 'J. Chapman sculp', 1798,
and published by J. Wilkes.

By 1777, when *Additional Observations* and *Two Tracts* appeared in print, it was not only with the criticisms of Markham and Edmund Burke that Price had to contend. The public mood regarding the American colonies had also changed. The intense support for the colonists' cause, so strong at the time Price published his *Observations* in 1776, had begun to wane with their Declaration of Independence and the start of hostilities. Commenting favourably on the course of events in the colonies had now become a more risky affair.

Price sensed this change by late August / early September 1776. Whereas in the fifth edition of his *Observations,* published in March, he confidently declared that he was happy to commit himself to the 'candour of the public', by November, as he prepared the *Additional Observations* for publication, he confessed to John Cartwright that he was now 'full of fears about the publication I have in view, sensible of the caprice of the public'.[15] Nevertheless, as *Additional Observations* was published, he put a brave face on things in a letter to William Adams: 'I expect that it will draw upon me a great deal more abuse; but as I don't deserve abuse it will make little impression on me.'[16]

By June Price's situation had become even more difficult. As he wrote to John Winthrop,'I have drawn *upon myself a vast deal of abuse* [his emphasis] . . . I am become a person so marked and obnoxious that prudence requires me to be very cautious. So true is this, that I avoid all correspondence with Dr Franklin, tho' so near me as Paris.'[17] The American Congress had elected Franklin as one of its commissioners to Paris in September 1776 with instructions to negotiate a treaty between America and France, his fellow commissioners being Silas Deane and Arthur Lee. In April 1777 Lee wrote to Price from Paris saying of the *Additional Observations* that he had never read 'any thing with more satisfaction'.[18] This letter from the enemy camp might well have entailed some risk to Price, although he noted in his later letter to John Winthrop that 'There is less danger in receiving than sending accounts.'[19]

In marked contrast to the criticism of Price at home, the Continental Congress, meeting in Philadelphia on 6 October 1778, resolved:

> That the Honourable Benjamin Franklin, Arthur Lee, and John Adams Esqrs or any one of them, be directed forthwith to apply to Dr. Price, and inform him, that it is the Desire of Congress to consider him a Cityzen of the united States, and to receive his Assistance in regulating their Finances. That if he shall think it expedient to remove with his family to America and afford such Assistance, a generous Provision shall be made for requiting his Services.[20]

The letter informing Price of this resolution arrived at Newington Green in mid-December 1778 from Franklin, Lee and Adams at Passy, near Paris. In a separate letter Commissioner Lee urged Price to accept the offered post. 'It is the voice of wisdom which calls you to the noblest of all works,' he wrote, 'the assisting to form a Government which means to make the principles of equal justice and the general rights the chief object of its attention. Generations yet unborn will bless the Contributors to this inestimable work, and among them I trust the names of Dr Price will hold a distinguished place.'[21]

That the members of Congress should consider Price for the position of financial secretary is no surprise since his *Observations on the Nature of Civil*

Liberty, which contained a lengthy analysis of Britain's debt problems, had been widely published in America. Also known, though not published there, was *Observations on Reversionary Payments*, Price's major work on annuities and life insurance. In the past Price had given financial advice to individual Americans, including Benjamin Franklin's son William on a proposed annuities fund.[22]

Gaining the benefit of Price's financial acumen was just one side of the American offer; the other was congressional concern over the state of America itself. Franklin, Lee and Adams had been appointed American representatives to Louis XVI's France with the paramount aim of obtaining practical and financial support for the Revolution. Two years into the war, America's financial needs were becoming acute, with the country suffering consequences common to any nation at war: a rampant inflation, a burdensome tax regime, and a black market economy by which some had already 'amassed fortunes' and were 'riding in chariots'.[23] There were even fears Congress might soon be unable to pay its bills or meet the needs of General Washington and the continental army. Clearly there would be much for a financial adviser to do in America but Price, having considered the offer, declined the position. 'It is not possible', he wrote in his formal third person reply to Congress on 18 January 1779, 'to express the sense he has of the honour which this resolution does him, and the satisfaction with which he reflects on the favourable opinion of him which has occasioned it. But he knows himself not to be sufficiently qualified for giving such assistance; and he is so con-nected in this country, and also advancing so fast into the evening of life, that he cannot think of a removal.' He felt, though, 'the warmest gratitude for the notice taken of him, and that he looks to the American States as *now* the hope, and likely *soon* to become the refuge of mankind'.[24]

On the same day as he sent his reply to Congress, via the commissioners in France, Price also answered the personal letter he had received from Arthur Lee. In this he was more fulsome in describing the offer from Con-gress, which he considered 'among the first honours of my life' and which emanated from an assembly 'the most respectable and important in the world'. He also clarified his reasons for not taking up the position. 'There is an indolence growing upon me as I grow older which will probably prevent me for ever from undertaking any public employment', he wrote. 'When I am in my study and among my books, and have nothing to en-cumber me I am happy; But so weak are my spirits that the smallest hurry and even the consciousness of having any thing to do which *must* be done, will sometimes distress and overpower me.'[25] As a man of fifty-five with a wife in frail health his decision is perhaps understandable. Less so is his protestation of a growing 'indolence': 1778 and the years immediately

Figure 16. 'The Politician', engraving by J. Ryder, 1782, after a painting by
Stephen Elmer. The figure portrayed is now known to be Benjamin Franklin,
who is seen reading the *Morning Post* dated 1 January 1776 while resting
his fist upon a copy of Price's *Observations on the Nature of Civil Liberty*.
Elmer thus makes clear the importance of Price's work, even though
the timing implied in the painting is impossible since the *Observations*
were not published in Britain until February 1776.

following it would be among the busiest and most controversial of his life.
This congressional offer of citizenship and employment had come to him,
after all, not only from one enemy, America, but via the capital of another,
France, which had entered the war with Britain in June 1778.

For some time prior to 1778 France had given clandestine help to the
Americans while remaining reluctant to aid them openly. Like most European
mainland states she was waiting for the American colonists to prove themselves
in their fight with Britain. That proof came in October 1777 when a British
army under General Burgoyne surrendered to a rebel army under Horatio

Gates at Saratoga. As a result, in January 1778 France provided America with a grant of 6 million livres, the start of a series of payments that would reach more than 20 million livres by 1783, a small fraction of the 1.3 billion livres (13 billion dollars today) it is estimated she eventually spent aiding America.[26] By February two treaties formally allying France and America had been signed, and these, lord Shelburne declared in the House of Lords on 13 March, rendered it almost impossible for Britain to avoid a war with France as well as America.

In his speech Shelburne also worried over Britain's preparedness for such a conflict, in particular the ability of her financial institutions to weather the coming storm. As the *Gentleman's Magazine* reported, he insisted that 'The Bank of England must be considered; every possible means must be exerted to assist the Bank and keep up the public credit. Sleeping and waking he had it ever in his mind; and Dr Price, with whom he had frequently conversed on the subject had convinced him of the urgent necessity of making the bank a primary object of attention and support.'[27] Prepared or not, the storm arrived in June 1778 when the French declared war on Britain, an outcome Price had first predicted as early as August 1776.

None of these seismic geopolitical shifts succeeded in weakening Price's support for the American cause. He and his followers were increasingly concerned, however, over the possibility of what Benjamin Franklin called the 'violence of government in consequence of his late excellent publications in favour of liberty'. Among Price's supporters was the earl of Shelburne; in December 1775, after the events at Bunker Hill, Price had sought import and export figures from Shelburne in order to complete his work on the financial aspects of the *Observations*. Shelburne had replied anxiously, 'I need not I am sure remind you, that all Office Informations require certain managements in the use that's made of them, least it should be trac'd to the Individual, who gives them, and who may be liable to suffer very unjustly.'[28] Shelburne was probably right to be cautious. Yet, it is also surprising how much detail concerning troop movements from Britain to America, as well as political news, Price freely imparts to his American correspondents. Once hostilities started in earnest his letters come perilously close to what could have been considered treasonable. In December 1775, for example, just a few months after Bunker Hill, he informs Charles Chauncy of the heavy recruiting going on in Britain with '4000 *Hanoverians* besides *Hessians* are to be sent' to America. He informs him too of the British attempt to raise a further 20,000 troops in Russia.[29]

Another concern was the possibility of his being the target of mob violence, particularly in the wake of the widespread and violent riots that erupted in London in the early summer of 1780. Between 1778 and 1779 two relief acts were passed in Parliament. The Catholic Relief Act of 1778 made modest changes to the life of Catholics in Britain, by allowing them the right to inherit and buy land for example, and the Dissenter Relief Act of 1779 finally removed the necessity for Dissenters to subscribe to the Thirty-Nine Articles of the Anglican Church (although they were still required to swear an oath, of which Price disapproved).

The Catholic Relief Act in particular provoked immediate hostility in a Britain now at war with Catholic France. Riots against the act began in Scotland but quickly spread to London where they were further whipped up by the parliamentary speeches of the wayward and erratic Lord George Gordon, a leader of the Protestant Association. On 2 June 1780 (by which time Britain was also at war with Spain) the anti-Catholic Gordon Riots erupted violently across the city. Although there was no comparable reaction to the Dissenter Relief Act, Price, aware of historic precedents, must have worried that his religious position, coupled with his very public support for America, and indirectly her Catholic allies, might make him a target of such violence.

Further criticism of Price did arise from the continuing misrepresentation or misunderstanding to which his published works and pulpit sermons were subject. This criticism was especially dangerous when it came from leading members of the British establishment such as Dr Lowth, the bishop of London. On Ash Wednesday, 17 February 1779, Lowth preached a sermon at the Chapel Royal in St James's Palace declaring Price to be a man 'whose study it has long been to introduce confusion, to encourage sedition, and to destroy all rule and authority, by traducing government, despising dominion, speaking evil of dignitaries, and assuming visionary and impractical principles as the only true foundation of a free government, which tend to raise discontents in the people, *to harden some in actual rebellion, and to dispose others to follow their example.*' Though it 'astonished' Price, coming as it did from a man whose character, learning and abilities he 'always used to venerate', such criticism could not remain unanswered and, in a published edition of a fast-day sermon he gave at Hackney in February 1779 Price answered Lowth by quoting back at the prelate his own words preached to the Assizes at Durham in 1764: 'The greatest and most important privilege that any people can possibly enjoy', Lowth had argued, 'is to be governed by laws framed by their own advice or consent.'[30]

Price used the publication of another fast-day sermon, in spring 1781, to further clarify his position regarding the American war by reminding his readers that he had predicted very early on 'that the colonies would be driven to form an alliance with France' and that a 'general war would be kindled'. Though he did 'not mean to boast of any sagacity' he did reflect on the abuse to which he had been subject as a result of these wholly correct observations:

> I am only one and one of the least of many who have stood forth on this occasion, yet it has happened that no one has fallen under a greater load of abuse. You will be sensible how improper an object of abuse I have been if you will consider,
>
> First, that detesting all abuse in political as well as religious discussion I have myself always avoided it.
>
> Secondly, that I have done no more than what is in a particular manner the duty of a Minister of the Gospel of peace to do; I mean, endeavoured to prevent the carnage of war and to promote peace and righteousness.
>
> Thirdly, what most of all justifies me is that events have proved that I was right in my opinion of the pernicious tendency of the measures against which I wrote.

'Upon the whole', he continued, 'I must repeat to you that there is nothing in the course of my life that I can think of with more satisfaction than the testimony I have borne and the attempts I have made to serve the cause of general liberty and justice, and the particular interest of this country at the present period. A period big with events of unspeakable consequences and perhaps one of the most momentous in the annals of mankind.'[31] It was a view grudgingly accepted by a reviewer of the sermon in the *Monthly Review* of April 1781 who declared Price's ideas to have been 'ridiculed when they were first published, as the dreams of a splenetic visionary; or execrated as the malignant effusions of a heart that only wished what it pretended to foresee. But however divided the world may be about Dr. Price's motives, there is something which all must agree in, what *was* speculation, is now a *fact*.'[32]

Beside the threat of house searches, mob violence and official condemnation, Price also had to contend with official interference in his mail. As Benjamin Vaughan told Franklin in Paris, 'All letters *to* this country are opened, and I suppose they are also opened *from* this country.'[33] Price's anxiety over State meddling with his correspondence had been growing for some time. As early as January 1775 Charles Chauncy had informed him: 'Tis easie to conceive that the news conveyed to the ministry by the [ship] *Scarborough* should be secreted, but not so easie to be accounted for that the private letters which went by her should be profoundly silent also.'[34] Price wrote back in December: 'The times are growing more and more serious; but I will not touch upon political affairs, because it is not possible to know into what hands any letters may fall, or what use may be made of them.'[35] Some letters received by Price were unsigned for this reason[36] and even when their delivery was entrusted to a particular friend or acquaintance there was no guarantee such people had not been 'cajoled'. Sarah, Price's wife, had even taken to having his mail packages delivered to a neighbour's house in case their own were subject to a surprise search. Price told some correspondents to write to him care of his nephew, the actuary William Morgan, at the 'Assurance office near Black-Fryars-Bridge', the headquarters of the Equitable Society.[37]

Correspondence with Franklin, a leading light of the American Revolution, was particularly dangerous while he was in Paris negotiating a treaty that would mean France joining with America in the war against Britain. Such correspondence ultimately necessitated the use of code numbers. 'The information which 176 gave last week to 64 of the capture of Dr Irving's vessel on the Mosquito Coast and its consequences are not true', Edward Bancroft wrote to Silas Deane from London on 7 February 1777; number 176 being Richard Price and number 64 Franklin.[38] Bancroft's letter is doubly interesting since aside from highlighting the fact that Price did not stop writing to Franklin, despite the dangers, it also reveals that some of the information Price obtained was no more than propaganda; this was a problem he was certainly aware of and which he acknowledged in a number of letters to his American correspondents.

Price's concern over tampering with his correspondence can also be seen in his reaction to receiving, one year late, a letter written from the Netherlands by Baron Joan Derk van der Capellen tot den Poll. When replying to the baron in January 1779 Price's first thought was to reassure him that the letter 'appeared plainly when it was brought to me, never to have been opened'.[39] Such suspicion is understandable since there were good reasons why the British government would be interested in letters coming to one of its principal political radicals from the Netherlands, and from van der Capellen in particular.

Van der Capellen came to British notice in 1776 when as a leader of the Dutch Patriots he helped persuade the Netherlands' parliament – the States-General – to refuse George III's request to his relative, the Stadholder William V of Orange, to borrow the mercenary Scotch Brigade for deployment in America. Van der Capellen was a keen supporter of the development of militias as a way to reduce the Stadholder's power as head of the army in the Netherlands.

He outlined in considerable detail the troubled political situation in the Netherlands in his first letter to Price, who, in his reply, was saddened to find it so similar to that in his own country:

> How melancholy is it to see human beings, crouching, as they do, under the yoke of tyranny, and acting as if they thought themselves only a body of beasts made to be disposed of at the discretion of a set of men who call themselves their

governours, but who in reality are their own Delegates or servants . . . I am sorry to find that Holland is not in a much better state. There it seems, as well as here, a sovereign power dispensing places and employments governs all; and the people either have no idea of their rights or are careless about them.[40]

Like Price, van der Capellen wished to educate his nation in the ideals of democracy and freedom he saw revealed in the American Revolution. To this end he had taken the liberty of translating *Observations on the Nature of Civil Liberty* into Dutch. 'What an honour have you done me by translating my Pamphlets and making yourself in the manner you relate an advocate for me?' Price replied.[41] Later, van der Capellen discussed in his 1781 publication *Aan Let Volk van Nederland* (To The People of the Netherlands) the disadvantages of a hereditary ruler and the need for a democratic society based on popular sovereignty, a text which helped inspire the Dutch patriots' ill-fated Batavian Revolution of 1787.

Aside from van der Capellen's radicalism, the fact that the Price/Capellen correspondence took place in 1779 would also have made it of interest to the British authorities for, in that year, there was growing evidence of covert Dutch aid to the American cause, which contravened the spirit of an Anglo-Dutch treaty of 1678. A further contentious issue was the free use of Dutch ports by American privateers, who were creating significant problems for British maritime trade at the time. The Dutch did nothing to exclude the privateers and the situation continued to deteriorate until Britain finally declared war on the Netherlands in December 1780.[42]

Price's correspondence with van der Capellen was not, in 1779 at least, an exchange with a declared enemy. A far greater risk in this regard, but one Price took throughout the war, was the sending of letters to America and to Americans living in France. The risk lay in the possibility such letters might be intercepted or otherwise fall prey to the widespread and efficient spy network Britain now had in place. That this could happen was made clear to Price on Sunday, 26 November 1780, when handbills appeared in London announcing the publication, in the following day's *Morning Post and Daily Advertiser*, of a letter by him to the American Congress. This raised 'painful apprehensions' in the minds of his friends but Price, 'knowing that there could be nothing genuine of that kind' which could do him harm or discredit, felt 'perfectly easy'.[43] In fact the letter was not by Price but was an extract from a letter Franklin had sent from Paris to the Foreign Affairs Committee of the American Congress informing them that 'Dr. Price, whose assistance was requested by Congress, has declined the service.'[44]

Why did the British press publish the letter and how did they obtain an obviously confidential missive to an American congressional committee from its Paris-based representative? The most likely reason was to discredit, or at least pressure into silence, a prominent government critic and vocal political radical. As Price noted himself, 'There was much malice in distributing the handbills.'[45] Less easily answered is how the press got hold of Franklin's letter. It certainly must have involved a British spy in the American camp at Paris. The proliferation of agents and double agents for the various sides in the conflict certainly increased the very real political risks involved in transatlantic correspondence at this time.

Edward Bancroft, later revealed to have been a double agent, probably had the greatest opportunity to obtain such a letter. A physician from New England, Bancroft lived in London prior to the Revolution where he became a close friend of Franklin, who sponsored him for election to the Royal Society in 1773. A fluent French speaker, Bancroft left London for Paris in 1776 and quickly became unofficial secretary to the American commission at Passy. In this capacity he had access to much of the commissioner's correspondence and could easily have seen Franklin's letter to Congress concerning Price.

Following France's entry into the war in 1778 the Americans were attempting to recruit spies in Britain. In 1779, for example, Commissioner Arthur Lee's brother, William, wrote from Paris to John Wilkes asking him to provide any information he could on British operations in the war, including military planning, shipping news and the results of cabinet meetings, the reward being a payment of £200 a quarter.[46] Lee couched his request to Wilkes in a kind of inverted patriotism. 'Every true Englishman', he suggested, would wish 'success to the enemy, until our liberties are secured'.[47] With Price's continuing support of the American cause we might wonder whether a similar appeal came his way. Though circumstantial, there is some evidence to suggest it did. A letter from Price to Benjamin Franklin in Paris on 14 October 1779 opens thus:

> Dear Sir
> Will you be so good as to get the inclosed letter convey'd to Mr A[rthu]r Lee, if he is near you and it can be done easily? If not, be so good as to burn it. Being obliged for particular reasons to avoid politics, it is a short acknowledgment of the favour he did me by a letter I received from him at the beginning of last summer, and contains nothing of much importance.[48]

There are a number of curious elements to this passage. First, despite declaring the letter contained 'nothing of much importance', it was clearly important enough for Price to risk sending it to Lee via Franklin in Paris, in spite of his refusal nine months earlier of a request from van der Capellen for an introduction to Franklin: 'It is scarcely in my power', Price had then replied. 'While in England he was one of my most intimate friends, but from mutual regard, we have since avoided writing to one another'.[49] Second, the passage contains the only instance in Price's surviving correspondence of his asking a recipient to burn an enclosed letter if it cannot be 'easily' passed on to the addressee. Third, Price's explicit desire 'for particular reasons to avoid politics' suggests the query was of a political nature and, were it to be revealed, would cause him problems at home. Finally, Price is replying to a letter sent by Arthur Lee at 'the beginning of last summer'. This effectively dates Lee's letter to June 1779, the same month in which his brother William wrote trying to recruit John Wilkes as a paid spy. Assuming, therefore, that Price is replying, via Franklin, to an invitation from Arthur Lee to take up a similar position, is it likely Price accepted? Again a firm answer is not possible, but from the tone of Price's cover letter to Franklin and his desire 'for particular reasons to avoid politics', it seems likely he refused. In doing so Price may well have remembered the declaration in his fast-day sermon earlier that year that 'a virtuous man must be a firm and determined patriot. Power cannot awe him. Money cannot bribe him.'[50]

Such caution, though, did not stop him associating (albeit at second hand) with Americans who had been imprisoned in Britain 'on suspicion of treason'. In the summer of 1780 Henry Laurens of South Carolina had been making his way to Amsterdam to negotiate a 10 million dollar loan on behalf of Congress when the British captured his ship off Newfoundland. Also recovered was a sack of papers Laurens had thrown overboard whose contents included the draft of a secret treaty between America and the Netherlands. Laurens was brought to London and committed to the Tower of London on 6 October. The previous day Price had written to John Temple (currently in Britain en route to Holland, Temple was born in Boston in 1732 and had been dismissed from his post of Surveyor General of the Customs of the Northern District of America by Lord North in 1774[51]) noting that 'Mr Lawrens [sic] is in town and has been examined', and he asked Temple 'to inform me, should you hear anything particular of him, or any other intelligence that may be learnt from him?'[52] Laurens was eventually released on 31 December 1781.

John Trumbull left America in May 1780 having obtained permission to come to Britain to study painting under the tutelage of Benjamin West. He was arrested on 19 November on suspicion of treason and confined to the Tothill Fields prison in Westminster. Horace Walpole noted the arrest and its ramifications for Price in a journal entry of 20 November:

Mr Trumbull, the son of the American Governor of Connecticut, was taken up
as a spy. His letters were immediately published, because, in one to his father,
he said Mr. Temple was intimate with the Duke of Richmond, and Mr David
Hartley, and Dr Price, who thence were represented as traitors. In reality the
Ministry hoped to discover that American agents had been at the bottom of the
late riots.

By December, though, the publication of Trumbull's letters showed 'the
court could prove nothing on them'.[53] In such an atmosphere of mistrust
and deceit Price must have worried over his position, but this did not stop
him expressing distress at the imprisonment of Trumbull in a further letter
to John Temple that same December. 'I am extremely grieved for the hard
fate of Mr. Trumbull. Should you ever see him I request the favour of you
to deliver to him my kind remembrances, and to inform him that I am
obliged by the advice of my friends, to do violence to my feelings by not
visiting him.'[54] Trumbull would survive his ordeal and his father, Jonathan
Trumbull, the governor of Connecticut, would later thank Price for the
consideration he had shown to his son. John Trumbull went on to produce
a number of famous paintings depicting key events and players in the
American Revolution that today adorn the rotunda of the Capitol Building
in Washington.

Price also associated in London with Patience Wright who modelled and
displayed waxwork figures of famous personages in the city while all the
time acting as an American spy. In a letter to Franklin of 7 May 1777, for
example, she discussed American prisoners in Britain. Their fate was a cause
of concern to Price too. In December 1782 he would lay before Shelburne
the 'case of three Natives of America now in Norwich Gaol'. Finding himself
'moved with compassion for these three men', he could not 'help earnestly
requesting Lord Shelburne's attention to their cases'.[55] In Wright's letter
to Franklin she also notes that Dr Price sends his 'hearty love', as did
'Mr Cartwright' and 'Major Peter Labelliere'.[56] Cartwright was already a
friend and correspondent of Price and it seems likely Price knew Labelliere
too. This was yet another potentially dangerous contact for in spring 1775
Labelliere had been accused of paying £1,500 to a force of men to seize the
Tower and the king. He had also been known to enter his soldiers' barracks
and urge them *not* to fight against their American brethren. On his death
Labelliere was buried on Box Hill in a perpendicular but head-downward
position because, he reasoned, he was leaving a topsy-turvy world and when
it righted itself he would be on his feet again.[57]

Exactly how much real danger Price was in at this time is impossible to
say; but clearly there were reasons for the British authorities to be suspicious

and watchful of him. Even though Price does not appear to have suffered physical abuse, being the object of such suspicion and watchfulness must have weighed heavily on a man of his moral sensibilities, as well as on his family. It says much for his courage that this never stopped him expressing his support for the American cause, in whose success he remained convinced and whose ideals he consistently supported. However, Price's activities in relation to America were not the only cause of concern to a suspicious and watchful state. There was also his participation in the growing calls for reform and change at home.

11

Reform and Contribution at Home

I have been lately so much talked of as a Politician, that I do not wonder you should have taken me for nothing else. But the truth is, that the study of politics has been a late deviation into which I have been drawn by the circumstances of the times and the critical situation of our public affairs.[1]

Any government facing war with four belligerents (America, France, Spain and the Netherlands) wants stability at home; what Lord North's administration faced was widespread, though not universal, disenchantment with Government and politicians. This was the mood to which Price gave voice in his 1779 fast-day sermon:

Among the persons to whom it is natural for us to look for the defence of our country, are those in high life, and among our senators, who have taken up the cry of public liberty and virtue, and oppose the oppressions of power. They seem, indeed, a glorious band; and it is impossible not to admire their zeal. But alas! how often have we been duped by their professions? How often has their zeal proved to be nothing but a cover for ambition, and a struggle for places? How many instances have there been of their forgetting all their declarations, as soon as they have got into power? How often do you hear of their extravagance and immoralities?

. . .

How mortifying is it to find the nation's best friends falling so short as they do of our wishes? What measures for restoring a dying constitution? What reformation of abuses, what public points do they hold forth to us, and pledge themselves to accomplish? How little does it signify who are in, or who are out of power, if the constitution continues to bleed, and that system of corruption is not destroyed, which has been for some time destroying the kingdom.[2]

By the end of the year demands for reform of this situation were coming from many parts of the country. In Ireland the Volunteers, established in

1778 to stave off possible invasion by France, were now 'demanding a free trade, and menacing a rebellion, if it [was] not granted'. Price apprehended the danger of this demand to a Britain burdened with increasing taxation and debt and anxious about its ability to trade in a climate of widespread war. 'I do not see how it can be granted without the danger of a rebellion among ourselves', he told van der Capellen on 26 October 1779. 'Such is the shocking dilemma into which our government has brought itself.'[3]

With calls for parliamentary reform continuing in the country, Price, for his part, now became a founder member of the Society for Constitutional Information. Formed in April 1780, its aim was to enable the people 'Thoroughly to inform themselves what the Constitution is; what is its present DANGER, and by what means it may be placed in Safety'.[4] Other members included Thomas Rogers, Price's neighbour at Newington Green and the Revd John Horne Tooke. It was with Horne Tooke that Price now collaborated on a pamphlet highly critical of North and his administration.

Described by a contemporary – Horace Walpole – as a 'knave', and by a more recent writer as a 'gadfly on the body politic',[5] Price's partnership with Horne Tooke seems an unlikely one. But balanced against Tooke's Anglicanism, his hostility to Catholics, his lack of support for the Dissenter cause, his philandering (he fathered three illegitimate children) and his card-playing, were many Pricean virtues: he taught himself medicine in order to aid his parishioners, and he was, like Price, a staunch defender of civil liberties and a strong advocate of economic and political reform. A one-time friend and supporter of John Wilkes, he even spent time in the Tower of London on a charge of libel for having drawn up an advert to raise money toward aiding widows, orphans and aged parents of Americans killed by British troops at Lexington and Concord. On his release, and with the demise of the Constitutional Society, which he had founded in 1771, Tooke joined the Society for Constitutional Information.

In their anonymously published pamphlet *Facts: Addressed to Landholders, Stockholders, Merchants, Farmers, Manufacturers, Tradesmen, Proprietors of Every Description, and Generally to All the Subjects of Great Britain and Ireland*, Price and Tooke set the tone early on. 'What now is our struggle?' they asked, before providing the answer: 'That those who make the laws shall no longer be prostituted to infamous, and sordid gain: that the legislature itself may be rescued from temptations which flesh and blood cannot withstand.' Horne Tooke's contribution to the work concentrated on attacking the civil list and the monarch's empty promise to economize, while demonstrating that the Government's largely unchecked spending effectively meant it was freeing itself from parliamentary control. He also recounted a number of financial scandals for which he held the North administration responsible.

Price, who contributed chapters two and eight to the work, concentrated on criticizing the Government's mishandling of financial matters, especially the negotiation of loans on highly unfavourable terms. As a consequence of this, taxation would have to increase substantially in order to fund repayments. Price sounded a warning note; there were limits, he argued, 'beyond which taxation cannot be carried with effect'. To exceed such limits raised the danger of open revolt.

The critical stance of *Facts* was popular and it went through eight editions in 1780. It also contributed toward the reduced majority suffered by North's administration in the general election of September/October that year, but the failure of the Government to fall was a frustration to Price. 'I have no hope from the new Parliament', he wrote to Shelburne on 16 October, 'nor while the representation of the kingdom continues such a mockery as it is, and subject both in its appointments and deliberations, to such an undue influence, is it to be expected that we should ever have any Parliaments that will be more than instruments of the crown.'[6]

Although weakened by the election, North's government lingered on. When its end finally came it was triggered not by events at home but by the news from America that General Cornwallis had surrendered to the American rebels at Yorktown on 19 October 1781. In the face of such a disaster North's position became untenable and in late March 1782 a new administration took office under lord Rockingham, with Price's friend Shelburne appointed Secretary of State for Home and the Colonies.

One consequence of jointly authoring *Facts* with Horne Tooke had been a rift between Price and Shelburne, who opposed the pamphlet's publication. Price had been willing to acquiesce in Shelburne's request not to publish, but Horne Tooke had not. Price's friendship with Shelburne ultimately survived the affair but ever afterwards Shelburne maintained a virulent dislike of Horne Tooke.[7]

Whatever cooling there had been in the friendship between Price and Shelburne, it appears to have been over by late March 1782, when Shelburne took up his position in the new Rockingham government. Price, 'anxious to improve the present moment', wasted no time in offering his lordship some advice. The public, he declared were 'against the *American* and *Dutch* wars, the extravagance that has prevailed in the expenditure of public money, the enormous influence of the crown, and that system of corruption by which our late ministers have supported themselves'.[8] He then proposed a threefold plan for the new ministers. First, 'secure the *salvation* of the country by a *general* Peace'. To do this, he argued, 'it is necessary that the nation should be *let down* and some humiliating concessions made . . . in our present circumstances, with a load of debt so heavy, taxes so multiplied, and resources

so strained, it is impossible to continue the war much longer without producing either total ruin or a horrid convulsion by which the men then in
power will be the greatest sufferers'. Second, it was necessary to acknowledge
'the independence of America' and, third, to move forward with reform of
'the representation of the kingdom'. If the administration carried through
these points successfully he was sure the ministers would 'fix themselves in
the hearts of the friends of humanity and liberty and make themselves objects
of the admiration of future ages. Should they *attempt* it and *fail*, they will
enjoy a satisfaction greater than any the emoluments of power can give in
the approbation of their own minds and in the grateful esteem of all the
honest and worthy part of the nation.'[9]

Moves towards peace in America would be made in due course but, for
the moment, Shelburne, in company with the likes of the younger Pitt,
remained content to put forward in May 1782 a parliamentary motion calling
for an enquiry into parliamentary representation. These proposals were
defeated, as were the main elements of the economical reforms proposed
by Edmund Burke as Paymaster in the new government. Price knew this
would not satisfy the public. 'Let new men give us a *real* represen[tat]ion',
he told Shelburne. 'This is the reformation we want, and this is the time for
accomplishing it. If it is put off to a time of tranquillity, it will never be
done.'[10]

By a 'real representation' Price did not mean universal male suffrage. His
more immediate aim was to see the removal of gross abuses of the electoral
system, especially such anachronisms as rotten boroughs and placemen in
Parliament. These he saw as among 'the most important of all the points of
Reformation, there can be no abuse so flagrant as that a few beggars, subject
to the treasury, Admiralty, &c. should possess the power of chusing the
majority of that Assembly which makes our laws, and disposes our lives and
fortunes'.[11] Some historians have argued that the 'corrupting' influence on
Parliament of the pensioners, placemen and other appointees present there
was of less significance than Price and reformers like him suggested. But the
reformers' concerns were unlikely to be based solely on the number of
placemen in Parliament. Their personal experience of having to live in a
system of patronage that extended through all levels of society must have
played a part, and it was a system to which Price was no stranger. As a public
figure and a well-known friend of Shelburne, he often found himself called
upon to act as an intermediary between the earl and those seeking preferment
and patronage. This was particularly the case following Shelburne's return
to political office in 1782. Such machinations were inherent in the patronage
system and in many cases unavoidable, however much petitioners and
petitioned disliked it.

Always closely allied to patronage for positional advancement was the prospect of monetary reward, though there is no evidence that Price benefited personally from acting as an intermediary in such solicitations. Indeed, on the one occasion when the power of patronage did place an offer of financial opportunity in his path he declined it in no uncertain terms. Sir Edmund Thomas, when seeking the Glamorgan parliamentary seat, had once canvassed Price for his vote. As an inducement Sir Edmund offered to 'procure' for Price the right to dispense the *regium donum* to his fellow Dissenters. The *regium donum*, founded in 1722 and administered in great secrecy by nine Dissenting ministers (the *regium donum* men), was originally designed to support any indigent colleagues and, more generally, the widows of Dissenting clergy. It could also be seen as a way of reassuring Dissenters of State toleration and thus as a tool for securing their general passivity.[12] Price, who had long resolved to have nothing to do with such a bribe/pension, replied that 'the best service Sir Edmund could render him or his brethren would be, to advise the king's ministers to discontinue a donation which could only be regarded by every independent dissenter as the price of his liberty'.[13] Price, though, was not above canvassing votes himself in the cause of friendship and reform, though never with any accompanying financial inducement or promise of patronage. During the election of 1780 he wrote to David Hartley: 'I am afraid I am now going to take an improper liberty with you; but the strong desire I feel to recommend to your vote and interest a friend whom I highly value urges me to it. The person I mean is Mr. Jones, who is offering himself a candidate to represent the University of Oxford at [the] next general election.'[14]

As the new Rockingham administration took office in March 1782 Price welcomed the prospect of reform at home and of peace with America and her co-belligerents. 'A great Revolution has at last taken place in this country', he informed Benjamin Franklin on 20 May. 'The opposers of the late measures have now the direction of our affairs. God grant they may succeed in extricating this country and . . . this war be soon terminated by an equitable and general peace.'[15] In the event it was not the war that was 'soon terminated' but Rockingham, who died on 1 July after three months in office, a casualty of a flu epidemic sweeping Europe that year. Shelburne now became Prime Minister and on 18 July Price seized the opportunity to point out to the earl the gravity of the situation he faced:

Some of my friends, who are likewise your Lordship's friends, tremble for the edge on which your Lordship now stands. They are afraid of the consequences of continuing the war. The country cannot bear much more. The last loan lies very heavy, and they apprehend that the difficulties and dangers attending another and a larger loan will be dreadful.[16]

In the pamphlet *Facts* Price had estimated the cost of the American war up to Christmas 1779 at £47,437,500 and he worried over the impact this figure must have on an already inflated national debt, when combined with the continued yearly loans. Shelburne shared these worries, and from October 1779 his surviving papers contain numerous submissions from Price on the servicing of such loans and their relation to the national debt. As Home and Colonial Secretary under Rockingham, and now as Prime Minister, Shelburne also received financial advice from other quarters and he often submitted this advice to Price for his opinion. At the same time he passed on Price's proposals to his other sources. As a result Price often met or corresponded with the likes of Francis Baring, founder of the finance house Baring Brothers and Co., and James Martin of the Martin banking family.

The same year, 1779, also saw Price return to the question of demography in 'An Essay on the Population of England and Wales since the Revolution [of 1688]', which he contributed to his nephew William Morgan's publication *The Doctrine of annuities and assurances on lives and survivorships stated, and explained.* In his essay, which was also published separately a year later, Price reached the conclusion (as he had for his earlier account of London) that the population of England and Wales was falling dramatically. More specifically, he suggested – in the face of reliable contemporary evidence to the contrary – that England's population of over six and a half million in 1690 had fallen to less than five million by 1777.

As a tireless advocate of the need for a regular census and the keeping of population statistics on a national basis, Price was aware of the general unreliability of much of his data. Indeed, prior to the first national census of 1801, which returned a population of 8,872,980, it could be truly said that nobody possessed accurate population data. But even allowing for all this we must ask why, in the face of the sound statistical evidence presented by writers such as William Wales, John Howlett, Arthur Young and William Eden, Price continued to maintain his opinion of a fall in population through-out the remainder of his life.

The answer must lie in his deep-held belief that 'The state in which mankind increase most, is that in which they lead simple lives, are most on an equality, and least acquainted with artificial wants. Luxury in society renders it a rank soil, which favours the growth of noxious plants and weeds.' Britain, a nation plagued by continental wars, a swollen army and navy, migration to the colonies, the high cost of provisions, engrossing of small farms by larger ones (which drove workers off the land and into cities) and, 'above all', the vices associated with luxury, public taxes and debt, profoundly lacked the simplicity and equality in life necessary for population increase.

By contrast, there was the situation he saw developing in America. From 1776 onward Price's published works and correspondence contain numerous examples of his vision of America as a form of Eden, a bountiful land with a growing population living under a government soon to be independent, mindful of civil liberties and supportive of religious and political freedom. This vision was confirmed for Price by the American demographics he gleaned from *The Interest of Great Britain Considered with Regard to her Colonies* by Benjamin Franklin and *A Discourse on Christian Union* by the New-England clergyman, Ezra Stiles. Both these authors had concluded that America's population was increasing, and growing faster in backwoods areas than in settled ones. This confirmed Price in his view of the superiority of simple country living over that of the city, and of the superiority of the American position to that of Britain. As D. O. Thomas has succinctly put it, 'In America a rapid increase in population was both caused by and proof of the possession of the virtues; in Britain a decline in population was caused by and proof of an increase in vice.'[17]

Although Price made valiant attempts to answer his critics on the subject of population decline, particularly in the third and fourth editions of his *Observations on Reversionary Payments*, it would be unfair to conclude that their criticism had no effect on him at all. 'I beg it may be remembered', he wrote in the fourth edition, 'that my opinion in this instance is by no means a clear and decided conviction.' Though he still believed there had been such a fall, in England at least, 'yet I wish to be considered as far from being decided in it, and therefore as open to receive any evidence which can be produced to overthrow it'. This evidence, he hoped, would come from the census he had so long advocated:[18]

> Some time or other, perhaps, the Legislature will think this a point worth its attention. Much light may be thrown upon it, and the state of our population kept constantly in view, by only ordering exact registers to be kept of the births, burials and marriages in the kingdom. It had lately been done in France; and the result has been a discovery that the population of FRANCE exceeds all that had been conjectured concerning it. Should a like discovery be the consequence of carrying such an order into execution here, it will give the kingdom an encouragement which at present it greatly wants; and I shall rejoice in my own confutation.[19]

Since to the end of his life Price continued to argue that there had been a fall in population we must conclude that not enough new evidence presented itself to satisfy him. Yet, such doubts as he felt over the issue certainly led to his recognition of what he later called his 'parental partiality' to a particular opinion and reluctance to oppose a settled opinion once reached. By linking his statistical analysis of population so closely to his political and puritan Dissenter vision of a just society Price's population studies represent one of the very rare instances when dogma overruled the reason and candour that were his life's more usual guiding lights.[20]

As well as contributing his population essay to William Morgan's book on annuities, Price also wrote an introduction for it in which he gave advice to an old acquaintance – the Society for Equitable Assurances. This, in turn, led to him making another important and lasting contribution to the Society, and to life assurance generally.

As actuary of the Equitable since 1775, William Morgan had carried into effect many of his uncle's earlier recommendations to the Society. As a result it had prospered and by 1780/1 plans were afoot to reduce the premiums payable by members and for a partial distribution among them of surplus profits. 'Different opinions have been entertained of this measure', Price notes in his introduction to Morgan's work, 'but the truth is, that (however safe and just the prosperous state of the Society then rendered it) it is in itself a measure of the most pernicious tendency . . . A repetition . . . might hurt the Society essentially, by withdrawing from it that security which it has been providing for many years, and bringing it back to infancy and weakness'. Furthermore, he argued, the Society should 'prevent the intrusion of bad lives' by appointing a medical assistant so as to prevent it becoming 'not a resource for the living and healthy, but a refuge for the sick and dying'. The Society should also be aware of 'the danger of employing unskilled calculators' who were less likely to undertake the 'long and laborious computations, which none but able mathematicians can make'. Finally, he recommended that the Society be 'Furnished with a set of [mortality] tables . . . more correct and elegant than it now uses . . . tables founded on observations . . . not among the bulk of the people in London, where life is particularly short but among mankind in general'. Heeding Price's advice, the Directors of the Society for Equitable Assurances selected tables calculated by him for the parish of All Saints in Northampton for the period 1735 to 1770 as the ones most fitted to their business needs.[21]

Achieving this involved Price in checking the selected tables against a local census made in the parish in 1746 before computing new tables to cover the period 1770 to 1780. From these tables, which now covered the period 1735 to 1780, William Morgan and his assistant, Thomas Cooper, produced a final set consisting of 'more than 20,000 computations'. This Herculean task was finished in November 1781 and although criticisms can be made of Price's part in it, such as his overestimation of the rate of mortality between 1735 and 1780, the tables became the Society's standard, for all purposes, for over fifty years. For his part in the production of what became known as the Northampton Tables, the General Court of the Equitable wished Price 'to accept some present from the Society as a lasting testimony of their respect'. This proved more difficult to achieve than they expected as no one could discover what present, if any, Price would willingly accept. In the end they prevailed upon him 'to accept one hundred guineas, or whatever sum the Society shall be pleased to appoint'.[22]

Despite his reluctance to accept any gift Price must have been pleased with the approbation of his work it represented and, as the summer of 1782 approached, he must have hoped too that, with his friend Shelburne now Prime Minister, the social, economic and political reforms at home and the peace with an independent America abroad he had so long desired might finally become a reality.

12

Peace with America

Permit me to congratulate you on the late Peace, and on the Revolution in favour of liberty which has taken place by the establishment of the independence of America. I cannot express to you the satisfaction this has given me. I have wished to live to see this issue of the contest with America; and I am thankful that I have seen it.[1]

On 22 March 1782, a few days after Shelburne took office as Secretary for Home and the Colonies in the short-lived Rockingham administration, a young British colonel, Lord Cholmondeley, took tea with Benjamin Franklin at Passy. Before departing, the colonel asked if there was any message Franklin wished to send to their mutual friend Shelburne. Franklin wrote a short note saying he wanted all to be made right between Britain and America. Shelburne received this note on 5 April and immediately dispatched an emissary to Passy in the person of Richard Oswald, a seventy-six-year-old Scot of liberal sentiment and placid character who got on well with Franklin from the start. This friendship, however, did not stop the two men from engaging in a game of diplomatic chess, with each weighing up the other's position. Oswald was keen to determine whether France would continue to fight against Britain if a peace was negotiated between Britain and America; Franklin was anxious to know what concessions Britain might eventually be willing to make to America.[2]

This impasse in the opening round of peace negotiations was broken in early July when the news of Rockingham's death and Shelburne's appointment as Prime Minister reached Franklin. Immediately he saw the opportunity this elevation of his old friend to the highest political office presented and, on 10 July, he passed Oswald a list of American terms for peace. These included the non-negotiable conditions of complete American independence, the evacuation of all British troops from America, the right of Americans to fish off Newfoundland and Nova Scotia and the ceding to America of all the lands east of the present colonies, up to the Great Lakes and the Mississippi.

By the end of July Shelburne had approved these terms as a basis for further negotiations but two problems then emerged with respect to Shelburne's own position regarding America. First was his desire to see her remain in the British empire on terms similar to those recently granted to the Irish – a relaxation in many trade restrictions and a grant of *almost* complete legislative independence. Second was Shelburne's reluctance to acknowledge American independence before negotiations on other points began. Neither of these positions was acceptable to the Americans. Franklin had already warned Oswald that America would never accept a position within the empire similar to that of Ireland. America also considered it impossible for Britain to grant them independence since their independence was a de facto position.[3]

Price watched the progress of these negotiations closely and despite having refused to become Shelburne's private secretary at around this time, he remained remarkably well informed on their progress. He also appears to have been among those who disagreed with Shelburne's suggestion that America adopt a position similar to Ireland's. Henry Laurens, for example, noted in a letter to Price on 31 August 1782 that 'It appeared clear to me that the new great Minister [Shelburne] had flattered himself with hopes of winning the United States, by proposing to them terms equal to those which had been extorted by Ireland, for I am intirely of your opinion Sir, in this article.' Laurens was also of the opinion 'that no solid or serious steps toward peace [had] yet been made', though convinced that 'all the contending parties earnestly wish to put an end to the War'.[4]

By the end of summer 1782 Franklin, who had played a prominent role in the peace negotiations from the very start, was incapacitated with severe gout and kidney stones; an illness which, it was thought at the time, might be his last. As a result the task of brokering peace that summer and early autumn fell to Commissioner John Jay, who had recently returned to Paris from Spain. Progress was made with a set of preliminary articles of peace agreed on 14 October. Although ill and frail, it was Franklin who wrote that day to Congress informing them that the articles had been sent to London for consideration but stressing that he did not hold out much hope of their being accepted. His prediction proved correct and negotiations resumed once more but now with a rejuvenated Franklin taking a larger part in the proceedings. John Adams, the third American peace commissioner newly returned from Amsterdam, where he had obtained a loan in support of the American cause, now joined Franklin and Jay in Paris.[5]

November 1782 saw the main phase of the peace negotiations and it quickly became apparent that the remaining points of contention were Shelburne's continuing desire to see British recognition of American independence as a treaty term, American access to fishing rights off Newfoundland

and Nova Scotia and the question of compensation to loyalists for their lost American property. By 18 November Price had heard that the first of these problems appeared to have been resolved. As he wrote to Franklin that day, 'One of the chief obstacles to Peace, is I hope, now removed by the acknowledgment of the independence of America.' His satisfaction at this outcome is evident:

> After many doubts and fears during the course of this war, I now see with un-speakable satisfaction this object secured, new constitutions of Government favourable to liberty civil and religious established in America, and a refuge there provided for the friends of truth and humanity. This is the consummation of the present contest which has been all along the object of my anxious wishes; and, I hope, I may now rejoyce with you on having lived to it.

The removal of this obstacle provided a cause for celebration but it also vindicated the position Price had adopted long before on the question of American independence:

> Could my wishes have had any influence, our new ministers upon the first change would have immediately acknowledged the independence of America, and on this ground open'd a negotiation for a *general* peace and made such concessions as would most probably have brought it about before this time. I have always deliver'd my sentiments freely to Lord Shelburne on these subjects. We have differ'd much in our opinions about them, but our friendship has continued.[6]

As early as March 1778 Price had tried to convince Shelburne 'immediately to recognise the independence of America', only to discover that the earl held to a different position:

> To this I know your Lordship is averse; and I am always grieved when I cannot adopt your sentiments. But situated, as this kingdom now is, I cannot in the present case, entertain any doubts. France has acknowledged the independence of America. Every power in Europe is ready to do it. All *real* authority is gone; and it cannot be expected that by any *nominal* authority we can bind them to anything that interferes with their interest. In these circumstances, all hesitation about yielding independence to them seem[s] unreasonable.[7]

By the third week of November 1782 Price, though more optimistic about a final settlement, still remained cautious: 'it is not yet certain how the present negotiations will terminate. God forbid that thro' the pride of this country there should be a continuation of the war'.[8]

In late November, with the extent and nature of reparations to the loyalists and the question of fishing rights off Newfoundland still to be dealt with, Price seems to have been asked to make a small contribution to the negotiations. 'Yesterday', he informed Shelburne, 'an account was sent me from the Continent, that in the negotiations for peace it is required by our court that *Congress* should make compensation to the Loyalists for their losses, and that this claim is likely to retard the peace, and even to be the means of breaking off the negotiation. I should think it very improper in me to take notice of this to your Lordship had I not been particularly desired to do it.' Price had some sympathy with the loyalists – 'these unhappy men' – but he did not believe their plight should stand in the way of a peace settlement. That would be 'sacrificing the Kingdom, on their account' and it was certain 'America may as easily be brought to unconditional submission, as to consent to take such enemies into its bosom and make compensation to them for their losses'. In raising this issue Price displayed a clear understanding of the developing political structure within the new America and the growing debate there over state and federal power. 'The states to which they [the loyalists] belong must determine concerning them', he continued to Shelburne. 'The jurisdiction of Congress does not extend to them. The acknowledgment of the independence of America is an acknowledgment that no injustice has been done them. They reckon'd upon sharing in confiscated estates, and they must not complain that the issues of war have disappointed them.' He then adds, in a postscript, 'I find I cannot send off this letter without adding to what I have said about the negotiations that I know that America is particularly jealous, and suspicious of the British Court at present and that this affords the strongest reason for being as fair and liberal as possible in negotiating with them in order to gain their confidence and to draw them off from France.'[9]

Within six days of Price's letter to Shelburne the outstanding issues in the negotiations had been resolved. American rights to fish off Newfoundland and Nova Scotia were granted, to the delight of Commissioner John Adams: 'Thanks be to God . . . our Tom Cod are safe in spite of the malice of enemies, the finesse of allies, and the mistakes of Congress',[10] and the question of loyalist reparations was agreed to be a state rather than a congressional matter. Congress would restrict itself to 'earnestly' recommending that each state return confiscated estates to their loyalist owners; something that predictably fell by the wayside after the peace had been signed. For their part the British recompensed many loyalists and helped those who wished to do so to move to Canada and Nova Scotia. With the resolution of these last problems the signing of preliminary peace terms took place on a snowy 30 November 1782 at a hotel in Paris.[11]

Excluded from the deal were the other belligerents in the dispute – Holland, Spain and France. The Americans – Franklin and Adams in particular – had left the French out of their negotiations with the British in flagrant disregard of both the terms of the Franco-American treaty of cooperation and the wishes of the American Congress. They did so after discovering the French intention to make concessions to the British, which would enable the British to adopt a tougher attitude to the Americans. Consequently, Vergennes, the French Foreign Minister would have no knowledge of the peace terms until the day before they were signed. Fortunately, this supporter and ally of the Americans at the French court took little umbrage once Franklin had admitted to the impropriety. Nor did he blanch when Franklin then took the opportunity to ask for a further loan from France; she provided the sum of 6 million livres. Vergennes's magnanimity of course belied the fact that he too had been negotiating with Britain behind the back of his American allies, such was the level of mistrust that so often existed between all parties to this affair. Nevertheless, on 20 January 1783 Vergennes summoned Franklin and Adams to his office in Versailles to watch as France and Spain signed their own peace preliminaries with Britain so establishing a welcome general peace.[12]

On the day France and Spain signed their peace terms Richard Price wrote to Shelburne:

> I cannot conclude without once more congratulating you on the Peace. My heart is now in a great measure at ease; and my resolution is to trouble myself as little for the future about Politics as possible. I reckon it enough that I have lived to see two great events which I have long been wishing for; I mean, the salvation of my country by a Peace, and a revolution in favour of the liberty of the world by the settlement with America.[13]

Such hopes proved premature on two counts. Price would find himself unable to withdraw from politics in the way that he wished and Shelburne, as Prime Minister, still faced the task of getting the peace treaties ratified by a parliament increasingly hostile to their terms, despite the fact that those terms generally favoured Britain.

In joining with the American rebels both France and Spain had entertained hopes, following a British defeat, of regaining much of the territory they had lost after the Seven Years War ended in 1763. But little was actually achieved in this regard under the terms of the peace treaties signed in January 1783. Although Britain ceded Florida and Minorca to Spain she retained control of strategically important Gibraltar, despite Spanish demands; and although France gained Senegal and Tobago, Britain's possessions in the

West Indies, India and Canada were almost untouched. Furthermore, despite Britain having suffered the undeniable trauma of losing her thirteen American colonies, this was ameliorated to a degree by the fact that their largely Anglophile population had been lost to independence rather than to another European power. The discoveries of James Cook in the South Seas in the 1770s had opened up new imperial possibilities, with Botany Bay in New South Wales providing a replacement for the penal colonies lost in America. In the event French support for America had in fact sown the seeds of the financial bankruptcy predicted by Turgot in 1776, and ultimately of her own revolution of 1789. The Dutch too, by their participation, had prepared the ground for their Batavian Revolution of 1784–7.

In such circumstances Shelburne might have been justified in expecting the treaties to pass relatively easily through Parliament but, instead, they proved a rallying point to those who distrusted and disliked him personally. Price had observed this dislike growing before the treaty with America had been signed, as he told Franklin in November 1782:

> I am sorry to observe so much distrust prevailing with respect to him, and I hope he will prove it to be groundless by restoring to this country the blessings of peace and using the power he now possesses to establish oeconomy in our finances and to produce such a reformation in our Parliament as shall make it a *real* representation instead of such a mockery and nu[i]sance as it is at present.[14]

Such was the rapid growth in this antipathy toward Shelburne that by February 1783 Price was intimating to the banker Francis Baring that 'the Friend who has saved this country *by a peace* and from whose noble views and those of his friends alone I expect a second salvation of it by a redemption of the public debts if that is yet possible, may not be the minister of this country another year'.[15] This prediction proved correct, though Price's time frame was too generous. Plagued by resignations over the treaty and by internal divisions in his government Shelburne attempted to keep a grip on power by entering into a coalition, first with Charles James Fox and then with Lord North but was unsuccessful in his approaches to both men. Instead, though sworn political enemies, Fox and North formed a coalition in opposition to Shelburne. In the light of this development Price offered Shelburne what consolation he could in a letter of 15 February. 'The present factious and shameful opposition will, I hope, be soon conquer'd. Hard it is to be opposed for saving a Kingdom. But such has been the fate of some of the best statesmen.'[16] In the face of a Fox/North coalition Shelburne had no hope of retaining power and he resigned as Prime Minister on 24 February 1783.

That same day Price called at Lansdowne House twice in the hope of talking with the earl but having met with no success wrote expressing his outrage at the course events had taken. 'The strange coalition of Lord North's party with the Rockingham party in order to condemn a Peace which has saved the kingdom, is one of the most scandalous events that ever happen'd.' Price saw in Shelburne's departure from office not only the possible demise of the peace settlement but also of his own hopes for economical and political reform. 'I have not sent your Lordship the remarks on the plan for the loan,' he continued, 'because I suppose it will not answer any end to think more of this subject. All my hopes of plans of redemption, Parliamentary reformation &c. will vanish with your Lordship.'[17] Price's anger is still evident in a letter of 10 March to Benjamin Franklin:

> Mr Fox, the pretended friend of the country, united to Lord North, the destroyer of the country – the Rockingham Party, a body of men who would be thought zealous whigs, united to Tories and the friends of despotism to oppose and censure a peace which has saved the kingdom – I hope foreigners see this in its true light; as, merely, a struggle of ambitious and disappointed men to get into power. May the united states take care to guard against the danger and misery of such factions.[18]

During the five-week political interregnum that followed Shelburne's resignation the king attempted to appoint anyone other than a member of the Fox/North coalition as Prime Minister. But when the handful of choices available to him, including the younger Pitt, had turned him down, George, who briefly considered abdication at this point, was left with no option but to ask the coalition to take office. This they did on 1 April 1783 with the duke of Portland as nominal premier, Charles James Fox as Foreign Secretary and Lord North as Home Secretary. In the aftermath of this, the peace terms passed through Parliament with few major changes and were signed in France on the morning of Wednesday, 3 September 1783. The Treaty of Paris between Britain and America was sealed at the Hotel de York, in the rue Jacob, and the Treaty of Versailles, establishing the general peace, at the office of the French Foreign Minister Vergennes.

Aside from seeing his long-held dream of American independence realized, the establishment of peace also meant for Price a welcome return to something approaching normality in his correspondence. Very quickly the content of his letters to and from America moved away from discussion of war and politics and returned to the familiar ground of matters scientific, philosophic and social. To Benjamin Rush, in Philadelphia, Price was soon forwarding a plan for observing meteors drawn up by Nevil Maskelyne, the Astronomer Royal, who had also requested Price to obtain from his American friends 'a list of all the Universities, Colleges and Philosophical Societies in the united states'.[19] There was also William Herschel's recent discovery of the new planet Georgium Sidus, later known as Uranus, to relate to Joseph Willard, corresponding secretary of the American Academy of Arts and Sciences. In the wake of the peace settlement he also discovered that the Corporation of Yale University had awarded him the degree of LLD on 24 April 1781 in sole company with George Washington, and that on 30 January 1782 he had been elected a Fellow of the American Academy of Arts and Sciences at Boston.

Perhaps the most welcome renewal of open and easy correspondence for Price was that with Benjamin Franklin, who had, at the start of the peace negotiations, supposed that 'we may now correspond with more Freedom, and I shall be glad to hear from you as often, as may be convenient to you'.[20] It was fitting too, and entirely in the character of their relationship, that after seven years of war Franklin's only intimation in his letter to Price of 16 September 1783 that a final peace had come a fortnight before was the simple statement: 'We have at length sign'd our Preliminary Articles as definitive.' The remainder of the letter he gave over to science and to introducing his friend into the new and fascinating world of 'Balloons fill'd with light inflammable Air, and the means of managing them so to give Men the Advantage of Flying'.[21] The Montgolfier brothers had flown in such a balloon in June 1783 and on 25 August Franklin had witnessed the ascent by chemist Jacques-Alexandre Charles from the Champ-de-Mars. Enclosed in Franklin's letter was a model balloon made of 'Gold-beaters Leaf . . . which being fill'd with inflammable Air . . . went up last Night, to the Ceiling in my Chamber, and Remained rolling about there for some time'.[22] It would be pleasant to think of Price trying out the model before passing it on to Joseph Banks, as Franklin requested. Price certainly appreciated the importance of ballooning. 'The discovery of air Balloons seems to make the present time a new Epoch', he told Franklin in April 1784, 'and the last year will, I suppose, be always distinguish'd as the year in which mankind begun to fly in France'.[23]

Despite the obvious enjoyment gained from his renewed correspondence with American friends, Price was enough of a realist to know that normal relations between Britain and America would not return for some time. As he remarked to Benjamin Rush, who sought his help in establishing a new college (Dickinson College) in Pennsylvania, 'I wish I could inform you that it is practicable to set on foot with success a subscription in this country for the purpose of assisting in establishing and endowing it. But I am afraid this cannot be done. It is too early a period of the peace for it. Friendship is not yet sufficiently restored between the two countries.'[24]

13

Advising Ireland, Scotland and America

My power is little; but such as it is, I am always glad to employ it as far as it can go in promoting the best interests of mankind.[1]

With the advent of an independent America the word 'revolution' truly entered the eighteenth-century mind as a potential consequence of government failings in the face of public grievance. One area of George III's kingdom where this seemed especially applicable was Ireland where, by October 1779, some were 'demanding a free trade and menacing a rebellion if it [were] not granted'.[2] Their demand arose out of the draconian restrictions imposed on Irish trade under the terms of Britain's navigation acts, which forbade Irish ships from carrying British or Irish exports to the remainder of the empire. There were also tight controls on the importation of some Irish goods into Britain. The result was significant hardship and poverty on the island.

Instrumental in demanding reform from outside parliament were the Irish Volunteers, an informal militia formed in 1778 and utilized in Ireland by the British government because of a shortage of regular troops resulting from deployments in America. Under pressure from the Volunteers, and worried that a troubled Ireland might be the back door for a French invasion of Britain, Lord North's government had already removed many of the Irish trade restrictions before his government fell in March 1782. Buoyed up by this success, the Volunteers next began to call for the legislative independence of the Irish parliament. Price noted this turn of events in a letter to Shelburne as the earl, who was born and initially educated in Dublin and owned extensive estates in County Kerry and Queen's County, took up his post as Secretary for Home and the Colonies in the new Rockingham government. The people of Ireland, Price declared, were acting under the conviction that the new government would be reform-minded and that 'new ministers, instead of opposing them, ought to assist them, and to grant them all they want to render their constitution of government as well as their trade perfectly free'.[3] How influential this letter proved to be is impossible to say but between May and July a Catholic Relief Act was passed and the Irish parliament gained almost complete legislative independence. In July 1783, however, the Volunteers demanded electoral reform, and formed an action committee under the chairmanship of a Lieutenant Colonel Sharman. He wrote to a number of prominent reformers in Britain asking for their advice. Price was among the recipients and his reply, along with those of the reformers Christopher Wyvill, John Jebb, the earl of Effingham and John Cartwright, was published in *A Collection of Letters which have been Addressed to the Volunteers of Ireland on the Subject of a Parliamentary Reform*. This appeared in Belfast on 4 October and in London on 27 October 1783.

Price, in his reply to Sharman, did not disguise his pleasure at the events taking place in Ireland:

> It is indeed with a satisfaction not to be expressed, I find the people of Ireland, after rescuing their trade and their legislature from the oppression of a sister kingdom, are now undertaking to rescue themselves from an *internal* oppression, no less inconsistent with liberty. The occasion is great, and the undertaking important and arduous in the highest degree. Should they be blest with success, they will have completed their own happiness, and exhibited an example which will for ever shine in the annals of mankind.[4]

By the time the Volunteers began demanding electoral reform there had been two further changes of government in Britain. The short-lived Rockingham administration, which took over from Lord North, had fallen in July 1782 and Shelburne had formed a new administration. As we have seen, by February 1783 Shelburne had been forced to resign in the face of a coalition headed by North and Fox. Price believed this 'odious Coalition' would be generally 'hostile to Reformation; and this will make it more difficult for the people of Ireland to succeed in their views; but *nothing can be difficult to a people determined to recover their rights* – IF UNANIMOUS AND FIRM'.[5]

The first priority, Price argued, must be to achieve a more equitable political representation. 'Is Ireland possessed of such a representation? Or is not, on the contrary, a vast majority of its House of Commons chosen, not by the people, (but as in England) by a few Grandees and Beggars?'[6] To remedy this situation many reformers who offered their advice to Sharman demanded an immediate and universal franchise but Price advocated a more pragmatic and gradualist approach. Even though 'The principles of civil liberty require, that every independent agent in a state (that is, every one who can be supposed to have a will and judgement of his own) should have a vote in the choice of his Governors . . . it has been seldom practicable to extend the right of voting so far.' Even in America, 'where new forms of government are established more liberal than any in the world', voting was still restricted to those who paid taxes or owned property. It was therefore necessary that, in order 'to avoid the danger of losing all by aiming at too much, the attempts of enlightened men should be governed by a regard to what is most practicable, considering present circumstances, and the attachment which always prevails in a country to old establishments'.[7] Also crucial was the question of votes for the disenfranchised Catholic majority in Ireland. Price favoured their being given the right to vote on the same qualifying terms as Protestants:

> I am so much an enemy to persecution that I cannot help wishing the right of voting, could be extended to Papists who possess property in common with Protestants. It is unjust to deprive any man of his Rights on account of his religion, unless self-defence makes it absolutely necessary.
>
> The danger from Papists is perhaps more produced by the Penal Laws against them, than by their religion. These detach them from the rest of the community, give them a separate interest, and make them enemies. Why should not a Papist be attached to the liberties of his country as well as a Protestant, if he is allowed to share in them? In truth, a country which allows him no rights, he cannot reckon his country. It is nothing to him whether it is enslaved or free; nor can he care what becomes of it.[8]

Once again he advocates gradual change. 'Ireland is peculiarly situated in two respects', he wrote in a postscript to Sharman. 'A great majority of the inhabitants are Papists; and a distribution of property, more unequal than in England or America, subjects them more to aristocratic tyranny. I have hinted, as a remedy for the former inconvenience, the admission of Papists to equal rights; but there may be stronger objections to this than I am aware of.'[9]

A further question, though 'of less consequence' than the reform of parliamentary representation, was the duration of parliaments. If people did not choose the make up of their parliament through the ballot then the duration of that parliament was of little consequence to them. But when people exercised their right to choose, short sessions were inevitable: 'for it is impossible that a People should not see that the long possession of power will corrupt, and that their security against the abuse of power depends on keeping their Representatives in a constant state of dependence and responsibility'.[10] Price favoured annual parliaments since they kept the representative body more subject to the control of its constituents and the representatives themselves would be chosen with less 'tumult and riot'.

Finally, Price believed that the Irish were setting an important example for the rest of Britain. 'By establishing an equal representation, may not the people of Ireland do their sister kingdom a most important service, by provoking its emulation, and rendering it ashamed of its own corrupt and mock representation?'[11]

Yet, as Price suspected, political reform proved to be as difficult to achieve in Ireland as it was in Britain. By Christmas 1783 he told Shelburne: 'The associated Volunteers in Ireland . . . are much exasperated against the Parliament there for rejecting their plan of reform. They are procuring an application by petition (or rather requisition) from all the Counties, Cities and towns; and should this likewise fail there will be great danger of a convulsion.'[12]

Reformist ideas were also developing in Scotland and in January 1784 Price wrote to Thomas McGrugar who, as secretary of the Committee of Citizens of Edinburgh, had forwarded to Price an account of their proceedings. Price felt himself honoured to be considered 'among the friends to the important cause in which they were engaged', namely, reform of the administration of the local burghs and of parliamentary representation. 'From the accounts you have sent me, I learn, that in *Scotland*, the state of the representation is worse than in *England*; and that the body of the people, particularly in the *Royal Burghs*, do not enjoy the *shadow* of *Liberty*.' As he had with the Irish reformers, so he offered his support to those in Scotland: 'May their zeal increase, and may the number of those men diminish who are for keeping mankind in abjection and servility.'[13]

Price was also preoccupied with American affairs. On 6 October 1783, as he had penned his letter of advice to Sharman and the Irish Volunteers so he wrote to the American Henry Marchant: 'America has made a noble stand against tyranny, and exhibited a bright example to the world.' Not only had she helped liberate one European country, Ireland, by her example but more would likely soon follow. 'God grant that the united states may wisely improve the liberty they have earned', he added, but they must 'take care to avoid the danger they are now in of fighting with one another and sinking into anarchy. This is the greatest danger that now threatens them; and should they not be able to guard against it, an event which might have proved a blessing to them and to the world may prove a curse. One of the fairest experiments in human affairs will fail, and the friends of liberty will be discouraged. You may, therefore, imagine that I have heard with distress of the dissensions among them, their prejudices against one another, and the reluctance of some of them in giving energy to the decisions of the delegation which forms their union, and in providing funds for maintaining their credit and redeeming their debts.'[14]

Price derived this gloomy outlook from his American correspondents and from the British press, which Benjamin Franklin believed 'monstrously magnified' American problems.[15] Franklin was undoubtedly right, but this could not disguise the fact that constitutional and practical problems did exist in America. The constitutional problems principally derived from the Articles of Confederation that had regulated relations between the various states since 1777. With independence from Britain it quickly became apparent that this loose constitutional arrangement was not up to the task of mediating between federal rights and those pertaining to the states. In addition, the way foreign powers viewed America had become an increasingly important issue. When considering trade issues, for example, were European countries dealing with a single entity called the United States or with a plethora of autonomous, independently trading states?

Price's thoughts on America's constitutional questions had a long gestation. As early as 1777 he records his disappointment that Pennsylvania had inserted a religious test into its newly written state constitution.[16] This required all members of the states' House of Representatives to acknowledge 'the divine inspiration of the Old and New Testament' before taking up their seat; an unpleasant reminder to Price of Britain's Test and Corporation Acts. He worried that if individual American states began imposing similar restrictions, such ills might be transposed into any federal constitution the Americans eventually developed. In the spring of 1778 Price had received a long letter from the ex-finance minister of France, Anne-Robert-Jacques Turgot, discussing this American situation while raising the question increasingly occupying Price. 'Can this new people,' Turgot asked, 'so advantageously placed for giving an example to the world of a constitution under which man may enjoy his rights, freely exercise all his faculties, and be governed only by nature, reason and justice – Can they form such a Constitution? Can they establish it upon a neverfailing foundation, and guard against every source of division and corruption which may gradually undermine and destroy it?'[17]

By 1779 Price began to consider 'taking the liberty to communicate' to the Americans 'a few additional observations' on their constitutional problems because, as he put it to Arthur Lee, 'The interests of mankind depends so much on the forms of government established in America that I have long thought it the duty of every man to contribute all he can towards improving them.'[18] Turgot had encouraged him to do this: 'All enlightened men – All the friends of humanity ought at this time to unite their lights to those of the *American* sages, and to assist them in the great work of legislation. This, sir, would be a work worthy of you. I wish it was in my power to animate your zeal in this instance.'[19] Price needed little encouragement: 'I am by no means qualified for such a work', he wrote, 'nor can I expect that any advice I can give will carry much weight with it, or be much worth their acceptance. I cannot however satisfy my own mind without offering it, such as it [is].'[20]

Price hoped to add his observations to those in Turgot's letter but in 1779 this proved impossible because Turgot insisted his letter remain private. Nor did he want Price to send him a detailed reply for he feared that the French authorities would open it and he would be 'found much too great a friend to liberty for a minister, even though a discarded minister'.[21] Turgot had been comptroller-general of the French finances until dismissed in May 1776. Perhaps with his own experience of State watchfulness in mind, Price abided by Turgot's request.

By 1783 some of Price's ideas on American constitutional issues began to appear in his correspondence. On New Year's Day, for example, he wrote to Benjamin Rush, a signatory of the Declaration of Independence, concerning 'a point of the last importance; I mean the federal union. The credit, the strength and even the existence of the united states seem to me to depend on the proper settlement of this point. It is obvious, that the greatest wisdom is required to find out such a plan as shall give due energy to the decisions of the delegation that forms the union without encroaching to much on the liberty and independence of the confederated states.'[22] Six months later, on June 26, he wrote to Rush again, this time concerning the need for 'a total separation of religion from state policy' in America while 'allowing an open field for improvement by a free discussion of all speculative points, and an *equal* protection, not only of all *christians*, but of all honest men of all opinions and religions'.[23] On 6 April 1784 Price told Franklin: 'I have been lately employing myself in writing *sentiments of caution and advice* which I mean to convey to them as a last offering of my good-will.'[24]

Price's 'sentiments of caution and advice' to America were contained in *Observations on the Importance of the American Revolution and the Means of Making It a Benefit to the World*, published in London in 1784. Of the Revolution's importance Price was in no doubt. The war of independence, he observed, 'did great good by disseminating just sentiments of the right of mankind and the nature of legitimate government, by exciting a spirit of resistance to tyranny'. Furthermore, as 'a sequestrated continent possessed of many singular advantages', America provided 'a place of refuge for opprest men in every region of the world' and it was in her that the foundations were being laid 'of an empire which may be the seat of liberty, science and virtue'. These 'sacred blessings' would, he hoped, 'spread till they become universal and the time arrives when kings and priests shall have no more power to oppress, and that ignominious slavery which has hitherto debased the world exterminated. I therefore think I see the hand of Providence at

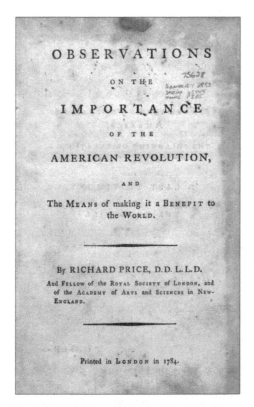

Figure 17. Title page of *Observations on the Importance of the
American Revolution and the Means of Making It a
Benefit to the World* (London, 1784).

work in the late war working for the general good.'[25] He even suggested
that 'next to the introduction of Christianity among mankind, the American
revolution may prove the most important step in the progressive course of
improvement'.[26]

The workings of providence – the kindly care and superintendence of
the world by God – formed one of the foundations of Price's religious
belief, and Price saw the American Revolution (as he would the later French
one) as part of a growing body of evidence for progress in human affairs;
progress that encompassed developments not only in political and social
reform but also in science, rational analysis and even morality. In common
with many Enlightenment thinkers, Price saw this progress as foreshadowing
the thousand years of peace prophesied in the Bible to precede the second
coming of Christ and the Last Judgement. Or, as he put it in his pamphlet:

Reason, as well as tradition and revelation, lead us to expect that a more improved and happy state of human affairs will take place before the consummation of all things. The world has hitherto been gradually improving. Light and knowledge have been gaining ground, and human life at present, compared with what it once was, is much the same that a youth approaching to manhood is compared with an infant.[27]

In Price's own time, and later, many criticized this millennialism as dangerously utopian, and Price was aware that some of his readers had interpreted his new pamphlet in this way. 'One of my correspondents in America who has been all along zealously attached to the American cause assures me that nothing can be more utopian than the expectations I have formed', he noted to Benjamin Rush in July 1785.[28] Such concerns would reach a peak in Price's case in the aftermath of his euphoric welcoming of the French Revolution in 1789. But for all his enthusiasm, Price never posits an earthly utopia as a real outcome. Though he believed in continual human improvement, the peaks and troughs of success and failure would always mark and mar human progress. 'Every present advance prepares the way for further advances . . . A dark age may follow an enlightened age but, in this case, the light, after being smothered for a time, will break out again with a brighter lustre.'[29]

Having, in the first part of the pamphlet, praised the importance of the American Revolution, Price used the second to outline his thoughts on *The Means of Promoting Human Improvement and Happiness in the United States*. Restricting himself to an opinion on 'a few great points', the first requirement he noted was for America to address the redemption of her debts and to make adequate compensation to the army that had carried her through the war. To achieve this, he recommended the establishment of a sinking fund. Surplus government funds would be placed in an inviolable account where they would gain the benefit of compound interest; this could then be used to redeem the debt over time. Price's concern with America's debt stemmed from his interest in that of Britain and, as he wrote his pamphlet on America, he was heavily involved in British attempts to deal with her own burgeoning national debt through the establishment of a similar sinking fund.

A further issue requiring America's attention was peace and the 'perpetuating of it'. To achieve this, a strong federal structure giving real power to Congress was crucial. He noted with concern that when disputes currently arose between the states they could 'order an appeal to Congress, an enquiry by Congress, a hearing, and a decision. But here they stop. What is most of all necessary is omitted. No provision is made for enforcing the decisions of Congress, and this renders them inefficient and futile . . . Without all doubt the powers of Congress must be enlarged. In particular, a power must be given it to collect, on certain emergencies, the force of the confederacy and to employ it in carrying its decision into execution.'[30] He was emphatic that this increase in congressional power should not take the form of standing armies, which were 'every where the grand supports of arbitrary power and the chief causes of the depression of mankind'. Instead, America should maintain an armed and trained militia. 'Free states ought to be bodies of armed citizens, well regulated and well disciplined, and always ready to turn out, when properly called upon, to execute the laws, to quell riots, and to keep the peace'.[31] He also advocated the taking of a regular census since this would enable any inequalities between the various states to be quickly seen and necessary help provided. It would also make a more equitable distribution of resources easier and so further reduce the likelihood of violence between the states.

Next, America must turn her attention to the question of liberty. Since the individual states had 'the distinguished honour of being the first states under heaven in which forms of government have been established favourable to universal liberty', this must include 'liberty of conduct in all civil matters, liberty of discussion in all speculative matters, and liberty of conscience in all religious matters'. Liberty of discussion also included the right to examine 'all public measures and the conduct of all public men, and of writing and publishing on all speculative points and doctrinal points'.[32] Liberty of conscience in religious matters was important because nothing was 'more disgraceful' to religion than it should show 'a disposition to call in the aid of civil power' in its defence. 'If it wants such aid it cannot be of God.'[33] For Price genuine religion is 'a concern that lies entirely between God and our own souls'.[34] Established religions impeded 'the improvement of the world' and were no more than 'boundaries prescribed by human folly to human investigation, and inclosures which intercept the light and confine the exertions of reason'.[35]

On education, the next issue of concern, Price opposed the prejudices which had 'prevailed against new lights', such as the discoveries of Newton and Galileo, and he disliked an education system whose 'principal object . . . (especially in divinity) is to teach established systems as certain truths, and to qualify for successfully defending them against opponents and thus to arm the mind against conviction and render it impenetrable to farther light':[36]

> The end of education is to direct the powers of the mind in unfolding themselves and to assist them in gaining their just bent and force. And, in order to this, its business should be to teach how to think, rather than what to think, or to lead into the best way of searching for truth, rather than to instruct in truth itself. [37]

Having stressed the importance of America's revolution and outlined the means of promoting its 'progress and improvement', Price turned, in the third and final part of his pamphlet, to alerting Americans to the dangers they and their revolution faced. These included not only the danger from increased public debts and the risk of internal war, to which he had already alluded, but also from banks and paper credit; from oaths, a multiplicity of which would 'render them too familiar' and result in 'a slight manner in administering them'; an unequal distribution of property and, finally, the danger from 'the Negro trade and slavery'.

Price's identification of unequal property distribution and slavery as potential dangers caused the most controversy in America and for that reason it is worth examining his views on them more closely.

In Price's opinion, man is happiest in 'the middle state between the savage and the refined, or between the wild and the luxurious'.[38] This state, he believed from his correspondence and reading, existed in some parts of America, such as Connecticut, where it revealed itself in the form of 'an independent and hardy yeomanry, all nearly on a level, trained to arms, instructed in their rights, clothed in homespun, of simple manners, strangers to luxury, drawing plenty from the ground'.[39] In such a society, where plenty existed for all rather than the few there was no unequal distribution of property and 'the rich and the poor, the haughty grandee and the creeping sycophant' were unknown. The danger, however, was that such a society would not last: 'simplicity and virtue will give way to depravity . . . equality will in time be lost' and 'the cursed lust of domineering shew itself'. Under such circumstances, liberty would languish and civil government degenerate into a tool of 'the few to oppress and plunder the many'.[40] Price did not feel wise enough to say how the Americans could avoid this happening, but there were three 'enemies to equality' against which he was sure they should be on their guard, namely: hereditary honours, primogeniture and foreign trade. The choice reveals the contemporary nature of Price's opinions on American affairs, since all three topics were the subject of current debate there. As we shall see, they were also of concern to America's representatives in Paris – Benjamin Franklin, John Adams and Thomas Jefferson, the latter having arrived in the city on 6 August 1784.

Price regarded 'with particular satisfaction' the declaration in the 1777 Articles of Confederation between the states that no titles of nobility would ever be granted by the United States. Americans, he said, should 'continue for ever what it is now their glory to be – a confederation of states, prosperous and happy, without lords, without bishops and without kings'.[41] His warning was timely, for many in America believed this situation to be under threat from the pressure being exerted to establish episcopacy in the country and from the establishment, in May 1783, of the Society of the Cincinnati.

Price had opposed an American episcopacy since the start of the revolution but it became a reality in 1787 when the archbishop of Canterbury first consecrated bishops for America. In contrast to the position of bishops in the mother country, however, these American bishops would never become part of an established church.

The Society of the Cincinnati was founded with a membership restricted to those American and French officers who had fought in the revolutionary war and it aimed to preserve the values of the revolution and to give succour in times of need to its members' families. The Society's rules, however, allowed for membership to be passed down to the eldest son, raising fears that its members might become a form of hereditary nobility and so undermine America's revolutionary values. Price's correspondence reflected this concern. William Hazlitt, senior, an old friend who went to live in America in 1783, before returning to England in 1786, wrote telling Price that Benjamin Rush, a man of impeccable revolutionary credentials and a long time Price correspondent, had become 'the tool of a party . . . who are labouring to destroy the present constitution of Pennsylvania, and to introduce in its room one which is in a great measure aristocratical and, in my opinion, very inimical to liberty'.[42] Later, it was even suggested that Washington, in his capacity as head of the Society of the Cincinnati, might attempt to establish a 'Dictatorship' or be tempted to assume a crown. In Paris, Franklin, Adams and Jefferson all opposed the new society, Franklin even going so far as to compose an eleven-page essay denouncing it.[43]

Primogeniture, Price's second enemy to equality, relates closely to hereditary honours since by passing land to the eldest son nobility maintained its grip on power and society; thus ensuring the continuation of many gross inequalities. In his essay on the Cincinnati Franklin criticized primogeniture as 'another pest to industry and improvement of the country' and in 1776 Jefferson introduced a bill in Virginia abolishing the 'entail', which controlled descent of property through the generations. In 1785 he also ensured that any form of feudal land tenure through primogeniture was abolished.[44]

Price's attitude to foreign trade, his third enemy to equality, is more complex, occasionally contradictory and unlike his views on hereditary honours and primogeniture, not always in accord with American aims and policies. Price advised America not to rely on foreign trade because in such a vast continent Americans could simply create 'a world within themselves'. A world in which it was possible to produce 'not only every necessary, but every convenience of life . . . Why should they look much further?' With a minimal risk of overseas invasion, 'What occasion have they for being anxious about pushing foreign trade, or even about raising a great naval force' to protect it?[45] Some Americans undoubtedly shared these views but Congress did not for it saw foreign trade as a means of restoring health to the nation's war-shattered economy. This was why Franklin, Adams and Jefferson were in Paris pursuing commercial trade treaties with Britain and other European powers. Price's adoption of a seemingly isolationist trade stance also appears self-contradictory for, in a letter written just two weeks after he signed the dedication of his pamphlet of advice to America, he informed the American Congregationalist minister Samuel Mather that 'There seems to be no probability of any settlement between us and America with respect to commerce. *I am strongly for having it as free and open as it was before the war*, but the prejudices in this country against a relaxation of the Navigation Act will not suffer this'[46] (emphasis added).

Price, in fact, did not oppose foreign trade per se. Indeed, he believed it had, 'in some respects, the most useful tendency'. It fostered good will between nations, produced 'mutual dependence' and it encouraged every man to consider himself a citizen of the world, so checking 'the excesses of that love of our country which has been applauded as one of the noblest, but which, really, is one of the most destructive principles of human nature'. What truly worried Price was not the actual trade but the effect it might have on America's revolutionary ideals. He feared it would create in America 'an increasing passion for foreign frippery' and that Americans would lose 'that simplicity of character, that manliness of spirit, that disdain of tinsel in which true dignity consists'. Instead, 'Effeminacy, servility, and venality will enter, liberty and virtue be swallowed up in the gulph of corruption.'[47]

The weakness of the American federal constitution compounded this worry. When dealing with old world states, for which trade was an instrument of power politics, a strong and unified front was imperative. All nations, he warned, were spreading snares for the Americans by 'courting them to a dangerous intercourse'.[48] Britain was doing this to America, as she had with Ireland, via the terms of her navigation acts that only allowed British ships, or those of her colonial traders, to conduct trade with British colonies. In addition, foreign goods destined for colonies such as the West Indies, a natural trading area for the Americans, had first to be imported into Britain where they were subject to import duties before being re-exported to the colony concerned. The act therefore gave considerable advantage to British trade and that of her colonies. This advantage America now lost by her independence, finding herself unable to trade directly with Britain or any British colonial possession. Furthermore, the protection given to British and colonial shipping by the Royal Navy had been withdrawn from American ships, which lay exposed to piracy. The latter was the reason Jefferson became convinced by 1785 that, contrary to Price's opinion, America needed her own blue-water navy to protect her international trade. Jefferson, though, understood Price's main point. That for a virtuous, yet still weak, 'New World' to enter into trade with a powerful and corrupt Old World would only gain America 'infection' and 'infinite mischief'. Before journeying to Paris, Jefferson had proposed in April 1784 to 'vest congress with so much power over [individual states'] commerce as will enable them to retaliate on any nation who may wish to grasp it on unequal terms'.[49]

At the end of his pamphlet Price turned to one last danger facing the Americans – the Negro trade and slavery. Until he wrote *Observations on the Importance of the American Revolution*, the word 'slavery' only appears in Price's writing in the context of citizens/subjects 'enslaved' by laws made without their participation, or by their living under an unrepresentative government, absolute monarchy or tyranny. But there is little doubt that the question of African-American slavery had been a topic of concern to him for a long time. He would certainly have been aware of the work of the British abolitionist Granville Sharp, a man with whom he became well acquainted. In 1783, he reviewed the plans of the entomologist Henry Smeatham to establish a colony of freed slaves in Sierra Leone. For Price, 'One of the blessings attending [the plan] would be the destruction of the slave trade.'[50] The subject may also have inspired debate at the Club of Honest Whigs, in earlier days, through Benjamin Franklin relating the story of King, one of the two household slaves he had brought with him to London on his second visit to the city between 1757 and 1762. Once in Britain, King had run away, only to be found sometime later at the home of a lady who had taught him to read, write and play the violin and French horn.[51]

As concern grew in Britain over Negro slavery, Price formulated to America a powerful, though still qualified, statement of opposition to the practice and the trade it fostered: ·

> The Negro trade cannot be censured in language too severe. It is a traffic which, as it has been hitherto carried on, is shocking to humanity, cruel, wicked and diabolical. I am happy to find that the united states are entering into measures for discountenancing it and for abolishing the odious slavery which it has introduced. Till they have done this, it will not appear they deserve the liberty for which they have been contending. For it is self-evident that if there are any men whom they have a right to hold in slavery, there may be others who have had a right to hold them in slavery. I am sensible, however, that this is a work which they cannot accomplish at once. The emancipation of the negroes must, I suppose, be left in some measure to be the effect of time and of manners. But nothing can excuse the united states if it is not done with as much speed, and at the same time with as much effect, as their particular circumstances and situation will allow.

I rejoice that on this occasion I can recommend to them the example of my own country. In Britain, a negro becomes a freeman the moment he sets his foot on British ground.[52]

Price's *Observations on the Importance of the American Revolution* appeared in London in 1784. He intended that all copies of this first London printing should be sent to America, as he informed Shelburne:

I have sent your Lordship the pamphlet which I mentioned to you. It will need your candour. You will probably think that I have carried my notions of liberty too far. What I have said, particularly on church establishments would give offence were the pamphlet to be publish'd here, but I have no thoughts of doing this. It is intended only for the American states . . .[53]

In fact, the danger of the work being pirated obliged him to publish it in Britain too, and a version appeared in 1785.

Many of the Americans to whom he sent copies appreciated its importance. George Washington read 'with the highest gratification . . . the doctor's excellent observations' and he felt it was 'Most devoutly . . . to be wished that reasoning so sound should take deep root in the minds of the revolutionists.'[54] Price had been particularly anxious that members of Congress should read the work, so he was no doubt pleased to hear from Richard Henry Lee, via John Adams in Paris, that its members had received their copies 'very thankfully and with the respect due to so able a defender of the liberties of Mankind, and the rights of human nature'.[55] In New Hampshire the pamphlet received approbation from the state's president, Meshech Weare. 'Give me leave to recommend to your Perusal, Doctor Price's Observations on the importance of the American Revolution', he informed the state's General Court in February 1785, 'tho' perhaps you may not fully agree with him in all his Sentiments, there are certainly many things in them, which deserve serious attention'.[56] Multiple copies also went to Benjamin Rush and to Henry Laurens, who distributed his six copies among members of the South Carolina legislature.

In Paris, Franklin considered the work 'excellent in itself' and something that would do Americans 'a great deal of good' and he passed a copy on to John Adams, who was soon to leave Paris to take up a position as America's first representative in Britain. In thanking Price for the work, Adams also expressed a desire 'to communicate' with him on various subjects and this led to a long-term friendship and correspondence between the two men.

The third American commissioner in Paris, Thomas Jefferson, wrote on 1 February 1785 to reassure Price that some of his concerns regarding

American federalism were actually being met. 'The want of power in the federal head was early perceived and foreseen to be the flaw in our constitution which might endanger its destruction', Jefferson noted. Concerning Price's warnings on foreign trade, Jefferson observed that 'Since the peace some nations of Europe, counting on the weakness of Congress and the little probability of a union in measure among the States, were proposing to grasp at unequal advantages in our commerce. The people are become sensible of this, and you may be assured that this evil will be immediately redressed, and redressed radically.'[57] Finally, he thanked Price for a work he had 'read . . . with very great pleasure, as have done others to whom I have communicated it. The spirit that it breathes is as affectionate as the observations themselves are wise and just. I have no doubt it will be reprinted in America and produce much good there.'

In sending his pamphlet to America, Price hoped that 'the warm part' he had taken in favour of the American cause would 'procure [him] a candid hearing'. The wide circulation the pamphlet enjoyed certainly made this likely. Following its appearance in Boston in 1784 it had, by 1785, been reprinted at Bennington, Hartford, New Haven, Philadelphia (twice), Trenton and, in 1786, at Charleston. It was also widely advertised, with the *Exchange Advertiser* of Boston declaring on 27 January 1785 that Price's *Observations on the Importance of the American Revolution* 'ought not to be passed over with a slight perusal – they ought to be written before every man's eyes, in *letters of gold*. They ought to be imprinted on the mind of every American, and be immediately carried into practice by all the legislatures of the United States. It would perhaps be saying too much to assert that every idea is practicable; but certain it is that most of his remarks are *sacred*, and to us, *interesting truths*.'[58] John Wheelock noted 'how great the applause is which its author receives throughout these states' and Price's old friend William Hazlitt, senior felt certain that 'no man living' could influence Americans so much as Price. He urged him to continue to 'meliorate and enlighten' them 'and to arouse them to improve and perfect their several forms of government'.[59] A candid hearing, though, usually implies a degree of censure as well as praise: this centred mainly on his warning to America of the dangers of slavery, and an unequal distribution of property.

Some of the criticism came from Henry Laurens, who, as a successful South Carolina planter and slave owner, might be expected to have taken issue with the entirety of Price's view of slavery, but this was not the case. Laurens told Price he had 'perused' the 'observations on the Negro trade and slavery' and found 'all well' until he came to Price's recommendation of the situation in Britain regarding slavery. 'If I did not know Dr Price to be a Man of Candour and Sincerity, I should suppose this intended as a bitter Sarcasm', Laurens declared. 'Britain is the fountain from whence We have been supplied with Slaves upwards of a century. Britain has passed Acts of Parliament for encouraging and establishing the Slave Trade, even for monopolizing it in her own Provinces.' Nor did Laurens think 'it quite a decided fact that the moment a negro sets his foot on British Ground, he becomes a free Man'.[60]

To Laurens's criticism of Britain's part in the slave trade no defence can be offered; as to whether a Negro became free once on British soil, both Laurens and Price were essentially right, thanks to the confused interpretations made of a 1772 judgement concerning a runaway slave named James Somerset. Having absconded while in Britain from his Virginian owner, Somerset had been caught and imprisoned on a ship soon to depart for Jamaica. Granville Sharp, the anti-slavery campaigner, brought the case to court and lord Mansfield had declared in his judgement that 'no master was ever allowed [in Britain] to take a slave by force to be sold abroad because he deserted from his service for any reason whatever'. This upholds Laurens's position since there is nothing here that actually implies the slave was free in Britain, only that he could not be forcibly returned to slavery once here, even if he had run away. However, when the legal codifier William Blackstone interpreted Mansfield's ruling he suggested that a Negro in Britain rendered his service to his master free of charge, in just the same way as an apprentice. This implied that the Negro was as free as the apprentice and could therefore leave his master's employ if he chose. It is presumably from this reading that Price drew his conclusion of a slave being free the moment he set foot in Britain. Whatever the truth of the matter, the official debate on slave 'ownership' clearly had more to do with property rights than any humanitarian concerns over slavery.[61]

Further criticism of Price's work came from members of the South Carolina legislature, to whom Laurens had distributed copies of the *Observations*. Price detailed their criticisms in a letter to Thomas Jefferson on 2 July 1785:

> Mr *Grimkey* the Speaker of the [South Carolina] House of Representatives and Mr *Izard* have agree'd in reprobating my pamphlet on the American Revolution because it recommends measures for preventing too great an inequality of property and for gradually abolishing the Negro trade and slavery; these being measures which . . . will never find encouragement in that state: and it appears that Mr *Grimkey* thought himself almost affronted by having the pamphlet presented to him . . .[62]

This worried Price because he felt that 'Should such a disposition prevail in the other united states, I shall have reason to fear that I have made myself ridiculous by speaking of the American Revolution in the manner I have done.'[63] Jefferson reassured him that though many in America still supported slavery, this stance should not be thought of as universal. It was certainly true that south of the Chesapeake 'few readers' would concur with Price's 'sentiments on the subject' but 'from the mouth to the head of the Chesapeak, the bulk of the people will approve it in theory, and it will find a respectable minority ready to adopt it in practice, a minority which for weight and worth of character preponderates against the greater number, who have not the courage to divest their families of a property which however keeps their consciences inquiet'.[64]

Henry Laurens illustrates Jefferson's characterization of the majority view in the continuation of his letter to Price. Of 'those Negroes who are called mine', Laurens noted, 'I shall speak very generally; they are as happy and as contented as labouring people can be, and some of them to whom I proffered absolute freedom wisely rejected it'. He then added a comment which encapsulates the view of many Americans on the subject at this time, including Jefferson and Washington: 'On my part, I am endeavouring to prevent their ever being absolutely Slaves, time is required for maturing my plan. You perceive Sir a whole country is opposed to me, it is necessary to proceed with discretion, to some of them I already allow Wages, to the whole every reasonable indulgence.'[65]

The modern reader will be quick to add '– except their freedom' to Laurens's last sentence, but doing so obscures the complex attitudes to slavery in men such as Laurens, Jefferson and Washington, all of whom, to their last days, remained slave owners while preaching equality. Even Price, who had no economic interest in slavery, by accepting that abolition in America was 'a work which they cannot accomplish at once' and that 'emancipation of the Negroes must, I suppose, be left in some measure to be the effect of time and manners', positioned himself, to a degree, with Jefferson, Laurens and Washington. This is why Laurens could so readily agree with the broad tone of Price's abolition statement. Such qualification is, of course, typical of Price's usually gradualist approach to reform, witnessed in his attitude to the extension of the franchise and the granting of votes to Irish Catholics. In the concluding paragraph of his pamphlet of advice to America, Price expressed a wish that he possessed 'a warning voice of more power'. The wish is of some poignancy when it is recalled that it took another eighty years and a bloody civil war before his hopes were to be answered on the subject of slavery.

14

Pitt and the Sinking Fund

It is of particular importance that the plan should be the most efficient that can be contrived; and it must require a good deal of deliberation to find out such a plan.[1]

Just over a year before writing *Observations on the Importance of the American Revolution,* in which he proposed the establishment of a sinking fund in order to deal with America's wartime debt, Price offered up a similar solution for Britain's own debt problems in a pamphlet entitled *The State of the Public Debts and Finances at Signing the Preliminary Articles of Peace in January 1783.* The establishment of this fund in Britain became a major preoccupation for him between 1782 and 1786.

As Chancellor of the Exchequer in 1716 Sir Robert Walpole had been the first to develop the idea of a fund designed to 'sink' or reduce the national debt. It was established in 1717, but Government raids on the fund for purposes other than debt redemption led to the scheme's abandonment. Price revived the notion, and by the early 1780s pinned his hopes for establishing a new sinking fund on the rise of his friend lord Shelburne to political power. Price had long advised Shelburne on financial matters and much of this advice had also been passed on to William Pitt. Now, as Chancellor, Pitt clearly thought the advice valuable, as a letter from Price to Shelburne in 1782 indicates: 'I feel a high respect for Mr. Pitt. He does me great honour by supposing me capable of being of any use to him. I shall be happy should I ever find this to be the case.'[2]

In November 1782 Shelburne sought Price's advice regarding the wording of a section on the sinking fund in the king's speech at the December opening of the new parliamentary session. Price suggested 'it should be intimated that the public debts ought not to be considered as irredeemable, there being still, notwithstanding their late great increase, reason to hope that such regulations may be establish'd and such savings made and future loans so conducted as to furnish the means of putting them into such a fixed course of redemption as will gradually bring them within the limits of safety'.[3] The finished speech was full of Pricean echoes, recommending that Parliament show 'immediate attention to the great objects of the public receipts and expenditure: and above all, to the state of the public debt. Notwithstanding the great increase of it during the war, it is to be hoped, that such regulations may still be established – such savings made – and future loans so conducted, as to promote the means of its gradual redemption, by a fixed course of payments.'[4]

By January 1783 Price believed that 'in consequence of the King's Speech and the late measures' the 'diffidence' with regard to the establishment of a sinking fund had finally begun 'to subside'.[5] As a result, he told Shelburne, 'Should the establishment of a general plan of redemption be resolved on, I shall be glad to be allowed to give my Ideas of the best method of proceeding in order to produce as quick and effectual a redemption as possible'.[6] Shelburne's resignation as Prime Minister at the end of February dashed these hopes; undaunted, Price put his concerns before the public in *The State of the Public Debts and Finances at Signing the Preliminary Articles of Peace in January 1783*.

The Fox/North coalition that replaced Shelburne's government made little or no progress on the sinking fund and Price's hope of action did not revive until December 1783 when the coalition government collapsed. William Pitt then travelled to the Palace to emerge as Prime Minister and Chancellor of the Exchequer. Having achieved a working majority in the general election that followed in March 1784 Pitt was secure in his position in office, but Price worried that as both Prime Minister *and* Chancellor, Pitt had taken on too much. 'There is much very important business to be done; and I do not know how to believe that Mr Pitt will be able to get thro' it without the aid of more experienced persons', he told Shelburne. Despite Price's worries Pitt's dual role was not unprecedented. Lord North had held both positions, as had Robert Walpole before him. In fact, taking on such a dual responsibility could be seen as emblematic of a strong Prime Minister, with Pitt signalling his desire to be seen in that mould. Nevertheless, Price remained concerned: 'I think I see a tendency in the tide of popularity to turn against him. He will be thought too ambitious, if he continues to hold both the posts he now enjoys. True wisdom would engage him to keep himself a little back.' Nor was Price clear as to Pitt's intent regarding the national debt and the sinking fund. 'Your Lordship must be much better informed than I am about Mr Pitt's intentions with respect to our finances. Indeed I know nothing of them. I have communicated my Ideas to the public and I leave them to be regarded or neglected just as events may turn out.'[7]

Figure 18. 'The Right Honourable William Pitt', drawn by L. Jackson
and engraved by H. Meyer, 1810, after a painting by I. Hoppner.

Price hoped that when Chancellor Pitt presented his first budget, he would
outline a plan to deal with the debt, and that this might include 'one or
two new taxes laid under the denomination of *Redemption* taxes to be in-
violably apply'd' to the sinking fund.[8] He also hoped such taxes would be
capital taxes rather than many 'little, vexatious and teasing taxes', which
were enough 'to make the kingdom mad'.[9] Pitt, however, although a keen
supporter of the sinking fund idea, was 'drinking the dregs' of the Fox/
North administration and the budgetary consequences of the American war.
The required million-pound surplus necessary for establishing a sinking fund

was simply not available. Furthermore, the budget of 30 June 1784 did end up imposing on a multiplicity of everyday and luxury items (ranging from ribbons and bricks to hackney carriages and gold) a range of the 'little' taxes Price so disliked.

Obliged now to wait for at least a year to see if these tax initiatives resulted in increased revenue, Price's interest in financial matters turned for a while to the situation developing in France, whose own debt had mushroomed as a result of her support of the American Revolution. This interest was fostered by his contacts with a number of Frenchmen interested in finance and by the pamphlets he sometimes received from Franklin in Paris; among them was a copy of the king of France's *Edict for Establishing a Sinking Fund*, published in August 1784. Franklin observed, in a letter of 13 September, that no one was better qualified than Price 'to make a sound Judgment of it', and asked him to 'drop me a few lines of your Opinion'.[10] Price replied in October that he admired the work's 'language and spirit and wisdom' but only 'a faithful execution of the plan establish'd by it can be necessary to extricate *France* from the embarrassments of its debts. This plan', he went on, 'is the same with that which I have been long writing about and recommending in this country to no purpose.'[11]

Price's frustration at Pitt's continuing inactivity regarding the debt issue finally boiled over in a letter to Shelburne that same month:

> The *French* are indeed getting the start of us fast, while we are wasting our time, as your Lordship says, with faction. Our funds are in a state of depression which I could scarcely have thought possible in a time of peace. No measures have been yet adopted for preserving us from the calamities with which they threaten us. I hear of nothing that Mr Pitt is doing for this purpose.[12]

Yet, some movement must have taken place since Price had noted in his earlier letter to Franklin that he had 'promised to draw up a table, during the next session of parliament', similar to 'the first in the French Edict, and marking as that does, distinctly for every year the progress of a Sinking fund in order to shew its powers, and I have some reason to expect that there will be a struggle in our parliament to get such a fund establish'd, and consigned to the care of Commissioners in order to render diversions of it less practicable'.[13] The resulting table was submitted to Pitt sometime before the end of April 1785. On 11 April Pitt announced in Parliament that he hoped during the coming year to obtain the one-million-pound revenue surplus to be used for debt redemption. This was not quick enough for Price who told Shelburne on 6 May: 'Mr Pitt in my opinion judges very wrong in delaying as he does the establishment of a plan of redemption.'[14]

By 29 November matters had at last begun to move forward more quickly. Pitt was 'much encouraged by the productiveness of the Revenue, and determined to establish a sinking Fund this winter'.[15] Pitt confirmed this in a letter to Price on 8 January 1786: 'The situation of the revenue certainly makes this the time to establish an effectual Sinking Fund.' He even enclosed an initial plan. 'Before I form any decisive opinion', he wrote, 'I wish to learn your sentiments upon it; and shall think myself obliged to you for any improvement you can suggest, if you think the principle a right one; or for any other proposal which from your knowledge of the subject you may think preferable.'[16] There followed a rapid and detailed correspondence between the two men with Price criticizing at length the proposals Pitt had sent him. On 15 January 1786, having found the criticisms 'on the whole very convincing', Pitt proposed a meeting at Downing Street as 'some points may occur which may be better explained in conversation than by writing, and I am anxious to avail myself to the utmost of your assistance, where it may be so material'.[17] After the meeting Pitt asked Price to submit his own plans for a sinking fund.

Working quickly, for the king had announced in Parliament on 24 January that a plan for the redemption of the debt would be introduced, Price sent Pitt 'Three Plans for Shewing the Progress and Effect during 40 Years of a Fund Consisting of a Million per ann. as is Therein Expressed and Apply'd to the Redemption of the Public Debts'. Each plan required the Government to place £1,000,000 per annum of surplus revenue into a fund. To this million, and depending on the plan adopted, further funds would be added from taxation, the buying of stock or the retirement of annuities. The resulting gains on the capital through the working of compound interest would mean that in forty years plan one would redeem £188,585,873 of debt, plan two £171,522,335 and plan three £126,070,401.[18] Price considered his first plan the most efficacious, even though it required imposing further taxes on the country. With a surplus of £919,290 confirmed by a House of Commons committee in 1786 the small sum required to make this up to a million was achieved by taxes introduced on spirits and hair powder for gentleman's wigs – the latter a possible irritation to Price as a lifelong wearer of full-bottomed wigs.[19]

With the required surplus assured, the bill to establish a sinking fund went ahead and on 29 March 1786 Pitt stood in the House of Commons and outlined the bill in a three-hour speech of some brilliance. In Parliament criticism of the sinking fund bill came principally from Pitt's brother-in-law, Earl Stanhope. He objected not to the bill's proposals but the fact that they did not go far enough. Price shared this view since the plan Pitt adopted (having baulked at the prospect of further taxes) bore most resemblance to

Price's third plan, the least effective of the three he submitted. Price and Stanhope also criticized a provision in the bill whereby the interest on stock purchased from the public would only be added to the fund until it reached a total of £4,000,000. Once this sum was reached the stock would simply be cancelled and no further interest paid. To Price this seriously undermined the working of compound interest on the fund just at the point where it became most effective and beneficial.

One proposal in the bill that met with Price's clear approval was the plan to place the fund in the Bank of England under the control of a board of commissioners. He also applauded the adoption of tight regulations designed to ensure that Government ministers could not raid the fund for uses other than debt redemption. On 26 May 1786 the bill received royal assent and 'The Sinking Fund Act' became a reality.[20]

Price's enthusiasm for the new fund is evident in a letter to Shelburne on 26 July: 'The public Funds, your Lordship sees, rise wonderfully. This is owing partly, I am afraid, to a decrease of trade; but chiefly to the expected operations of the plan of redemption'.[21] However, Price was not content just to see the plan introduced. He now voluntarily monitored its operation from 1786 until 1789, two years before his death. He had planned to publish the results of his monitoring in a 'Comparison of the Debts Redeemed with the Debts Contracted from the Commencement of the Year 1786 to the Year 1789', and this, in turn, was to form part of a fifth edition of his *Observations on Reversionary Payments*. But the work was not ready by the time he died, and the data eventually appeared in William Morgan's *A Review of Dr. Price's Writings on the Subject of the Finances of this Kingdom* in 1792.

As D. O. Thomas has shown, Price discovered that in the first three years of its operation the fund incurred more debt than it redeemed, a conclusion confirmed in 1791 by a select committee enquiry into the public finances of 1786 to 1791. The committee also confirmed Price's conclusion that the current tax level was too low to maintain the fund properly, an issue Price had raised with Pitt from the very beginning. Significantly, these years were a time of peace in Britain and only after the nation had endured the twenty-year long Napoleonic wars, which began in 1793, did the fund's major problem really became apparent. Both Pitt and Price had made provision in their plans for the Government to borrow money, when circumstances dictated, in order to continue to finance the fund. In the short term this produced few problems, but in the long term, and with the country at war, debt increasing rapidly and money expensive to borrow, the board of commissioners found themselves borrowing to finance the fund at a higher rate of interest than the fund itself actually paid. Astonishingly, this situation went unnoticed for a long time and Government continued to resolutely support the fund. Only when this 'ruinously expensive' policy became apparent did the fund fall into disrepute and it was finally abandoned in 1828.

Price has occasionally been blamed for his part in the mismanagement of the fund. D. O. Thomas concludes, for example, that:

> Price's writings had played a part in fostering the delusions that allowed the Sinking Fund to be operated for so long in such a disadvantageous way: the belief that the Sinking Fund could be effectively maintained by borrowing alone; the belief that the operation of compound interest had a mysterious efficacy quite independent of taxation and annual surpluses; and the belief that it is possible to redeem at compound interest by borrowing at simple interest.[22]

It is worth bearing in mind, however, that criticism of the fund's working relates mostly to its mode of operation in the years following Price's death. During his lifetime it is clear from the letters and plans he submitted to Pitt that Price both addressed and forewarned Pitt of some of the problems that later came to light, including the need for proper provision by surplus revenue obtained from adequate taxation. Similarly, Price envisaged Government borrowing to support the fund as a short-term stopgap; he did not advocate borrowing over the long-term. Finally, had he lived, it is extremely unlikely that a man who voluntarily monitored the sinking funds operation between 1786 and 1789, and noted its failings, would have remained silent in the face of the ludicrous borrowing regime that held sway after his death. We can be confident he would have made his opinion known in another candid pamphlet.

One question remains: how indebted was Pitt to the ideas of Richard Price? William Morgan, Price's nephew, was in no doubt that Pitt owed a considerable debt to his uncle's ideas and had been ungenerous in not publicly acknowledging this fact. So incensed was Morgan that he penned a pugnacious defence of his uncle in *A Review of Dr. Price's Writings on the Subject of the Finances of this Kingdom*, published in 1792. The controversy is almost impossible to resolve at this distance, but D. O. Thomas's succinct views on the issue present a balanced and justified resolution:

> It is likely that the confidence which the public came to have in Pitt as a financial administrator played a large part in the restoration of British financial credit, and that this confidence owed much to the intention, embodied in the Sinking Fund Act, of redeeming the public debts. Just how much was owed to the renewal of Sinking Fund operations cannot now be determined with any precision, but if

it is rightly supposed that the faith which the public came to have in Pitt's financial skills was a major factor in the avoidance of disaster it must, I think, be conceded that Price had no small part to play in the creation of confidence and its attendant prosperity.[23]

Although the sinking fund issue occupied a considerable amount of Price's time through the 1780s he still found time to involve himself in many of his other interests, particularly while he had waited for William Pitt to stir himself over the sinking fund issue between 1784 and 1786.

In July 1784 he had visited Birmingham to see Joseph Priestley, who had moved there after leaving Shelburne's employ. He also continued his literary endeavours, writing long letters to the Scot lord Monboddo discussing natural philosophy,[24] and penning a postscript to a paper written by his nephew, George Cadogan Morgan, for the Royal Society on 'Observations on the Light of Bodies in a State of Combustion'. But Price's principal contributions during this period were made in other fields that had long interested him – annuities, demographics, civil liberties and finance.

Although Price had included a significant amount of new data in the two-volume fourth edition of his *Observations on Reversionary Payments* published in 1783, he had not produced anything wholly new on annuities since writing the introduction to William Morgan's book on the subject in 1779. He rectified this in 1784 with a short pamphlet containing his letters of advice to an unidentified correspondent in Edinburgh, who wished to establish an annuities scheme for widows and orphans in that city.[25] In 1786 he also involved himself in the plan of the Devon vicar John Acland to give pensions to the poor through the establishment of friendly societies. Acland outlined his ideas in *A Plan for Rendering the Poor Independent of Public Contribution: Founded on the Friendly Societies Commonly Called Clubs*. Price favoured the scheme, which made contribution compulsory for everyone between 21 and 30 years of age, with those over 30 contributing on a voluntary basis; this offered a distinct advantage over the earlier, entirely voluntary, scheme of Francis Maseres in which Price had also been involved. The select committee supervising the parliamentary bill designed to establish Acland's scheme charged Price with compiling the actuarial tables needed for it to operate on a sure footing. Even as late as 1788 he was working on these tables and it would not be until 8 June 1789 that a bill 'for the more effectual relief of the poor' came before Parliament. It passed through the Commons safely but failed in the Lords. Even so, Price's work acted as a positive influence on many later schemes.[26]

Price's last published work on demography had been his controversial *Essay on Population* in 1779. In the second half of 1785 his correspondence with Joseph Clarke, a physician at the Lying-In Hospital in Dublin, was published. It concerned various statistical studies Clarke had undertaken in response to Price's assertion in *Observations on Reversionary Payments* that male mortality exceeded that of the female in all the life stages. Clarke's letters on the issue were read to the Royal Society on 30 March 1786 and later published in the *Philosophical Transactions*.[27] Accompanying them was Price's reply in which he 'took Clarke's findings to support his own hypothesis'.[28]

Civil liberties also received Price's attention at this time, not least because among the issues distracting Pitt from tackling the sinking fund issue was his private members' bill on parliamentary reform. Amongst other things the bill provided for an end to the anachronistic 'rotten boroughs', a limited extension of the franchise and the better running of elections. Price had long been an advocate for all of these, and he rejoiced 'to find that Mr Pitt is so much in earnest and reforming the Representation of the Kingdom'.[29] The earnest desire for reform proved insufficient, however, and this bill too was defeated in Parliament.

If there were a more hopeful reformist agenda to be found it appeared to be developing in America where, in 1786, the State of Virginia passed an act to ensure religious freedom. Written by Thomas Jefferson, it encapsulated almost all of the religious freedoms Price and many other Dissenters dreamed of establishing in Britain. As Jefferson's original draft stated that:

> no man shall be compelled to support any religious worship, place, or ministry whatsoever; nor shall be forced, restrained or molested, or burthened in his body or goods, nor shall otherwise suffer on account of his religious opinions or belief. But that all men shall be free to profess, and by argument maintain, their opinion in matters of religion; and that the same shall in no wise diminish, enlarge, or affect their civil capacities.[30]

Price obtained a copy of what he called this 'example of legislative wisdom and liberality never before known'. He then 'industriously circulated' it in Britain, together with a prefatory note of his own.

15

The Watershed Years (1786–8)

My life is coming to its dregs. Times of severe trial, pining, sickness, sharp pains etc., may lie before me this year, or I may be to struggle through my last conflict. My resolution is to maintain as much tranquillity as possible and to let it come when it will come. I consider the work of my life as done. I hope I have been in some measure useful.[1]

Four months after helping mastermind Pitt's sinking fund, Richard Price experienced a personal tragedy that for a short time threatened to end his further contribution to public life. Since 1762 his wife Sarah had suffered periodic bouts of ill health, but in May 1783 her condition worsened and, by October, a 'suppreset gout' had 'brought upon her . . . some paralytic symptoms' that Price thought 'very threatening'.[2] Though she rallied, Sarah was left unable to read or write easily and Richard now began, 'almost every afternoon', to sit down 'for an hour or two with the utmost patience and even cheerfulness to play cards with her'.[3] By the time his *Observations on the Importance of the American Revolution* appeared in print in October 1784 a fourth attack of the palsy had worsened Sarah's condition still further. 'For some time now', Price told Shelburne, 'she could hardly either speak or swallow or turn in bed, and I lived under the dismal apprehension of losing a companion, partner and friend to whom for 27 years the happiness of my life has been in a great measure owing'.[4] By July 1786 her state was 'a great weight' on his spirits. He feared too that his own health 'might sink under it' and, if it proved possible, he planned to leave Sarah 'for a few weeks' to partake of the rejuvenating sea air and swimming at Eastbourne or Brighton.[5] But Price was at home in Newington Green on the morning of 20 September when his wife died at the age of fifty-eight.

That Sarah's death marks a watershed in Price's life is evident from his correspondence. 'The anguish I feel on this occasion is inexpressible', he wrote to Shelburne on the day she died. 'I am now to wait by myself till some distemper takes me after her.'[6] Price's friends were soon offering their

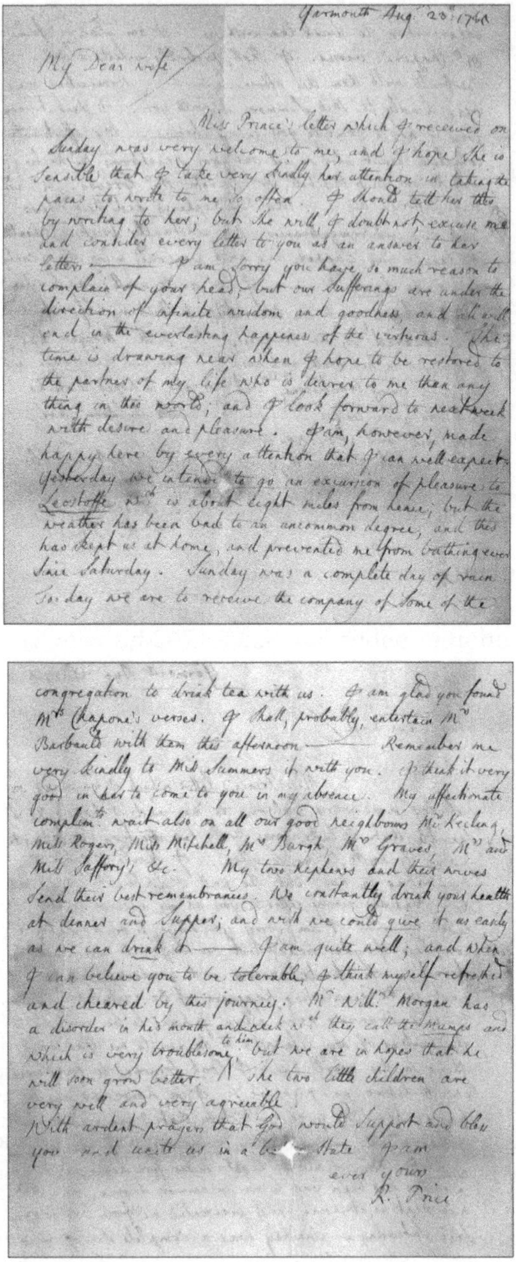

Figure 19. Letter from Richard Price to his wife Sarah dated 'Yarmouth,
Aug. 23, 1785'. Price's wife died on 20 September 1786,
a little over a year after this letter was written.

condolences, lord Shelburne among the first. His letter, written from his country estate of Bowood, the day after Sarah's demise, reveals the depth of his friendship:

> I have no need when I write to you, particularly on this occasion, to wait for reflection, I am not afraid to let my heart dictate. Let me beseech you to command me in any shape. I will go instantly to London if I can contribute to your comfort, or will be happy to see you here, where no one shall come, but such as are agreeable to you.[7]

A week later he wrote again, repeating his offer of a stay at Bowood, 'where every person about the house reveres and respects you, and you'll make us very happy, which is the next thing to being happy yourself'.[8] Price politely declined for although he had first thought of retiring to Wales and his relations there, he decided instead to stay 'at a little lodging of my nephew Morgan's at Sydenham to which I fled, leaving to him the management of all that was necessary to be done. Tomorrow', Price continued, 'I return to Newington Green where I hope to be able to spend the winter.'[9]

Shelburne next tried to revive Price's flagging sprits by insisting he struggle against misfortune and turn his thoughts to work: 'I think it the duty of every friend you have to incite you to exert yourself, to prevent the calamity which you have lately undergone taking too much hold on your mind.'[10] Joseph Priestley urged the same. 'Your retirement from the pulpit, for some time, is certainly very proper; but I would not have you *as yet* think of doing it altogether. You have still great vigour of constitution, and can hardly employ it better; and it may even have a greater effect if you be not confined to constant duty.'[11]

Price hardly needed such advice, for by 9 October, two weeks after Sarah's death, his thoughts had turned to the prosecution of two works that had been 'in hand for some time'. These were a third edition of his treatise on morals and a compilation of various sermons he had delivered at the Old Gravel Pit chapel in Hackney, whose congregation urged him to publish them. He hoped these occupations, together with his routine preaching, his correspondence, his monitoring of the performance of the sinking fund and a new lecturing post to which he had committed himself, would help divert his attention through the winter.[12] But notwithstanding such distractions, the general dilapidation of his house at Newington Green as well as the death of various friends and neighbours and the absence of Sarah persuaded him by the spring of 1787 to move to a new home in St Thomas's Square, Hackney. Hackney had been where he and Sarah spent their first year of married life together, but it was also closer to the London societies to which

Price belonged, and to his nephew, George Cadogan Morgan, who also came to live there at this time.

With Price still in low spirits his friends and relations rallied around again, now offering practical as well as emotional support. On 1 April Joseph Priestley visited from Birmingham and preached the morning sermon at Gravel Pit, while Price restricted himself to administering the Eucharist. In the afternoon his nephew George Cadogan Morgan preached to 'a reasonable audience' and George now became his uncle's principal helper at the chapel following the retirement of Price's co-pastor. Familial help also arrived from Wales as Price's widowed sister, Sarah Morgan, moved up from Bridgend to act as his housekeeper; her daughter would later join her.[13]

Prior to his wife's death Price's correspondence and published works are generally lacking in emotional revelation or personal anecdote but this now changed. Her demise seems to have awakened in him a desire to take stock of his life, a desire that came to a head in 1789. 'I see that my life is drawing fast to an end', he told Shelburne. 'This has led me to consider how it has been spent, and lately to resolve to write some reflections on the transaction of it and my conduct in it. I have begun since I have been here [south Wales] to execute this resolution and I hope I shall not find it an unprofitable or uncomfortable employment.'[14]

Price's autobiographical notes have not survived. We have been left instead one of the two portraits for which he reluctantly agreed to sit between 1787 and 1788, and a journal in which he recorded some private thoughts and views on various public events during his last few years. These, along with the volume of sermons he edited for publication in the months following Sarah's death, provide us with a glimpse of the man he had become by his sixty-fifth birthday in 1788.

Price had long resolved 'to descend to the grave without consenting to sit for any picture', a consequence of his puritan Dissenter dislike of personal vanity. This was a cause of some frustration to his many friends and admirers but in the winter of 1787/8 he consented 'to sit to a Mr. H( )t for a miniature portrait', despite the colds and stomach problems that plagued him. The artist is probably John Hazlitt, brother to the famous essayist and critic William Hazlitt and son of the Unitarian minister William Hazlitt, senior, a close friend of Price. No trace of this miniature has ever been found so we must be thankful that Price's doctor, a 'Mr Watkins', suggested his friend and patient pose once again but this time for a fuller portrait 'taken in the best manner' and by 'one of the first painters'. Price agreed but not without some agitation on account of the cost to Mr Watkins, who offered to pay for it, and with further anxious reflections on the problem of vanity. As he wrote in his journal, 'I have vanity enough but not this sort of vanity. I have felt at the time of sitting so embarrassed and distressed that I must have been an insufferable subject. I am, however, now it is over reconciled to it and inclined to feel the vanity that I suppose is usual on such occasions.'[15]

Benjamin West, the artist chosen to undertake the new portrait, was an American and Pennsylvanian Quaker who had left America for Italy in 1760 before coming to London in 1763. Having established himself as a painter of portraits and historical works he found favour with George III and, on the death of Joshua Reynolds in 1792, became president of the Royal Academy. His 'somewhat heavy, formal style' tended toward the 'Grand Manner' and occasioned contrary opinions among his viewing public. 'I have seen West's famous painting', noted Jane Austen of 'Christ Rejected', a vast canvas painted in 1814, 'and prefer it to anything of the kind I ever saw before . . . [it] is the first representation of our Saviour which ever at all contented me'.[16] William Hazlitt, junior disagreed and, in a critique of 'Christ Rejected' that was to establish his fame as an art critic and essayist, he took a more disparaging view of the artist's representation of the human form. 'Mr. West', he concluded, 'makes no use whatever of the moveable frame of the countenance, the only language it possesses; he sees and feels nothing in the human face but bones and cartilages: or if he does avail himself of this flexible machinery it is only by rule and method.' West's pictures, he concluded, 'are not of the epic but the didactic kind, not poetry, but prose'.[17]

This didactic, instructional mode suffuses West's portrait of Richard Price, who is seen sitting beside a bookcase of weighty tomes (a setting much favoured today by television interviewers wishing subliminally to reflect the intellectual authority of their interviewee). Price's arm rests on a volume entitled 'Butler's Analogy': this is Joseph Butler's *Analogy of Religion, Natural and Revealed, to the Constitution and Course of Nature* (1736), about which Price once remarked: 'I reckon it happy for me that this book was one of the first that fell into my hands. It taught me the proper mode of reasoning on moral and religious subjects, and particularly the importance of paying due regard to the imperfections of human knowledge.'[18] Finally, in a clear reference to his involvement in public affairs and his controversial support of the American rebels, Price is pictured holding a sheaf of papers that on examination prove to be a letter from Benjamin Franklin.

On the more personal side, and despite Hazlitt's strictures, West does catch something of the wiry physicality attributed to Price by his con-temporaries, one of whom described him as being 'slim in person, and rather below the common size, but possessed of great muscular strength and remark-able activity' – a physique to which a daily round of horse-riding, swimming and cold baths contributed.[19] One may also find, beyond the broad forehead and thick black eyebrows that give him a slightly quizzical look beneath his by then old-fashioned full-bottomed wig, a degree of introspection. It is a face that reveals, as the French writer Henri Laboucheix suggests, 'intelligence, self-control and energy' and, perhaps, a 'trace of almost malicious self-satisfaction'.[20] But this is as far we can go in reading Price's more intimate character from West's portrait. In other respects the artist maintains a distance between viewer and subject, by adopting, for example, the three-quarter-length pose. It is perhaps significant too that Price is portrayed in that instant when, having read Franklin's letter, he has removed his glasses or pince-nez and seems about to enter into a moment of reflection on the import of its contents. In doing so he does not look directly at the viewer. Instead, his contemplative gaze is off to our left and in consequence his eyes, those windows onto the soul, are lost to us.

As a man generally averse to self-revelation, Price was no doubt pleased with West's concentration on the prose of his life – his physical appearance and intellectual contribution – rather than the poetry of his inner emotions. But it means that if we are to glimpse that inner life more fully we must leave pictorial images and turn instead to Price's writings and those of his contemporaries.

Price began keeping his occasional journal on 25 March 1787, just as he moved into his new house in Hackney. It reveals much that reflects the age and stage of life he had now reached. There is, inevitably, a desire for a reduced workload, but also, more touchingly, a growing timorousness reflected in his worries about being alone in the house and having his sleep interrupted by noises whose origin he cannot explain. There are worries too over his increasing frailty and the illnesses that now afflict him more than ever before.[21] And yet the diary also clearly reveals a man of enormous energy who continually takes on more and more work, whether in preparing his own works for publication, lecturing, working on annuities tables for Parliament or editing and revising the work of his friends. We see a man still interested in and reacting to public events, both at home and abroad, such as the revolt of the Dutch Patriots in the United Provinces in 1787, when he felt 'the efforts of the independent citizens in Holland to gain a free constitution' were being 'crushed by [Britain's] interposition'. He worried too that this would inflame France and 'provoke her into a confederacy with the [Holy Roman] Emperor, Russia and Spain' and so draw Britain 'into a continental war'.[22]

And yet, as its editors have sensitively put it, there is much here that is profoundly revealing. 'Most poignantly of all [Price's] journal reveals with great candour – so that to decipher his shorthand seems to be an intrusion upon his privacy – his desire to serve God by being useful, his confidence that the virtuous will be rewarded with eternal life, and his hope that he will, and his fears that he will not, be numbered among them.'[23]

Price's insurance against failing to achieve eternal life had always been to live his life according to the demands of virtue. In a sermon written in the months following Sarah's death he outlined what living such a life had actually entailed. The sermon is titled 'Of the Security of a Virtuous Course' and in virtue, Price says, 'there is SAFETY' for:

Uprightness signifies the same with integrity or sincerity. It implies a freedom from guile, and the faithful discharge of every known duty. An upright man allows himself in nothing that is inconsistent with truth and right. He complies with all the obligations he is under, and avoids every kind of prevarication and falsehood. He maintains an equal and uniform regard to the whole of righteousness. He hates alike all sin, and practises every part of virtue, from an unfeigned attachment to it established in his soul. This is what is most essential to the character of an upright man. He is governed by no sinister ends, or indirect views, in the discharge of his duty. It is not the love of fame, or the desire of private advantages, or mere natural temper that produces his virtuous conduct; but an affection to virtue *as* virtue; a sense of the weight and excellence of the obligations of righteousness; and a zeal for the honour of God and the happiness of mankind.[24]

It included too 'faithfulness in all our transactions with *ourselves*' and 'candour, fairness and honesty in all our transactions with our fellow-creatures'. This was, in short, a reiteration of the creed of virtue he had outlined as long ago as 1758 in his *Review of Morals*. It was the creed by which he had attempted to live his whole life (though even the most virtuous can slip: on the afternoon of 27 May 1787, for example, he used in the company of others a 'hasty and indiscreet expression . . . concerning a minister in the city. I have since reflected on this with concern and pain').[25]

Sometimes his attempt to follow a virtuous course conflicted with his natural inclinations and desires, such as his wish, often expressed over the years, to withdraw from public life in order to concentrate on his ministry and theological writing. In part this reflected a common eighteenth-century neurosis. Socializing and entertaining in one's home or through one's correspondence made up a far larger part of eighteenth-century life than it does today and it was a responsibility many found irksome, especially as they grew older. For the seventy-three-year-old Thomas Jefferson his 'greatest oppression' was 'a correspondence afflictingly laborious'.[26] In London, Benjamin Franklin had a mirror fitted outside his front door that allowed him to remain hidden yet see who was calling.[27] He could then decide if he wished to receive the visitor or not. Price suffered similar frustrations and felt 'Greatly encumbered by my engagement and obligation to visit, to dine from home, and to answer letters . . . I long for more rest and quiet than I can at present enjoy.'[28] But it was not only in old age that Price had wished to withdraw from or minimize his contribution to society. He had, as we have seen, fought against the desire all his adult life.

That he returned to the fray so often throughout his life suggests that Price had a constitutional inability to withdraw from public life in a society where the need to *act* was acute. As his neighbour Samuel Rogers noted, Price was 'the most humane of men; to see distress was in him to feel an impulse to relieve it'.[29]

To live life as virtuously as Price attempted requires great strength of character, and it is perhaps the coupling of this inner strength with a commitment to virtue that gave rise to the 'malicious self-satisfaction' Henri Laboucheix believed he saw reflected in Price's portrait. It does not, however, seem to have resulted in arrogance for humility, another cardinal element of virtue, is ascribed to Price by all his contemporaries. Nor did this humility result in sycophancy. The unassuming and respectful manner of Price's letters to persons of a higher social status could lead to an impression of him as an overly respectful subordinate to the likes of lord Shelburne or William Pitt. However, Price was never afraid to speak truth to power or privilege, as his trenchant criticisms of Lord North and his disagreements with lord Shelburne over American independence bear witness.

A further danger for someone possessing a strong character linked to a virtuous nature is an attraction to dogma and certainty, something to which Price was not wholly immune. He never questions his belief in God the creator in quite the same way he does the divinity of Christ. Nor can he entirely escape a charge of dogmatism in relation to his demographic studies and his refusal to countenance a rising rather than falling population in Britain and London. These, though, are exceptional instances. More often than not, he welcomed doubt and constructive criticism imparted in a civilized manner. Criticism based on personality or the sort of silent criticism meted out to him by Samuel Johnson, however, was less welcome. At Oxford James Boswell had once been present 'when Dr Price, even before he had made himself generally obnoxious by his zeal for the French Revolution, came into a company where Johnson was, who instantly left the room'; Johnson being 'particularly resolute in not giving countenance to men whose writings he considered as pernicious to society'.[30]

Price's nephew, William Morgan, credits him with intense powers of concentration but in attesting to those powers he also notes that Price was not a good multitasker for, 'when engaged in one pursuit, he never could apply his mind to any other'. Such single-mindedness also meant Price could, at times, be 'very absent, and [so he] had many adventures'. When out riding in his 'blue greatcoat and black spatterdashes' he was often thrown from his white horse.[31] On another occasion, when sea-bathing, a boat had to be sent out to rescue him after he swam out of his depth, 'knowingly', he would later argue. When out walking Price often fell into a deep reverie, 'his eyes fixed on the ground, one hand in his pocket and the other swinging by his side'.[32] At such times, 'he was apt to forget all his surroundings' – although in 1773 he remained aware enough to jump into the river at Newington to save a drowning man.[33] Price also suffered from a degree of absent-mindedness and his neighbour, Samuel Rogers, recalled him once going down 'to supper an hour after he had eaten it'.[34] A slightly more embarrassing lapse concerned the commission Price received from John Adams, the new American ambassador to Britain, on behalf of Thomas Jefferson in Paris.

John Adams and his family had left France for London on 20 May 1785 and in early July Jefferson wrote asking Adams to enquire into the cost of insuring the life of French sculptor Jean Antoine Houdon, who was to journey to America in order to make a likeness of George Washington. Adams replied on 4 August noting that although he had been given a quote for the insurance Dr Price would enquire further into the matter and 'endeavour to reduce it a little'. A delay then ensued for Price forgot to make the necessary arrangements and it was not until October that Adams could tell Jefferson the business had been concluded. The insurance was eventually taken out with the Society for Equitable Assurances with Price's nephew, William Morgan, named as Jefferson's agent in the matter.[35]

A very warm friendship developed between Price and John Adams and his wife Abigail on their arrival in London. They were particularly grateful for this since despite Adams's respectful welcome from George III he and his wife were largely snubbed by London society. So close did the friendship become that the second letter Price wrote on the occasion of Sarah's death was to Adams. The ambassador duly paid a call at Newington Green a few days later, though he missed Price who had gone to stay at Sydenham. The Adamses often attended Price's meeting house in Hackney and Abigail sometimes entertained her husband, a future American president, with edifying extracts from Price's sermons and works: 'Treachery venality and villainy must be the Effects of dissipation, voluptuousness and impiety says the Great Dr. Price and adds, these vices sap the foundation of virtue, they render Men necessitous and Supple, ready at any time to sacrifice their consciences. Let us remember these Truths in judging of Men.'[36] Following his return to America Adams wrote telling Price: 'There are few portions of my life that I recollect with more satisfaction than the hours I spent at

Hackney, under your guidance, and in private society, and conversation with you at other places.'[37]

Price's generosity toward Adams was commensurate with his attitude to friends in general. We have already seen how he took on the editing of Priestley's work on electricity; he also supported some of Priestley's experiments financially. He helped find offers of employment for Mary Wollstonecraft when she was heavily in debt, even going so far as to take over some of her debts when her creditors came pressing. 'He has been uncommonly friendly to me', she wrote. 'I have the greatest reason to be thankful – for my difficulties appeared insurmo[u]ntable.'[38]

As a result of this willingness to help, Price received a large number of requests from individuals and institutions and his journal reveals the toll these appeals took of him as he aged. The prison reformer John Howard's account of European and British prisons was one such labour of friendship.[39] On 24 June 1787 Price confided to his journal: '*Mr. H*[owar]*d's* manuscript lies a burden upon me. I have got through one third of it.'[40] In September we find him working on it while on holiday at Eastbourne and, on 6 October, he was clearly relieved to have 'finished the correction of *Mr. H*[owar]*d's* manuscript which has indeed perplexed me and taken up much of my time'.[41] This proved a false dawn for by 28 October he was 'Employed again in revising the manuscript of *Mr. H*[owar]*d's*'.[42] Escape presumably came a little later as there are no further mentions of the work. Instead, in June 1788, we find him 'Employed in correcting Mr. H[owar]d's account of the Protestant Charter'.[43]

In 1786 the American poet, radical and statesman Joel Barlow, who would soon become intimately involved with France and its revolution, submitted his 'Vision of Columbus: A Poem in Nine Books' to Price in the hope that he might be able to offer help or advice on getting the work published in Britain. Price thought the poet 'a very rising genius' but took advice on the poem from Thomas Day, a poet, writer and political reformer. Day was not enamoured of the work; his reply to Price is interesting chiefly because of his percipient assessment of Price's reaction to appeals for help. 'There may be one reason why you should not implicitly trust the dictates of your own mind', Day wrote, 'and that is, the great goodness of your mind, which inclines you to undertake a task that most other people would have declined at the first offer.'[44] Such advice went unheeded. For the rest of his life Price remained unable to refuse giving help or advice to those who approached him for it. As he confessed in his journal in 1790, 'I cannot be easy without endeavouring to be civil to everybody.'[45]

Aside from giving personal advice Price also subscribed to the books of various authors and organized the purchase of equipment for various institutions, to many of which he also supplied copies of his own works. Abroad, these included the American Academy of Arts and Sciences, Dartmouth College and Harvard University, whose corporation thanked him as 'a Patron of humanity, a benevolent Asserter of the civil and religious liberties of mankind, and a warm Friend to the United States of America'.[46] At Benjamin Franklin's request Price also drew up a list of suitable books 'on religion and government' for a new parochial library in the Massachusetts township of Franklin. The citizens had wanted to build a steeple in their namesake's honour for which they hoped the great man would provide a bell. 'Sense being preferable to Sound', Franklin had asked the township to accept books instead.[47] Having completed his list, Price sent it to Franklin together with 'a present to the parish . . . of such of my own publications as I think may not be unsuitable'.[48]

Serious although he appears in his published works and his reaction to the demands made upon him by his acquaintances and friends, Price did not lack a sense of humour. Anyone whose social life included membership of numerous clubs and societies, and friendship with the likes of Benjamin Franklin, a well-known wit; Horne Tooke, who Samuel Rogers declared to be a 'most pleasant and most witty' man; and John Adams, whose conversation had 'a good deal of amusement' and 'a considerable degree of wit and humour',[49] is unlikely to have been humourless himself. Nor, in true eighteenth-century style, was his wit, and appreciation of it in others, always of the most refined or intellectual kind. Take the letter he received from Benjamin Franklin in September 1783 discussing balloon flights in Paris and the light inflammable air that filled them. Discussion of this inflammable air had put Franklin 'in mind of a little jocular Paper' he had written some years earlier and he forwarded a copy to Price.[50] The paper, now known as an 'Essay on Perfumes', concerned a means to 'discover some drug . . . that shall render the natural discharges of wind from our bodies, not only inoffensive, but agreeable as perfumes'. In April 1784 Price thanked Franklin for his bagatelle: 'I convey'd this to Dr Priestley, and we have been entertained with the pleasantry of it and the ridicule it contains.'[51] The following extract illustrates what tickled Price, the serious-minded philosopher, mathematician and scientist:

What comfort can the vortices of Descartes give to a man who has whirlwinds in his bowels! The knowledge of Newton's mutual Attraction of the particles of matter, can it afford Ease to him who is rack'd by their mutual repulsion, and the cruel distensions it occasions? The pleasure arising to a few philosophers, from seeing, a few Times in their life, the threads of light untwisted, and separated by the Newtonian prism into seven colours, can it be compared with the ease

and comfort every man living might feel seven times a day, by discharging freely
the wind from his bowels? Especially if it be converted into a perfume: for the
pleasures of one sense being little inferior to those of another, instead of pleasing
the sight he might delight the smell of those around him, and make numbers
happy, which to a benevolent mind must afford infinite satisfaction . . . And
surely such a liberty of Ex-pressing one's Scent-iments, and pleasing one another,
is of infinitely more Importance to human happiness than that Liberty of the
Press, or the abusing of one another, which the English are so ready to fight &
die for. – In short, this invention completed, would be, as Bacon expresses it,
bringing philosophy home to Men's business and bosoms. And I cannot but
conclude, that in comparison therewith, for universal and continual UTILITY,
the Science of the Philosophers above mentioned . . . are all together, scarcely
worth a FART-HING.[52]

Besides taking stock of his private life in the years following his wife's
death, Richard Price also reviewed his public one, drawing together in
his publications the ideals he had continually expressed throughout his life.
The process would reach a climax in his enthusiastic and public reception
of the French Revolution of 1789, but it began with a sermon preached
in April 1787, less than a year after Sarah's passing.

In December 1785 Price had joined a committee charged with establishing
a new Dissenter college to replace several that had recently closed. Founded
in April 1786, New College was sited in Hackney and, despite Joseph
Priestley's advice not to take on such a heavy duty, Price agreed to become
a tutor. He would lecture on morals, mathematics and philosophy but also
expected to contribute to courses on 'the higher mathematics, fluxions etc.
N[ewto]n's discoveries, and of assurances, life annuities, public finances
etc'.[53]

The following year, on the first anniversary of the college's founding, he
preached a sermon at London's Old Jewry meeting house to a congregation
made up of those who had subscribed funds. Published in London in 1787
and in Holland in 1788, the sermon – *The Evidence for a Future Period of
Improvement in the State of Mankind, with the Means and Duty of Promoting It*
– reflected the millennialist belief in progress he had expressed in his *Observations
on the Importance of the American Revolution*. It also drew together the pre-
occupations of his public life – education, religious toleration, reason, science,
virtue, civil liberty, political reform, free will and progress.

In philosophical and natural knowledge, Price told his audience, we
stand on the shoulders of Newton 'and assisted by his discoveries we see
farther than he did. How daring then would be the man who should say
that our successors will not see farther than we do?' He also believed that
this increase in natural knowledge must produce 'more enlarged views and

liberal sentiments in religion'.[54] Such progress, coupled with the spread of the principles of humanity, would surely lead to the alleviation of the horrors of war.

Providence had a hand in these improvements and the most common means it employed to carry out its ends were 'the investigations and active exertions of enlightened and honest men'. Also vital were candour and virtue since 'Inactivity and sleep' were 'fatal to improvement. It is only (as the prophet Daniel speaks) by running to and fro, that is, by diligent enquiry, by free discussion and the collision of different sentiments, that knowledge can be increased, truth struck out, and the dignity of our species promoted.'[55]

Education was crucial to continued discovery and progress, an importance reflected in the character of educational institutions: 'Seminaries of learning are the springs of society which, as they flow foul or pure, diffuse through successive generations depravity and misery, or, on the contrary, virtue and happiness.' The education they provided was crucial because 'On the bent given to our minds as they open and expand depends their subsequent fate, and on the general management of education depends the honour and dignity of our species.'[56]

Price continued to interest himself in the issues of concern in America even though, at this stage in his life, he could not always accede to American requests to contribute to them in the way he had in the past. In August 1785 Jefferson urged Price to address an exhortation to the young men of William and Mary College in Williamsburg on the question of slavery. Price, on this occasion, declined.

In 1786 Benjamin Rush requested a small pamphlet addressed by Price 'to the Congress, and the legislature of each of the States' upon the subject of education.[57] Though flattered by the request, Price did not feel up to this task either. Significantly, though, in replying to this request he noted his unwillingness to subject himself to the self-censorship Rush considered necessary in the proposed publication. 'You observe, that in writing to the citizens of America it would be necessary that I should be silent about the disputed doctrines of Christianity, and particularly the Trinity', Price replied:

> I am afraid that were I to write again, I should find this a hard restraint. I am likely soon, in consequence of a petition from the congregation to which I preach, to publish in this country a free discussion of these doctrines: and I hope your countrymen will learn not only to bear but to encourage such discussions. It is only vice and error that can suffer by them.[58]

The free discussion to which Price refers in his reply to Rush appeared in 1786 in *Sermons on the Christian Doctrine*, in which he also outlined the nature of the virtuous life quoted earlier. Over six thousand copies were sold in six months and its British publisher, Thomas Cadell, noted that sales would have been a lot better if Price had not been so controversial. The book appeared in Philadelphia in 1788 with the order of the sermons changed, the more controversial ones being relegated to its latter half; this Philadelphia edition also listed over ninety subscribers, among them the cream of American society. George Washington took four copies and Benjamin Franklin six and the list also included eleven delegates and two wives of delegates to the American Constitutional Convention of 1787.[59]

Benjamin Rush first mentioned to Price the possibility of such a convention in April 1786 and, in May, he explained why it was necessary:

> Most of the *distresses* of our country, and of the *mistakes* which Europeans have formed of us have arisen from a belief that the American revolution is *over*. This is so far from being the case, that we have only finished the first act of the great drama. We have changed our forms of government, but it remains yet to effect a revolution in our principles, opinions and manners, so as to accommodate them to the forms of government we have adopted.

More immediately, however, the convention 'at Annapolis' would concern itself with 'agreeing upon certain commercial regulations, and of suggesting such alterations in the Confederation [of States] as will give more extensive and coercive powers to Congress'.[60]

The strengthening of the federal constitution and the whole question of foreign trade had been significant elements in Price's *Observations on the Importance of the American Revolution* and the news of the convention gave him 'particular pleasure'. However, this first convention attempt failed when the necessary quorum could not be reached, although Rush reassured a worried Price that 'Whatever form of political existence may be before us, I am fully satisfied that our independence rests upon a firm basis, and that Great Britain will never recover from any of our changes in opinion or government her former dominion or influence in this country.'[61] This last point was important because, as Price noted in his reply to Rush, America's internal problems formed 'subjects of triumph' in Britain:

> The conclusion is, that you are falling to pieces and will soon repent your independence. But the hope of the friends of virtue and liberty is . . . that, whereas the kingdoms of Europe have travelled to tranquillity through seas of blood, the United States are travelling to a degree of tranquillity and liberty that will make them an example to the world, *only* through a sea of blunders. God grant this may prove the truth.[62]

America next addressed this 'sea of blunders' between May and September 1787 when the first and (so far) only American Constitutional Convention got underway in Philadelphia. The convention debates proved vigorous, hard-fought affairs but on 17 September George Washington, as president of the convention, presented to Congress the agreed, if not yet ratified, Constitution of the United States. Price received a copy sometime between October 1787 and March 1788, perhaps in November, the same time as Jefferson received his in Paris.[63] In March the following year Price informed Arthur Lee: 'I must own to you that the new federal constitution, in its principal articles, meets my Ideas, and that I wish it may be adopted.'[64]

Unquestionably there was a lot for Price to welcome in the constitution. The federal government had been strengthened and provisions made for Congress to have the power 'to regulate trade with foreign nations', just as he hoped. A two-chamber mode of government was also to be adopted through the creation of a House of Representatives and a Senate, which fitted with Price's belief in balanced government. The constitution provided for a census to be taken within three years and, thereafter, every ten years. This in particular was a provision Price had long wanted but failed to see adopted in Britain. He would have noticed too that, in line with his warnings and recommendations in *Observations on the Importance of the American Revolution*, 'No Title of Nobility' was to be granted in the United States and that the presidential oath – 'I do solemnly swear (or affirm) that I will faithfully execute the Office of President of the United States, and will to the best of my Ability, preserve, protect and defend the Constitution of the United States' – was commendably short and couched in terms acceptable to his ideal of the separation of religion and state. A militia to 'execute the laws of the Union, suppress Insurrections and repel Invasions' was also established, and though the accompanying provision for Congress 'To raise and support armies' was less welcome, the restricting of monetary appropriations for such a purpose to two years was not. On one issue above all others, however, the constitution failed – the issue of slavery.

As the Constitutional Convention took place, Benjamin Franklin had informed Price that:

From a most grateful sense of the Zeal and abilities with which you have long and successfully defended the rights of Mankind, the [Pennsylvania] Society [for promoting the abolition of slavery and the relief of free Negroes unlawfully held in bondage] have done themselves the honour of enrolling your name in the number of their corresponding members, and they earnestly request the continuance of your labours in the great objects of their Institution, for in this business the friends of humanity in every Country are of one Nation and Religion.[65]

Price welcomed his election to the Pennsylvania Society, but declining health and his many work commitments, meant he could not accept election to the committee of the newly formed London Society for the Purposes of Effecting the Abolition of the Slave Trade. In August 1787 he wrote to the anti-slavery publisher James Phillips concerning the matter:

> I think myself much honoured by the [invitation] of your Committee to add me to their number. No one [can] more devoutly wish success to their endeavours, or more heartily detest the diabolical traffick which they desire to abolish. But being already engaged in a greater variety of other important business than it is possible for me properly to attend to, I am under the necessity of begging to be excused.[66]

He nevertheless remained a member of the Society and contributed to its funds until his death in 1791.

Despite the lack of a clause concerning slavery in the American constitution, Price's general acceptance of it, and his desire to see it ratified by the various states, reflects his belief in progress and his pragmatism. As he said in a letter to Ezra Stiles on 22 March 1788, 'There *may* be omissions and there *must* be defects in this constitution, the removal of which it is at present best to trust to future time and experience.'[67]

Having now reviewed both his private and public lives in the wake of Sarah's death, Price felt by 1788 that his life was running toward its close. In October 1787 he was distressed by his obligation to teach at New College in Hackney and he only continued there on the understanding that his nephew, George Cadogan Morgan, could take over the burden whenever necessary. In June 1788 he chose to resign from the post, though he remained actively involved with the institution up until his death. Illness, too, was now taking its toll. The day after his sixty-fifth birthday he expressed surprise 'that disorders showing decay [had] not appeared sooner'. Foregoing his usual cold baths through the winter of 1787/8 gave little relief from his various complaints; in fact, he felt the omission only took from him what 'health and vigour' he had been accustomed to feel. In May 1788 horse-riding too came to an end when he found himself without his own mount for the first time in forty years. Through the first half of 1788 he devoted time to drawing up the actuarial tables required by Parliament to accompany the Bill for the More Effectual Relief of the Poor based on John Acland's scheme, but by the end of July he was glad to set off for Wales. There, if he found 'things agreeable', he would make a pretty long stay. Having set out 'dispirited with a cough, a languor, loss of spirits, appetite and sleep', the combination of sea air and bathing at Southerndown

'perfectly recovered' him and he did not return to London until the end
of September.[68]

On his return two events occupied his attention. First, there was the
question of the 'King's insanity'. George III suffered his first bout of what
some believe to have been porphyria in 1762, with a further attack occur-
ring in 1765. Its recurrence now, in 1788, raised the question of the need
for a Regency Act, and under what terms the Prince of Wales might become
regent in his father's place. Price wrote an undated document for lord
Shelburne outlining the pros and cons of these questions and concluded in
favour of the Prince of Wales becoming regent. He was even 'inclined to
favour the measure of a permanent regency' but one 'temper'd by a temporary
regency for a few months in order to obtain surer ground'. He also suggested
conditions might be attached in order to 'bind [the regent] to such points
as are most desired by the kingdom and most necessary to its welfare'.[69] This
was a qualification clearly attempting to ensure the implementation of the
political and social changes he wished to see in Britain. In the event, the
king recovered and the Prince of Wales resumed his waiting role.

The second issue of interest to Price on his return to London was the
question of France. Despite feeling, in 1788, that his life was 'coming to its
dregs', the events taking place across the Channel very quickly reanimated
his spirits.

Plate 1a. 'Richard Price, D.D. F.R.S.'
by Benjamin West, 1784.

Plate 1b. 'Benjamin Franklin', 1783,
after Joseph Duplessis.

Plate 2a. 'Joseph Priestley' by Ellen Sharples, *c.*1797.

Plate 2b. 'William Petty, 1st Marquis of Lansdowne
(Lord Shelburne)', 1766, after Sir Joshua Reynolds.

Plate 3a. 'Mary Wollstonecraft' by John Opie, 1797.

Plate 3b. 'John Horne Tooke' by Thomas Hardy,
before 1791.

Plate 4a. 'Smelling out a rat; or the atheistical-revolutionist
disturbed in his midnight "calculations"'
attributed to James Gillray, 1790.

Plate 4b. 'The doctor indulged with his favourite scene'
by Isaac Cruikshank, December 1790(?).

16

Revolution in France

Be encouraged, all ye friends of freedom and writers in its defence! The times are auspicious. Your labours have not been in vain. Behold kingdoms, admonished by you, starting from sleep, breaking their fetters and claiming justice from their oppressors! Behold, the light you have struck out, after setting America free, reflected to France and there kindled into a blaze that lays despotism in ashes and warms and illuminates Europe![1]

'What is now passing in France is an object of my anxious attention', Price told America's representative in Paris, Thomas Jefferson, in October 1788. 'I am by no means properly informed about the nature and circumstances of the struggle; but as far as it is a struggle for a free constitution of government and the recovery of their rights by the people I heartily wish it success whatever may be the consequences for this country, for I have learnt to consider myself more as a citizen of the world than of any particular country, and to such a person every advance that the cause of public liberty makes must be agreeable.'[2]

Two aspects of French affairs interested Price between 1786 and 1788. First was the country's burgeoning national debt and the attempts being made to deal with it, an interest that mirrored his perennial concern with Britain's own debt problems. Second were the political and social changes which, by 1788, were essential adjuncts to fiscal reform in a nation of absolute monarchy, a nobility with immense taxation privileges forming the Second Estate and a powerful clergy forming the First Estate. The Third Estate, or *Tiers État*, comprised the rest of France, in the shape of the mostly unrepresented but increasingly restless commoners. Stimulating his interest further were the numerous pamphlets he received from Paris on these issues, and his correspondence and meetings with men at the very heart of French affairs.

Price's letter to Jefferson marks the beginning of a series of letters between the two men in which Jefferson, 'as an interested spectator, with no other bias than a love of mankind', detailed for Price the unfolding of events that culminated in the French Revolution later in the year. In his first reply to Price, on 8 January 1789, Jefferson reviewed developments and expressed the belief that he saw at work in the country the influence of America's own revolution. Not only did this appear 'to have awakened the thinking part' of France 'from the sleep of despotism in which they were sunk' but French officers returning from America 'were mostly young men, less shackled by habit and prejudice, and more ready to assent to the dictates of common sense and common right'. Jefferson also notes that the level of France's national debt remained her most immediate problem, resulting mainly from 'the dissipations' of a court that 'had exhausted the money and credit of the state'.[3]

What Jefferson did not mention was that the court's largest 'dissipation' had been the financing of the American Revolution, achieved mainly through loans raised by Jacques Necker, the French finance minister from 1776 to 1781. Necker had disguised the extent of the resulting French liability by calling the interest charged on the loans ordinary expenditure and saying that he had found the money for America through various financial economies. As a result, none of the loans was underwritten by new taxation and it was left to the financier and statesman Charles Alexandre de Calonne, who took over as minister of finance in 1783, to announce a deficit in 1786 of 112 million livres, a quarter of the government's likely income.[4]

Jefferson outlined the minister's attempts at fiscal reform: 'M. de Callonnes found himself obliged to appeal to the nation and to develop to it the ruin of their finances. He had no ideas of supplying the deficit by economies; he saw no means but new taxes. To tempt the nation to consent to these some douceurs were necessary.'[5] Two such 'douceurs' or inducements were the proposal to create new provincial assemblies and a promise to convene an Assembly of Notables to discuss the nation's financial problems. Calonne would not survive in post to carry the reforms forward for although at the Assembly of Notables convened in February 1787 'The leading vices of the constitution and administration were ably sketched out, good remedies proposed, and under the splendor of these propositions a demand for more money was couched', the Notables and the clergy 'adroitly avoided the demand of money, got him displaced and one of the leading men placed in his room'.[6]

The new man – Brienne, archbishop of Toulouse – took over on 1 May 1787 and 'by . . . the hopes formed of him' and by further borrowing he was able to reform 'considerably the expenses of the court'. He also continued to implement Calonne's proposals, including the establishment of the new provincial assemblies. 'Notwithstanding the prejudices since formed against him', Jefferson continued, 'he appeared to me to pursue the reformation of the laws and constitution as steadily as a man could do who had to drag the

MIRABEAU *l'Ainé.*

Figure 20. 'Mirabeau L'Ainé' (Honoré Gabriel Riquetti, Comte de Mirabeau), engraved by Jacques-Louis Copia, *c.*1791, after a painting by Louis-Marie Sicardi. French writer, revolutionary and leading member of the National Assembly, Mirabeau translated Price's *Observations on the Nature of Civil Liberty* into French and later met him in London.

court after him, and even to conceal from them the consequences of the measures he was leading them into.'[7]

Jefferson believed that Brienne was more or less obliged to continue with Calonne's reforms by 'the public clamours excited by the writings and workings of the Patriots', who kept 'up the public fermentation at the exact point which borders on resistance without entering on it'.[8] The French Patriots were men of liberal sentiment derived from the nobility, clergy and France's small but well-educated middle class, some of whom formed what became known as the 'Committee of Thirty'. Among its members were Condorcet and Mirabeau, both nobles who had communicated with or met

Price and men destined to achieve great prominence in the events leading up to the revolution of 1789. Mirabeau, who had translated Price's *Observations on the Importance of the American Revolution* into French, was a leading light in the Assembly of Notables when, in 1787, it demanded the creation of a permanent commission to undertake a complete audit of the French finances. This demand proved too much for the king, who saw it as an infringement of his royal prerogative. He vetoed the proposal and by May 1787 the Assembly of Notables had been dissolved.

Jefferson's letter to Price informed him of various events between May and September, following the dissolution of this assembly, and in particular, a crucial confrontation between Brienne and the French *parlements*. Acting as the principal law courts in the realm, the *parlements* of France, of which there were thirteen spread throughout the country, possessed a crucial legislative power. For any new law to be enacted they had first to register it in their records, their objections to any proposed legislation being made known via a remonstrance sent to the king. This system gave the *parlements* a means to delay implementation of unpopular legislation and by the end of July 1787 the Paris *Parlement* was doing just that with regard to some of Brienne's proposals, in particular those relating to new taxes. On 6 August the king and his government then tried to enforce registration of the required laws at a *lit de justice* – a gathering held in the name of the king, and sometimes in his presence, at which the *parlements* could be overruled by royal decree. On this occasion, the Paris *parlement* declared the king's attempt at enforced registration illegal and as a consequence the whole *parlement* was exiled from the city. Uproar followed: as the government sought to maintain order troops appeared on the streets of Paris. By September, with order largely restored, an event outside the borders of the country in 1787/8 provided a distraction for those politically involved in France.

The event was another attempt by 'patriots' in the Dutch Republic to curb the power of their ruler – the Stadholder, William V of Orange.[9] Many in Britain believed that, as on that earlier occasion, France would support the Dutch Patriots in their new reform effort but, as Price noted in his journal, 'Britain, Our Britain (to *awe* the *French* and to prevent them from interposing) immediately began to arm and at the same time suggested to *France* that its interposition would be a declaration of war.'[10]

Because of her financial predicament France found herself unable to come to the aid of the Patriots and Price realized that 'The desertion of *Holland* by *France* and its suffering itself to be . . . *threatened* [by Britain] in consequence of its [financial] *embarrassments* lets it down exceedingly and is felt as a severe humiliation which probably will not be long submitted to.'[11] He was right. The sense of embarrassment felt in France led to renewed criticism of the government and this, coupled with the risk of further civil unrest, made finding a solution to the country's financial crisis all the more urgent. In pursuit of this solution a royal session convened in Paris on 19 November 1787 to discuss Brienne's proposal to raise further loans and the need for new taxes. The king attended the session but after lengthy debate and with no foreseeable resolution in the offing he controversially used the occasion to again order the *parlements* to register Brienne's new taxes, as if the royal session were actually a *lit de justice*. Members of the session, including the duc d'Orléans, the king's cousin, protested that the king's order was illegal. A second tool of autocratic kingly power, a *lettre de cachet*, exiled the duke and various other vocal opponents.

Through the remainder of 1787 and on into the summer of 1788 periodic rioting and disorder shook France and it was against this background that the *parlements* now joined with the French Patriots in calling for the Estates General to be convened. This body, in which the First, Second and Third Estates of France would be represented, had not met since 1614 and it was only after much prevarication that Brienne agreed it should meet. On 8 August he announced that it would meet on 1 May the following year but on 16 August events overtook him, when the finances he had been trying to rescue finally collapsed and all payments from the French treasury were stopped. State bankruptcy, long predicted by Price as a consequence of too high a national debt, had come to France. Brienne resigned and by 26 August Jacques Necker, the master of creative accounting, had returned to office.

Necker immediately faced issues beyond the pressing financial ones, including increasing social unrest exacerbated by less controllable events, such as the freak hailstorm that swept across the Paris basin in July 1788 destroying a substantial part of the annual harvest. Bread prices were rising rapidly and although Necker acted quickly to try to control them by taking over the grain trade, they would reach their peak on 14 July 1789, the day of the Bastille's fall.

A second challenge Necker faced concerned the form under which the promised Estates General should meet, their method of voting and the numbers of representatives to be assigned to each of the Three Estates. To consider these issues, which would prove crucial to subsequent events, he re-convened the Assembly of Notables between 6 November and 12 December 1788. In his letter to Price of January 1789 Jefferson outlined the man-oeuvrings into which the royal court and the Three Estates then entered:

> The court was well disposed to the people, not from principles of justice or love to them. But they want'd money. No more can be had from the people. They are squeezed to the last drop. The clergy and nobles, by their privileges and

influence, have kept their property in a great measure untaxed hitherto. They then remain to be squeezed, and no agent is powerful enough for this but the people. The court therefore must ally itself with the people. But the Notables, consisting mostly of privileged characters, had proposed a method of composing the states, which would have rendered the voice of the people, or tiers etat, in the states general, inefficient for the purposes of the court.[12]

The inefficiency alluded to by Jefferson resulted from the fact that when acting together in the Estates General the First and Second Estates, the clergy and the nobles, could always outvote the third, whose alliance the court needed. Consequently, the Court

determined that the tiers etat shall have in the States general as many votes as the clergy and nobles put together. Still a great question remains to be decided: that is, shall the states general vote by orders or by persons? Precedents are both ways. The clergy will move heaven and earth to obtain the suffrage by orders, because that parries the effect of all hitherto done for the people. The people will probably send their deputies expressly instructed to consent to no tax, to no adoption of the public debts, unless the unprivileged part of the nation has a voice equal to that of the privileged; that is to say unless the voice of the tiers etat be equalled to that of the clergy and nobles.[13]

The winter of 1788/9 proved a particularly harsh one and served to deepen the crisis. Jefferson noted the 'Siberian degree of cold' in Paris, while in London Price, who usually loved frosty weather, found this particular winter 'too severe' as his thermometer fell below 10 degrees Fahrenheit (-12°C). But while London enjoyed a frost fair and 'fires on the Thames',[14] the consequences of the weather in France were dire. With increasingly scarce and costly bread taking an ever-greater proportion of the commoners' meagre income many of the poor died of the cold. At the same time the lack of money for goods other than bread resulted in falling demand and rising unemployment. This in turn reduced the government's badly needed tax revenue and exacerbated the already parlous financial state of the country.

Delegates to the Estates General finally gathered at Versailles on 5 May 1789. On 19 May, in a second letter from Paris, Jefferson informed Price that 'The great preliminary question, Whether they shall vote by orders or persons' remained undecided. Nevertheless, 'the votes already given in the separate chambers . . . show that the Tiers etat are unanimous for voting by persons, a good majority of the clergy of the same disposition, and only 54 of the noblesse against 190 of the same body who are for voting by orders'.[15] This voting problem began to resolve itself in dramatic fashion on 17 June when the members of the Third Estate, having failed to persuade the other two orders to join with them, voted by an overwhelming majority to declare themselves a National Assembly and the sole legislative body in France. They also declared all present taxes to be illegal, although allowable until a new system of taxation could be decided upon. A short time later a majority of the First Estate – the clergy – voted to join the Assembly, which left only the nobles isolated.

On Saturday, 20 June the deputies of the new National Assembly arrived at their usual meeting place to find its doors locked and posters put up announcing a royal session to be held on the following Monday. Infuriated, and suspecting an imminent attempt to dissolve their fledgling Assembly, the delegates adjourned to a nearby tennis court. There, in what became known as the 'Tennis Court Oath', they swore not to disband until a French constitution had been agreed.

At the advertised royal session, which took place on Tuesday, 23 June, the king attempted to negate the power of the self-declared Assembly by offering a mix of concessions, including some on tax, while asserting that nothing decided by the Assembly could be valid without his approval. He then ordered the deputies to disperse and to meet separately in their constituent Estates. The nobles obliged and left the session chamber but the clergy and the *Tiers État* remained behind, with Mirabeau declaring that only bayonets would remove them. The king acquiesced and allowed them to remain in session. In doing so he allowed power to move to the Assembly and so effectively ended absolute monarchy in France. Following this act of defiance toward the king, those clergy who had so far refused to join their brethren within the National Assembly now did so, as did a few of the nobles. The king finally accepted the reality of this situation on 27 June when he ordered all the remaining nobles to join what now became the first unified French National Assembly.

It was at this crucial juncture that Price began receiving intelligence from another and more personal source in France. On 14 June he had noted in his journal that his nephew, George Cadogan Morgan, was preparing a trip to Switzerland. The first part of this journey took George through France from Calais to Marseilles in the first weeks of the Revolution and, fortuitously, his time in Paris corresponded with the dramatic opening events of the 1789 revolution.

George Morgan and his travelling companions, Dr Edward Rigby, a Norwich physician, and two younger men – probably Morgan's tutees, Samuel Boddington and Olyett Woodhouse – arrived at Calais on 3 July. Having been informed that they 'should find Paris perfectly free from disturbance', they arrived there on the evening of 7 July and took up lodgings in

Figure 21. 'The Marquis de Lafayette Presiding over the French National Assembly,
13–14th July 1789', unattributed French engraving, *c.*1830. Richard Price's
nephew, George Cadogan Morgan, visited the National Assembly on
11 July and witnessed Lafayette presenting the Bill for the Declaration
of the Rights of Man and Citizen, which was passed in August.

the Grand Hotel adjacent to the Palais Royal at the extravagant rent of 'two
guineas a week'. Recently built and owned by the duc d'Orléans, a man
at the centre of political events, the Palais had been thrown open to the
Parisian public, who turned it into a centre of social, political and ultimately
revolutionary activity. 'The first night of our arrival', Morgan recorded in
his journal, 'we had scarcely finished our tea when we hastened to the inner
part of the Palais, where crowds of Parisians meet every evening to talk
politics, to drink coffee or to sup.'[16]

After a few days of sightseeing the party travelled to Versailles on the
morning of 11 July in order to attend a session of the National Assembly.
They arrived, as Dr Rigby noted, in time 'to hear La Fayette make the
motion for a declaration of rights, which will be considered one of the most
prominent events of this revolution'.[17] Lafayette had placed before the
Assembly his 'Declaration of the Rights of Man and Citizen', one of many
submitted to the Committee on the Constitution which had been appointed
by the National Assembly on 7 July to formulate a French constitution and
a declaration of rights. Writing to Price on 12 July, the day after Lafayette's

presentation, Jefferson outlined for him the remit of the constitutional committee, 'because it will shew you they mean to begin the building at the bottom, and know how to do it'. Their remit included the preparation of a: 'Declaration of the rights of man. Principles of the monarchy. Rights of the nation. Rights of the king. Rights of the citizens. Organisation and rights of the national assembly. Forms necessary for the enaction of laws. Organisation and functions of the provincial and municipal assemblies. Duties and limits of the judiciary power. Functions and duties of the military power.'[18] Such proposals could not fail to excite so doughty a campaigner for civil liberties as Richard Price. Nor were they uncongenial to his nephew George who wrote of being delighted at the spectacle at Versailles of 'the representatives assembled to establish liberty in one of the first nations on earth'.[19]

By noon that same Sunday the party had returned to Paris where during lunch in the Rue St Michel they were asked whether they had heard of Necker's flight. 'As we had just arrived from Versailles our positive assurances satisfied those who were present that the rumour was false.' In fact, the king had dismissed Necker on 11 July while Morgan and his party were at Versailles, yet, as Morgan later noted, the action had not been 'whisper'd in the neighbourhood of the Palace'.[20]

Necker, despite his Protestantism, remained popular in Paris for his attempt to keep the bread price in check and when news of his dismissal reached the city, crowds quickly began to gather in the streets. Later, and as a mark of mourning for the king's dismissal of their champion, these same crowds forced the closure of the Paris theatres, including the one attended by Morgan and his friends.[21] Leaving the theatre, Morgan and his party tried to return to the Palais Royal, 'But every street was almost blocked up with inhabitants' and from 'several companies of the mob we heard the cry "Aux Armes".' At the Palais all was 'a boiling and unsettled state of commotion'. Learning that 'the barriers of the town were on fire' and that 'the Swiss Guards had fired and that fifty of the populace had fallen', the group decided to return to 'the citadel' of their hotel. Sitting in his room at 4 a.m. on the morning of 13 July, Morgan describes in a letter to his wife how he has spent the whole night surveying the mob as it passed to and fro in front of the hotel with 'increasing destruction and rage'. All around the sky was 'red with fires, the air full of the reports of guns and of the cries of women'. At one particularly alarming moment, 'the doors of a gunsmith living just beneath [his] rooms were violently assailed', though the assault came to nothing since 'the arms had already been seized by another party'.[22]

The next day, 14 July, the party went to visit 'the gardens of the duc d'Orléans at Monceaux' and so missed seeing the Bastille fall. On their return they heard of the attack on the prison, and in the Rue St Honore they were met by a large crowd 'bringing a Paper on which was written La Bastille est prise & les Portes sont ouvertes'. This was followed, as Samuel Boddington records, by 'The heads of the Governor and Commandant of the Bastile just cut off from their bodies carrying in triumph'.[23]

By this point the party felt their own 'situation becoming a very serious one' and as a semblance of order returned to the city over the next few days they made numerous attempts to obtain a passport to leave. Unsuccessful in this, they heard on 16 July that the king was to come to Paris, an event they decided to witness. The next day, having found a position on a balcony overlooking the scene, Morgan watched the king arrive at the Hôtel de Ville from Versailles. On 19 July, having finally secured a passport, the travellers left the city.

As these events unfolded Morgan described them for Price in two letters written between 12 and 21 July. Neither has survived.[24] Nevertheless, a sense of Morgan's excitement can be gleaned from two extracts published elsewhere. 'The spirit of the people in this place is inconceivably great', he wrote, 'and has abolished all the proud distinctions which the King and the Nobles had usurped in their minds.' He summed up the week's events grandiloquently:

> Paris was the scene of action, which to a mind whose first anxieties are for the general rights of man, must render all the subsequent objects of my transient survey very flat and insipid: the capital of the first empire in the world all in arms for liberty; a king DRAGGED *in submissive triumph by his conquering subjects*; the Bastille in ruins, and every monument of slavery in flames – these are appearances of grandeur which seldom rise in the prospect of human affairs, and which, during the remainder of my life, I shall think of with wonder and *gratification*.[25]

Price's joy at reading of such events is evident in his ebullient reply to Jefferson on 3 August when he too expressed his 'wonder and gratification' at

> one of the most important revolutions that have ever taken place in the world. A Revolution that must astonish Europe; that shakes the foundation of despotic power; and that probably will be the commencement of a general reformation in the governments of the world which hitherto have been little better than usurpations on the rights of mankind, impediments to the progress of human improvement, and contrivances for enabling a few grandees to oppress and enslave the rest of mankind. Glorious patriots! How has my heart been with them? And how ardently do I wish they may finish the great work they have begun in a manner that shall be most honourable to themselves and most beneficial to the world to which they are giving an example.[26]

In his enthusiasm Price saw the French Revolution not only as a successor to Britain's Glorious Revolution of 1688 and the American Revolution of 1776 but as an event that touched upon almost every one of his life's principal interests and concerns. Did the Revolution not originate in large part from a debt crisis of the kind he had consistently warned against? Had he not warned, in his contribution to the pamphlet *Facts* with Horne Tooke, that too high a level of taxation in order to address such a debt would lead to rebellion? And now that revolution was upon the people of France, were they not addressing its future progress through reason and free enquiry in an assembly elected by one of the most complex yet fairest elections ever held in Europe? And was the National Assembly not attempting to develop a constitution and governmental framework along lines similar to those he had advocated in his writing on civil liberties? Had not an autocratic king been made subject to the will of his people, to whom, according to Price, even as the highest magistrate in the land he was rightly a servant? Were not the vested interests and wealth of the landed and untaxed aristocracy being addressed and the priestly power of the First Estate swept aside, so removing the power of patronage and religion from government? All of these developments had been the subject of Price's quill over many years and his joy on seeing them come to fruition in what had been, despite the violence witnessed by his nephew in Paris, a largely bloodless revolution is understandable. In the face of such developments Price inevitably compared the situation developing in France with that existing at home in Britain. As he told Jefferson:

I scarcely believe we are capable of making such an exertion as the French nation is now making with a spirit of unanimity altogether wonderful. We are duped by the forms of liberty. A representation so partial as to be almost a mockery and so venal as to be little better than a nuisance bears the name of a *real* representation. Our Patriots are vicious men, and their opposition in general is nothing but a vile struggle for power and its emoluments. It is happy for the people of *France* at this crisis that they have no forms to deceive them, and that their struggle is with absolute power avowed, and not with a power apparently limited but really absolute in consequence of an undue influence which overturns the constitution and spreads corruption thro' every corner of the kingdom.[27]

Shortly after writing these words Price travelled to Southerndown on the coast of south Wales where he would now spend all his holidays until his death in 1791. Once there he kept in touch with French developments through the *London Gazetteer*, which he received 'every morning from London' and whose news was 'often very delightful' to him. He did not return to London until early September, to be entertained by the traveller's tales of his nephew George, who returned home on 9 September, having travelled through France to Geneva, the Alps, Lausanne, Strasbourg, Dusseldorf and Holland.

With Morgan back in London, Price relied once again on Jefferson's letters for first-hand accounts of developments across the Channel and on 13 September he received a letter that could not fail to cheer him. 'The outlines of their constitution have now been fixed by the National assembly', Jefferson wrote:

> They have decided that their legislative assembly shall be of constant existence. Opinions vary whether the elections shall be annual, biennial, or triennial: that it shall consist of a single body: but they are still free to divide that body into two or three sections, or to establish a council of revision with only powers of advice: and that the king shall have a negative, which may suspend a law till reconsidered and passed again by a subsequent assembly in which case it will become law.[28]

Although Jefferson acknowledged that these outline proposals needed bolstering with more concrete resolutions, such developments suggested the French were moving toward a position for their monarch and legislature akin to those of Britain's constitutional monarchy. Less welcome was the suggestion to make the Assembly a unicameral legislature. Price had always advocated a bicameral legislature so as to ensure proper scrutiny of proposed legislation and for the protection of minorities, whose rights could so easily be overwhelmed by a single chamber. Also less welcome would have been the news from Jefferson that factions with 'very dangerous views' were beginning to develop in the Assembly. Price disliked all factions and parties in politics.

By the end of September, with his nephew back in London and Jefferson having left Paris for America, Price had to resort to the British press to learn of events in France. Nothing he read appears to have undermined his generally positive view of the Revolution, despite the development of factions and the treatment of King Louis and his family who, between 5 and 6 October, had been forced by a mob to move from Versailles to Paris during what became known as the October Days. The king would never return to Versailles and when the National Assembly also moved to Paris a few days later the city became the centre of the Revolution with, as one observer put it, the king and his family 'more like prisoners than Princes'. For Price, though, writing in his journal two weeks after this event, 'The affairs of *France* continue interesting in the highest degree through forming a new constitution there which will be an example and instruction to the world.'[29]

Not only did French affairs continue to be interesting they also helped to revive his spirit and energies. He now accepted an invitation to preach a sermon to the London Revolution Society on 4 November, the anniversary of William III's landing in England in 1688. He had refused a similar invitation the previous year, the one-hundredth anniversary of the revolution, on account of his age, increasing infirmity and a desire to be away from public life. But now, animated anew by the events in France, he accepted and hoped that God would guide him 'to such language as may have a tendency to serve the cause of justice and liberty'.[30] This sermon, entitled *A Discourse on the Love of our Country* and given before a congregation 'numerous and respectable' in the familiar surroundings of Old Jewry in the City of London, ignited what has been called the most crucial ideological debate ever carried on in English.

17

On the Love of our Country[1]

May heaven grant that it may be the means of promoting the interest of truth, and liberty and justice.[2]

The great debate unleashed by Price's *Discourse on the Love of our Country* stirs up issues still at the heart of societies today: most fundamentally, perhaps, the true extent of the sovereignty of the people, and the nature and value of civil liberties and citizens' rights in the face of aristocratic privilege or tyrannous rule. Yet, the real tinder for this debate only came toward the very end of Price's sermon, when he briefly touched upon the relationship between the monarch and the people, and on his own enthusiasm for the recent events in France. For the main part his *Discourse* actually centred on a consideration of the nature of society in both a national and an international context.

As events began to unfold in France Price had informed Thomas Jefferson in Paris that he 'heartily' wished success to French attempts at reform and the securing of their rights, whatever the consequences for his own country, since he had come to consider himself 'more as a citizen of the world than of any particular country'.[3] His *Discourse,* nonetheless, is essentially an attempt to reconcile national loyalty with internationalist aspiration through a form of universal patriotism. It is, in the words of the historian Martin Fitzpatrick, 'perhaps the most influential tract on patriotism in the late eighteenth century'.[4] The *Discourse* thus ranks alongside the *Review of Morals, Observations on Reversionary Payments* and *Observations on the Nature of Civil Liberty* as among Price's most important contributions, not only to the society of which he was a part but also to our own understanding of the society to which we belong, and its place in the world.

Love of country, Price argued, did not imply a passion for 'the soil or spot of earth on which we happen to have been born'. Rather, it was a contractual bond to the community or communities of which we are a part and which seek to ensure and defend our civil liberties, including those of

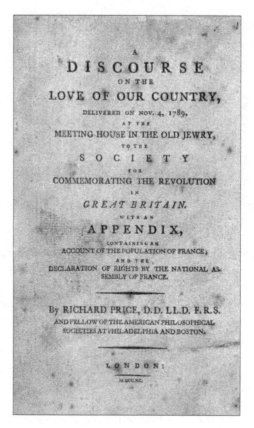

Figure 22. Title page of *A Discourse on the Love of our Country* (London, 1790) in which Price welcomed the opening events of the French Revolution. His comments began the 'revolution controversy' in Britain and provoked Edmund Burke into voicing his opposition to the Revolution, and Price's 'wicked principles', in *Reflections on the Revolution in France*, published in 1790.

freedom of worship, of expression, of enquiry and of political debate and participation. So, although 'Our regards, according to the order of nature, begin with ourselves, then our families, and benefactors, and friends and only after them our country', it was to the latter that our other interests were really subordinate, since our liberties were usually to be obtained and protected at the level of the nation. But even though, as individuals, 'we can do little for the interests of mankind at large' this did not mean we had no responsibility toward the wider communities of which we are a part. In Price's philosophy of patriotism, and his capacity as a citizen of the world, 'the noblest principle in our nature is the regard to general justice and that good will which embraces all the world'. Thus, 'in pursuing the interests of our country, we ought to carry our views beyond it'.[5]

The danger here is that any desire to export ideas in pursuit of our country's interests generally leads to imposition of those ideas on other peoples. Price addresses this problem by arguing that although love of our country is a noble passion, 'like all other passions it requires regulation and direction' because 'everything related to us we are disposed to overvalue'. Above all, the love of our country must never 'imply any conviction of the superior value of it to other countries, or any particular preference of its laws and constitution of government'. Nor should patriotism descend into narrow nationalism and 'that spirit of rivalship and ambition which has been common among nations. What has the love of their country hitherto been among mankind? What has it been but a love of domination, a desire for conquest, and a thirst for grandeur and glory, by extending territory and enslaving surrounding countries?'[6]

Long ago, Price had declared his belief in the right of any people to self-determination. British attempts at empire-building in India during his lifetime had appalled him. 'Turn your eyes to India', he had written in *Observations on the Nature of Civil Liberty* in 1776. 'There Englishmen, actuated by the love of plunder and the spirit of conquest, have depopulated whole kingdoms and ruined millions of innocent people by the most infamous oppression and rapacity.'[7] Price's position here contrasts markedly with that of Edmund Burke, who, as we shall see in the next chapter, would come to lead the opposition to the views expressed by Price in the *Discourse*. In 1784 Burke had opposed British withdrawal from India, because we were put there 'by the Sovereign Disposer and we must do the best we can'.[8] It may not be too much to suggest that Price's position was so radically opposed to the dominant trend in nineteenth-century imperial Britain that it contributed to the dramatic erosion of his reputation at that time.

For Price, 'the noblest principle in our natures' was concern for 'general justice and that good will which embraces all the world'. It was through such 'universal benevolence' that we should seek our country's improvement and benefit, by considering ourselves citizens of the world and by taking care 'to maintain a just regard to the rights of other communities.' He considered all wars of invasion and conquest for the purposes of 'dominion, or to gratify avarice' as 'wicked and detestable'. Only defensive wars were 'just wars'.

But if invasion, conquest and enforced conformity to our ways were anathema, 'by what means', he asks, 'might we best promote the interests of our country?' To answer this question Price returned to three of the guiding principles of his life – truth, virtue and liberty – 'the chief blessings of human nature'.

Truth came in the form of enlightenment through the power of reason and education, because ignorance was 'the parent of bigotry, intolerance, persecution and slavery. Inform and instruct mankind, and these will be excluded.' Virtue follows knowledge and is directed by it, for 'virtue without knowledge makes enthusiasts and knowledge without virtue makes devils, but both united elevates to the top of human dignity and perfection. We must, therefore, if we would serve our country, make both these the objects of our zeal.' Liberty is inseparable from knowledge and virtue, so 'an enlightened and virtuous country must be a free country. It cannot suffer invasions of its rights, or bend to tyrants.'[9]

Based on these three attributes a country might influence others not by threat or domination but by the example of its freedom for the individual, by its toleration, by its allowance of free enquiry and its commitment to community; in short, by its establishment and guardianship of civil liberties.

The possibility of taking action where a need for change was still perceived to exist remained important, but this did not mean a carte blanche freedom to disobey or overturn rules or rulers. Love and duty towards our country also implied a requirement 'to obey its laws and to respect its magistrates for reasons beneficial to our community as well as to ourselves'. In giving obedience to our governors, he argued, we must be careful to avoid two extremes. The first of these is 'a proud and licentious contempt' for those in power, born of 'a disdainful pride derived from a consciousness of equality, or, perhaps, superiority, in respect of all that gives true dignity to men in power and producing a contempt of them, and a disposition to treat them with rudeness and insult'.[10] The second, its extreme opposite, is servility and adulation toward those in power, since adulation is 'always odious' as well as dangerous in that it gives to the powerful 'improper ideas of their situation'. Price then illustrated these points by reference to a recent address made by his fellow Dissenters to George III, on the occasion of the monarch's recovery from his latest bout of madness. Price believed that these Dissenters had 'appeared more like a herd crouching at the feet of a master than like enlightened and manly citizens rejoicing with a beloved sovereign'.[11] Were he to have been present he would have addressed the king in very different language, honouring him 'as almost the only lawful King in the world, because the only one who owes his crown to the choice of the people' – a reference to the fact that George's kingship derived from Protestant resistance to the Catholic James II, the invitation of leading aristocrats to William and Mary to defend 'the people's religion, liberties and properties' and the subsequent invasion by William and abandonment of his throne by James. Furthermore, in consequence of these events in 1688 Price would have urged the king to consider himself 'more properly the *servant* than the sovereign' of the people.[12]

'Civil governors', Price argued, 'are properly the servants of the public and a King is no more than the first servant of the public, created by it, maintained by it, and responsible to it; and all the homage paid him is due to him on no other account than his relation to the public. His sacredness is the sacredness of the community. His authority is the authority of the community, and the term *Majesty*, which it is usual to apply to him, is by no means his own majesty, but the majesty of the people.' This form of kingship he had seen created in France when Louis gave up his divine and absolute right to rule. For Price, it was the public office of monarch that was crucial, not the man who occupied it. Whatever the king may be 'in his private capacity and though, in respect of personal qualities, not equal to or even far below many among ourselves – for this reason I say (that is, as representing the community and its first magistrate) he is entitled to our reverence and obedience'.[13] This obedience did not mean a sycophantic worship. 'Men in power', Price warned his congregation, 'are always endeavouring to extend their power. They hate the doctrine that it is a trust derived from the people and not a right vested in themselves.' This was why every government, even 'the best constituted', tended toward 'despotism'. Citizens should always be 'ready to take alarms, and determined to resist abuses as soon as they begin'.[14] Any failure of such vigilance brought the danger of our being enslaved by those most properly our servants. During the Glorious Revolution this vigilance had been seen in the actions of the British people, but it was essential that the principles underpinning that revolution were never forgotten. These same principles, he was pleased to say, the London Revolution Society had adopted as its own: 'First, the right to liberty of conscience in religious matters. Secondly, the right to resist power when abused. And Thirdly, the right to chuse our own governors, to cashier them for misconduct, and to frame a government for ourselves.'[15] But simple celebration of the past was not enough. The Glorious Revolution of 1688, though a great work, was neither perfect nor complete. Not only did religious intolerance and discrimination still exist in Britain, as exemplified by the Test and Corporation Acts which 'deprive of eligibility to civil and military offices all who cannot conform to the established worship', but there was the fundamental grievance of an inadequate parliamentary representation without which 'government is nothing but an usurpation'.[16]

Price then entered on a peroration in which he exhorted his audience to take action. The increasing luxury that entailed abuses of power in Britain, the monstrous weight of debt that crippled it and the vice and venality that were bringing down God's displeasure demanded such action, just as it had in revolutionary America and now France. It was time for Britons to redress these iniquities as a duty to themselves and on behalf of their communities 'for when the community prospers the individuals that compose it must prosper with it'. Britain, he warned, was 'everyday more reconcilable to encroachments in the securities of its liberties'. This must change, he argued, and, in the light of the French and American revolutions, the 'present times' were eminently favourable for 'all exertions in the cause of public liberty'.[17]

It was only after this comprehensive outline of a universalist patriotism that Price expressed his more euphoric welcome of the revolutions that seemed to combine so many of these ideas and ideals:

> What an eventful period this is! I am thankful I have lived to see it, and I could almost say, *Lord, now lettest thou thy servant depart in peace, for mine eyes have seen the salvation*. I have lived to see a diffusion of knowledge which has undermined suspicion and error. I have lived to see the rights of men better understood than ever, and nations panting for liberty, which seemed to have lost the idea of it. I have lived to see thirty millions of people, indignant and resolute, spurning at slavery, and demanding liberty with an irresistible voice, their king led in triumph, and an arbitrary monarch surrendering himself to his subjects. After sharing in the benefits of one Revolution [1688], I have been spared to be a witness to two other Revolutions, both glorious. And now, methinks, I see the ardour for liberty catching and spreading, a general amendment beginning in human affairs, the dominion of kings changed for the dominion of laws, and the dominion of priests giving way to the dominion of reason and conscience.[18]

Afterwards, members of the Revolution Society adjourned to the London Tavern for a celebratory dinner. There, Price received the thanks of the meeting 'for his excellent sermon', coupled with a request that he publish it in full. When it appeared on 5 December the entire edition sold out the same day. A second edition appeared on 11 December and a further four during 1790. It was during this celebratory dinner that Price gave further ammunition to his opponents by moving the adoption of a congratulatory address to the National Assembly:

> The Society for Commemorating the [Glorious] Revolution in Great Britain, disdaining National partialities, and rejoicing in every triumph of Liberty and Justice over Arbitrary Power, offer to the National Assembly of France their Congratulations on the Revolution in that Country, and on the prospect it gives to the two first Kingdoms in the World, of a common participation in the blessings of Civil and Religious Liberty.
>
> They cannot help adding their ardent wishes of an happy settlement of so important a Revolution, and at the same time expressing the particular satisfaction with which they reflect on the tendency of the glorious example given in France

to encourage other Nations to assert the unalienable rights of Mankind, and thereby to introduce a general reformation in the governments of Europe, and to make the World free and happy.[19]

The text of this address was transmitted to the French National Assembly, where it was read out on 25 November and received 'with lively applause'. According to the duc de la Rochefoucauld-Liancourt, the Assembly saw in it 'the dawn of a glorious day, in which two nations who have always esteemed one another not withstanding their political divisions and the diversity of their governments, shall contract an intimate union, founded on the similarity of their opinions and their common enthusiasm for liberty'.[20]

Despite this, and many other congratulatory accolades from France and organizations such as the Society for Constitutional Information at home, which dubbed him 'the friend of the Universe', Price now became aware of growing antagonism to the Revolution in Britain. As he informed Shelburne on 5 December, 'I find that the opposition [in Parliament] as well as the Court dislike what is passing in France.'[21] That opposition would soon find a powerful voice to challenge Price both personally and intellectually. But, as the New Year of 1790 dawned, reflections on the French situation were not Price's most immediate concern; rather, they were those of a man fast approaching his allotted threescore year and ten.

In April 1790 Price turned sixty-seven and though he thought it 'wonderful' that he was in reasonable health, certain 'weaknesses and incapacities' were nevertheless increasing – the rheumatism affecting his knee and hip, and a night-time tendency to think of things he needed to do or had 'omitted to do', all of which interrupted his sleep.

More poignant are his remarks concerning the passing away of acquaintances, such as Adam Smith,[22] and close friends including John Howard and Benjamin Franklin. John Howard died in Russia from an infection caught while investigating the state of that nation's prison system. He had been a friend since they first met at Newington Green over forty years before. Price had spent many hours editing and revising Howard's groundbreaking works on prisons and prison reform, which he considered 'an example of benevolence and humanity hardly ever before known'. Howard had 'gone to receive his reward', Price noted, before adding, somewhat wistfully, 'We are . . . separated but I hope not for ever.'[23]

News of Benjamin Franklin's demise at the age of eighty-four came in June 1790 just as Price finished reading a copy of his autobiography. Franklin's grandson had sent it to a mutual friend, Benjamin Vaughan, with instructions that Price should also read it. When noting in his journal Franklin's death from 'pleurisy and suppurated lungs', Price also recorded his friend's long battle with bladder stones, an ailment they had in common.[24] In 1785/6 Franklin, while still living in Paris, had been particularly troubled by 'the stone' and Price had sympathized from personal experience. 'What a sad calamity it is to be visited in the last stage of life by so dreadful a distemper?' he wrote. 'Dreadful I know it to be from experience. I have, however, been so happy as to discharge the stone.'[25]

With the loss of such close friends Price reflected on his own final hours. 'O! why am I not more diligent in preparing for my own end?' he confides to his journal. 'I have now lived beyond the age in which my father and brother died but I hope not lived quite in vain'. Keeping him going in the face of such melancholy rumination were his belief in the Christian promise of a resurrection and his resolve, even though old, tired and increasingly frail, to ensure that the 'small portion' of life remaining to him would 'be devoted to such further attempts of service as [he might] be capable of'.[26]

A number of projects kept him busy in 1790. Early in the year we find him chasing up a batch of scientific instruments missing from a consignment he had sent to Yale University. In April, despite disliking public dispute, he involved himself in a controversy concerning the election of his nephew William Morgan to the Royal Society. In 1789 Morgan had been awarded the Society's highest honour, the Copley Medal, for his work on annuities; an anonymous letter to Joseph Banks, the Society's president, opposed electing to the Society 'the nephew of a celebrated dissenting patriot who, presuming on the acquisition of a medal, is emboldened to become a petitioner for more constant honours'.[27] Banks showed this letter to Price who believed it to have been written by the physician and chemist Dr Adair Crawford, another member of the Society. Morgan had severely criticized a paper by Crawford 'on animal heat and combustion' and although Crawford answered the criticisms, Price felt they had left him 'with a resentment in his mind which makes him very averse to Mr M[orga]n and is perfectly unworthy of a Philosopher'.[28]

One philosopher with whom Price often argued in a gentlemanly manner was Joseph Priestley, who had also taken to reflecting on his own life's course at this time. The result was a short autobiography written during one of his 'summer excursions'. Forwarding a copy to Price in August 1790 he urged his celebrated friend to 'remember that life is precarious' and to employ one of his own holidays in the same way.[29] Price received the work while taking such a holiday in Wales, and had already recorded in his journal an intention to spend some time while there 'writing reflections on my past life'. These he hoped 'to prefix to a second volume of sermons'. On returning to London on 2 October, after what proved to be his last visit home to Wales, Price began preparing this second volume of sermons for publication; as well as adding to his autobiographical notes and making alterations and additions to a fifth edition of *Observations on Reversionary Payments*, his major work on annuities.

Besides literary endeavours Price also found his time taken up with numerous visitors, including sisters and nieces from Wales and various Frenchmen who arrived with introductions from the duc de La Rochefoucauld-Liancourt. There also came the likes of 'Mr Hobhouse', 'a late convert to the Dissenters and the cause of civil liberty and religious liberty', whose three-week stay put Price 'out of [his] way and burdened [his] spirits'. The greatest burden, however, remained his correspondence, which now included letters to be written to numerous societies in France on behalf of the London Revolution Society, onto whose correspondence committee he had been drafted the previous December. Price maintained a very active interest in the progress of the Revolution. In January 1790, for example, he was gratified to learn that three translations of his Old Jewry *Discourse* and his congratulatory address to the National Assembly were available in France (a third edition also appeared in Britain at this time). He now found himself 'more a public man than ever' with 'engagements and encumbrances' increasing just as his 'capacity for bearing them . . . continually diminished'.[30]

In May 1790 he anxiously waited to hear the result of the debates taking place in the French National Assembly over whether or not 'the power of making war and peace shall be delegated by the nation to the king'. Should the determination be against such a delegation, he noted, 'a glorious example will be given to the world, and we may hope that the time will come when the aspirations of kings and the intrigues of *courts* will be no longer capable of proclaiming wars and delighting the rich'.[31] On 6 June the Assembly duly voted 'not to grant the king the power of making peace and war' and some of Price's apprehension over the safety of the Revolution dissipated. 'This glorious revolution', his journal records, 'becomes more and more likely every day to be happily settled.'[32] This satisfaction was enhanced by the Assembly's later decisions to renounce foreign conquest and abolish nobility in France.

By 1790 Price had good reason for considering that he had, in some way, contributed to the changes taking place in France. His work on moral philosophy and his *Four Dissertations* had both been well received in the country. His *Observations on the Nature of Civil Liberty* had been quickly translated and published there by Mirabeau, a man now at the very heart of proceedings in the National Assembly. In financial matters his writing on Britain's national debt had been read and referenced in the run up to the Revolution by Frenchmen concerned about their own country's burgeoning debt problems. On the subject of annuities, too, his expertise had been sought during the establishment of the Compagnie Royale d'Assurrance in 1787, the first French life-assurance company.[33] And now, in 1790, nearing the end of his life, he received three further proofs of the esteem in which he and his ideas were held in France.

First, a letter from a 'T. Procter', an Englishman living in France, informed him that his *Discourse* to the Revolution Society was 'justly celebrated' in the country and 'quoted by the Writers of the day in support of the principles of liberty'.[34] Second, in June, la Rochefoucauld-Liancourt wrote to encourage Price to attend the planned celebrations in Paris of the first anniversary of the fall of the Bastille. The Feast of the Federation, as it came to be called, took place just outside the city on the Champ de Mars in the presence of the king and before a crowd estimated at 300,000. Price did not doubt it would be a glorious day, one that 'ought to contribute greatly to sustain the patriotic ardour which has freed France from bondage',[35] but he could not attend. Instead, he went to a Bastille-Day celebration dinner in London arranged by his neighbour Samuel Rogers on behalf of a new society, The Friends of the Revolution in France.

This boisterous celebration was held at the Crown and Anchor tavern in London with Price acting as one of the stewards. In this capacity he found himself called upon to offer up a toast in front of a 'most numerous and respectable company of gentlemen'. But before doing so, Price made a short speech. In it he advocated an alliance 'for maintaining and perpetuating peace' between Britain and revolutionary France, a peace that would help avoid the expensive wars between the two nations that had so contributed to the scale of Britain's national debt. Such an alliance would lay an axe to the passions of kings and ministers and the intrigues of courts for embroiling nations in war. Much as he had done in 1776, Price also presented his vision of a family of European states, a confederation to include not only Britain and France but 'HOLLAND, and other countries on this side of the globe, and the United States of AMERICA on the other', so that 'when alarms of war come, they will be able to say to contending nations, PEACE, and there will be PEACE'. He then made his toast, to 'An alliance between France and Great Britain for perpetuating peace, and making the world happy.'[36]

In the wake of this Bastille-Day celebration, the third confirmation of his celebrity status in France arrived in the form of a letter from the Citizens of the District of Quimper in Brittany describing how they had 'been affected even to tears' when reading of his speech and toast. They applauded his idea of an alliance between Britain and France and should any 'rash and daring' ministers oppose such a move 'the friends of liberty in the two countries would recognize one another, and, far from fighting, would cement by fraternal embraces that union which ought ever to subsist between two nations destined to exhibit to the astonished world an example of all the social virtues'. They were happy too to give Price a 'testimony of [their] admiration' because 'Principles so excellent when professed by you, cannot but fail to draw together, throughout the world, all the true friends of mankind.'[37]

Hopes for such a political alliance were premature, and destined to fail, but alliances had certainly started at a social level. In January 1790 Price learnt of the formation in Paris of the Society of 1789. By May he had received the Society's by-laws from la Rochefoucauld-Liancourt, coupled with a request that the London Revolution Society be affiliated to them.[38] Another attempt at *entente cordiale* occurred in the summer of 1790 when representatives from Nantes arrived in London. Price and his nephew George Cadogan Morgan attended a dinner in their honour and Price played his part in replying to the visitors' address, which took place under a banner bearing sentiments close to his heart – 'Pacte universal' and 'a l'union de la France and [*sic*] d'Angleterre'.[39]

In the context of the broad alliance of nations Price had outlined in both his *Discourse* and his Bastille-Day speech, these international links were undoubtedly encouraging, as were similar attempts being made, with varying degrees of success, to forge links between the different reformist societies within Britain itself. At the Bastille-Day celebration in London the Society for Constitutional Information and several Whig clubs were represented. Despite the plethora of loyal toasts and the singing of patriotic songs that accompanied such gatherings, however, they increasingly worried those who distrusted revolutionary France and the ideas it had unleashed. There were concerns even within the ranks of the Revolution Society itself: Earl Stanhope, who had chaired the Society's meeting of November 1789, personally struck his name off the membership list in the wake of London's Bastille-Day celebrations and prior to the next meeting of the Society on 4 November 1790, which took place at the London Tavern. Reporting on this meeting, *The Times* noted that 'Dr Price, or rather according to their own principles, Mr Richard Price', was in the chair, and he offered up a radical toast 'To the Parliament of Britain, May it become a National Assembly.' According to *The Times* again, 'When Mr. Richard Price gave "the National Assembly" as a toast . . . he might, with the most perfect consistency, have added, "and many thanks to them for having confirmed the Family Compact, and for arming against Britain without the smallest provocation!"'[40] It was at this time that Price once again found his *Discourse* the target of opposing and sometimes venomous quills.

Of the many pamphlets published in opposition to the *Discourse* most relied on poorly argued appeals to tradition and the status quo, as this extract from *Observations on Doctor Price's Revolution Sermon* by Edward Sayer illustrates:

> The freedom or liberties of the people are principally guarded by the frame of our legislature, and by the acts which have distinguished that legislature for many centuries. Some defects may, upon speculative principles, be found in its constitution, but they have existed from the beginning with it. They have grown with its growth, have accompanied its success, and afford at this time no other symptoms of decay, than they have for ages long since past without misfortune.[41]

Sayer felt this argument to be greatly strengthened 'by the consideration that it cannot be ascertained, except by weak conjecture, whether these very defects do not contribute to the existence of the state, in which they appear, not as ulcerous blotches, but as gentle humours that pervade the whole of the body, and flow through the veins of the healthiest constitution'.[42] Sayer's 'gentle humours' were, of course, the constitutional defects that had been the subject of Price's lifelong reformist zeal: the limited franchise, the unequal political representation across the country, the baneful influence of placemen and royal pensioners in a parliament where vested interest could so often scupper attempts at meaningful social and political reform and, finally, the continuing treatment of Dissenters and other religious groups outside the Established Church as second-class citizens. Betraying a rhetorical ignorance of Price's position on these matters, Sayer went on to ask: 'what motive is it that can animate the Doctor to blow his trumpet in Sion, to beat his drum ecclesiastic, and to proclaim reforms for evils that do not exist?'[43]

One man who had no doubt as to Price's motive was the Whig politician, MP and parliamentarian Edmund Burke. He believed Price and the London Revolution Society acolytes wanted nothing less than a British revolution akin to that in France, and were plotting the overthrow of the British constitution, monarchy and state.

18

Burke and his Reflections

The Revolution in *Fr*[an]*ce* will for ever distinguish the last year and will form an epoch of the greatest importance in the history of human kind. It is an event wonderful and *unparalleled*. I am refreshed and animated whenever I turn my thoughts to it and I *exult* in the hope that possibly I may have contributed a little towards producing and confirming it.[1]

Edmund Burke's reaction to the early events of the French Revolution had been one of bemused private interest. 'Like all England', he gazed with astonishment at a French struggle for liberty, unsure whether to 'blame or to applaud'. There was something 'mysterious and paradoxical' in the Revolution. Though he could admire its spirit, he worried that 'the old Parisian ferocity' had broken out in a 'shocking manner'. Were this to prove a one-off 'explosion' it would mean little; but should it prove to be 'character rather than accident' then the French people were 'not fit for liberty, and must have a strong hand like that of their former masters to coerce them. Men must have a certain fund of natural moderation to qualify them for freedom, else it becomes noxious to themselves and a perfect nuisance to every body else.'[2]

As events continued to unfold it seemed to Burke that 'character' rather than 'accident' had indeed prevailed, and by the end of 1789 his position hardened into one of outright opposition to the Revolution. In the wake of the October Days, when a violent and threatening mob forced Louis and his family to move from Versailles to effective imprisonment in Paris, Burke wrote to his son Richard expressing concern that with the elements comprising human society dissolving, a 'world of monsters' was now 'to be produced in the place of it – where Mirabeau presides as the Grand Anarch, and the late Grand Monarch makes a figure as ridiculous as pitiable'.[3]

Burke's private disquiet at the Revolution turned to public condemnation in February 1790 when he argued in a parliamentary debate that the French had shown themselves to be 'the ablest architects of ruin'. In an amazingly short time 'they had completely pulled down to the ground, their monarchy, their Church, their nobility, their law, their revenue, their army, their navy, their commerce and their manufacture'. It was therefore necessary 'to keep the distemper of France from the least countenance in England where some wicked persons had shown a strong disposition to recommend an imitation of the French spirit of reform'.[4]

One such 'wicked person' was Richard Price and the crucial spur to Burke making public his opposition to the Revolution had been his reading in mid-January 1790 of Price's *Discourse on the Love of our Country*. Almost immediately he began composing a pamphlet repudiating Price's ideas. By February the first pages of text were being sent to a friend, who advised against a war of words with Price. The completed text, written in the form of a letter to a young Parisian friend, and highly critical of Price, would be published on 1 November 1790 under the title *Reflections on the Revolution in France*.

Richard Price believed, with some qualification, in the virtues of a balanced constitution achieved through the effective operation of its three principal institutions – monarchy, Lords and Commons. Burke shared this belief. In his *Discourse*, however, Price argued that ultimate political sovereignty did not rest in these institutions but in the hands of those they were created to serve – the people. Even the king was 'no more than the first servant of the public, created by it, maintained by it, and responsible to it'. Royal authority stemmed not from the institution of monarchy itself but from 'the majesty of the people'. When state institutions failed to operate properly they should be reformed; the power to demand and instigate that reform also lay with the people. Taking his cue from the principles underpinning the London Revolution Society, Price argued that this situation derived from the consequences of the 1688 Glorious Revolution, which gave to the people of England and Wales prior to 1707, and to all of Britain thereafter, 'the right to chuse our own governors, to cashier them for misconduct, and to frame a constitution for ourselves'. Finally, he became the first person to link the progress made in civil liberties in Britain at the time of the Glorious Revolution with that more recently achieved by the Americans in 1776 and the French in 1789. The citizens of America and France, he had argued, were now ahead of those in Britain in the possession of civil liberties derived from the natural rights of the individual. If the British people wished to regain their eminence in this field they needed to emulate America and France by instigating reform.

Such claims incensed Burke, and he made clear in *Reflections* that his own belief in the balanced constitution did not rest on the 'rights of man' divined from 'the nakedness and solitude of metaphysical speculation', nor on the 'spirit of innovation' that arose from the 'selfish temper and confined views' he ascribed to Price. Instead, he appealed to prescriptive rights – 'that grand title which supersedes all other title' – and by which he meant the rights of an established hierarchy. These are the rights of privilege based on property, with hereditary and aristocratic position as qualifications for political leadership.

The French Revolution, with its emphasis on reason, natural rights and the growing importance and dominance of the Third Estate, directly challenged these prescriptive rights by attacking the pillars of the hierarchical and aristocratic society Burke lauded. Not only had the monarchy in France been undermined (though not yet overthrown) but nobility, which acted for Burke as 'a graceful ornament to the civil order' and as 'the Corinthian capital of polished society', had been outlawed in June 1790 as he was writing *Reflections*. Such consequences of the Revolution, he argued, 'reflected only a sour, malignant, envious disposition . . . that sees with joy the unmerited fall of what had long flourished in splendour and honour'.[5]

Britons, Burke confidently asserts, were 'resolved to keep an established Church, an established monarchy, an established aristocracy, and an established democracy' each 'in the degree it exists and in no greater'.[6] This position seems to preclude any hope of change, progress or reform, yet Burke also asserted that he did not oppose reform. Change, though, must be gradual, so as not to undermine the institutions and above all the stability of the society which undertook it. Burke feared that reformists like Price, with their adherence to ideas derived from rational philosophy, were too quick to move from speculation and philosophizing to radical and fundamental change of long-established institutions and modes of living.

As to the more specific constitutional ideas Price expressed in his *Discourse*, Burke argued that it was incorrect to conclude that the Glorious Revolution gave to the people a right to choose their governors. Were that to be the case, Britain's hereditary monarchy would have become elective, something it clearly was not. The dethronement of Catholic James II and enthronement of Protestant William and Mary at the Glorious Revolution of 1688 merely interrupted the hereditary line. It did not end it. Nor, he believed, did 1688 give the people a right to cashier their governors for what Price called 'misconduct'. To use so vapid a word to describe the transgressions of Catholic James II, who had attempted to 'subvert the Protestant Church and State and their fundamental unquestionable laws', would only lead people to cashier their governors on the very weakest of pretexts. Price also erred in implying that the events of 1688 established in the people a right to frame their own government. On the contrary, in removing James and establishing the Bill of Rights that accompanied the accession of William and Mary, those in charge of events in 1688/9 sought only to restore the ancient constitution existing at James's accession. They did not seek to fashion a new one: 'the very idea of the fabrication of a new government' ought to be 'enough to fill us with disgust and horror'.

Nor did Burke agree with Price's assertion that political power lay, by right, in the hands of the people. 'As to the share of power, authority and direction which each individual ought to have in the management of the state, that I must deny to be amongst the direct, original rights of man in civil society', he wrote.[7] It was inherently dangerous to link, as casually as Price had done, political power, civil liberties, natural rights and calls for reform. Doing so would simply unleash 'a swinish multitude' (a term applicable to the Parisian mob) which would overturn all established order and institutions. This, he firmly believed, was what Price and his fellow members of the Revolution Society were actively encouraging.

As for the two urgently needed constitutional reforms Price had mentioned in his *Discourse* – parliamentary reform through an expansion of the franchise and religious toleration through repeal of the Test and Corporation Acts – Burke opposed both. 'Our representation', he insisted, with regard to the franchise, 'has been found perfectly adequate to all the purposes for which a representation of the people can be devised or desired. I defy the enemies of our constitution to show the contrary.'[8]

His opposition to religious toleration, however, surprised many Dissenters for they believed it represented a change from his previous position of qualified support. Burke believed that 'In a Christian commonwealth the church and state are one and the same thing, being different integral parts of the same whole.'[9] In Britain, the Protestantism of the Church of England remained the established religion, so although toleration of Dissent may be possible, the established State religion still needed solid protection. By 1790 he had come to believe that the Dissenters, Price eminent among them, were actively seeking to undermine this symbiotic and sacred union of Church and State. He also worried that the appeal to natural rights derived from reason, espoused so freely by Dissenters like Price and the French revolutionaries, would ultimately lead to atheism. For all these reasons, when a motion for the repeal of the discriminatory Test and Corporation Acts came before the British parliament in March 1790, he felt unable to support it. He even went so far as to declare in a parliamentary speech on the motion that the publications of the likes of Price, Priestley and other Dissenters were evidence of their 'warm, animated, and acrimonious hostility against the Church establishment'. His argument was that they already had religious toleration and that he could not support them further until they came to see that the Church was no more than 'a jealous friend to be reconciled, and not an adversary that must be vanquished'.[10]

During this same debate Burke's friend Charles James Fox also spoke. As a sponsor of the motion and supporter of the Dissenter cause, Fox, in contrast to Burke, mentioned with approval both the French Revolution and Price. Although critical of Price's use of the pulpit for political purposes, Fox declared himself happy to see a 'neighbouring nation' restoring the rights of men, and an 'enlightened philosopher' at home rising above 'local attachments' to demand freedom for humankind. This was generous, especially given that Price had publicly criticized Fox's lifestyle and moral veracity, expressing his hope that men 'who opposed tyranny' would disdain low passions in themselves and so 'avoid insulting the virtuous part of the community by an open exhibition of vice'.[11] Though Fox is not mentioned by name in the published version of the *Discourse,* contemporary comment suggests Price had been more forthright in the actual sermon.

Burke's criticism of Price however, which was published, is a good deal more acrimonious than this. Though conceding that Price was a 'nonconforming minister of eminence', whose sermon contained 'some good moral and religious sentiments . . . not ill expressed', his ideas were nevertheless 'mixed up in a sort of porridge of various political opinions and reflections'. This pernicious porridge was a recipe cooked up by Price and all those 'who came reeking from the effect of [his] sermon . . . literary caballers and intriguing philosophers and political theologians and theological politicians, both at home and abroad'. They have 'set him up as a sort of oracle', Burke claims, 'because, with the best intention in the world he phillipizes, and chants his prophetic song in exact unison with their designs'.[12] This was not a new argument. Even at the height of the American Revolution, Price stood accused of being little more than a 'tool of Benjamin Franklin'. The accusation, however, was but one salvo in Burke's attempt to floor this 'political preacher' and 'Archpontiff of the Right's [*sic*] of Man' spouting 'a barbarous philosophy'.

Following Fox, Burke also accused Price of using his pulpit to make a 'political sermon' when 'no sound ought to be heard in the church but the healing voice of Christian charity'. The 'cause of civil liberty and civil government', Burke felt, gained 'as little as that of religion by this confusion of duties'. Then, despite a grudging nod to the value of Price's work on annuities and population studies, he goes on to portray their author as one of a new and unwelcome breed of cold, unfeeling and calculating rationalists who were ushering in a time when 'sophisters, oeconomists and calculators' would reign, and the old 'Glory of Europe' would be 'exhausted forever'. Finally, Burke makes an invidious and dangerous insinuation. By linking together Britain's Glorious Revolution of 1688 with that of republican America (though Burke does not explicitly discuss the American Revolution) and an increasingly anti-monarchical and revolutionary France, Price had revealed himself to be no more than an unpatriotic sower of sedition and a revolutionary republican. Burke bolstered this accusation by connecting Price's name to those of the regicides who had brought about the execution of Charles I. Price's *Discourse*, Burke argued, followed a strain established by Hugh Peters, who preached on behalf of the parliamentary forces and was executed for treason following the restoration of Charles II. Peters also rode in the procession that saw Charles I brought to London as a prisoner of Parliament. Burke found echoes of this in Price's *Discourse,* when he expressed thanks for having lived to see not only the rights of man better understood, but the vast kingdom of France 'spurning at slavery, and an arbitrary monarch led in triumph and surrendering himself to his subjects'. Burke also cites for good measure the sentiments expressed by George Cadogan Morgan in his published letters to Price from France; the sight of 'A king dragged in submissive triumph by his conquering subjects . . . is one of those appearances of grandeur which seldom rise in the prospect of human affairs.' All such 'leading in triumph', Burke opined, is 'a thing in its best form unmanly and irreligious' and the fact that it filled Price 'with such unhallowed transports, must shock . . . the moral taste of every well born mind'.[13]

To be publicly accused of sedition and revolutionary republicanism represented nothing new for Price. Much the same charges had been levelled against him for his support of the American revolutionaries, and now, as then, they did nothing to change his belief that Britain should emulate America and France. On 4 November 1790, just three days after publication of Burke's *Reflections*, he made this clear publicly at the London Revolution Society's next dinner in celebration of Britain's 1688 Revolution. As chairman of the occasion Price clambered onto a table, despite his rheumatics, and offered up a toast – 'to the parliament of Great Britain, may it become a national assembly'.[14]

Whether he had read Burke's *Reflections* by the time he made this toast is unclear, though it seems likely he had, for many other toasts made that day made clear reference to the *Reflections*, its author and its contents. What is certain is that Price felt a need to answer Burke's charges. His brief reply to them duly appeared in the preface, footnotes and appendix he added to a fourth edition of his *Discourse,* which was published toward the end of November 1790. Here Price makes it clear that he had not intended to suggest that the British monarchy became elective in the wake of the Glorious Revolution. Rather, it had been to show that the events of 1688 had fundamentally changed the relationship between Crown, Parliament and people. As a result of 1688 the Crown became subject to statute. The monarch was no longer an absolute ruler but one governed by the will of Parliament and, through Parliament, the people (despite their limited representation). In fact, Price argued, Burke had cited 'as authority against the right of the people to choose their own governors the very act for settling the crown on William and Mary which was an exercise of that right'.[15]

With regard to his use of the word 'misconduct' to describe the actions of James II, Price reiterates his belief that the acts of Parliament overthrowing James and enthroning William and Mary most certainly *did* establish a change in the succession as a result of the monarch's *misconduct*. Nor can it be supposed that such acts were 'intended to deprive the nation for ever of the power' to change the line of succession when circumstances dictated. Contrary to Burke's assertion that the reformers' intention in 1688 had simply been to restore the old hierarchies and constitution, 'It cannot be supposed that it was the intention of the act to subject the nation for ever to any tyrants that might happen to arise in the new line of succession.'[16]

To Burke's use of extracts from the *Discourse* and the letters written by George Cadogan Morgan from Paris, Price took great exception. Through such selective quotation he felt Burke had portrayed him as 'a barbarian delighted with blood profaning scripture, and exulting in the riot and slaughter at Versailles' when the king and queen had been forced to move to Paris during the October Days. Price rightly asserts that the letters from which Burke quoted did not relate to the events of October but to those witnessed by his nephew in Paris in July when, 'after the conquest of the Bastille, the King of France sought the protection of the National Assembly . . . by his own desire'. Price declared himself surprised 'that Mr Burke could want candour so much as to suppose that [he] had any other events in view'.[17]

In his brief reply of November 1790 Price concentrated on countering Burke's constitutional criticisms and took little notice of the often vituperative attacks on his character. Even today these are scarcely worth refuting, since Burke's portrayal of the cold, rational (yet also dangerously bloodthirsty) instigator of societal anarchy seems very far from the loving husband, and affectionate, sociable and generous friend revealed in Price's letters and diaries.

Equally unfounded is the suggestion that Price was an enemy of the Established Church. He certainly believed in the superiority of Dissenting Protestantism and was aware too that some Dissenters harboured more radical views regarding the Church than he did. His friend Joseph Priestley, for example, had preached a sermon on 5 November 1785 declaring that rational Dissenters were 'laying gunpowder, grain by grain under the old building of error and superstition', namely the Church establishment. In time a spark might ignite this gunpowder and produce 'an instantaneous explosion' so that the 'work of ages, may be overturned in a moment, and so effectually as the same foundation can never be built upon again'.[18] Price, though highly critical of the actions of the Church and its establishment could still write that 'The Church Establishment in England is one of the mildest and best sort.' None of this made him an 'enemy' of the Church of England, as Burke claimed, and though Price had good reason to dislike them for voting down many of the reforms he championed, he maintained a close friendship with a number of bishops. Moreover, his wife Sarah remained a devout Anglican throughout her life, in marked contrast to Burke's wife who abjured her Catholicism on her marriage. The one personal criticism to ring true in Burke's characterization of Price's personality is that he used his pulpit for political preaching.

What, though, of the political concerns Burke also raised in *Reflections*? Among his accusations, Burke notes that Price had not adequately defined what he meant by 'the people' to whom he willingly gave the power to amend the nation's constitution. He also argues that Price's style of rationalist philosophizing would lead to a dangerous 'Spirit of Innovation', which would lead to impetuous demands for ill-considered reforms detrimental to established institutions and hierarchies. Finally, he claims that Price and his like-minded followers desired to see French revolutionary ideas spread into Britain, and that this would unleash the mob just as surely as it had in France.

There were some grounds for Burke's concern over the lack of a definition of 'the people' in Price's *Discourse*. If 'the people' possessed the right to fundamentally change the constitution it was essential to know who 'the people' actually were and the rules within which they could legitimately act. Were the people to be considered en masse, as in a true democracy? Or were they to be seen as particular groups of people, such as freeholders or landowners; or were they elected representatives acting on behalf of the people as a whole? Burke saw in that lack of definition the possibility of an arbitrary power being created; a democracy of the people with no con-stitutional or legal limits. More disingenuously, however, he framed his argument in *Reflections* in such a way as to imply that this was precisely what Price wished to see created in Britain.

Price, however, always expressed his constitutional ideas in terms of the importance of parliamentary and representative government. In this respect, 'the people' are already defined and their actions limited by law and prece-dence; in no sense did he ever support a democracy of the people en masse. On the contrary, throughout his life Price championed a two-chamber legislature precisely to avoid the tyranny that a single chamber could exert over minorities.

Nor was Burke really justified in suggesting that Price and his rationalist ideas reflected a spirit of impetuous innovation and reform. Price had spent his adult life attempting reasoned and reasonable reform through the only institution available to him – an unreformed parliament. The more realistic question is: with the advent of revolution so near to home did Price now believe the time had come for impetuosity to overcome a lifetime's restraint? Given the fiery language of the *Discourse*, Burke can be forgiven for thinking *this* might be the case.

In April 1784 Price had told Benjamin Franklin that 'an equal represen-tation' in Britain, a major article in his reformist agenda, was 'a blessing which probably we shall never obtain till a convulsion comes which will dissolve all governments and give an opportunity for erecting a new frame'.[19] Did he believe such a moment had now arrived with the Revolution in France? Is this the reason he asked in his *Discourse* sermon 'Why are the nations of the world so patient under despotism? – Why do they crouch to tyrants and submit to be treated as if they were a herd of cattle' before reflecting on 'the favourableness of the present times to all exertions in the cause of public liberty'. The ringing closing paragraph of the sermon could, as it doubtless did to Burke, sound decidedly like a threat:

> Tremble all ye oppressors of the world! Take warning all ye supporters of slavish governments and slavish hierarchies! Call no more (absurdly and wickedly) reformation, innovation. You cannot now hold the world in darkness. Struggle no longer against increasing light and liberality. Restore to mankind their rights and consent to the correction of abuses, before they and you are destroyed together.[20]

The sentiments expressed here were clearly formulated by September 1789. 'If I mistake not', he declares in a letter to Shelburne, 'a day of Judgement is coming upon slavish governments and Hierarchies; and their abettors were they wise would prepare for it, and by yielding in time and consenting to reform gradually would endeavour to lessen the violence of their fall.'[21] All that differentiates the thoughts expressed here from those he published is the more qualified tone he adopts – were slavish government wise they would 'prepare for change' and by 'yielding in time' they might 'lessen the violence of their fall'. But Price also suggests in his letter to Shelburne that change will not come to Britain quite yet. 'Sometime or other, perhaps, Britain ashamed to be left behind, will catch the contagion and demand with an irresistible voice like that of France a correction of abuses, and particularly an equal and virtuous representation in the room of the partial and corrupt one with which it is now mocked.'[22]

One might see in such qualifications a degree of ambiguity in Price's position. On the one hand he exults in revolutionary change abroad, hopes to see it spread throughout Europe and warns those who oppose it of the imminence of their rout; on the other hand he is more circumspect about events in Britain. This ambiguity can also be seen in relation to another of Burke's criticisms, that Price was a revolutionary republican and regicide intent on 'cashiering kings'.

When replying to Burke in November 1790 Price did not directly address this charge, perhaps because it was not new. In March 1790, just as Burke composed *Reflections*, Price was busy writing to the MP William Smith rebutting the very same accusation: 'I think it very hard to be charged, as I now am, with being a Republican, after repeatedly in my publications declaring the contrary.'[23] His most recent repudiation of the charge had been in April 1787, in his sermon on *Evidence for a Future Improvement* given to supporters of New College in Hackney. 'So far am I from preferring a govern-ment purely republican, that I look upon our own constitution of government as better adapted than any other to this country, and in THEORY excellent.'[24] All he desires is to restore that constitution 'to purity and vigour by removing the defects in our representation, and establishing that independence of the three estates on one another in which its essence consists'.[25] This qualification repeats an earlier one in which the ambiguity of his position is perhaps even more evident. In *Observations on the Importance of the American Revolution*, written in 1785, Price urged the Americans not to 'produce a proud and tyrannical aristocracy' but to 'continue for ever what it is now their glory to be – a confederation of states prosperous and happy, *without lords, without bishops and without kings*' (emphasis added).[26] To these clearly republican sentiments he adds a footnote, at the word 'bishops': 'I do not mean by "bishops" any officers among Christians merely spiritual, but lords spiritual, as distinct from lords temporal, or clergymen raised to pre-eminence and invested with civil honours and authority by a state establishment. I must add that by what is here said I do not mean to express a general preference of a republican constitution of government.' Any suggestion of republicanism in Britain is quickly stifled in the next sentence: 'There is a degree of political degeneracy which unfits for such a [republican] constitution. Britain, in particular, consists too much of the high and the low, (of scum and dregs) to admit of it. Nor will it suit America should it ever become equally corrupt'.[27]

There may be a number of reasons for Price's differently expressed opinions on republicanism at home and abroad, not least the possibility that privately he did in fact favour republican over monarchical government, even in Britain. Many people at this period held more radical private sentiments than they uttered in public. Mary Wollstonecraft's most radical opinions, for example, only became known posthumously after her husband, William Godwin, printed some of her previously unpublished works. An alternative reason may simply be that he saw the subject in the light of this passage from his 1758 *Review of Morals*:

> Many practices, very warrantable and proper under one form of government, or in the first establishment of a community, or amongst a people of a particular genius, and where particular regulations and opinions prevail, may be quite wrong on another state of things, or amongst a people of other characteristics and customs.[28]

Burke was therefore right to be worried over areas of imprecision in the language Price used and the dangers that could result. But he was hardly justified in presenting those consequences as Price's actual intent.

19

The Close

His loss I greatly regretted. It was a national one – a loss to all mankind.[1]

There were those who came to believe that Burke's criticism contributed to Price's demise. In 1795 Abigail Adams wrote to her husband, Vice-President John Adams, that one of Burke's insinuations had 'killed Good Dr. Price'.[2] At home, Christopher Wyvill, in his *Defence of Dr. Price and the Reformers of England*, published in 1792, felt that Price's 'feeling mind was too much hurt by the unmerited insults of his opponent, and the injustice of the Public, and his gray hairs were soon brought with sorrow to the grave'. Among those closest to Price, however, sentiments were markedly different. According to his nephew William Morgan, 'the rancorous invectives of Mr. Burke . . . neither disturbed the tranquility of his mind, nor had any other effect on him other than convincing him that the violent passions of the author had deranged his understanding'.[3] Price's conduct in the last months of his life confirms this assertion. Replying to a letter from Joseph Priestley of 27 January 1791, he remarked:

> You endeavour very kindly to comfort me over Mr. Burke's abuse but I have not been much impressed by it. Though it could seem to entertain the worst opinion of me it may in the end do me more good than harm. One lady, an acquaintance of yours, Mrs M. calls me a fool. Such has been the fate of most persons who have aimed at mending the world and opposed the corruption of the world. The apostles were charged with turning the world upside down.[4]

In January 1791 Joseph Priestley published *Letters to the Right Honourable Edmund Burke, Occasioned by his Reflections on the Revolution in France*, a pamphlet written partly to defend Price. Priestley, though, was not the first to undertake such a defence. Among the earliest had been Mary Wollstonecraft in *A Vindication of the Rights of Men in a Letter to the Right Honourable*

Edmund Burke; Occasioned by his Reflections on the Revolution in France, published in November 1790, four weeks after Burke's *Reflections* first appeared.

Between 1784 and 1786, while in her mid-twenties, Wollstonecraft lived and taught in her own school at Newington Green and she frequently attended Price's meeting house. Her pamphlet gives us a glimpse of the man she called 'Le Sage':

> I could almost fancy that I now see this respectable old man, in his pulpit, with hands clasped, and eyes devoutly fixed, praying with all the simple energy of unaffected piety; or, when more erect inculcating the dignity of virtue, and enforcing the doctrines his life adorns; benevolence animated each feature, and persuasion attuned his accents; the preacher grew eloquent, who had only laboured to be clear; and the respect that he exhorted, seemed only the respect due to personified virtue and matured wisdom.[5]

In *A Vindication of the Rights of Men* Wollstonecraft attacked Burke for his personalized assault on so virtuous a man as Price: 'Is this the man you brand with so many opprobrious epithets? He whose private life will stand the test of the strictest enquiry – away with such unmanly sarcasms, and puerile conceits.'[6] Profoundly influenced by Price's views on morality, virtue and politics, her writing reveals the devotion his ideas could inspire in others:

> Granting for a moment Dr. Price's political opinions are utopian reveries, and that the world is not yet sufficiently civilized to adopt such a sublime system of morality they could, however, only be the reveries of a benevolent mind. Tottering on the verge of the grave, that worthy man in his whole life never dreamt of struggling for power or riches; and, if a glimpse of the glad dawn of liberty rekindled the fire of youth in his veins, you [Burke], who could not stand the fascinating glance of a great Lady's eyes, when neither virtue nor sense beamed in them, might have pardoned his unseemly transport, – if such it must be deemed.[7]

The reference to 'a great Lady's eyes' refers to a much-quoted passage in *Reflections*, in which Burke lavished praise on Marie Antoinette. Wollstonecraft's staunch defence of Price's character is followed by a detailed, almost point-by-point, refutation of Burke's principal arguments.

Though she chose to publish her pamphlet anonymously, Wollstonecraft nevertheless forwarded a copy to Price. In writing to thank her on 12 December 1790 he declared that he had 'not been surprised to find that a composition which he had heard ascribed to some of our ablest writers appears to come from Miss Wollstonecraft'. He felt 'happy in having such an advocate' and requested 'her acceptance of his gratitude for the kind and handsome manner in which she . . . mentioned him'.[8]

By far the most famous tract to oppose Burke's *Reflections* appeared at the end of February 1791. Tom Paine's *Rights of Man* reflects many of Price's ideas and hopes but takes them in a more overtly republican and revolutionary direction. Paine denounced monarchy and aristocracy. He even denied the existence of a British constitution since, being unwritten, it could not be produced for scrutiny in the way the constitutions of America or France could. Paine also noted that Burke, 'not sufficiently content with abusing the National Assembly', spent 'a great part of his work . . . abusing Dr. Price (one of the best hearted men that lives) and the two societies in England known as the Revolution and the Constitutional Societies'.[9] The bracketed sentiment suggests a personal friendship with Price, which could extend back to 1774, when Paine first made the acquaintance of Price's friend Benjamin Franklin in London. Certainly Price and Paine knew each other from 1787, the year Paine joined the Society for Constitutional Information. He also had dinner with Price in Hackney in early September 1789 and found him 'all joy and happiness at the progress of the revolution'.[10]

As a substantial pamphlet war erupted in the wake of publication of his *Discourse* Price turned to more mundane matters. Despite having given up his teaching post at New College in Hackney there were still problems to concern him there. In addition, Joseph Priestley, whom Price had just aided with 'a generous benefaction', sought an opinion on a controversial sermon he intended to give and solicited help in presenting a paper of new experiments to the Royal Society.[11] At the same time, Priestley began to receive regular updates, from various sources, on the state of Price's health for this had now truly begun to fail.

Having preached a sermon at a friend's funeral on a particularly cold day in February 1791 Price came away uttering one of his most prescient phrases. Such a service, he declared, was a 'sure way of sending the living after the dead'.[12] On 6 February he made what turned out to be the last entry in his private journal. It reveals a man committed, even in his frailty and decline, to faith in a creator and to usefulness and contribution: 'May God make whatever *remainder* of life I am to expect as easy and useful as possible. I refer myself to the disposal of that wisdom and goodness which governs all things.' His last sentence, though, shows how difficult daily life was becoming: 'I should be much happier than I am had I no letters to write. They are indeed a sad burden upon me.'[13] Having informed his congregation at the Gravel Pit chapel in Hackney of his decision to resign as their pastor, he preached his last sermon there on Sunday, 20 February.

In March he spoke at the graveside of another friend and having taken no shelter from the inclement weather quickly developed a severe fever. Ten days later he had recovered enough to ride out in a carriage for the benefit of the open air but the very next day was 'seized with a complaint in the neck of the bladder', a reappearance of the trouble he shared with Dr Franklin. This marked the onset of his last illness. Unable this time to pass the bladder stones, the pain from them assumed a severity only matched by the treatment undertaken to relieve it.

The surgical extraction of bladder stones involved the doctor making an incision in the perineum, the area between the scrotum and the anus, in order to reveal the bladder and bladder neck. Forceps were then inserted into the neck to extract the stone or stones and to root around for any remaining debris. In pre-anaesthetic times the pain induced was excruciating. Over the course of the next month Price underwent the operation 'two or three times a day' until the surgeon attended 'almost constantly' in order to provide relief. According to William Morgan, 'These dreadful agonies were borne . . . with a resignation which never uttered a sigh nor a murmur; and to the last hour of his life this good man retained the same placid and benevolent temper of mind which prevailed throughout the whole course of it.' Price, apparently, even restrained himself from groaning, saying 'he would not contract the habit'.[14]

The news that the 'dangerous' radical Dr Price was ill proved of interest to London society. Some heard of it with sorrow, and there were many callers at his Hackney home to enquire after him. Others welcomed the news as an insurance against revolution. When commenting in his journal on the death of Mirabeau, in France, on 2 April, Horace Walpole noted: 'Dr Price is dying also – fortunate omens for those who hope to die in their beds too.'[15]

Despite the severity of his illness Price did not finally take to his own bed until April, declaring as he did so 'that all was now over'. He then refused further aid from the doctor. On 18 April he lay with 'the faculties of his mind entire' from six o'clock in the afternoon until midnight when the final change came and he died a few minutes before three o'clock in the morning of 19 April 1791, aged sixty-eight. The day was the sixteenth anniversary of the shots fired at Lexington and Concord and the start of the War of Independence in America he had done so much to champion.

In the following days, between 19 and 21 April, an autopsy was performed, seemingly in Price's home in Hackney. It revealed 'his viscera' to be 'very diseased – one kidney quite gone – the other very unsound'. As Thomas Belsham noted, 'it is wonderful that he did not suffer more than he appears to have done'.[16]

Figure 23. Price's tomb in Bunhill Fields cemetery in the City of London.
Price's friend Thomas Bayes is buried nearby.

Price had requested a quiet funeral and his family dutifully planned an evening interment, a common practice at the time, in the Dissenting burial ground at Bunhill Fields in the City of London. But such was the clamour from his friends and associates for a more public affair the family were ultimately forced to agree, though they did draw the line at a proposal for the funeral cortege to proceed 'through some of the most public streets of London' for fear the event would degenerate 'into a pageant very unsuitable to the remains of the modest and humble person who was to be the subject of it'.[17]

Despite these precautions the funeral proved to be a substantial affair and one in which the London Revolution Society played a full part. Four days after Price's demise the committee of the Society, meeting at the King's Head tavern in London, resolved that 'on the melancholy Event of the Decease of so distinguished a Friend to the Rights of Mankind as the Rev. Dr. Price, every public mark of respect is due to his memory from this society and all the Friends of Freedom'. Printed handbills were then sent out correcting a previous mistake in the date of the funeral and recommending every member of the Society to wear mourning for eight days and issue hatbands of black crepe to their servants. On the day of the funeral 'proper persons' were stationed at appropriate positions in order to direct carriages coming from the City of London or the West End to their correct position in the gathering cortège which, when it finally departed for the cemetery at eleven o'clock on 26 April, was led by six horsemen 'in their proper habiliments' and comprised twenty coaches of family and friends and thirty of gentlemen mourners. On entering Bunhill Fields cemetery, through the spiked gate erected to prevent the activities of body snatchers, the pall over the coffin was borne by six of Price's fellow Dissenting ministers, among them Joseph Priestley. At one o'clock he was laid to rest in a grave already containing the remains of his beloved wife Sarah and his Uncle Samuel, who had proved so helpful to him in his early London days.[18]

In the weeks following the funeral the London Revolution Society received paeans in praise of Price from a veritably alphabetic list of the Jacobin clubs and societies of the Friends of the Constitution in France. Even the Jacobin Club in Paris is believed to have gone into mourning. To the members of these societies, Price appeared as the implacable enemy of tyranny, an apostle and defender of liberty and the great benefactor of the human race. The Society in Nantes, whose emissaries Price had helped welcome to London just a few months earlier, vowed to declare a part of their town 'le Quartier de Richard Price' and to place his bust in their meeting hall, along with a copy of France's 'Declaration of the Rights of Man' (which Price had appended to the published version of his *Discourse*).[19]

At home, many were convinced of his lasting fame. Andrew Kippis, in his graveside eulogy, expressed a belief that Price's virtues would unite him 'with the Lockes, and the Hoadlys, and the more eminent benefactors of mankind'.[20] Even those less enamoured of his views concurred. The *Gentleman's Magazine* in its lengthy obituary cited a more radical pantheon of association than Kippis: 'Whenever history shall rise above the prejudices which may for a time darken her page, and celebrate the eras when man began to open their eyes to behold their own rights' the name Richard Price would be linked to those of 'Franklin, Washington, Fayette and Paine'.[21] But this was not to be. The prejudices and condescension of history have converged to largely remove Richard Price's name from the accepted Enlightenment pantheon. For decades, he would be most commonly perceived as the unfortunate Dr Price who was bested by Edmund Burke. Even his key role linking the British revolution of 1688 and those in America and France, a major factor in Burke's criticism of him, would be usurped. In 1987, at the 250th anniversary celebrations of Tom Paine's birth at the United Nations, it was claimed that Paine, not Price, 'supplied the link between the three revolutionary movements of the epoch, in America, France and Britain'.[22]

Various factors have contributed to the forgetting of Richard Price. In the late eighteenth and early nineteenth centuries there was a growing opposition to, and eventual clamp down on, reform in Britain, largely as a result of the escalation of violence and terror during the course of the Revolution in France. Perhaps more tellingly, Burke came to be perceived as the man who had accurately predicted the direction of the Revolution and this undermined the more optimistic faith in rationalism and natural rights that Price and others had expounded.

In a surprising claim Edmund Burke once said that in writing *Reflections on the Revolution in France* he intended 'no controversy with Dr. Price or Lord Shelburne or any other of their set'. Instead, he had two different aims in mind. First, 'to set in full View the danger from their wicked principles and black hearts' by stating 'the true principles of our constitution in Church and state upon grounds opposite to theirs'; second, he wanted 'to expose [Price and his companions] to the hatred, ridicule and contempt of the whole world', as he would 'always expose such calumniators, hypocrites, sowers of sedition, and approvers of murder and all its Triumphs'.[23] In his brief reply to *Reflections* Price had effectively countered Burke's 'true principles' while choosing to ignore his more disingenuous and vituperative personal attacks. It is a measure of the success of Burke's approach that even in 1790/1 Price is already seen as the Burkean caricature – a seditious revolutionary republican bent on cashiering kings and undermining the Established Church and religion.

That is seen nowhere better than in the caricatures of Price published in 1790/1. In Gillray's 'Smelling out a Rat or The Atheistical Revolutionist Disturbed in his Midnight Calculation' (Plate 4a) we see (an equally ridiculous, large-nosed) Burke, crown and cross in hand, sniffing out a startled Price who has been busy writing a tract bearing the title 'On the benefits of anarchy, regicide, atheism . . .' On the floor, alongside his *Discourse* sermon, is another treatise 'on the ill effects of order & government on Society and on the absurdity of serving God and honouring the King'. And, lest there be any doubt as to Price's position as a potential regicide, the picture on the wall behind him is titled the 'Death of Charles the First, or the Glory of Great Britain'. In 'The Doctor Indulged with his Favourite Scene' (Plate 4b) Price kneels upon the crown of France, has a devil on his back and peers though a peephole into the boudoir of Marie Antoinette as it is ransacked by a Parisian mob. Finally, in 'Tale of a Tub. Every Man has his Price', which forms the cover to this book, Richard Price appears in a barrel of political gunpowder (a veiled reference to Swift's satire or Priestley's gunpowder sermon). The barrel pulpit rests on a book of 'Calculations' and the papers from which Price reads bear the words 'bind their kings with chains'.

These are not Price's words, of course, but those Burke used when comparing Price's *Discourse* sermon to the works of the Cromwellian Hugh Peters.

Such visual satire was (and still is) the lot of many in public life, and Gillray himself, when it suited him, was no respecter of Church and Crown. But the images certainly helped to reinforce a particular notion of Price and his legacy with a wider public. As late as 1797, doggerel reflecting the sentiments of the earlier caricatures was being published:

> Let our vot'ries then follow the glorious advice,
> In the Gunpowder Legacy left us by Price,
> Inflammable matter to place grain by grain
> And blow up the state with the torch of Tom Paine![24]

A growing hostility to reform, and to the Dissenting reformers particularly, also contributed to the changing view of Price in Britain. Public hostility to reform had been muted at the time of his death and a month later, on 28 May 1791, the Constitutional Society felt bold enough to denounce the 'indecent virulence' of Burke's attacks on the 'illustrious patriots of France'. However, these words formed part of a much longer resolution on reform that some London newspapers considered 'not safe' and so refused to print. Concern over a possible public backlash against the reformers was evident at the next London Bastille-Day celebration, held shortly after the unsuccessful royal flight to Varennes. Not only were fewer members present at the London Bastille dinner than the year before, when Price had made his speech in favour of France, but attendees were asked not to wear the French cockade and the meeting ended early.

Although the London Bastille-Day dinner passed off with no more than a few broken windows, it was a different matter in Birmingham where the home, laboratory and meeting house of Price's friend Joseph Priestley were attacked and all but destroyed. The perpetrators were a 'Church-and-king' mob, angry at Priestley's fiery sermons attacking the Established Church and his continuing support for revolutionary France. Priestley believed that had Price still been alive his house and meeting place in Hackney would have suffered the same treatment.[25]

By April 1794 the reformers' situation had deteriorated so much that Priestley felt it necessary to take his family to America. In doing so, he gave substance to Price's prescient declaration of 1773 that '*America* is the country to which most of the friends of liberty in this nation are now looking; and it may be in some future period the country to which they will all be flying.'[26] Price's own nephew, George Cadogan Morgan, also considered emigration at this time. In May the Habeas Corpus Act was suspended. William Stone, a reformist member of Price's Hackney congregation, found himself in prison; Jeremiah Joyce, an ex-student of Price's at New College, was called before the Privy Council; and Horne Tooke, Price's former collaborator, was arrested and put on trial for treason. Burke meanwhile had taken to advocating 'A general war against Jacobins and Jacobinism' as 'the only chance of saving Europe from a frightful Revolution'. In 1795 the Seditious Meetings Bill and Treasonable Practices Bill were introduced with the aim of stifling the radical reform movement. They came to be known as Pitt's 'Gagging Bills' and proved largely effective.

In great part these events were consequent upon those in France. By April 1792, just a year after Price's death, the guillotine began its work. In the same year the French monarchy would be abolished and a National Convention convened. In 1793 Louis was executed and war declared on Britain, the Dutch Republic and Spain. Tom Paine was declared an outlaw in Britain for publishing *Rights of Man*, after he escaped to France. Welcomed as a hero and already a French citizen, Paine entered into the great Convention debate on the fate of Louis XVI. Having spoken against execution he found himself arrested and by 1794 languished in the Luxembourg prison awaiting the guillotine at Robespierre's pleasure. In this year too Price's correspondent Condorcet probably poisoned himself, having been discovered in hiding by Robespierre's police. He later died in prison, another victim of the Terror.

The violence of the Terror in France would have appalled Price, not only because of its often arbitrary nature but because it was carried out in the name of virtue, one of the three guiding principles of his life. In a speech in 1794 on the principles of political morality, Robespierre addressed one of the overwhelming problems facing the Revolution, namely how to defend it against those who opposed its values and ideals and who sought to destroy it through legal, illegal or even violent means. 'If the basis of popular government in peacetime is virtue', he told the National Convention, 'its basis in a time of revolution is both virtue and terror – virtue, without which terror is disastrous, and terror, without which virtue has no power . . . Terror is merely justice, prompt, severe, and inflexible. It is therefore an emanation of virtue, and results from the application of democracy to the most pressing needs of the country.'[27]

Such declarations only fed the perception in Britain that Burke had been right. The deceitful dreams and visions of equality and natural rights peddled by the likes of Price had ended, as Burke predicted, 'in base oligarchy' – the rule of the few as epitomized in France by Robespierre and the Committee of Public Safety. The 'oppression of the minority', Burke had argued, 'will extend to far greater numbers, and will be carried on with much greater

Figure 24. Richard Price memorial railings in his birthplace,
Llangeinor, south Wales.

fury, than can almost ever be apprehended from the dominion of a single sceptre'.

Seen in this light Price's lifelong belief in reason and the concept of natural rights can seem impossibly naive. Yet, as far back as his 1758 *Review of Morals*, Price had seen that 'actions may have all the form of virtue without any of its realities'. Price had always understood that things could go wrong because he understood the frailties of human nature when under the influence of the passions. It was a crucial element of his moral philosophy, and underpinned his belief that we must continually educate ourselves and constantly question our motives and actions. It is this philosophy that underpins the kind of society he outlined in his *Discourse*.

The modern French critic, Henri Laboucheix,[28] has described the dialogue between Price and Burke as one which, in dealing with a revolutionary period:

> must be placed amongst the intellectual, social, political, and religious forces which are at the very source of British civilization. This great debate is seen finally to be a dialogue between science and law, between philosophy and literature, between reason and feeling, between the human sciences and aesthetics, between evolutionism and traditionalism, between thought and life . . . Price asks us to respect, first of all, individual liberties guided by reason. Burke asks us to respect, first of all, social life ordered by customs. In this double respect for life and for the intelligence which illuminates it, British eighteenth-century thought perhaps reveals to us the secret of true wisdom.[29]

Price's contribution to this debate is not to be seen as a simple advocacy of one side over the other. His approach is a balanced one where all discussion and debate are to be welcomed as helping foster understanding and progress. Nor can his contribution be understood in relation to the rhetoric of a single sermon or a single book. His contribution is his entire life's work and his dogged and brave championing of truth, liberty, virtue and all those rights and civil liberties we now perhaps too easily take for granted. Burke is remembered today for his prescience about the course of the French Revolution. Price is largely forgotten beyond the realms of academia. Yet, it is the natural rights and civil liberties championed by Price, rather than Burke's narrow prescriptive rights, which lie at the heart of our modern society.

Notes

Introduction: Rediscovering Richard Price

1 CC, p. 5.
2 Leslie Stephen, *History of English Thought in the Eighteenth Century* (2nd edn., 2 vols., London, 1881), I, p. 429.
3 *Travels*, p. 7.
4 Richard Price, *Four Dissertations* (3rd edn., London, 1772), p. 138n.
5 J. G. A. Pocock, 'Radical Criticisms of the Whig Order in the Age between Revolutions', in Margaret C. Jacob and James R. Jacob (eds.), *The Origins of Anglo-American Radicalism* (1984), p. 48.
6 Yong-june Park (ed.), *Slavoj Žižek, Demanding the Impossible* (paperback edn., Cambridge, 2014), rear-cover text.
7 Richard Price, 'A Discourse on the Love of our Country', in *PW*, p. 180.
8 Paul Frame and Geoffrey W. Powell, '"Our first concern as lovers of our country must be to enlighten it": Richard Price's Response to the French Revolution', in Mary-Ann Constantine and Dafydd Johnston (eds.), *'Footsteps of Liberty & Revolt': Essays on Wales and the French Revolution* (Cardiff, 2013), p. 61.

1. A Background of Dissent

1 Extract from Charles II's 'Declaration of Breda', taken from 'Constitutional Documents of the Puritan Revolution', no. 105: 'Declaration of Breda', *www.constitution.org/eng/conpur105.htm*.
2 Ibid.
3 See W. S. K. Thomas, *Stuart Wales* (Llandysul, 1988), pp. 123–4.
4 Ibid.
5 *HM*, pp. 1–3.
6 Originally a farm of 30 acres called *Ty yn y Ton*, see map in Glamorgan Archives Service, Merthyr Mawr Archive, DN/E/1/7b. Today known as Tynton, *Tyn* is a contraction of *tyddyn*, meaning homestead, smallholding, croft, (small) farm etc. The pronunciation would support this as the 'y' is short not long as it would be in *tŷ* (with thanks to Gwen Gruffudd for this information).

7   I am indebted to David Perry and John Morgan for sharing their as yet unpublished ancestral researches into the Price family tree.

8   See Richard Brinkley, 'The Library of Richard Price', *The Price-Priestley Newsletter*, 4 (1979), 6.

9   Caroline E. Williams, *A Welsh Family from the Beginning of the 18th Century* (2nd edn., London, 1893), pp. 136–7.

10 *Memoirs*, p. 5.

11 Whether Thomas Morgan knew Richard Price personally is not known, but his letter book indicates he wrote in February 1775 to Richard's stepbrother Samuel Price at 'Park near Cardiff'. Morgan also knew and corresponded with some of Price's closest friends, including Joseph Priestley whose ordination he had attended in 1763. The Thomas Morgan papers are held at the National Library of Wales: NLW 5457E, Henllan Papers, 6: A Notebook; NLW 5456A, Henllan Papers, 5: A Diary; NLW 5455A, Henllan Papers, 4: A Notebook; NLW 5453C, Henllan Papers, 2: Letter Book 1762–94.

12 See Gwyn Walters, 'Richard Price and the Carmarthen Academy', *The Price-Priestley Newsletter*, 4 (1980), 69.

13 See *CRP*, III, pp. 212–13, Ezra Stiles to Richard Price, 10 April 1789; ibid., pp. 214–17, Ezra Stiles to Richard Price, 13 April 1789; ibid., pp. 241–7, Richard Price to Ezra Stiles, 31 July 1789.

14 See *HM*, p. 8 n. 8 for the controversy surrounding the actual site of the school; also pp. 1–10 for general family history.

15 *Memoirs*, p. 6.

16 *Sermons*, p. 132.

17 *Memoirs*, p. 6.

18 Details of Rice Price's will from *HM*, pp. 9–10, and D. O. Thomas, 'Rice Price's Will', *The Price-Priestley Newsletter*, 2 (1978), 98–107.

2. A London Life

1   Emrys Jones, 'The Age of Societies', in *idem* (ed.), *The Welsh in London 1500–2000* (Cardiff, 2001), p. 81.

2   George Smeeton, *Doings in London or Day and Night Scenes of the Frauds, Frolics, Manners and Depravities of the Metropolis* (London, 1828), p. 3.

3   P. W. Clayden, *The Early Life of Samuel Rogers* (London, 1887), p. 9.

4   *Memoirs*, p. 10.

5   *HM*, p. 11.

6   *Memoirs*, p. 11.

7   See H. McLachlan, *English Education under the Test Acts* (Manchester, 1931); J. H. Overton, *History of the Church of England in the Eighteenth Century* (2 vols., London, 1878), II, p. 44.

8   *HM*, p. 11.

9   *CC*, pp. 12–13.

10 *Memoirs*, p. 10.

11 *CRP*, III, p. 201, Richard Price to the marquis of Lansdowne, 21 January 1789.
12 Giacomo Casanova, *History of my Life*, trans. W. R. Trask (paperback edn., 12 vols., Baltimore, 1997), IX, p. 251.
13 See Liza Picard, *Dr. Johnson's London* (paperback edn., London, 2003), pp. 278, 297.
14 Clayden, *Early Life of Samuel Rogers*, p. 10.
15 See plate in Picard, *Dr. Johnson's London*, p. 266.
16 For an example of such guides, see *Harris's List of Covent Garden Ladies or Man of Pleasure's Kalendar* (1771).
17 *CRP*, III, p. 147, Richard Price to Benjamin Rush, 24 September 1787.
18 Ibid., I, p. 48, Richard Price to Miss A. Burrows, 4 April 1767.
19 The contemporary slang 'a threepenny upright' probably refers to this. See Peter Ackroyd, *London: The Biography* (London, 2000), p. 374; F. A. Pottle (ed.), *Boswell's London Journal 1762–1763* (London, 1950), p. 255.
20 *CRP*, III, p. 202, Richard Price to the marquis of Lansdowne, 21 January 1789.
21 The monument's function as an observatory was short-lived due to the problem of vibration in the lenses and mirrors caused by the passing of innumerable heavy carts and wagons.
22 Ben Weinreb and C. Hibbert (eds.), *The London Encyclopedia* (London, 1983), pp. 525–6.
23 *Memoirs*, p. 22n.
24 Samuel Rogers, *Recollections of the Table-Talk of Samuel Rogers* (2nd edn., London, 1856), p. 4.
25 See John Stephens, 'Richard Price, A Sermon on Revelation 21.3', *E&D*, 12 (1993), 78–91.
26 Picard, *Dr. Johnson's London*, pp. 294–8.
27 See Clayden, *Early Life of Samuel Rogers*, p. 18.
28 Joseph Priestley, *A Discourse on Occasion of the Death of Dr. Price* (London, 1791).
29 See, for example, the letter from Richard Price to Sarah in Paul Frame, 'A Further Seven Uncollected Letters of Richard Price', *E&D*, 27 (2011), 156–8; also this volume, Fig. 19 (with thanks to Nicola Bennetts for providing this).
30 Built in 1658, and so predating the Fire of London, the row forms the oldest surviving brick terrace in London. In 2008 it was suggested that Price lived in what is now number 54. See Alex Allardyce, *The Village that Changed the World: A History of Newington Green London N16* (London, 2008), p. 20.
31 Newington Green chapel is the oldest Nonconformist place of worship still in use in London.
32 On 23 March 1781 Fanny Burney noted in her journal: 'I met a small party, consisting only of Mrs. Price, who was a *Miss Evelyn*, Miss Benson, Dr. Johnson and Mrs. Carter.' She went on to declare Mrs Price to be 'a very sensible, shrewd, lofty, and hardheaded woman'. Whether this actually refers to Sarah Price is uncertain, though her comparison of 'Mrs. Price' with 'Miss Evelyn', a character in Fanny's novel *Evelina*, is suggestive in the sense that Evelyn suffered from ill heath and spent some of her life under the care of a reverend gentleman (Arthur Villars). Only a single letter from Price to his wife has been found; see 29n above.

33 Allardyce, *Village that Changed the World*, p. 20.

34 Rogers, *Recollections of the Table-Talk*, p. 3.

35 Richard Price, *A Review of the Principal Questions and Difficulties in Morals* (London, 1758).

3. The Virtues of Virtue

1 Richard Price, 'A Review of the Principal Questions and Difficulties in Morals', in Raphael, p. 266.

2 Ibid., p. 239.

3 *Idem*, 'Dissertation 1: On Providence', in *Four Dissertations* (3rd edn., London, 1767), pp. 28–9.

4 *Idem*, 'Review of Morals', p. 292.

5 He also attempted it in a separate essay entitled *On the Being and Attributes of the Deity*. This did not appear in public until 1787, as an appendix to the third edition of his *Review of Morals*, but it had actually been written much earlier. He intended to include it in the first edition of the *Review of Morals* in 1758. See Raphael, p. 111.

6 Clarke had outlined his own thoughts on the necessity of God's existence in his Boyle lectures of 1704 and 1705; these were published as *The Beings and Attributes of God* and the *Evidences of Natural and Revealed Religion* and, later, combined into a book. Named after the Irish scientist Robert Boyle (1627–91), the Boyle lectures allowed academics to discuss, candidly, the existence of God. They were revived in February 2004 at St Mary Le Bow church in London.

7 Price, 'Review of Morals', p. 287.

8 Ibid., p. 292.

9 Ibid., pp. 290, 291n. As Price acknowledges in this note he is quoting here from the 'general Scholium' at the end of Newton's *Principia*.

10 Ibid., p. 290.

11 *Idem*, 'Dissertation IV: On the Nature of Historical Evidence and Miracles', in *Four Dissertations*, p. 436.

12 See chapter 5 for fuller details of Price first coming to know Priestley. For a detailed comparison of the two thinkers, see Jack Fruchtman, Jr., *The Apocalyptic Politics of Richard Price and Joseph Priestley: A Study in Late Eighteenth-Century English Republican Millennialism* (Philadelphia, 1983).

13 Joseph Priestley, *Disquisitions Relating to Matter and Spirit* (London, 1777).

14 *Idem, The Doctrine of Philosophical Necessity* (London, 1777).

15 *Idem, A Free Discussion of Materialism and Philosophical Necessity in a Correspondence between Dr. Price and Dr. Priestley* (London, 1778).

16 Ibid., see 'Dedication'.

17 Ibid., p. xxxvii.

18 See Robert E. Schofield, *The Enlightened Joseph Priestley, A Study of his Life and Work from 1773 to 1804* (Pennsylvania, 2004), p. 65.

19 Ibid., p. 85.

20 For a discussion of Price and his relations with David Hume in regard to this
debate, and concerning the existence of miracles (which Hume denied and Price
defended), see letters from and to David Hume in *CRP*, I, pp. 45–7; see also ibid.,
45 nn. 1–2. Also, H. S. Price, 'A Few Observations on David Hume and Richard
Price on Miracles', *E&D*, 5 (1986), 21–37; Bernard Peach, 'On What Point Did
Richard Price Convince David Hume of a Mistake? With a Note by Henri
Laboucheix', *The Price-Priestley Newsletter*, 2 (1978), 76–81.

21 Price, 'Review of Morals', p. 43.

22 Ibid., p. 20.

23 Ibid., p. 100.

24 Ibid., p. 62.

25 Ibid., p. 267.

26 Ibid., p. 142.

27 Ibid., p. 149.

28 Ibid., p. 151.

29 Ibid., p. 152.

30 Ibid., p. 153.

31 Ibid., p. 157.

32 Ibid., p. 100.

33 Ibid., pp. 100, 171–4.

34 Ibid., p. 181.

35 Schofield, *Enlightened Joseph Priestley*, p. 81.

36 Ibid., p. 80.

37 Price, 'Review of Morals', p. 181.

38 *Idem*, 'Sermon V: On the Omnipresence of God', in William Morgan (ed.), *Sermons
on Various Subjects, by the late Dr. Richard Price, D.D. F.R.S.* (London, 1816), p. 120.

39 *HM*, p. 38.

40 Richard Price, 'Sermon VII', in Morgan (ed.), *Sermons on Various Subjects*, p. 135.

41 Ibid., 'Sermon XV', pp. 281–2.

42 Ibid., 'Sermon IX', p. 165.

43 *Sermons*, p. 21.

44 *CRP*, III, p. 256, Richard Price to the marquis of Lansdowne, 9 September 1789.

45 Price, 'Review of Morals', p. 175.

46 Ibid., pp. 172–3.

47 Ibid., p. 173.

48 See Price's discussion in 'Sermon VII, Of The Christian Doctrine as Held by
Trinitarians and Calvinists', *Sermons*, pp. 119–43.

49 *Idem*, 'Sermon IV', in Morgan (ed.), *Sermons on Various Subjects*, p. 78.

50 See CC, pp. 23–4.

51 Schofield, *Enlightened Joseph Priestley*, p. 80.

52 Richard Price, *The Nature and Dignity of the Human Soul. A SERMON PREACHED
AT St. THOMAS'S, January the First, 1766. For the Benefit of the Charity-School in
Gravel-Lane* (London, 1766).

53 *Idem*, 'Britain's Happiness and the Proper Improvement of It', in *PW*, pp. 2–3.

54   Ibid., p. 3.
55   Ibid., pp. 6–7.
56   Ibid., p. 7.
57   Ibid., p. 4.
58   Ibid., p. 5.
59   Ibid., p. 10.
60   Ibid.
61   Ibid., pp. 10–11.
62   Ibid., p. 13.
63   The sermon was published as *Britain's Happiness and the Proper Improvement of It* at the end of 1759 to limited public response. No further edition appeared until July 1791, shortly after Price's death, and then in a heavily and controversially edited form.

4. The Equitable Life

1   In writing this chapter the author is particularly indebted to the work of D. O. Thomas (*HM*) and M. E. Ogborn (Ogborn).
2   *CRP*, I, pp. 125–6, Benjamin Franklin to Richard Price, 11 February 1772; ibid. p. 125n.
3   *Memoirs*, p. 25.
4   Ibid., p. 27.
5   In his *Memoirs* William Morgan mentions the invitation to be a preacher at Lewin's Mead in Bristol but, as D. O. Thomas, *HM*, p. 128n, has pointed out, no such invitation is recorded in the minute book of the Lewin's Mead meeting place for this period. Thomas concluded that if the invitation happened at all it must have been made informally.
6   See *Memoirs*, p. 21. Poor Jewry Lane (or Street) is in EC3 in London. Price's earlier position in Old Jewry is in EC2.
7   Ogborn, pp. 88–9.
8   *CRP*, I, p. 9, Richard Price to John Canton, 10 November 1763.
9   Royal Society, EC/1765/21. Price was elected as a member of the Council of the Society in 1785; see *The Times* newspaper online archive for 2 December 1785, *http://www.thetimes.co.uk/tto/archive*.
10   G. A. Barnard, 'Thomas Bayes's Essay Towards Solving a Problem in the Doctrine of Chances', *Biometrika*, XLV (1958), 293–315.
11   See Sharon Bertsch McGrayne, *The Theory That Would Not Die: How Bayes' Rule Cracked the Enigma Code, Hunted Down Russian Submarines and Emerged Triumphant from Two Centuries of Controversy* (New Haven, 2011), p. 11.
12   *ORP*, I, p. v.
13   *CRP*, I, p. 278, Richard Price to John Edwards, 22 August 1768.
14   Ibid., p. 281, Richard Price to the Equitable Life Board, 5 January 1769.
15   Ogborn, p. 91.
16   *HM*, p. 217n.
17   Ogborn, p. 91.

18 Ibid., pp. 101–2, 205. On William Morgan's retirement as actuary in 1830 his son Arthur Morgan replaced him. Arthur Morgan would remain actuary, and so continue the familial link with the Society, for a further forty years; see ibid., pp. 204–5.

19 See *ORP*, I, p. vi.

20 See *HM*, pp. 227–8, for European efforts.

21 See CC, p. 126 n. 1.

22 Peter Ackroyd, *London: The Biography* (London, 2000), p. 519, noted that a one million population was only achieved in 1800. Other sources put the figure for 1801 at 922,000; see Roy Porter, *English Society in the Eighteenth Century* (revised edn., London, 1991), p. 364.

23 See *ORP*, I, p. 377.

24 From Price's arrival in London in 1740 to his death in 1791 coal imports to London almost doubled, rising from 484,000 (1740–9) to 825,000 (1785–94) chaldrons; a chaldron being a dry weight measurement of coals (one chaldron = 85lbs). See Porter, *English Society*, p. 365.

25 *ORP*, I, pp. 351 n. (a), 377.

26 See Edmund S. Morgan, *Benjamin Franklin* (New Haven, 2002), p. 106.

27 See ORP, I, p. 375

28 See *www.medicine.ox.ac.uk/bandolier/booth/booths/risk.html*. Part of this site is dedicated to Richard Price, who 'pioneered the gathering of information on death, thus becoming at the same time a founder of epidemiology'.

29 *ORP*, I, p. 287.

30 See ibid., p. 83.

31 Ibid., p. 135.

32 *CRP*, I, pp. 101–2, Richard Price to George Walker, 3 August 1771.

33 Ibid., pp. 118–20, Richard Price to Alexander Webster, 21 October 1771.

34 *Bibliography*, p. 52.

35 *ORP*, I, pp. 181–235.

36 Ibid., p. 181.

37 See *CRP*, I, pp. 101–2, Richard Price to George Walker, 3 August 1771.

38 Ibid., pp. 96–7, Richard Price to [Mrs Montagu], 22 March 1771.

39 Ibid., pp. 114–15, Richard Price to Joseph Priestley, [between 3 and 9 October 1771].

40 See *Memoirs*, p. 39.

41 To give it its full title: *The General Body of Protestant Dissenting Ministers of the Three Denominations in and about the Cities of London and Westminster.*

42 *CRP*, I, p. 101, Richard Price to [an unidentified correspondent], 15 July 17[71].

43 It also appeared later in the *Lewes Journal* of 14 and 21 October 1771; see *HM*, pp. 140–2. See *CRP*, I, pp. 99–100, for further detail of Price's involvement with the Maseres's scheme, in particular the consultation with Price prior to publication of the scheme in *The Public Enquirer.*

44 Published as an *Account of a Scheme for Providing Relief for Protestant Dissenting Ministers of the Three Denominations in Old Age, Which was Laid before the General Body in*

London, at a Meeting Held at Dr. Williams's Library in Red-Cross Street on 20th Nov. 1771.

45 See *HM*, pp. 141–2.

46 Ibid., p. 214.

47 Andrew Kippis, *An Address, Delivered at the Interment of the Late Rev. Dr. Richard Price, on the twenty-sixth of April, 1791* (London, 1791), p. 10.

5. Science and Society

1 David Hume (1748), quoted in E. C. Mossner, 'Introduction', in *idem* (ed.), *David Hume: A Treatise of Human Nature* (Harmondsworth, 1985), p. 21.

2 Read to the Royal Society on 10 May 1770 and printed in *Philosophical Transactions*, LX (1770), 268–76.

3 The first mention of Maskelyne in Price's correspondence is in a letter to Thomas Reid written sometime in 1772/3, but there is little doubt that Price knew him earlier than this date; see *CRP*, I, p. 153.

4 Quoted in Richard Hough, *Captain James Cook: A Biography* (paperback edn., London, 1995), p. 44.

5 Quoted in *Bibliography*, p. 29.

6 Richard Price, 'A Letter from Richard Price, D.D. F.R.S. to Benjamin Franklin, LL.D. F.R.S. on the Effect of the Aberration of Light on the Time of a Transit of Venus over the Sun', *Philosophical Transactions*, LX (1770), 536–40.

7 See *CRP*, I, p. 37 n. 1.

8 Joseph Priestley, *The History and Present State of Electricity with Original Experiments* (London, 1767).

9 Ibid.

10 Franz Ulrich Theodor Aepinus, a German natural philosopher from Rostock in Saxony, published his *Tentamen Theoriae Electricitatis et Magnetisimi* in 1759 in St Petersburg, where he worked at the Imperial Academy of Sciences.

11 See *CRP*, I, p. 54 n. 2, Joseph Priestley to Richard Price, 16 January 1768.

12 Ibid., p. 116, Joseph Priestley to Richard Price, 19 October 1771; ibid., p. 121, Joseph Priestley to Richard Price, 23 November 1771.

13 See Priestley, *History and Present State of Electricity*, part VIII, section VIII, 'Experiments on Animals', pp. 653–4; ibid., part VIII, section IX, 'New Experiments in Electricity made in the Year 1766', p. 659.

14 *CRP*, I, p. 114, Richard Price to Joseph Priestley [between 3 and 19 October 1771].

15 Ibid., p. 123, Joseph Priestley to Richard Price, 5 December 1771.

16 Ibid., p. 124, Richard Price to Joseph Priestley [December 1771]. Canton's comment may be a veiled reference to the patrician arrogance that some contemporaries did not like in Banks. In the event, Banks was destined not to sail. Having been instrumental in demanding Cook add various top-heavy structures to the ship *Endeavour* (mainly in order to accommodate Banks's entourage and pets), the ship threatened to become unseaworthy. In a choice between space for Banks or seaworthiness, the needs of the ship prevailed and Banks did not sail.

[17] Ibid., p. 133, Joseph Priestley to Richard Price, 21 July 1772.

[18] Shelburne, who became marquis of Lansdowne in 1784, bought this Robert Adam designed house from lord Bute in 1768. A substantial part of it was later demolished but two rooms, in either of which Price could have been entertained at his first meeting with Shelburne, survive in America. The vast drawing room resides in the Art Museum of Philadelphia and the dining room, in which Shelburne is known to have entertained prominent Dissenters, including Price, is preserved in the New York Metropolitan Museum of Art.

[19] *CRP*, I, p. 96, Richard Price to [Mrs Montagu], 22 March 1771.

[20] During renovations at Bowood House in 1956 its original dining room was purchased by Lloyd's of London and removed to its London headquarters in 1958. There it served as the council chamber until 1986 when it was moved to the new Lloyd's building designed by Richard Rodgers where it remains today.

[21] *CRP*, I, p. 98, Richard Price to Shelburne, 22 May 1771.

[22] Ibid., p. 133, Joseph Priestley to Richard Price, 21 July 1772.

[23] Ibid., p. 145, Richard Price to Shelburne, 31 October 1772.

[24] Richard Price, *Four Dissertations* (3rd edn., London, 1767), p. 151.

[25] Ibid., pp. 150–1.

6. Freedoms Denied

[1] Richard Price, 'Evidence for a Future Period of Improvement in the State of Mankind', in *PW*, p. 171.

[2] *Idem*, 'Observations on the Nature of Civil Liberty', in *PW*, p. 30.

[3] For the background to the Wilkes affair and the nature of George III's involvement I am indebted to Peter D. G. Thomas, *John Wilkes: A Friend to Liberty* (Oxford, 1996), and Stanley Ayling, *George the Third* (London, 1972).

[4] Quoted in Thomas, *John Wilkes*, pp. 27–8.

[5] Ibid., p. 29.

[6] See Roy Porter *Enlightenment: Britain and the Creation of the Modern World* (paperback edn., London, 2001), p. 272.

[7] Like 'Satan preaching against sin' was Lord Despenser's verdict on Sandwich reading out the poem. The motto of the Hell-Fire Club was the Rabelaisian *Fay ce que voudra* (Do what you will; this seems to be the consensus for the Hell-Fire Club spelling of the motto).

[8] See Ayling, *George the Third*, p. 158.

[9] *CRP*, II, p. 219, Richard Price to Benjamin Franklin, 12 July 1784; see also ibid. n. 3.

[10] Ibid., p. 275, Richard Price to John Wilkes, 28 April 1785.

[11] See Thomas Somerville, *My Own Life and Times 1741–1814* (Edinburgh, 1861), p. 146.

[12] Richard Price, 'Additional Observations on the Nature and Value of Civil Liberty', in *PW*, pp. 98–9.

13 *Idem, Four Dissertations* (3rd edn., London, 1767), p. 366n.
14 Ibid., p. 366. Price made this argument while opposing the need for censorship to protect the Christian religion.
15 See Ayling, *George the Third*, p. 114.
16 Ibid.
17 Ibid., p. 157.
18 Ibid., p. 151.
19 *CRP*, I, pp. 268–70, Richard Price to William Adams, 11 February 1778.
20 See Ayling, *George the Third*, p. 166.
21 Ibid., p. 159. See also H. T. Dickinson, 'George III and Parliament', *Parliamentary History*, 30 (2011), 395–413.
22 *CRP*, I, p. 129, Richard Price to the earl of Chatham, 13 May 1772.
23 See ibid., p. 131 n. 1. See also G. M. Ditchfield, '"How Narrow will the Limits of this Toleration Appear?" Dissenting Petitions to Parliament, 1772–1773', *Parliamentary History*, 24 (2005), 91–106; *idem*, 'The Subscription Issue in British Parliamentary Politics, 1772–1779', *Parliamentary History*, 7 (1988), 45–80.
24 To be unwilling to prosecute.
25 See Ayling, *George the Third*, p. 189.
26 *CRP*, I, p. 131, Richard Price to the earl of Chatham, 22 May 1772.
27 Ibid., pp. 158–9, Richard Price to the earl of Chatham, 11 March 1773.
28 Richard Price, 'A Review of the Principal Questions in Morals', in Raphael, p. 180n.
29 Most Dissenters were in fact unwilling to extend toleration to Roman Catholics because they saw Catholicism as inconsistent with the safety of the state.
30 D. O. Thomas, 'Proposed Protest Concerning Dissenters: Richard Price and the Earl of Chatham', *Transactions of the Unitarian Historical Society*, XXIV, no. 2 (1976), 57.
31 Richard Price, 'Discourse on the Love of our Country', in *PW*, p. 184.
32 *CRP*, I, p. 159, Richard Price to the earl of Chatham, 11 March 1773.

7. *Price, Franklin and the Club of Honest Whigs*

1 *CRP*, I, p. 79, Richard Price to Benjamin Franklin, 3 April 1769.
2 Franklin had previously visited the city in 1724 when he stayed for two years and worked as a printer.
3 See *CRP*, I, pp. 52–3, Benjamin Franklin to Richard Price, 1 August 1767; ibid., p. 53 n. 4.
4 Not the University of Glasgow as intimated by William Morgan in his *Memoirs on Price*, p. 42.
5 The discovery in the Marischal College minute book for 7 August 1769 that Price was actually nominated for the degree by Dr Alexander Gerard, the Professor of Divinity at the College, may cast some doubt on Morgan's suggestion of a fee having been paid. See *HM*, p. 143 n. 4. Marischal was also the home of a school of 'common sense' philosophy and the 'Wise Club' (the Philosophical Society of

Aberdeen founded in 1758) that opposed, like Price, the scepticism of David Hume. Among its members was Thomas Reid a correspondent of Price. See Sophia Rosenfeld, *Common Sense, A Political History* (Cambridge, Massachusetts, 2011), pp. 56–89.

[6] See Liza Picard, *Dr. Johnson's London* (paperback edn., 2003), pp. 210–11, for a detailed description of the pool.

[7] Such names include Brynmawr, Narberth, Tredyffrin, Uwchlan, Radnor, North Wales, Upper Gwynedd, Haverford, Gladwynne, Penn Wynne and Lower Merion. Some of these names are younger than the eighteenth century in origin but Bala Cynwyd is believed to have begun life as two settlements, Bala and Cynwyd, founded by Welsh Quakers from north Wales in 1682. See also Charles H. Browning, *Welsh Settlement of Pensylvania* [*sic*] (Philadelphia, 1912).

[8] W. Macdonald (ed.), *The Autobiography of Benjamin Franklin* (London, n.d.), pp. 47–8.

[9] Full details of these publications can be found in C. William Miller, *Benjamin Franklin's Philadelphia Printing 1728–1766: A Descriptive Bibliography* (Philadelphia, 1974), pp. 10–13, and in William Williams, 'More About the First Three Welsh Books Printed in America', *National Library of Wales Journal*, III, (1943–4), 19–22.

[10] See Lawrence Henry Gipson, *Lewis Evans* (Philadelphia, 1939), pp. 1–14.

[11] See John Adams, 'Novanglus; or, A History of the Dispute with America, from its Origin, in 1754, to the Present Time', in C. Bradley Thompson (ed.), *The Revolutionary Writings of John Adams* (Indianapolis, 2000), pp. 246–54. For Franklin's references to Wales and the American situation, see, for example, papers at *www.franklinpapers.org*: 'Notes on Parliamentary Precedents (call no. 1232a)', 'The Colonists Advocate II (1714a)' and 'Marginalia (17380a)'.

[12] I am indebted to Dr Peter Davies for the information regarding Price's possible membership of the Masons. Recent work on the Price family tree by John Morgan and David Perry (personal communication) has shown, however, that there is also a surgeon named Richard Price (1736–93) who is descended from Price's aunt, Jennet. It is therefore possible that this surgeon is the Price indicated in the Masons' documents.

[13] Jasper Ridley, *The Freemasons* (paperback edn., London, 2000), p. 93. Ridley, pp. 77–9, also records that John Wilkes became a Freemason at the time of his imprisonment in the King's Bench prison, but not without considerable controversy.

[14] Besides swim flippers Franklin is also credited with the invention of, among other things, the lightning conductor, bifocal spectacles and the catheter – the latter developed for use in his own treatment.

[15] *CRP*, I, p. 38, Joseph Priestley to Richard Price, 8 March 1766.

[16] 7, Craven Street (alongside Charing Cross station), one of the two houses in the street in which Franklin lived, was opened to the public as The Franklin House Museum on 17 January 2006 in commemoration of the tercentenary of Franklin's birth.

[17] Peter Ackroyd, *London: The Biography* (London, 2000), p. 360, notes the seventeenth-century diarist Samuel Pepys as being the first person to use the word 'clubbing'.

18   Ibid., p. 361.
19   See CC, p. 154.
20   See J. Dybikowski, *On Burning Ground: An Examination of the Ideas, Projects and Life of David Williams* (Oxford, 1993), pp. 49–60.
21   Ibid., for discussion of relationship to Price and his works (e.g. pp. 166–75, 226–7) and to France (e.g. pp. 194–215).
22   Ben Weinreb and C. Hibbert (eds.), *The London Encyclopedia* (London, 1983), p. 471.
23   Possibly including Franklin's physician and friend Dr John Fothergill.
24   James Boswell, in Frank Brady and Frederick A. Pottle (eds.), *Boswell in Search of a Wife 1766–1769* (London, 1957), pp. 318–19.
25   See P. W. Clayden, *The Early Life of Samuel Rogers* (London, 1887), p. 10.
26   Burgh, a teacher and notable political philosopher, was also Price's neighbour at Newington Green. He published *The Dignity of Human Nature* in 1754 and *Political Disquisitions* in 1774–5 (3 vols.).
27   See Verner W. Crane, 'The Club of Honest Whigs: Friends of Science and Liberty', *The William and Mary Quarterly*, 3rd series, XXIII, no. 2 (1966), 210–33.
28   Macdonald (ed.), *Autobiography of Benjamin Franklin*, p. 54.
29   See CC, p. 55.
30   Macdonald (ed.), *Autobiography of Benjamin Franklin*, p. 52.
31   Thomas Paine, 'The Age of Reason', in Eric Foner (ed.), *Thomas Paine, Collected Writings* (New York, 1995), p. 666.
32   Ibid., pp. 686–7.
33   Historians argue over the exact date of the beginnings of the Industrial Revolution but changes were underway in British society by the mid-eighteenth century, including Abraham Derby's first use of coke in smelting (1709), the innovations that resulted from James Hargreaves's spinning jenny of 1763 and the improvement of Thomas Newcomen's steam engines by James Watt in 1765.
34   Thomas Paine, *The Age of Reason, Part III. Appendix – My Private Thoughts on a Future State* (London, 1818), p. 55.
35   Dybikowski, *On Burning Ground*, p. 51.
36   Macdonald (ed.), *Autobiography of Benjamin Franklin*, p. 52
37   Ibid., p. 81.
38   *CRP*, III, p. 299, Richard Price to Benjamin Franklin, *c.*30 May 1790.
39   Macdonald (ed.), *Autobiography of Benjamin Franklin*, p. 73.
40   Edmund S. Morgan, *Benjamin Franklin* (New Haven, 2002), p. 21.
41   Macdonald (ed.), *Autobiography of Benjamin Franklin*, p. 73.
42   Quoted in Crane, 'Club of Honest Whigs', 210–33.

8. On a Perilous Edge

1   *CRP*, I, p. 187, Richard Price to the earl of Chatham, 9 February 1775.
2   See Peter D. G. Thomas, *Revolution in America: Britain & the Colonies 1763–1776* (Cardiff, 1992), pp. 11–12.

3   Ibid., pp. 12–14.
4   Ibid., pp. 69–70.
5   The letters were published in Philadelphia in 1768 as *Letters from a Farmer in Pennsylvania to the Inhabitants of the British Colonies.*
6   See Thomas, *Revolution in America*, pp. 70–1.
7   Hancock was destined to be the first to sign the Declaration of Independence in 1776 and he did so in a signature large enough to ensure that King George might see and read it.
8   *CRP*, I, p. 77, Richard Price to Benjamin Franklin, 3 April 1769; ibid. n. 11.
9   Ibid., p. 151, Henry Marchant to Richard Price, 21 November 1772.
10 Ibid., p. 164, Richard Price to Henry Marchant, 2 November 1773.
11 Ibid., p. 170, Charles Chauncy to Richard Price, 30 May 1774.
12 Ibid., p. 172, Charles Chauncy to Richard Price, 18 July 1774.
13 The Administration of Justice Act allowed government officials in America who were accused of capital crimes to be sent to a different state or back to Britain for trial. Many colonists felt this gave British troops a licence to kill them without fear of punishment and unsurprisingly they dubbed it 'the Murder Act'. The Massachusetts Government Act placed local government in the hands of the governor, a policy that undermined completely the colonies' own charter and colonial assembly.
14 *CRP*, I, pp. 175–6, John Winthrop to Richard Price, 20 September 1774.
15 Ibid., p. 178 n. 1, Richard Price to Josiah Quincy, junior, 9 December 1774.
16 Ibid., p. 199, Ezra Stiles to Richard Price, 10 April 1775.
17 Ibid., p. 89, Charles Chauncy to Richard Price, 22 March 1770.
18 Ibid., pp. 165–6, Richard Price to Ezra Stiles, 2 November 1773.
19 Ibid., p. 181, Richard Price to the earl of Shelburne, 29 December 1774.
20 Ibid., pp. 182–3, Charles Chauncy to Richard Price, 10 January 1775.
21 Ibid., pp. 186–7, Richard Price to the earl of Chatham, 9 February 1775.
22 Price was wrong in this; North's administration, which won the election in October 1774, would go on, even with a reduced majority, until 1782.
23 *CRP*, I, pp. 188–91, Richard Price to Charles Chauncy, 25 February 1775.
24 Ibid., p. 189.
25 Ibid., p. 191.
26 Ibid., p. 201, John Winthrop to Richard Price, 10 April 1775.
27 Ibid., p. 202.
28 Ibid., p. 207, Richard Price to Josiah Quincy, junior, April or May 1775.
29 Ibid., p. 208, John Winthrop to Richard Price, 6 June 1775.
30 Ibid., pp. 209–10.
31 Ibid., pp. 211–12. Winthrop's postscript is dated 30 June 1775.
32 Ibid., p. 212.
33 Ibid., p. 222, Charles Chauncy to Richard Price, 22 July 1775.
34 Ibid.
35 Ibid., p. 223.
36 Ibid., p. 231, the earl of Shelburne to Richard Price, 15 October 1775.
37 Ibid., p. 232, Richard Price to [James Bowdoin], [October 1775].

9. Revolution in America

1 Richard Price, 'Observations on the Nature of Civil Liberty', in *PW*, p. 27.
2 See Ian Davidson, *Voltaire in Exile* (London 2004), p. 70 (as translated by Davidson).
3 See CC, p. 76.
4 Ibid., p. 77.
5 Ibid.
6 Price, 'Observations on the Nature of Civil Liberty', p. 58.
7 See CC, p. 77.
8 *CRP*, I, p. 248, Richard Price to William Adams, 14 August 1776.
9 See *Bibliography*, pp. 57–76, for all known editions.
10 *CRP*, I, p. 248, Richard Price to William Adams, 14 August 1776.
11 Price, 'Observations on the Nature of Civil Liberty', p. 20.
12 After an initial short collection of *Fragments* published in 1760, Macpherson's 'translations' of Scots Gaelic verse owed increasingly more to his own imagination than to his sources; a fierce and long-lived debate on their authenticity polarized opinion in the last quarter of the eighteenth century. See Fiona Stafford, *The Sublime Savage: A Study of James Macpherson and the Poems of Ossian* (Edinburgh, 1988).
13 Wesley's *Some Observations on Liberty; Occasioned by a Late Tract* was also published in 1776.
14 *CRP*, I, p. 246, Richard Price to [John Winthrop], 14 May 1776.
15 Ibid., pp. 248–9, Richard Price to William Adams, 14 August 1776.
16 Ibid., p. 247, Richard Price to [Jon Winthrop], 14 May 1776.
17 P. W. Clayden, *The Early Life of Samuel Rogers* (London, 1887), p. 33.
18 See Roland Thomas, *Richard Price: Philosopher and Apostle of Liberty* (London, 1924), p. 69.
19 See *CRP*, I, p. 243 n. 1.
20 Thomas, *Richard Price*, p. 69; Clayden, *Early Life of Samuel Rogers*, p. 33.
21 Price, 'Observations on the Nature of Civil Liberty', p. 23.
22 Ibid., p. 22.
23 Ibid., p. 23.
24 Ibid., pp. 23–4.
25 Ibid., p. 24.
26 *CRP*, II, p. 189, Richard Price to Lieutenant Colonel Sharman, 7 August 1783.
27 Richard Price, 'Review of Principal Questions in Morals', in Raphael, p. 261.
28 *Idem*, 'Observations on the Nature of Civil Liberty', pp. 28–9.
29 Ibid., p. 24.
30 Ibid., p. 25.
31 Ibid., p. 33.
32 Ibid., p. 30.
33 Ibid., p. 28.
34 Ibid., p. 66.
35 Ibid., p. 37.

36 Ibid., p. 38.
37 Ibid., p. 39.
38 Ibid.
39 Ibid., p. 40.
40 Price, 'Review of Principal Questions in Morals', p. 157.
41 *Idem*, 'Observations on the Nature of Civil Liberty', p. 68.
42 Ibid., p. 69.
43 Richard Ketchum, *The Winter Soldiers: George Washington and the Way to Independence* (London, 1973), p. 7.
44 Ibid.
45 Merrill D. Peterson (ed.), *Thomas Jefferson: Writings* (New York, 1984), p. 13.
46 CC, p. 79.
47 Ketchum, *Winter Soldiers*, p. 18.
48 Jefferson purchased a copy of Price's *Observations* prior to 29 July 1776. See P. H. Smith (ed.), *Letters of Delegates to Congress, 1774–1789* (25 vols., Washington D.C., 1976–2000), IV, p. 562, Thomas Jefferson to Richard Henry Lee, 29 July 1776.
49 See *Bibliography*, p. 71.
50 Smith (ed.), *Letters of Delegates to Congress*, IV, p. 415, John Adams to Samuel Chase, 9 July 1776.
51 Henri Laboucheix, *Richard Price as Moral Philosopher and Political Theorist*, trans. Sylvia and David Raphael (Oxford 1982), p. 107.
52 David McCullough, *John Adams* (London, 2001), p. 97. See also Ketchum, *Winter Soldiers*, p. 5.
53 Thomas Paine, *Common Sense* (London, 1986), pp. 65–7.
54 See Ketchum, *Winter Soldiers*, p. 12.

10. Reaction at Home and Abroad

1   *CRP*, I, p. 259, Richard Price to John Winthrop, 15 June 1777.
2   Ibid., p. 249, Richard Price to William Adams, 14 August 1776.
3   John Shebbeare, *An Essay on the Origin, Progress and Establishment of National Society* (London, 1776).
4   Richard Price, 'Observations on the Nature of Civil Liberty', in *PW*, p. 29.
5   *Idem*, 'Additional Observations on the Nature of Civil Liberty', in *PW*, p. 80.
6   Ibid., pp. 80–1.
7   *Idem*, 'Two Tracts, General Introduction', in *PW*, p. 16.
8   *Idem*, 'Observations on the Nature of Civil Liberty', p. 24.
9   *Idem*, 'Two Tracts, General Introduction', p. 17.
10 Ibid., pp. 17–18.
11 Ibid., p. 15.
12 CC, p. 86.
13 Edmund Burke, 'Speech on American Taxation', in E. J. Payne, *Selected Works* (4 vols., Oxford, 1922), I, p. 154.

14 Ibid., pp. 156–7.
15 *CRP*, I, p. 251, Richard Price to John Cartwright, 27 November 1776.
16 Ibid., p. 252, Richard Price to William Adams, 20 February 1777.
17 Ibid., pp. 258–9, Richard Price to John Winthrop, 15 June 1777.
18 Ibid., pp. 253–5, Arthur Lee to Richard Price, 20 April 1777.
19 Ibid., pp. 258–9, Richard Price to John Winthrop, 15 June 1777.
20 Ibid., II, pp. 29–30, Benjamin Franklin, Arthur Lee and John Adams to Richard Price, 7 December 1778.
21 Ibid., p. 31, Arthur Lee to Richard Price, 28 December 1778. See also CC, p. 88.
22 *www.franklinpapers.org*, no. 626098 = 019–416b, Benjamin Franklin to William Franklin, 2 December 1772; *CRP*, I, p. 142, Richard Price to Benjamin Franklin, 30 September 1772; ibid. n. 17.
23 See David McCullough, *John Adams* (London, 2001), p. 219.
24 *CRP*, II, pp. 34–5, Richard Price to Benjamin Franklin, Arthur Lee and John Adams, 18 January 1779.
25 Ibid., p. 35, Richard Price to Arthur Lee, 18 January 1779.
26 For details of the payments made by France to America, see J. A. Leo Lemay (ed.), *Franklin Writings* (New York, 1987), p. 1490; Stacy Schiff, *Benjamin Franklin and the Birth of America* (paperback edn., London, 2006), p. 5.
27 See *Gentleman's Magazine*, 48 (1778), 103.
28 *CRP*, I, p. 236, the earl of Shelburne to Richard Price, December 1775.
29 Ibid., p. 235, Richard Price to Charles Chauncy, December 1775(?). See also ibid., nn. 4 and 5.
30 Richard Price, *A Fast Sermon Delivered to a Congregation of Protestant Dissenters, at Hackney, on 10th February Last* (London, 1779). See *CRP*, II, p. 42 n. 1, for discussion.
31 Richard Price, 'A Fast Sermon' (1781), in *PW*, p. 114.
32 Quoted in *Bibliography*, p. 110, with reference to the *Monthly Review*, LXIV, 315–16 (1781).
33 *www.franklinpapers.org*, no. 627429 = 023–241b, Benjamin Vaughan to Benjamin Franklin, 27 January 1777.
34 *CRP*, I, p. 181, Charles Chauncy to Richard Price, 10 January 1775.
35 Ibid., p. 234, Richard Price to Charles Chauncy, [12 December 1775].
36 Ibid.: 'Yesterday I received an anonymous letter dated Philadelphia September 12th. It contains a chronicle of facts many of them important and interesting . . .'
37 See CC, p. 92; Caroline E. Williams, *A Welsh Family from the Beginning of the 18th Century* (2nd edn., London, 1893), p. 57; *CRP*, II, p. 86, Richard Price to the earl of Shelburne, 4 December 1780.
38 See CC, p. 93.
39 *CRP*, II, p. 37, Richard Price to Baron J. D. van der Capellen, 25 January 1779.
40 Ibid., p. 38.
41 Ibid., p. 37.

42 See N. A. M. Rodger, *The Command of the Ocean* (paperback edn., London, 2005), p. 348.
43 *CRP*, II, p. 85, Richard Price to the earl of Shelburne, 4 December 1780.
44 See ibid., p. 85, Benjamin Franklin to The Committee for Foreign Affairs, Passy, 26 May 1779; ibid., n. 1.
45 Ibid., p. 85, Richard Price to the earl of Shelburne, 4 December 1780.
46 Peter D. G. Thomas, *John Wilkes: A Friend to Liberty* (Oxford, 1996), p. 174.
47 Ibid.
48 *CRP*, II, p. 53, Richard Price to Benjamin Franklin, 14 October 1779.
49 Ibid., p. 38, Richard Price to Baron J. D. van der Capellen, 25 January 1779.
50 Price, *A Fast Sermon* (1779).
51 *CRP*, II, p. 39 n. 2, Charles Chauncy to Richard Price, 20 May 1779.
52 Ibid., p. 80, Richard Price to John Temple, 5 October 1780.
53 A. Francis Steuart (ed.), *The Last Journals of Horace Walpole during the Reign of George III, from 1771–1783 with Notes by Dr. Doran* (2 vols., London, 1910), II, pp. 337–8, 340.
54 *CRP*, II, p. 86, Richard Price to John Temple, 8 December 1780.
55 Ibid., p. 159, Richard Price to the earl of Shelburne, 14 December 1782.
56 See Charles Coleman Sellers, *Patience Wright, American Artist and Spy in George III's London* (Connecticut, 1976).
57 Others suggest he was buried upside down in emulation of his namesake St Peter.

11. Reform and Contribution at Home

1 *CRP*, II, p. 65, Richard Price to lord Monboddo, 2 to 12 August 1780.
2 Richard Price, *A Sermon Delivered to a Congregation of Protestant Dissenters, at Hackney* (London, 1779).
3 *CRP*, II, p. 55, Richard Price to Baron J. D. van der Capellen, 26 October 1779.
4 *HM*, p. 286.
5 See CC, p. 132.
6 *CRP*, II, p. 82, Richard Price to the earl of Shelburne, 16 October 1780.
7 See CC, p. 133.
8 *CRP*, II, p. 116, Richard Price to the earl of Shelburne, 26 March 1782.
9 Ibid., pp. 116–17.
10 Ibid., p. 117. See also *HM*, pp. 286–7.
11 *CRP*, II, p. 158, Richard Price to Christopher Wyvill, 12 December 1782.
12 See John Stephens, 'Samuel Chandler and the Regium Donum', *E&D*, 15 (1996), 57–70.
13 See *Memoirs*, p. 36. Also *CRP*, II, p. 179, Richard Price to the earl of Shelburne, 18 April 1783, for evidence of Price's resolve 'to have nothing to do with' the payment.
14 *CRP*, II, p. 60, Richard Price to David Hartley the Younger, 30 May 1780.

15 Ibid., p. 124, Richard Price to Benjamin Franklin, 20 May 1782.
16 Ibid., p. 131, Richard Price to the earl of Shelburne, 18 July 1782.
17 D. O. Thomas, 'Richard Price and the Population Controversy', *The Price-Priestley Newsletter*, 4 (1980), 46.
18 See ibid., 55.
19 See ibid.
20 For this account of Price's population controversy I am particularly indebted to Dean Peterson, 'The Origins of Malthus's Data on Population: The Political and Religious Biases in the American Sources', *Journal of the History of Economic Thought*, 19 (1997), 114–26, and to Thomas, 'Richard Price and the Population Controversy'.
21 See Ogborn, pp. 108–10.
22 Ibid., pp. 111–12.

12. Peace with America

1 *CRP*, II, p. 177, Richard Price to Benjamin Franklin, 10 March 1783.
2 See Stacy Schiff, *Benjamin Franklin and the Birth of America* (paperback edn., London, 2006), pp. 289–90.
3 Ibid., pp. 301–2.
4 *CRP*, II, p. 137, Henry Laurens to Richard Price, 31 August 1782.
5 Schiff, *Franklin and Birth of America*, pp. 303–8.
6 *CRP*, II, pp. 149–51, Richard Price to Benjamin Franklin, 18 November 1782.
7 Ibid., I, pp. 273–5, Richard Price to the earl of Shelburne, 21 March 1778.
8 Ibid., II, p. 150, Richard Price to Benjamin Franklin, 18 November 1782.
9 Ibid., pp. 155–6, Richard Price to the earl of Shelburne, 24 November 1782.
10 Quoted in Stanley Ayling, *George the Third* (London, 1972), p. 295.
11 Schiff, *Franklin and Birth of America*, p. 312.
12 Ibid., pp. 313–18.
13 *CRP*, II, p. 169, Richard Price to the earl of Shelburne, 20 January 1783.
14 Ibid., p. 150, Richard Price to Benjamin Franklin, 18 November 1782.
15 Ibid., p. 173, Richard Price to Francis Baring, 14 February 1783.
16 Ibid., p. 175, Richard Price to the earl of Shelburne, 15 February 1783.
17 Ibid., pp. 175–6, Richard Price to the earl of Shelburne, 24 February 1783.
18 Ibid., p. 177, Richard Price to Benjamin Franklin, 10 March 1783.
19 Ibid., p. 163, Richard Price to Benjamin Rush, 1 January 1783.
20 Ibid., p. 128, Benjamin Franklin to Richard Price, 13 June 1782. Price was also elected to the American Philosophical Society in 1785.
21 Ibid., p. 193, Benjamin Franklin to Richard Price, 16 September 1783.
22 Ibid.
23 Ibid., p. 214, Richard Price to Benjamin Franklin, 6 April 1784.
24 Ibid., p. 162, Richard Price to Benjamin Rush, 1 January 1783.

13. Advising Ireland, Scotland and America

1 Rémy Duthille, 'Thirteen Uncollected Letters of Richard Price', *E&D*, 27 (2011), 104, Richard Price to Thomas McGrugar, 27 January 1784.
2 *CRP*, II, p. 55, Richard Price to Baron J. D. van der Capellen, 26 October 1779.
3 Ibid., p. 117, Richard Price to the earl of Shelburne, 26 March 1782. For the Irish context, see David Lammey, 'The Growth of the "Patriot Opposition" in Ireland during the 1770s', *Parliamentary History*, 7 (1988), 257–81.
4 *CRP*, II, p. 188, Richard Price to Lieutenant Colonel Sharman, 7 August 1783.
5 Ibid.
6 Ibid., p. 192, 'A: Price's Appendix', *To the Associated Volunteers of Ireland*.
7 Ibid., p. 189, Richard Price to Lieutenant Colonel Sharman, 7 August 1783.
8 Ibid., p. 190.
9 Ibid., p. 191.
10 Ibid., p. 190.
11 Ibid., pp. 192, 'A: Price's Appendix', *To the Associated Volunteers of Ireland*.
12 Ibid., p. 207, Richard Price to the earl of Shelburne, 30 December 1783.
13 Duthille, 'Thirteen Uncollected Letters of Richard Price', 107.
14 *CRP*, II, p. 199, Richard Price to Henry Marchant, 6 October 1783.
15 Quoted in Stacy Schiff, *Benjamin Franklin and Birth of America* (paperback edn., London, 2006), p. 341.
16 See Richard Price, 'Two Tracts, General Introduction', in *PW*, p. 19 n. 1.
17 *CRP*, II, pp. 12–13, A. Turgot to Richard Price, 22 March 1778.
18 Ibid., p. 36, Richard Price to Arthur Lee, 18 January 1779.
19 Ibid., p. 17, A. Turgot to Richard Price, 22 March 1778.
20 Ibid., p. 215, Richard Price to Benjamin Franklin, 6 April 1784.
21 Ibid., p. 18, A. Turgot to Richard Price, 22 March 1778.
22 Ibid., p. 162, Richard Price to Benjamin Rush, 1 January 1783.
23 Ibid., p. 186, Richard Price to Benjamin Rush, 26 June 1783.
24 Ibid., p. 215, Richard Price to Benjamin Franklin, 6 April 1784.
25 Richard Price, 'Observations on the Importance of the American Revolution', in *PW*, pp. 117–18.
26 Ibid., p. 119.
27 Ibid., p. 118.
28 *CRP*, II, p. 294, Richard Price to Benjamin Rush, 22 July 1785.
29 Price, 'Observations on the Importance of the American Revolution', p. 118.
30 Ibid., pp. 122–3.
31 Ibid., p. 123.
32 Ibid., p. 125.
33 Ibid., p. 128.
34 Ibid., p. 131.
35 Ibid., p. 132.
36 Ibid., p. 139.
37 Ibid., pp. 137–8.

38 Ibid., pp. 144–5.
39 Ibid., p. 145.
40 Ibid.
41 Ibid., p. 146.
42 *CRP*, II, p. 321, William Hazlitt to Richard Price, 15 November 1785.
43 Schiff, *Franklin and the Birth of America*, pp. 355–7.
44 William Howard Adams, *The Paris Years of Thomas Jefferson* (New Haven, 1997), p. 148.
45 Price, 'Observations on the Importance of the American Revolution', p. 147.
46 *CRP*, II, p. 221, Richard Price to Samuel Mather, 22 July 1784.
47 Price, 'Observations on the Importance of the American Revolution', p. 148.
48 Ibid.
49 Adams, *Paris Years of Thomas Jefferson*, p. 175.
50 See Paul Frame, 'A Further Seven Uncollected Letters of Richard Price', *E&D*, 27 (2011), 143–60.
51 Gary B. Nash, 'Franklin and Slavery', *Proceedings of the American Philosophical Society*, 150, part 4 (2006), 618–35.
52 Price, 'Observations on the Importance of the American Revolution', p. 150.
53 *CRP*, II, p. 230, Richard Price to the earl of Shelburne, October 1784.
54 Ibid., pp. 324–5, George Washington to Richard Price, November 1785. See also ibid., p. 271, Richard Price to George Washington [March 1785].
55 Edmund C. Burnett (ed.), *Letters of Members of the Continental Congress* (8 vols., Washington, 1921– 36), VIII, p. 174, cited in CC, p. 111.
56 *CRP*, II, p. 304, John Wheelock to Richard Price, 13 August 1785; ibid. n. 3.
57 Ibid., p. 261, Thomas Jefferson to Richard Price, 1 February 1785.
58 See CC, p. 112.
59 *CRP*, II, pp. 320–1, William Hazlitt to Richard Price, 15 November 1785.
60 Ibid., p. 263, Henry Laurens to Richard Price, 1 February 1785.
61 For full discussion, see Norman S. Poser, *Lord Mansfield, Justice in the Age of Reason* (Montreal, 2013), pp. 292–300.
62 *CRP*, II, p. 290, Richard Price to Thomas Jefferson, 2 July 1785.
63 Ibid.
64 Ibid., p. 298, Thomas Jefferson to Richard Price, 7 August 1785. The first American census in 1790 revealed that there were almost 700,000 Negro slaves in America and that over 90% were in the Chesapeake area and to the south. See Joseph J. Ellis, *Founding Brothers: The Revolutionary Generation* (New York, 2002), p. 102.
65 *CRP*, II, pp. 264–5, Henry Laurens to Richard Price, 1 February 1785.

14. Pitt and the Sinking Fund

1 *CRP*, II, p. 331, Richard Price to William Pitt, 9 January 1786.
2 Ibid., p. 133, Richard Price to the earl of Shelburne, 6 August 1782.
3 Ibid., p. 157, Richard Price to the earl of Shelburne, 28 November 1782.

4 Ibid., p. 157 n. 1.

5 Ibid., p. 165, Richard Price to the earl of Shelburne, 6 January 1783.

6 Ibid., p. 168, Richard Price to the earl of Shelburne, 20 January 1783.

7 Ibid., pp. 216–17, Richard Price to the earl of Shelburne, 8 May 1784.

8 Ibid., p. 277, Richard Price to the marquis of Lansdowne, 6 May 1785. Note: Shelburne became marquis of Lansdowne in 1784 but, to avoid confusion, 'Shelburne' has been used throughout the main text of the current work.

9 Ibid., p. 279, Richard Price to the marquis of Lansdowne, 2 June 1785.

10 Ibid., pp. 226–7, Benjamin Franklin to Richard Price, 13 September 1784.

11 Ibid., p. 240, Richard Price to Benjamin Franklin, 21 October 1784.

12 Ibid., p. 230, Richard Price to the earl of Shelburne, [October 1784].

13 Ibid., pp. 240–1, Richard Price to Benjamin Franklin, 21 October 1784. See also ibid., p. 241 n. 3.

14 Ibid., p. 277, Richard Price to the marquis of Lansdowne, 6 May 1785.

15 Ibid., p. 324, Richard Price to the marquis of Lansdowne, 29 November 1785.

16 Ibid., p. 330, William Pitt to Richard Price, 8 January 1786.

17 Ibid., p. 334, William Pitt to Richard Price, 15 January 1786.

18 See CC, p. 145; also ibid., pp. 142–51.

19 See William Hague, *William Pitt the Younger* (paperback edn., London, 2005), p. 226; also ibid., pp. 223–7.

20 See *HM*, pp. 234–59, for a very detailed survey of the sinking fund issue.

21 *CRP*, III, p. 48, Richard Price to the marquis of Lansdowne, 26 July 1786.

22 *HM*, p. 256.

23 Ibid., p. 259; also ibid., pp. 256–9, for an account of the funds problems and their relation to Price.

24 See, for example, *CRP*, II, pp. 65–8, 87–90, 99–101, 106–8, 194–5.

25 See *Bibliography*, pp. 128–9.

26 Ibid., pp. 133–4.

27 See *Philosophical Transactions*, LXXVI (1786), 349–64.

28 See *Bibliography*, pp. 130–1.

29 *CRP*, II, pp. 256–7, Richard Price to Christopher Wyvill, 6 January 1785.

30 See ibid., III, pp. 45–6, Richard Price to Sylvanus Urban, editor of the *Gentleman's Magazine*, 26 July 1786; ibid. n. 1.

15. The Watershed Years (1786–8)

1 6 January 1788 in 'Journal', 383.

2 See *CRP*, II, p. 200, Richard Price to Henry Marchant, 6 October 1783; also ibid., p. 182.

3 *Memoirs*, pp. 116–17.

4 *CRP*, II, p. 230, Richard Price to the earl of Shelburne, October 1784.

5 Ibid., III, p. 48, Richard Price to the marquis of Lansdowne, 26 July 1786.

6 Ibid., p. 59, Richard Price to the marquis of Lansdowne, 20 September 1786.

7   Ibid., p. 60, the marquis of Lansdowne to Richard Price, 21 September 1786.
8   Ibid., p. 64, the marquis of Lansdowne to Richard Price, 29 September 1786.
9   Ibid., pp. 65–6, Richard Price to the marquis of Lansdowne, 2 October 1786.
10 Ibid., p. 63, the marquis of Lansdowne to Richard Price, 29 September 1786.
11 Ibid., p. 73, Joseph Priestley to Richard Price, 23 October 1786.
12 Ibid., pp. 67–9, Richard Price to the marquis of Lansdowne, 9 October 1786.
13 27 May 1787 in 'Journal', 378.
14 *CRP*, III, p. 256, Richard Price to the marquis of Lansdowne, 9 September 1789.
15 4 May 1788 in 'Journal', 384; ibid. n. 71.
16 See *http://www.jasnaeastpa.org/agm.html*, Jane Austen to Martha Lloyd, 2 September
    1814.
17 Quoted in A. C. Grayling, *The Quarrel of the Age: The Life and Times of William
    Hazlitt* (London, 2001), p. 178.
18 Richard Price, 'Observations on the Importance of the American Revolution',
    in *PW*, p. 142.
19 P. W. Clayden, *The Early Life of Samuel Rogers* (London, 1887), p. 10.
20 Henri Laboucheix, *Richard Price as Moral Philosopher and Political Theorist*, trans.
    Sylvia and David Raphael (Oxford, 1982), p. 34.
21 22 June 1788 and 17 January 1789 in 'Journal', 385 and 392, for example.
22 16 December 1787 in ibid., 382.
23 'Introduction', in ibid., 366.
24 See *Sermons*, pp. 9–12.
25 27 May 1787 in 'Journal', 378.
26 See Merrill D. Peterson, (ed.), *Thomas Jefferson, Writings* ([New York], 1984),
    p. 1373, Thomas Jefferson to Charles Thomson, 9 January 1816.
27 Clayden, *Early Life of Samuel Rogers*, p. 308.
28 27 May 1787 in 'Journal', 377.
29 Quoted in Caroline E. Williams, *A Welsh Family from the Beginning of the 18th
    Century* (2nd edn., London, 1893), p. 59.
30 Clayden, *Early Life of Samuel Rogers*, p. 311.
31 Ibid., pp. 9, 34.
32 Williams, *Welsh Family*, p. 61.
33 See Alan Ruston, 'Richard Price as a Man of Action', *E&D*, 10 (1991), 113–14.
34 Clayden, *Early Life of Samuel Rogers*, p. 10.
35 See *CRP*, II, p. 308 n. 1, for detailed discussion.
36 See *http://www.masshist.org/digitaladams*, Abigail Adams to John Adams, 19 October
    1783.
37 *CRP*, III, p. 225, John Adams to Richard Price, 20 May 1789.
38 See Lyndall Gordon, *Mary Wollstonecraft: A New Genus* (London, 2005), pp. 76, 78.
39 See John Howard, *Account of the Principal Lazarettos in Europe with Various Papers
    Relative to the Plague: Together with Further Observations on Some Foreign Prisons
    and Hospitals: And Additional Remarks on the Present State of Them in Great Britain
    and Ireland* (London, 1789). According to Samuel Rogers, *Recollections of the Table-
    Talk of Samuel Rogers* (2nd edn., London, 1856), pp. 151–2, 'People are not

aware that Dr. Price wrote a portion of it'. See also R. W. England, 'Who Wrote John Howard's Text? The State of the Prisons as a Dissenting Enterprise', *British Journal of Criminology*, 33, no. 2 (1993), 203–15; also CC, pp. 60–1, for a full account.

[40]   24 June 1787 in 'Journal', 378.
[41]   6 October 1787 in ibid., 380.
[42]   28 October 1787 in ibid., 381.
[43]   29 June 1788 in ibid., 386.
[44]   *CRP*, III, p. 16, Thomas Day to Richard Price, 8 April 1786.
[45]   1 August 1790 in 'Journal', 395.
[46]   *CRP*, II, p. 265, President and Fellows of Harvard to Richard Price, 3 March 1785.
[47]   Ibid., p. 266, Benjamin Franklin to Richard Price, 18 March 1785.
[48]   Ibid., p. 282, Richard Price to Benjamin Franklin, 3 June 1785.
[49]   David McCullough, *John Adams* (London, 2001), p. 471.
[50]   *CRP*, II, p. 193, Benjamin Franklin to Richard Price, 16 September 1783.
[51]   Ibid., p. 214, Richard Price to Benjamin Franklin, 6 April 1784.
[52]   Benjamin Franklin, 'To The Royal Academy of *****', in J. A. Leo LeMay (ed.), *Benjamin Franklin* (New York, 1987), pp. 952–5.
[53]   21 October 1787 in 'Journal', 380.
[54]   Richard Price, 'The Evidence for a Future Period of Improvement in the State of Mankind', in *PW*, p. 161.
[55]   Ibid., pp. 163–4.
[56]   Ibid., p. 166.
[57]   *CRP*, III, p. 31, Benjamin Rush to Richard Price, 25 May 1786.
[58]   Ibid., pp. 54–5, Richard Price to Benjamin Rush, 30 July 1786.
[59]   See CC, p. 108 n. 18.
[60]   *CRP*, III, p. 30, Benjamin Rush to Richard Price, 25 May 1786.
[61]   Ibid., p. 76, Benjamin Rush to Richard Price, 27 October 1786.
[62]   Ibid., pp. 115–16, Richard Price to Benjamin Rush, 26 January 1787.
[63]   Ibid., p. 151, Richard Price to Joseph Willard, 10 October 1787; ibid., p. 170, Richard Price to Arthur Lee, 24 March 1788. See also Peterson (ed.), *Thomas Jefferson, Writings*, p. 1522.
[64]   *CRP*, III, p. 170, Richard Price to Arthur Lee, 24 March 1788.
[65]   Ibid., p. 134, Benjamin Franklin to Richard Price, 9 June 1787.
[66]   Ibid., p. 142, Richard Price to James Phillips, 23 August 1787.
[67]   Ibid., p. 164, Richard Price to Ezra Stiles, 22 March 1788.
[68]   27 July and 28 September 1788 in 'Journal', 386.
[69]   See 'Appendix IV' in ibid., 400.

16. Revolution in France

[1]   Richard Price, 'A Discourse on the Love of our Country', in *PW*, pp. 195–6.
[2]   *CRP*, III, p. 182, Richard Price to Thomas Jefferson, 26 October 1788.

[3] Ibid., p. 196, Thomas Jefferson to Richard Price, 8 January 1789.
[4] See William Doyle, *The Oxford History of the French Revolution* (paperback edn., Oxford, 1990), p. 69.
[5] *CRP*, III, p. 196, Thomas Jefferson to Richard Price, 8 January 1789.
[6] Ibid., pp. 196–7.
[7] Ibid., p. 197.
[8] Ibid.
[9] For a detailed discussion of this event, see Simon Schama, *Patriots and Liberators, Revolution in the Netherlands 1780–1813* (paperback edn., London, 2005), pp. 64–135.
[10] 4 November 1787 in 'Journal', 381.
[11] Ibid.
[12] *CRP*, III, p. 198, Thomas Jefferson to Richard Price, 8 January 1789.
[13] Ibid., pp. 198–9.
[14] See William Howard Adams, *The Paris Years of Thomas Jefferson* (New Haven, 1997), p. 270; 21 December 1788, 4 January 1789 and 25 January 1789 in 'Journal', 388–90.
[15] *CRP*, III, pp. 223–4, Thomas Jefferson to Richard Price, 19 May 1789.
[16] See *Travels*, p. 51.
[17] Lady [Elizabeth] Eastlake (ed.), *Dr Rigby's Letters from France &c. in 1789* (London, 1880), p. 38.
[18] *CRP*, III, p. 233, Thomas Jefferson to Richard Price, 12 July 1789.
[19] *Travels*, p. 52.
[20] Ibid., p. 49.
[21] Ibid.
[22] Ibid., pp. 49–50.
[23] Ibid., p. 17.
[24] Nor do copies of the *London Gazetteer* for 13 August and 14 September 1789, in which the letters were originally reprinted, appear to have survived.
[25] See *Gentleman's Magazine*, 60 (1790), 1097.
[26] *CRP*, III, p. 247, Richard Price to Thomas Jefferson, 3 August 1789.
[27] Ibid., pp. 247–8.
[28] Ibid., pp. 257–8, Thomas Jefferson to Richard Price, 13 September 1789.
[29] 18 October 1789 in 'Journal', 391.
[30] Ibid.

17. On the Love of our Country

[1] In writing this chapter the author is indebted to the work of Martin Fitzpatrick, 'Patriots and Patriotisms: Richard Price and the Early Reception of the French Revolution in England', in Michael O'Dea and Kevin Whelan (eds.), *Nations and Nationalisms: France, Britain and Ireland and the Eighteenth-Century Context* (Oxford, 1996), pp. 211–30; *idem*, 'Richard Price and the London Revolution

Society', *E&D*, 10 (1991), 35–50; and D. O. Thomas, 'Neither Republican nor Democrat', in *The Price-Priestley Newsletter*, 1 (1977), 49–60. See also Paul Frame and Geoffrey W. Powell, '"Our first concern as lovers of our country must be to enlighten it": Richard Price's Response to the French Revolution', in Mary-Ann Constantine and Dafydd Johnston (eds.), *'Footsteps of Liberty and Revolt': Essays on Wales and the French Revolution* (Cardiff, 2013), pp. 53–68.

2   6 December 1789 in 'Journal', 392.

3   *CRP*, III, p. 182, Richard Price to Thomas Jefferson, 26 October 1788.

4   Fitzpatrick, 'Patriots and Patriotisms', p. 211.

5   Richard Price, 'Discourse on the Love of our Country', in *PW*, pp. 177–89.

6   Ibid., pp. 178–9.

7   Ibid., p. 71.

8   Quoted in Stanley Ayling, *Edmund Burke* (paperback edn., London, 1990), p. 162.

9   Price, 'Discourse on the Love of our Country', pp. 181–4.

10   Ibid., pp. 185, 187.

11   Ibid., p. 185.

12   Ibid., p. 186.

13   Ibid., pp. 185–6.

14   Ibid., p. 187.

15   Ibid., pp. 189–90.

16   Ibid., p. 192.

17   Ibid., pp. 194–5.

18   Ibid., p. 195.

19   'Appendix I' in 'Journal', 397.

20   *CRP*, III, p. 260, le duc de la Rochefoucauld to Richard Price, 2 December 1789. Note that in the index to vol. III of Price's published correspondence, *CRP*, III, p. 364, the duke is identified as 'la Rochefoucauld d'Enville'. However Rémy Duthille, 'Thirteen Uncollected Letters of Richard Price', *E&D*, 27 (2011), 93 n. 24, has shown that Price's correspondent was actually la Rochefoucauld-Liancourt.

21   *CRP*, III, p. 261, Richard Price to the marquis of Lansdowne, 5 December 1789.

22   See ibid., p. 326, Richard Price to le duc de la Rochefoucauld, [14 October 1790], and ibid. n. 12, on Smith's attitude to Price. See also CC, p. 59, for Price's possible contribution to Smith's *Wealth of Nations*.

23   4 April 1790 in 'Journal', 393.

24   6 June 1790 in ibid., 394.

25   *CRP*, II, p. 215, Richard Price to Benjamin Franklin, 6 April 1784. See also remedies being offered in ibid., pp. 318–19, Richard Price to Benjamin Franklin, 5 November 1785, and ibid., III, pp. 116–17, Richard Price to Benjamin Franklin, 26 January 1787, and ibid., p. 117 n. 2.

26   6 June 1790 in 'Journal', 394.

27   See *CRP*, III, p. 279, Richard Price to Sir Joseph Banks, 17 April 1790; ibid. n. 1.

28   Ibid., p. 280.

29   Ibid., p. 317, Joseph Priestley to Richard Price, 29 August 1790.

[30] 17 January 1790 in 'Journal', 392.
[31] 23 May 1790 in ibid., 394.
[32] 6 June 1790 in ibid., 394.
[33] Fitzpatrick, 'Richard Price and the London Revolution Society', 40 n. 22.
[34] *CRP*, III, p. 265, T. Procter to Richard Price, 12 January 1790.
[35] Ibid., p. 306, Richard Price to le duc de la Rochefoucauld [extract], 2 July 1790.
[36] 'Appendix III' in 'Journal', 398–9.
[37] *CRP*, III, pp. 313–14, Citizens of the District of Quimper in the Department of Finisterre to Richard Price, 4 August 1790.
[38] Ibid., pp. 288–9, le duc de la Rochefoucauld to Richard Price, 2 May 1790.
[39] Fitzpatrick, 'Richard Price and the London Revolution Society', 44.
[40] Ibid., 45. See also *The Times*, 6 November 1790.
[41] Edward Sayer, *Observations on Doctor Price's Revolution Sermon* (London, 1790), pp. 9–10.
[42] Ibid., p. 11.
[43] Ibid.

18. Burke and his Reflections

[1] 17 January 1790 in 'Journal', 393.
[2] Quoted in Conor Cruise O'Brien (ed.), *Edmund Burke, Reflections on the Revolution in France* (paperback edn., London, 2004), pp. 13–14. See also Carl B. Cone, *Burke and the Nature of Politics: The Age of the French Revolution* (Lexington, 1964), pp. 294–5.
[3] See Stanley Ayling, *Edmund Burke* (paperback edition, London, 1990), p. 194.
[4] See *The Parliamentary History of England* (36 vols., London, 1816), XXVIII, p. 356.
[5] Edmund Burke, *Reflections on the Revolution in France, and on the Proceedings in Certain Societies in London Relative to that Event* (London, 1790), p. 205.
[6] Ibid., pp. 135–6.
[7] Ibid., p. 87.
[8] Ayling, *Edmund Burke*, p. 211.
[9] Ibid., p. 53.
[10] Ibid., p. 198.
[11] Richard Price, 'Discourse on the Love of our Country', in *PW*, p. 193, and ibid. n. 1.
[12] Burke, *Reflections on Revolution in France*, p. 13.
[13] Ibid., p. 99.
[14] Quoted in Martin Fitzpatrick, 'Richard Price and the London Revolution Society', *E&D*, 10 (1991), 45.
[15] Price, 'Discourse on the Love of our Country', p. 190 n. 23.
[16] Ibid.
[17] Ibid., p. 177. See also *Travels*, pp. 11, 51, for a discussion of George's letters to Price.
[18] Joseph Priestley, *The Importance and Extent of Free Inquiry in Matters of Religion: a*

Sermon, Preached before the Congregations of the Old and New Meeting of Protestant Dissenters at Birmingham. November 5, 1785. To Which are Added, Reflections on the Present State of Free Inquiry in this Country (Birmingham, 1785), pp. 40–1.

[19] *CRP*, II, p. 215, Richard Price to Benjamin Franklin, 6 April 1784.

[20] Price, 'Discourse on the Love of our Country', p. 196.

[21] *CRP*, III, p. 257, Richard Price to the marquis of Lansdowne, 9 September 1789.

[22] Ibid., p. 256.

[23] Ibid., p. 273, Richard Price to [William Smith], 1 March 1790.

[24] Richard Price, 'Evidence for a Future Period of Improvement in the State of Mankind', in *PW*, pp. 164–5.

[25] Ibid., p. 165 n. 19.

[26] Price repeats these last words in the closing paragraph of his 'General Introduction' to the *Two Tracts* of 1778 without any footnote qualification. See *idem*, 'General Introduction, Two Tracts', in *PW*, p. 19.

[27] *Idem*, 'Observations on the Importance of the American Revolution', in *PW*, p. 146, and ibid. n. 16.

[28] *Idem*, 'A Review of the Principal Questions in Morals', in Raphael, p. 175.

19. The Close

[1] *CRP*, III, p. 332, Alexander Christie to Richard Price, 25 October 1790.

[2] *http://www.masshist.org/digitaladams*, Abigail Adams to John Adams, 21 January 1795.

[3] *Memoirs*, p. 164.

[4] *CRP*, III, p. 337, Richard Price to Joseph Priestley, after 27 January 1791.

[5] Mary Wollstonecraft, *A Vindication of the Rights of Men, in a Letter to the Right Honourable Edmund Burke, Occasioned by his Reflections on the Revolution in France* (2nd edn., London, 1790), pp. 35–6.

[6] Ibid., p. 36.

[7] Ibid., pp. 34–5.

[8] See Paul Frame, 'A Further Seven Uncollected Letters of Richard Price', *E&D*, 27 (2011), 143–60.

[9] Thomas Paine, 'Rights of Man', in Eric Foner (ed.), *Thomas Paine, Collected Writings* (New York, 1995), p. 436.

[10] See Jenny Graham, *The Nation, The Law and The King, Reform Politics in England, 1789–1799* (2 vols., Lanham, 2000), I, p. 131; ibid. n. 33.

[11] *CRP*, III, p. 339, Joseph Priestley to Richard Price, 16 February 1791.

[12] *Memoirs*, p. 175.

[13] 6 February 1791 in 'Journal', 396.

[14] *Memoirs*, p. 176.

[15] Quoted in CC, p. 199.

[16] Thanks to Tony Rail and Martin Fitzpatrick for this information. See Tony Rail, 'A Previously Unpublished Letter from Thomas Belsham to Samuel Fawcett, 21 April 1791', *E&D*, 30 (forthcoming).

[17] *Memoirs*, p. 180.

[18] Martin Fitzpatrick, 'Richard Price and the London Revolution Society', *E&D*, 10 (1991), 49.

[19] Oliver Stutchbury, 'Nantes and the Death of Richard Price', *E&D*, 11 (1992), 158, concludes that though there is no surviving evidence in Nantes that this proposal was carried out, 'this is not to say that these events did not happen at the time'. No maps of the time were found and the town records Stutchbury saw appeared to be 'fair copies of earlier documents, and it does not need a particularly suspicious mind to suspect that on one of the many changes of central government which France enjoyed in the next century, the town elders found it convenient to omit this episode from their history'.

[20] See Andrew Kippis, *An Address, Delivered at the Internment of the Late Rev. Dr. Richard Price, on 26 April 1791* (London, 1791), p. 23.

[21] See *Gentleman's Magazine*, 61 (1791), 389–90.

[22] Michael Foot, 'Thomas Paine and the Democratic Revolution', in Joyce Chumbley and Leo Zonneveld (eds.), *Thomas Paine: In Search of the Common Good* (Nottingham, 2009), p. 27.

[23] Quoted in CC, pp. 187–8.

[24] Ibid., p. 197.

[25] See Graham, *The Nation, The Law and The King*, I, p. 238; ibid. n. 104.

[26] *CRP*, I, p. 164, Richard Price to Henry Marchant, 2 February 1773.

[27] Quoted in Ruth Scurr, *Fatal Purity: Robespierre and the French Revolution* (paperback edn., London, 2007), p. 275.

[28] Henri Laboucheix was 'a professor at the Sorbonne and Director of a Centre there for the History of Ideas in the Anglo-American World'; see Henri Laboucheix, *Richard Price as Moral Philosopher and Political Theorist*, trans. Sylvia and David Raphael (Oxford, 1982), p. 1.

[29] Ibid., p. 137.

Select Bibliography

The following bibliography includes a separate listing of the principal works by Price and all material referenced in the text and chapter notes. In some cases titles have been abbreviated and joint authorship indicated in parentheses. Where a Price work is believed to have only appeared in the *Philosophical Transactions of the Royal Society* the relevant journal volume is referenced, otherwise the published London offprint is indicated.

There is no published edition of Price's complete works currently available but a full listing of them, together with all their various British and overseas editions can be found in *Bibliography*. That work also references most of the material published on, or relating to Price up to *c.*1993. Modern editions of Price's most important writings can be found in Raphael on moral philosophy, *PW* on politics and civil liberties (all references to Price's major works on civil liberty are made to this easily accessible volume), and for Price's extensive correspondence see *CRP*, Duthille, 'Thirteen Uncollected Letters of Richard Price', and Frame, 'A Further Seven Uncollected Letters of Richard Price'. The reader is also referred to *The Price-Priestley Newsletter*, 1–4 (1977–80) and the journal *E&D*, 1– (1982–), which contain numerous articles relating to Price and those with whom he lived and worked. All past and current editions of *E&D* can now be accessed free and online at *http://www.english. qmul.ac.uk/drwilliams/journal/intro.html*.

A chronological listing of Richard Price's main published works

Price, Richard, *A Review of the Principal Questions in Morals* (London, 1758).
—— *Britain's Happiness and the Proper Improvement of It* (London, 1759).
—— 'An Essay Towards Solving a Problem in the Doctrine of Chances. By the Late Rev. Mr. Bayes, F.R.S. Communicated by Mr. Price in a Letter to John Canton A.M.F.R.S.', *Philosophical Transactions*, LIII (1763), 370–418.

—— 'A Supplement to the Essay on a Method of Calculating the Exact Probability of All Conclusions Founded on Induction', *Philosophical Transactions*, LIV (1765), 296–325.

—— *The Nature and Dignity of the Human Soul* (London, 1766).

—— *Four Dissertations* (London, 1767).

—— *Observations on the Expectations of Lives, The Increase of Mankind, The Influence of Great Towns on Population, and Particularly the State of London, with Respect to Healthfulness and Number of Inhabitants. Communicated to the Royal Society, April 27, 1769. In a Letter from Mr. Richard Price, F.R.S. to Benjamin Franklin, Esq; LL.D. and F.R.S.* (London, 1769).

—— *The Vanity, Misery, and Infamy, of Knowledge without Suitable Practice* (London, 1770).

—— 'Observations on the Proper Method of Calculating the Values of Reversions', *Philosophical Transactions*, LX (1770), 268–76.

—— 'A Letter from Richard Price, D.D. F.R.S. to Benjamin Franklin, LL.D. F.R.S. on the Effect of the Aberration of Light on the Time of a Transit of Venus over the Sun', *Philosophical Transactions*, LX (1770), 536–40.

—— *Observations on Reversionary Payments; on Schemes for Providing Annuities for Widows, and for Persons in Old Age; on the Method of Calculating the Values of Assurances on Lives; and on the National Debt* (London, 1771).

—— *A Letter from the Rev. Dr Webster, of Edinburgh, to the Rev. Dr Price, of London, and Dr Price's Answer, Relative to the Establishment for a Provision to the Widows and Children of the Ministers and Professors of Scotland* (Edinburgh, 1771).

—— (with Revd Andrew Kippis), *Account of a Scheme for Providing Relief for Protestant Dissenting Ministers of the Three Denominations in Old Age* (London 1771).

—— *An Appeal to the Public, on the Subject of the National Debt* (London, 1772).

—— 'Farther Proofs of the Insalubrity of Marshy Situations', *Philosophical Transactions*, LXIV, part I (1774), 96–8.

—— 'Observations on the Difference between the Duration of Human Life in Towns and in Country Parishes and Villages', *Philosophical Transactions*, LXV, part I (1775), 424–5.

—— *Observations on the Nature of Civil Liberty, the Principles of Government, and the Justice and Policy of the War with America* (London, 1776).

—— *Additional Observations on the Nature and Value of Civil Liberty, and the War with America* (London, 1777).

—— *Two Tracts on Civil Liberty, the War with America, and the Debts and Finances of the Kingdom: with a General Introduction and Supplement* (London, 1778).

—— (with Joseph Priestley), *A Free Discussion of the Doctrines of Materialism and Philosophical Necessity, in a Correspondence between Dr. Price and Dr. Priestley* (London, 1778).

—— *A Sermon Delivered to a Congregation of Protestant Dissenters, at Hackney, on the 10th February Last Being the Day Appointed for a General Fast* (London, 1779).

—— 'Essay, Containing an Account of the Progress from the Revolution, and the Present State, of Population in England and Wales', in William Morgan, *The Doctrine of Annuities and Assurances on Lives and Survivorships, Stated and Explained* (London, 1779).

—— (with John Horne Tooke but published anonymously), *Facts: Addressed to the Landholders, Stockholders, Merchants, Farmers, Manufacturers, Tradesmen, Proprietors of Every Description, and Generally to All the Subjects of Great Britain and Ireland* (London, 1780).

—— *A Discourse Addressed to a Congregation at Hackney, on February 21st, 1781, Being the Day Appointed for a Public Fast* (London, 1781).

—— *The State of the Public Debts and Finances at Signing the Preliminary Articles of Peace in January 1783. With a Plan for Raising Money by Public Loans, and for Redeeming the Public Debts* (London, 1783).

—— *Proceedings Relative to the Ulster Assembly of Volunteer Delegates: on the Subject of a More Equal Representation of the People in the Parliament of Ireland, to which are Annexed, Letters from the Duke of Richmond, Dr. Price, Mr. Wyvill, and Others* (Belfast, 1783).

—— *Observations on the Importance of the American Revolution, and the Means of Making It a Benefit to the World* (London, 1784).

—— Postscript to George Cadogan Morgan, 'Observations on the Light of Bodies in a State of Combustion', *Philosophical Transactions*, LXXV, part I (1785), 211.

—— (with Revd John Acland), *A Plan for Rendering the Poor Independent on Public Contribution; Founded on the Basis of the Friendly Societies Commonly Called Clubs. By the Rev. John Acland . . . to which is Added a Letter from Dr. Price, Containing his Sentiments and Calculations on the Subject* (London, 1786).

—— A prefatory letter to Thomas Jefferson, *Statute of Virginia* (broadsheet; London, 1786). See *Gentleman's Magazine*, 57 (1787), 74–5.

—— *Sermons on the Christian Doctrine as Received by the Different Denominations of Christians. To which are Added, Sermons on the Security and Happiness of a Virtuous Course, on the Goodness of God, and the Resurrection of Lazarus* (London, 1787).

—— *The Evidence for a Future Period of Improvement in the State of Mankind, with the Means and Duty of Promoting It* (London, 1787).

—— *Sermons on the Security and Happiness of a Virtuous Course, on the Goodness of God and the Resurrection of Lazarus. To which are Added Sermons on the Christian Doctrine as Received by the Different Denominations of Christians* (Philadelphia, 1788).

—— *A Discourse on the Love of our Country, Delivered on Nov. 4, 1789, at the Meeting House in Old Jewry, to the Society for Commemorating the Revolution in Great Britain. With an Appendix, Containing the Report of the Committee of the Society; an Account of the Population of France. And the Declaration of Rights by the National Assembly of France* (London, 1789).

Selected references

Ackroyd, Peter, *London, The Biography* (London, 2000).
—— *Newton* (London, 2006).
Acland, John, *A Bill for the More Effectual Relief of the Poor, and Ascertaining the Settlement of Bastard Children* (Exeter, 1786).
Adams, William Howard, *The Paris Years of Thomas Jefferson* (New Haven, 1997).
Allardyce, Alex, *The Village that Changed the World, A History of Newington Green London N16* (London, 2008).
Andrews, Stuart, '"Insects of the Hour": Dr Price's Revolutions', *History Today*, 41, no. 5 (1991), 48–58.
Aqvist, Lennart, *The Moral Philosophy of Richard Price* (Copenhagen, 1960).
Ayling, Stanley, *Edmund Burke* (paperback edn., London, 1990).
—— *George the Third* (London, 1972).
Bahar, Saba, 'Richard Price and the Moral Foundations of Mary Wollstonecraft's Feminism', *E&D*, 18 (1999), 1–15.
Bailyn, Bernard, *To Begin the World Anew, The Genius and Ambiguities of the American Founding Fathers* (New York, 2004).
Barnard, G. A., 'Thomas Bayes's Essay towards Solving a Problem in the Doctrine of Chances', *Biometrika*, XLV (1958), 293–315.
Barnes, W. H. F., 'Richard Price – A Neglected Eighteenth Century Moralist', *Philosophy*, XVII (1942), 159–73.
Bellhouse, D. R., 'On Some Recently Discovered Manuscripts of Thomas Bayes' (unpublished University of Western Ontario MSc thesis, 1991).
Black, Jeremy, 'Edmund Burke: History, Politics and Polemic', *History Today*, 37, no. 12 (1987), 42–7.
—— and Roy Porter, *A Dictionary of Eighteenth-Century World History* (Oxford, 1994).
Brady, Frank, and Frederick A. Pottle (eds.), *Boswell in Search of a Wife 1766–1769* (London, 1957).
Brewer, John, *The Sinews of Power: War, Money and the English State 1688–1783* (London, 2002).
Brinkley, Richard, 'The Library of Richard Price', *The Price-Priestley Newsletter*, 4 (1980), 4–15.
Browning, Charles H., *Welsh Settlement of Pensylvania* [*sic*] (Philadelphia, 1912).
Brumwell, Stephen, and W. A. Speck, *Cassell's Companion to Eighteenth-Century Britain* (London, 2001).
Burke, Edmund, *A Letter from Edmund Burke, Esq., One of the Representatives in Parliament for the City of Bristol, to John Farr and John Harris, Esqrs., Sheriffs of that City, on Affairs in America* (Bristol, 1777).
—— *Reflections on the Revolution in France, and on the Proceedings in Certain Societies in London Relative to that Event* (London, 1790).
—— *Thoughts on the Present Discontents* (London, 1770).

Burnett, Edmund C. (ed.), *Letters of Members of the Continental Congress* (8 vols., Washington, 1921–36).

Butler, Joseph, *Analogy of Religion, Natural and Revealed, to the Constitution and Course of Nature* (London, 1736).

Canovan, Margaret, 'Two Concepts of Liberty – Eighteenth-Century Style', *The Price-Priestley Newsletter*, 2 (1978), 27–43.

Casanova, Giacomo, *History of my Life*, trans. W. R. Trask (paperback edn., Baltimore, 1997).

Claeys, Gregory, *The French Revolution Debate in Britain, The Origins of Modern Politics* (Basingstoke, 2007).

Clayden, P. W., *The Early Life of Samuel Rogers* (London, 1887).

Cone, Carl B., *Burke and the Nature of Politics, The Age of the American Revolution* (Lexington, 1957).

—— *Burke and the Nature of Politics, The Age of the French Revolution* (Lexington, 1964).

—— *Torchbearer of Freedom: The Influence of Richard Price on 18th Century Thought* (Lexington, 1952).

—— 'Richard Price and Pitt's Sinking Fund of 1786', *Economic History Review*, 2nd series, IV (1951), 243–51.

—— 'Richard Price and the Constitution of the United States', *American Historical Review*, LIII (1947–8), 726–47.

Constantine, Mary-Ann, and Paul Frame (eds.), *Travels in Revolutionary France & A Journey Across America by George Cadogan Morgan & Richard Price Morgan* (Cardiff, 2012).

Crane, Verner W., 'The Club of Honest Whigs, Friends of Science and Liberty', *William and Mary Quarterly*, 3rd series, XXIII, no. 2 (1966), 210–33.

Crowder, Colin, 'Berkeley, Price and the Limitations of the Design Argument', *E&D*, 8 (1989), 3–24.

Cua, Antonio S., *Reason and Virtue: A Study in the Ethics of Richard Price* ([Athens], 1966).

Davidson, Ian, *Voltaire in Exile* (London, 2004).

Davies, Leonard Twiston, and Averyl Edwards, *Welsh Life in the Eighteenth Century* (London, 1939).

Davies, John, *A History of Wales* (London, 1993).

Davies, Russell, *Hope and Heartbreak: A Social History of Wales and the Welsh, 1776–1871* (Cardiff, 2005).

Dickinson, H. T., *The Politics of the People in Eighteenth-Century Britain* (Basingstoke, 1994).

—— 'George III and Parliament', *Parliamentary History*, 30 (2011), 395–413.

—— 'Richard Price on Reason and Revolution', in William Gibson and Robert G. Ingram (eds.), *Religious Identities in Britain, 1660–1832* (Aldershot, 2004), pp. 231–54.

Ditchfield, G. M., '"How Narrow will the Limits of this Toleration Appear?" Dissenting Petitions to Parliament 1772–1773', *Parliamentary History*, 24 (2005), 91–106.

—— 'The Subscription Issue in British Parliamentary Politics, 1772–1779', *Parliamentary History*, 7 (1988), 45–80.

Doyle, William, *The Oxford History of the French Revolution* (Oxford, 1990).

Duthille, Rémy, 'Richard Price on Patriotism and Universal Benevolence', *E&D*, 28 (2012), 24–41.

—— 'Thirteen Uncollected Letters of Richard Price', *E&D*, 27 (2011), 83–142.

D. W. (Lledrod), 'Byr-gofiant' [A brief memoir of Richard Price], *Seren Gomer* (1836), 65–7.

Dybikowski, J., *On Burning Ground: An Examination of the Ideas, Projects and Life of David Williams* (Oxford, 1993).

—— 'A Bibliography of D. O. Thomas', *E&D*, 19 (2000), 214–23.

Earman, John, 'Bayes, Hume, Price and Miracles', *Proceedings of the British Academy*, 113 (2002), 91–109.

Eastlake, Lady [Elizabeth] (ed.), *Dr Rigby's Letters from France etc. in 1789* (London, 1880).

Eden, William, *Four Letters to the Earl of Carlisle, the Third Edition. To which is Added. A Fifth Letter, on Population; on Certain Revenue Laws and Regulations Connected with the Interests of Commerce; and on Public Oeconomy* (London, 1780).

Elazar, Yiftah, 'The Liberty Debate: Richard Price and his Critics on Civil Liberty, Free Government, and Democratic Participation' (unpublished Princeton University PhD thesis, 2012).

Ellis, Joseph J., *Founding Brothers, The Revolutionary Generation* (New York, 2002).

England, R. W., 'Who Wrote John Howard's Text? The State of the Prisons as a Dissenting Enterprise', *British Journal of Criminology*, 33, no. 2 (1993), 203–15.

Faulkner, John, 'Burke's Perception of Richard Price', in Lisa Plummer Crafton (ed.), *The French Revolution Debate in English Literature and Culture* (Westport, 1997), pp. 1–26.

Ferguson, Adam, *Remarks on a Pamphlet Lately Published by Dr. Price* (London, 1776).

Fitzpatrick, Martin, 'Enlightenment, Dissent and Toleration', *E&D*, 28 (2012), 42–72.

—— 'Natural Law, Natural Rights, and the Toleration Act in England, 1688–1829', in Diethelm Klippel (ed.), *Naturrecht und Staat, Politische Funktionen des Europäischen Naturrechts* (Munich, 2006), pp. 35–58.

—— 'Patriots and Patriotisms: Richard Price and the Early Reception of the French Revolution in England', in Michael O'Dea and Kevin Whelan (eds.), *Nations and Nationalisms: France, Britain and Ireland and the Eighteenth-Century Context* (Oxford, 1996), pp. 211–30.

—— 'Richard Price and the London Revolution Society', *E&D*, 10 (1991), 35–50.

—— 'The Patriotism of a Philosophe: the case of Richard Price', in Williams (ed.), *Richard Price and the Atlantic Revolution*, pp. 36–57.

——, Peter Jones, Christa Knellwolf and Ian McCalman (eds.), *The Enlightenment World* (London, 2007).

Flavell, Julie, *When London was Capital of America* (New Haven, 2010).

Foner, Eric (ed.), *Thomas Paine, Collected Writings* (New York, 1995).

Foot, Michael, 'Thomas Paine and the Democratic Revolution', in Joyce Chumbley and Leo Zonneveld (eds.), *Thomas Paine: In Search of the Common Good* (Nottingham, 2009), pp. 23–31.

Foster, R. F., *The Oxford History of Ireland* (Oxford, 1992).

Fothergill, Irene, M., and David Williams, 'French Opinion Concerning Dr. Richard Price', *Bulletin of the Board of Celtic Studies*, V (1929), 72–4.

Frame, Paul, 'A Further Seven Uncollected Letters of Richard Price', *E&D*, 27 (2011), 143–60.

—— and Geoffrey W. Powell, '"Our first concern as lovers of our country must be to enlighten it": Richard Price's Response to the French Revolution', in Mary-Ann Constantine and Dafydd Johnston (eds.), *'Footsteps of Liberty and Revolt': Essays on Wales and the French Revolution* (Cardiff, 2013), pp. 52–68.

Franklin, Benjamin, *The Interest of Great Britain Considered with Regard to her Colonies* (London, 1761).

Fruchtman, Jack, Jr., *The Apocalyptic Politics of Richard Price and Joseph Priestley: A Study in Late Eighteenth-Century English Republican Millennialism* (Philadelphia, 1983).

Gipson, Lawrence Henry, *Lewis Evans* (Philadelphia, 1939).

Gordon, Lyndall, *Mary Wollstonecraft, A New Genus* (London, 2005).

Graham, Jenny, *The Nation, The Law and The King, Reform Politics in England, 1789–1799* (2 vols., Lanham, 2000).

Grayling, A. C., *The Quarrel of the Age. The Life and Times of William Hazlitt* (London, 2001).

Hague, William, *William Pitt the Younger* (paperback edn., London, 2005).

Hoecker, James J., 'Joseph Priestley and the Reification of Religion', *The Price-Priestley Newsletter*, 2 (1978), 44–75.

Holmes, Richard, *The Age of Wonder, How the Romantic Generation Discovered the Beauty and Terror of Science* (London, 2009).

Hough, Richard, *Captain James Cook* (London, 1995).

Howard, John, *Account of the Principal Lazarettos in Europe with Various Papers Relative to the Plague: Together with Further Observations on Some Foreign Prisons and Hospitals: And Additional Remarks on the Present State of Them in Great Britain and Ireland* (London, 1789).

Howlet, J., *An Examination of Dr Price's Essay on the Population of England and Wales; and the Doctrine of an Increased Population Established by Facts* (Maidstone, 1781).

Hudson, W. D., *Reason and Right: A Critical Examination of Richard Price's Moral Philosophy* (London, 1970).

Hunt-Bull, Nicholas, 'Richard Price and Frances Hutcheson – Does a Moral Sense Theory Make Ethics Arbitrary', *E&D*, 23 (2004–7), 24–44.

Irving, Isla June, 'The Life and Times of Richard Price', in Williams (ed.), *Richard Price and the Atlantic Revolution*, pp. 73–6.

Israel, Jonathan, *A Revolution of the Mind, Radical Enlightenment and the Intellectual Origins of Modern Democracy* (Princeton, 2010).

—— *Democratic Enlightenment: Philosophy, Revolution and Human Rights 1750–1790* (Oxford, 2011).

Jenkins, Geraint H., *Literature, Religion and Society in Wales 1660–1730* (Cardiff, 1978).

—— *The Foundations of Modern Wales 1642–1780* (Oxford, 1987).

Jones, E., 'The Age of Societies', in *idem* (ed.), *The Welsh in London 1500–2000* (Cardiff, 2001), pp. 54–87.

Jones, Whitney R. D., *David Williams. The Anvil & the Hammer* (Cardiff, 1986).

Kellner, Peter (ed.), *Democracy: 1,000 Years in Pursuit of British Liberty* (Edinburgh, 2009).

Kenyon, J. P., *The Stuarts* (London, 1973).

Ketchum, Richard M., *The Winter Soldiers, George Washington and the Way to Independence* (London, 1973).

Kippis, Andrew, *An Address Delivered at the Internment of the Late Dr. Richard Price* (London, 1791).

Kruckeberg, Robert Dale, junior, 'Dr Richard Price, The Marquis de Condorcet, and the Political Culture of Friendship in the Late Enlightenment' (unpublished University of North Texas MA thesis, 2001).

Laboucheix, Henri, *Richard Price as Moral Philosopher and Political Theorist*, trans. Sylvia Raphael and David Raphael (Oxford, 1982).

Lammey, David, 'The Growth of the "Patriot Opposition" in Ireland during the 1770s', *Parliamentary History*, 7 (1988), 257–81.

Langford, Paul, *The Eighteenth Century* (Oxford, 2002).

Lemay, J. A. Leo (ed.), *Benjamin Franklin, Writings* (New York, 1987).

Lewis, Gwynne, 'Richard Price: Revisionism and the French Revolution', in Williams (ed.), *Richard Price and the Atlantic Revolution*, pp. 1–9.

Linton, Marisa, *The Politics of Virtue in Enlightenment France* (Basingstoke, 2001).

Lock, F. P., *Edmund Burke, Volume 1: 1730–1784* (Oxford, 1999).

—— *Edmund Burke, Volume 2: 1784–1797* (Oxford, 2006).

Loughran, Trish, 'Disseminating *Common Sense*: Thomas Paine and the Problem of the Early National Bestseller', *American Literature*, 78 (2006), 1–28.

McCulloch, David, *1776, America and Britain at War* (London, 2005).

—— *John Adams* (London, 2001).

Macdonald, W. (ed.), *The Autobiography of Benjamin Franklin* (London, 1904).

McGrayne, Sharon Bertsch, *The Theory that Would Not Die: How Bayes' Rule Cracked the Enigma Code, Hunted Down Russian Submarines and Emerged Triumphant from Two Centuries of Controversy* (New Haven, 2011).

McLachlan, H., 'The Old Hackney College 1786–1796', *Transactions of the Unitarian Historical Society*, 3, no. 3 (1925), 185–205.

—— *English Education under the Test Acts* (Manchester, 1931).

Macpherson, James, *The Rights of Great Britain Asserted against the Claims of America; Being an Answer to the Declaration of the General Congress. 6th Edition. To which is Now Added a Refutation of Dr. Price's State of the National Debt* (London, 1776).

Malone, Edward (ed.), *The Life of Samuel Johnson LLD by James Boswell Esq.* (Edinburgh, n.d.).

Markham, William, *A Sermon Preached before the Incorporated Society for the Propagation of the Gospel in Foreign Parts . . .* (London, 1777).

Maseres, Francis, *A Proposal for Establishing Life-Annuities in Parishes for the Benefit of the Industrious Poor* (London, 1772).

—— *Considerations on the Bill Now Depending in the House of Commons for Enabling Parishes to Grant Life Annuities to Poor Persons, upon Purchase in Certain Circumstances, and under Certain Restrictions . . .* (London, 1773).

Miller, C. William, *Benjamin Franklin's Philadelphia Printing 1728–1766: A Descriptive Bibliography* (Philadelphia, 1974).

Miller, Peter (ed.), *Political Writings: Joseph Priestley* (Cambridge, 1993).

Millican, Peter (ed.), *David Hume, An Enquiry Concerning Human Understanding* (paperback edn., Oxford, 2007).

Molivas, Gregory I., 'Richard Price, the Debate on Free Will, and Natural Rights', *Journal of the History of Ideas*, 58, no. 1 (1997), 105–23.

Morgan, Edmund S., *Benjamin Franklin* (New Haven, 2002).

Morgan, George Cadogan, 'Observations on the Light of Bodies in a State of Combustion', *Philosophical Transactions*, LXXV, part I (1785), 211.

Morgan, William, *A Review of Dr. Price's Writings, on the Subject of the Finances of the Kingdom: To which are Added the Three Plans Communicated by Him to Mr. Pitt in the Year 1786 for Redeeming the National Debt: And Also an Enquiry into the Real State of the Public Income and Expenditure, from the Establishment of the Consolidated Fund to the Year 1791* (London, 1792).

—— *Memoirs of the Life of the Rev. Richard Price* (London, 1815).

—— *Sermons on Various Subjects, by the Late Dr. Richard Price, D.D. F.R.S.* (London, 1816).

Mossner, Ernest C. (ed.), *David Hume, A Treatise of Human Nature* (Harmondsworth, 1985).

Mullett, Charles F., 'The Legal Position of the English Protestant Dissenters 1767–1812', *Virginia Law Revue*, 25, no. 6 (1939), 671–97.

Nagai, Yoshio, 'Jeremy Bentham on Richard Price', *E&D*, 1 (1982), 83–7.

Nash, Gary B., 'Franklin and Slavery', *Proceedings of the American Philosophical Society*, 150, part 4 (2006), 618–35.

O'Brien, Conor Cruise, *Edmund Burke* (paperback edn., London, 2002).

—— (ed.), *Edmund Burke, Reflections on the Revolution in France* (London, 2004).

Ogborn, Maurice Edward, *Equitable Assurances: The Story of Life Assurance in the Experience of the Equitable Life Assurance Society, 1762–1962* (London, 1962).

Overton, J. H., *History of the Church of England in the Eighteenth Century* (2 vols., London, 1878).

Owen, David, 'Hume Versus Price on Miracles and Prior Probabilities: Testimony and the Bayesian Calculation', *The Philosophical Quarterly*, 37 (147), 187–202.

Paine, Thomas, *Common Sense* (paperback edn., London, 1986).

—— *The Age of Reason, Part III. Appendix – My Private Thoughts on a Future State* (London, 1818).

—— 'The Age of Reason', in Foner (ed.), *Thomas Paine, Collected Writings*, pp. 665–830.

Park, Yong-june, *Slavoj Žižek, Demanding the Impossible* (paperback edn., Cambridge, 2014).

Payne, E. J. (ed.), *Burke, Selected Works. Volume 1: Thoughts on the Present Discontents & The Two Speeches on America* (Oxford, 1922).

Peach, W. Bernard, 'Hume's Mistake', *Journal of the History of Ideas*, XLI, no. 2 (1980), 331–4.

—— 'On What Point Did Richard Price Convince David Hume of a Mistake? With a Note by Henri Laboucheix', *The Price-Priestley Newsletter*, 2 (1978), 76–81.

—— 'Richard Price, Josiah Tucker, John Locke and D. O. Thomas', *E&D*, 19 (2000), 45–59.

—— 'The Indefinability and Simplicity of Rightness in Richard Price's Review of Morals', *Philosophy and Phenomenological Research*, XIV, no. 2 (1954), 370–85.

—— (ed.), *Richard Price and the Ethical Foundations of the American Revolution* (Durham, North Carolina, 1979).

—— and D. O. Thomas (eds.), *The Correspondence of Richard Price* (3 vols., Durham, 1983–94).

Peterson, Dean, 'The Origins of Malthus's Data on Population: the Political and Religious Biases in the American Sources', *Journal of the History of Economic Thought*, 19 (1997), 114–26.

Peterson, Merrill D. (ed.), *Thomas Jefferson, Writings* (New York, 1984).

Peterson, Susan Rae, 'The Compatibility of Richard Price's Politics and Ethics', *Journal of the History of Ideas*, 45 (1984), 537–47.

Picard, Liza, *Dr. Johnson's London* (London, 2003).

Pocock, J. G. A., 'Radical Criticisms of the Whig Order in the Age between Revolutions', in Margaret C. and James R. Jacob, *The Origins of Anglo-American Radicalism* (1984).

Poitias, Geoffrey, 'Richard Price, Miracles and the Origin of Bayesian Decision Theory', *The European Journal of the History of Economic Thought*, 20, part 1 (2013), 29–57.

Porter, Roy, *Blood and Guts, A Short History of Medicine* (London, 2003).

—— *English Society in the 18th Century* (London, 1991).

—— *Enlightenment: Britain and the Creation of the Modern World* (London, 2001).

Poser, Norman, S., *Lord Mansfield: Justice in the Age of Reason* (Montreal, 2013).

Pottle, F. A. (ed.), *Boswell's London Journal 1762–1763* (London, 1950).

Price, H. S., 'A Few Observations on David Hume and Richard Price on Miracles', *E&D*, 5 (1986), 21–37.

Priestley, Joseph, *An Essay on the First Principles of Government, and on the Nature of Political, Civil and Religious Liberty* (London, 1768).

—— *A Discourse on Occasion of the Death of Dr. Price, Delivered at Hackney, on Sunday, May 1, 1791* (London, 1791).

—— *The History and Present State of Discoveries Relating to Vision, Light and Colours* (London, 1772).

—— *The History and Present State of Electricity with Original Experiments* (London, 1767).

—— *The Importance and Extent of Free Inquiry in Matters of Religion: A Sermon, Preached Before the Congregations of the Old and New Meeting of Protestant Dissenters at Birmingham. November 5, 1785. To Which are Added, Reflections on the Present State of Free Inquiry in this Country* (Birmingham, 1785).

—— 'Letter V: Of the Revolution Society in England, and Mr. Burke's Reflexions on Dr. Price', in *idem, Letters to the Right Honourable Edmund Burke, Occasioned by his Reflections on the Revolution in France, &c.* (Birmingham, 1791), pp. 43–8.

—— 'On the Noxious Quality of the Effluvia of Putrid Marshes', *Philosophical Transactions*, LXIV, part 1 (1774), 90–5.

Raphael, D. D. (ed.), *A Review of the Principal Questions in Morals by Richard Price* (Oxford, 1974).

—— 'Ethics and Aesthetics in the British Moralists', *E&D*, 23 (2004–7), 131–47.

Raynor, David, 'Hume's Mistake – Another Guess', *Hume Studies*, VII (1981), 164–7.

Rees, W. J., 'Richard Price 1723–1791', *Efrydiau Athronyddol*, LV (1992), 68–77.

Revolution Society, *An Abstract of the History and Proceedings of the Revolution Society in London. To which is Annexed a Copy of the Bill of Rights* (London, 1789).

—— The Minute Book of the London Revolution Society, British Library Add 648814.

Ridley, Jasper, *The Freemasons* (paperback edn., London, 2000).

Rifkin, Jeremy, *The Empathic Civilization, the Race to Consciousness in a World in Crisis* (paperback edn., Cambridge, 2013).

Rodger, N. A. M., *Command of the Ocean, A Naval History of Britain 1649–1815* (London, 2005).

Rogers, Samuel, *Recollections of the Table-Talk of Samuel Rogers* (2nd edn., London, 1856).

Rosenfeld, Sophia, *Common Sense: A Political History* (Cambridge, Massachusetts, 2011).

Ruston, Alan, 'Price and Priestley at Gravel Pit Chapel, Hackney', *The Price-Priestley Newsletter*, 4 (1980), 26–9.

Rutt, J. T. (ed.), *The Life and Correspondence of J. Priestley* (2 vols., London, 1831–2).

—— *The Theological and Miscellaneous Works of Joseph Priestley* (25 vols., London, 1817–31).

Sayer, Edward, *Observations on Dr. Price's Revolution Sermon* (London, 1790).

Schama, Simon, *Citizens, A Chronicle of the French Revolution* (paperback edn., London, 2004).

—— *Patriots and Liberators, Revolution in the Netherlands 1780–1813* (paperback edn., London, 2005).

Schiff, Stacy, *Benjamin Franklin and the Birth of America* (paperback edn., London, 2006).

Schofield, Robert E., *The Enlightened Joseph Priestley: A Study of his Life and Work from 1733–1773* (Pennsylvania, 1998).

—— *The Enlightened Joseph Priestley: A Study of his Life and Work from 1773–1804* (Pennsylvania, 2004).

Scurr, Ruth, *Fatal Purity: Robespierre and the French Revolution* (paperback edn., London, 2007).

Sellers, Charles Coleman, *Patience Wright, American Artist and Spy in George III's London* (Connecticut, 1976).

Shebbeare, John, *An Essay on the Origin, Progress and Establishment of National Society; in which the Principles of Government, the Definitions of Physical, Moral, Civil, and Religious Liberty, Contained in Dr. Price's Observations, etc. Are Fairly Examined and Refuted . . .* (London, 1776).

Simpson, T., *Treatise on the Doctrine of Annuities and Reversions* (London, 1742).

Smeeton, George, *Doings in London or Day and Night Scenes of the Frauds, Frolics, Manners and Depravities of the Metropolis* (London, 1828).

Somerville, Thomas, *My Own Life and Times 1741–1814* (Edinburgh, 1861).

Stafford, Fiona, *The Sublime Savage: A Study of James Macpherson and the Poems of Ossian* (Edinburgh, 1988).

Stephen, Leslie, *History of English Thought in the Eighteenth Century* (2nd edn., 2 vols., London, 1881).

Stephens, John, 'Conscience and the Epistemology of Morals: Richard Price's Debt to Joseph Butler', *E&D*, 19 (2000), 133–46.

—— 'Richard Price, A Sermon on Revelation 21.3', *E&D*, 12 (1993), 78–91.

—— 'Samuel Chandler and the Regium Donum', *E&D*, 15 (1996), 57–70.

—— 'The London Dissenting Ministers and Subscription', *E&D*, 1 (1982), 43–72.

—— 'When Did David Hume Meet Richard Price?', *The Price-Priestley Newsletter*, 4 (1980), 30–9.

Steuart, Francis (ed.), *The Last Journals of Horace Walpole during the Reign of George III, from 1771–1783 with Notes by Dr. Doran* (2 vols., London, 1910).

Stiles, Ezra, *A Discourse on Christian Union* (Boston, 1761).

Stutchbury, Oliver, 'Nantes and the Death of Richard Price', *E&D*, 11 (1992), 158.

Tannahill, Reay (ed.), *Paris in the Revolution, A Collection of Eye-Witness Accounts* (London, 1966).

Temple, Nora, *The Road to 1789: From Reform to Revolution in France* (Cardiff, 1992).

Thomas, Beryl, 'Richard Price's Shorthand', *The Price-Priestley Newsletter*, 4 (1980), 40–2.

—— and D. O. Thomas, 'Richard Price's Journal for the Period 25 March 1787 to 6 February 1791. Deciphered by Beryl Thomas with an Introduction by D. O. Thomas', *National Library of Wales Journal*, XXI, no. 4 (1980), 366–413.

Thomas, D. O., *Richard Price and America* (Aberystwyth, 1975).

—— *The Honest Mind: The Thought and Work of Richard Price* (Oxford, 1977).

—— *Ymateb i Chwyldro / Response to Revolution* (Cardiff, 1989).

—— 'Francis Maseres, Richard Price and the Industrious Poor', *E&D*, 4 (1985), 65–82.

—— 'Memoirs of the Life of the Rev. Richard Price by William Morgan', *E&D*, 22 (2003), 1–134.

—— 'Neither Republican Nor Democrat', *The Price-Priestley Newsletter*, 1 (1977), 49–60.

—— 'Proposed Protest Concerning Dissenters: Richard Price and the Earl of Chatham', *Transactions of the Unitarian Historical Society*, XV1, no. 2 (1976), 49–62.

—— 'Rice Price's Will', *The Price-Priestley Newsletter*, 2 (1978), 98–107.

—— 'Richard Price: A Sketch of Proposals for Discharging the Public Debts, Securing Public Liberty, and Preserving the State', *E&D*, 1 (1982), 91–105.

—— 'Richard Price and Edmund Burke: The Duty to Participate in Government', *Philosophy*, 34 (1959), 308–22.

—— 'Richard Price and the Population Controversy', *The Price-Priestley Newsletter*, 4 (1980), 43–62.

—— 'Richard Price and the Freedom of the City of London', *E&D*, 8 (1989), 90–109.

—— 'Was Richard Price a Radical?', in Williams (ed.), *Richard Price and the Atlantic Revolution*, pp. 58–70.

—— (ed.), *Richard Price: Political Writings* (Cambridge, 1991).

——, John Stephens and P. A. L. Jones, *A Bibliography of the Works of Richard Price* (Aldershot, 1993).

Thomas, Peter D. G., *John Wilkes, A Friend to Liberty* (Oxford, 1996).

—— *Politics in Eighteenth-Century Wales* (Cardiff, 1998).

—— *Revolution in America: Britain & The Colonies 1763–1776* (Cardiff, 1992).

Thomas, Roland, *Richard Price: Philosopher and Apostle of Liberty* (Oxford, 1924).

Thomas, W. S. K., *Stuart Wales* (Llandysul, 1988).

Tomaselli, Sylvana (ed.), *Mary Wollstonecraft, A Vindication of the Rights of Men and A Vindication of the Rights of Woman* (Cambridge, 1995).

Thompson, C. Bradley, *The Revolutionary Writings of John Adams* (Indianapolis, 2000).

Thornbury, William, et al., *Old and New London: A Narrative of its History, its People, and its Places* (6 vols., London, n.d.).

Trask, Willard R. (trans.), *Giacomo Casanova, History of My Life* (12 vols., Baltimore, 1997).

Tully, James (ed.), and Michael Silverthorne (trans.), *Samuel Puffendorf, On the Duty of Man and Citizen* (Cambridge, 1991).

University College of Wales, *Richard Price 1723–1791: An Exhibition to Commemorate the United States Bicentennial* (Aberystwyth, 1976).

—— *Richard Price 1723–1791: An Exhibition to Mark the Bicentenary of his Death* (Aberystwyth, 1991).

Vidal, Gore, *Inventing a Nation, Washington, Adams, Jefferson* (New Haven, 2003).

Wales, William, *An Enquiry into the Present State of Population in England and Wales; and the Proportion which the Present Numbers of Inhabitants Bears to the Number of Former Periods* (London, 1781).

Walters, Gwyn, 'Richard Price and Carmarthen Academy', *The Price-Priestley Newsletter*, 4 (1980), 69.

Webb, Robert K., 'Price among the Unitarians, *E&D*, 19 (2000), 147–70.

Weinreb, Ben, and Christopher Hibbert (eds.), *The London Encyclopedia* (London, 1983).

Wesley, John, *Some Observations on Liberty; Occasioned by a Late Tract* (London, 1776).

West, Tessa, *The Curious Mr. Howard: Legendary Prison Reformer* (Hook, 2011).

Williams, Caroline E., *A Welsh Family from the Beginning of the 18th Century* (2nd edn., London, 1893).

Williams, Chris (ed.), *Richard Price and the Atlantic Revolution* (Bridgend, 1991).

Williams, Howard, 'Karl Marx and Richard Price', *E&D*, 3 (1984), 91–8.

Williams, J. Gwyn, 'Richard Price and Rice Price', *The Price-Priestley Newsletter*, 2 (1978), 107.

Williams, William, 'More about the First Three Welsh Books Printed in America', *National Library of Wales Journal*, III (1943–4), 19–22.

Wollstonecraft, Mary, *A Vindication of the Rights of Man, in a Letter to the Right Honourable Edmund Burke, Occasioned by his Reflections on the Revolution in France* (London, 1790).

Wood, Gordon S., *Empire of Liberty: A History of the Early Republic, 1789–1815* (Oxford, 2009).

Wyvill, Christopher, *A Defence of Dr. Price and the Reformers of England* (London, 1792).

Young, Arthur, *Political Arithmetic, Containing Observations on the Present State of Great Britain and the Principles of her Policy in the Encouragement of Agriculture* (London, 1774).

Zebrowski, Martha K., "'We may venture to say, that the number of Platonic Readers is considerable": Richard Price, Joseph Priestley, and the Platonic Strain in Eighteenth-Century Thought', *E&D*, 19 (2000), 193–213.

Žižek, Slavoj, with Jean Ducange (ed.) and John Howe (trans.), *Virtue and Terror, Maxililien Robespierre* (London, 2007).

Principal websites utilized

Benjamin Franklin letters at *http://www.yale.edu/franklinpapers/index.html*.

Constitutional documents at *http://www.constitution.org*.

E&D at *http://www.english.qmul.ac.uk/drwilliams/journal/intro.html*.

Eighteenth Century Collections Online (ECCO) at *http://quod.lib.umich.edu/e/ecco*.

Jane Austen material at *http://www.jasnaeastpa.org*.

John and Abigail Adams letters at *http://www.masshist.org/digitaladams*.

Library of Congress, American Memory pages (Thomas Jefferson Papers, George Washington Papers, Letters of Delegates to Congress and Chronology of Congress) at *http://memory.loc,gov/ammem/index.html*.

Oxford Dictionary of National Biography at *http://www.oxforddnb.com*.

The Times Newspaper Online Archive at *http://www.thetimes.co.uk/tto/archive*.

Welsh Biography Online at *http://wbo.llgc.org.uk*.

Index